Latin Palaeography

Antiquity and the Middle Ages

Latin
Palaeography

Antiquity and the Middle Ages

BERNHARD BISCHOFF

TRANSLATED BY
DÁIBHÍ Ó CRÓINÍN AND DAVID GANZ

PUBLISHED IN ASSOCIATION WITH
THE MEDIEVAL ACADEMY OF IRELAND

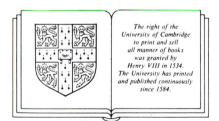

The right of the
University of Cambridge
to print and sell
all manner of books
was granted by
Henry VIII in 1534.
The University has printed
and published continuously
since 1584.

CAMBRIDGE UNIVERSITY PRESS

Cambridge
New York   Port Chester   Melbourne   Sydney

Published by the Press Syndicate of the University of Cambridge
The Pitt Building, Trumpington Street, Cambridge CB2 1RP
40 West 20th Street, New York, NY 10011-4211, USA
10 Stamford Road, Oakleigh, Melbourne 3166, Australia

Originally published in Berlin as *Paläographie des romischen
Altertums und des abendländischen Mittelalters*
by Erich Schmidt Verlag 1979; 2nd rev. ed. 1986
and © Erich Schmidt Verlag
First published in English by Cambridge University Press 1990 as
Latin Palaeography: Antiquity and the Middle Ages
Reprinted 1990

Printed in Great Britain at the University Press, Cambridge

British Library Cataloguing in Publication Data

Bischoff, Bernhard
Latin Palaeography: Antiquity and the Middle Ages
1. Palaeography to 1500
I. Title II. (Paläographie des römischen
Altertums und des abendländischen
Mittelalters.) *English*
417′.7

Library of Congress Cataloguing in Publication Data

Bischoff, Bernhard.
[Paläographie des römischen Altertums und des abendländischen Mittelalters.
English]
Latin Palaeography: Antiquity and the Middle Ages / Bernhard Bischoff;
translated by Dáibhí Ó Cróinín and David Ganz.
p.   cm.
Translation of: Paläographie des römischen Altertums und des
abendländischen Mittelalters.
Bibliography: p.
Includes indexes.
ISBN 0 521 36473 6. — ISBN 0 521 36726 3 (pbk.)
1. Paleography, Latin. 2. Manuscripts. Latin—History. 3. Manuscripts, Latin
(Medieval and modern)—History. 4. Manuscripts, Medieval—History. 5.
Paleography. I. Title.
Z114.B5713 1989
417′.7—dc 19   88-34649 CIP

ISBN 0 521 36473 6 hardback
ISBN 0 521 36726 3 paperback

Contents

Contents

vi

Abbreviations

Abh.   Abhandlungen

Arch.   Archiv

Arch. f. Dipl.   *Archiv für Diplomatik, Schriftgeschichte, Siegel- und Wappenkunde*

Arch. f. Urk.   *Archiv für Urkundenforschung*

Arch. Pal. Ital.   *Archivio Paleografico Italiano* (edd.: Ernesto Monaci et al., Rome 1882 ff.)

Arch. stor. ital.   *Archivio storico italiano*

Arndt–Tangl   Wilhelm Arndt/Michael Tangl, *Schrifttafeln zur Erlernung der lateinischen Paläographie* 1/2 (4th ed.), 3 (2nd ed.) (Berlin 1904–06)

Baesecke, *Lichtdr.*   Georg Baesecke, *Lichtdrucke nach altdeutschen Handschriften* (Halle/S. 1926)

Battelli, *Lezioni*[3]   Giulio Battelli, *Lezioni di paleografia*, 3rd ed. (Vatican City 1949)

Becker, *Catalogi*   Gustavus Becker, *Catalogi bibliothecarum antiqui* (Bonn 1885)

Bibl. Éc. Chartres   *Bibliothèque de l'École des Chartes*

Bischoff, *Kalligraphie*   Bernhard Bischoff, *Kalligraphie in Bayern. Achtes bis zwölftes Jahrhundert* (Wiesbaden 1981)

Paläographie   Paläographie, in: Wolfgang Stammler (ed.), *Deutsche Philologie im Aufriß* 1[2] (Berlin–Bielefeld–Munich 1957), cols 379–452; also separately printed

Paléographie   *Paléographie de l'antiquité romaine et du moyen âge occidental* (transl. by Hartmut Atsma and Jean Vezin; Paris 1985)

Schreibschulen   *Die südostdeutschen Schreibschulen und Bibliotheken in der Karolingerzeit. 1. Die bayrischen Diözesen*, 3rd ed. (Wiesbaden 1974; 1st ed. Leipzig 1940); *Die vorwiegend österreichischen Diözesen* (Wiesbaden 1980)

Bruckner, *Scriptoria*   Albert Bruckner, *Scriptoria medii aevi Helvetica*, to date 14 vols (Geneva 1935–78)

Bull.   Bullettino

Catal. manoscr. datati   *Catalogo dei manoscritti in scrittura latina datati o databili* 1

vii

	(ed. Viviana Jemolo; Turin 1971); 2 (ed. Francesca di Cesare; Turin 1982)
Catal. mss. datés	Charles Samaran/Robert Marichal, *Catalogue des manuscrits en écriture latine portant des indications de date, de lieu ou de copiste,* to date vols 1–3, 4/1, 5–7 (Paris 1959 ff.)
Catal. of dated MSS., Switzerland	*Catalogue of the dated manuscripts written in the Latin script from the beginnings of the Middle Ages to 1550 in the libraries of Switzerland* 1 (Beat Mathias von Scarpatetti). Text and plates (Dietikon-Zürich 1977)
Cavallo, *Libri*	Guglielmo Cavallo, *Libri e lettori nel medioevo* (Bari 1977)
Cencetti, *Compendio*	Giorgio Cencetti, *Compendio di paleografia latina* (Naples 1963)
Lineamenti	*Lineamenti di storia della scrittura latina* (Bologna 1954)
Pal. lat.	*Paleografia latina* (Guide 1; Rome 1978)
Chatelain, *Pal. class. lat.*	Émile Chatelain, *Paléographie des classiques latins* 1/2 (Paris 1884–1900)
ChLA	Albert Bruckner/Robert Marichal et al., *Chartae Latinae Antiquiores,* 1–15, 17–18, 20–22 (Olten-Lausanne 1954–67; Zürich 1975)
Chroust, *Monumenta*	Anton Chroust, *Monumenta palaeographica, Denkmäler der Schreibkunst des Mittelalters,* ser I and II (Munich 1902–17); ser III (Leipzig 1931–40)
CLA	Elias Avery Lowe, *Codices Latini Antiquiores,* 1–11 and Suppl. (Oxford 1934–71); 2² (ibid. 1972). Addenda by B. Bischoff and V. Brown, *Mediaeval Studies* 47 (1985) 317–366, with 18 plates (cited as CLA Addenda).
Clm	*Codex Latinus Monacensis*
Crous-Kirchner, *Schriftarten*	Ernst Crous/Joachim Kirchner, *Die gotischen Schriftarten* (Leipzig 1928)
Datierte Hss.	*Datierte Handschriften in Bibliotheken der Bundesrepublik Deutschland* (ed. Johanne Autenrieth) 1. Frankfurt am Main (Gerhard Powitz; Stuttgart 1984)
Degering, *Schrift*	Hermann Degering, *Die Schrift. Atlas der Schriftformen des Abendlandes vom Altertum bis zum Ausgang des 18. Jahrhunderts* (Berlin 1929)
Écr. lat.	Jean Mallon/Robert Marichal/Charles Perrat, *L'Écriture latine de la capitale romaine à la minuscule* (Paris 1939)
Ehrle–Liebaert, *Specimina*	Franz Ehrle/Paul Liebaert, *Specimina codicum Latinorum Vaticanorum* (Bonn 1912)
Exempla scripturarum 1 (II, III)	Bruno Katterbach/Augustus Pelzer/Carolus Silva-Tarouca, *Codices Latini saeculi XIII* 1, Vatican City 1928); B. Katterbach/C. Silva-Tarouca, *Epistolae et instrumenta saeculi XIII* (II, ibid. 1930); Iulius Battelli, *Acta pontificum²* (III, ibid. 1965)
Fichtenau, *Mensch und Schrift*	Heinrich Fichtenau, *Mensch und Schrift im Mittelalter* (Vienna 1946)

Fischer, *Schrifttafeln*	Hanns Fischer, *Schrifttafeln zum althochdeutschen Lesebuch* (Tübingen 1966)
Foerster, *Abriß*²	Hans Foerster, *Abriß der lateinischen Paläographie*, 2nd revised and enlarged edition (Stuttgart 1963)
Gumbert, *Utrechter Kartäuser*	J.P. Gumbert, *Die Utrechter Kartäuser und ihre Bücher* (Leiden 1970)
It. Med. e Um.	*Italia Medioevale e Umanistica*
Jahrb.	*Jahrbuch*
John, *Lat. Pal.*	James J. John, Latin Paleography, in: James M. Powell (ed.), *Medieval Studies, An Introduction* (Syracuse, N.Y. 1976) 1–68
Katal. d. dat. Hss., Österreich	*Katalog der datierten Handschriften in lateinischer Schrift in Österreich*, 1–4 (F. Unterkircher) 5 (Franz Lackner), 6 (Maria Mairold) (Vienna 1969 ff.)
Katal. d. dat. Hss., Sweden	*Katalog der datierten Handschriften in lateinischer Schrift vor 1600 in Schweden* 1/2 (Monica Hedlund) Text and plates (Stockholm 1977)
Ker, *Catal. of MSS.*	Neil R. Ker, *Catalogue of Manuscripts containing Anglo-Saxon* (Oxford 1957)
Engl. MSS.	*English Manuscripts in the Century after the Norman Conquest* (Oxford 1960)
Kirchner, *Script. Goth. libr.*	Joachim Kirchner, *Scriptura Gothica libraria* (Munich–Vienna 1966)
*Script. Lat. libr.*²	*Scriptura Latina libraria*, ed. alt. (Munich 1970)
Koehler, *Karol. Min.*	Wilhelm Koehler (Köhler), *Die karolingischen Miniaturen*, 1–3 (Berlin 1930–60)
Koehler/Mütherich, *Karol. Min.*	Wilhelm Koehler/Florentine Mütherich, idem 4–5 (Berlin 1971ff.)
Koennecke, *Bilderatlas*	Gustav Koennecke, *Bilderatlas zur Geschichte der Deutschen Nationalliteratur* (Marburg 1887)
Lehmann, *Erforschung*	Paul Lehmann, *Erforschung des Mittelalters*, 1–5 (Stuttgart 1959–62; 1: 1st edition Leipzig 1941)
Lesne, *Livres*	Émile Lesne, *Les livres, «scriptoria» et bibliothèques du commencement du VIIIe à la fin du XIe siècle* (Histoire de la propriété ecclésiastique en France 4, Lille 1938)
Lindsay, *Notae Latinae*	W.M. Lindsay, *Notae Latinae. An account of abbreviations in Latin manuscripts of the early minuscule period (ca. 700–850)* (Cambridge 1915; reprinted Hildesheim 1965)
Litterae Textuales	*Litterae Textuales* [= *Codicologica* 1976 ff.]; ed. by J.P. Gumbert et al. (Amsterdam 1972–76; Leiden 1976 ff.)
Lowe, *Palaeographical Papers*	Elias Avery Lowe, *Palaeographical Papers 1907–1965* 1/2 (Oxford 1972)
Mallon, *De l'écriture*	Jean Mallon, *De l'écriture, receuil d'études* (Paris 1982)
Paléographie romaine	*Paléographie romaine* (Madrid 1952)
Mazal, *Gotik*	Otto Mazal, *Buchkunst der Gotik* (Graz 1975)

Romanik	*Buchkunst der Romanik* (Graz 1978)
Mittelalt. Bibliothekskat.	*Mittelalterliche Bibliothekskataloge Deutschlands und der*
Deutschl.	*Schweiz*, vols. 1 and 2 ed. Paul Lehmann; vol. 3 ed. Paul Ruf; 4, 1 ed. Christine Elisabeth Ineichen-Eder; vol. 4, 2 ed. Günter Glauche and Hermann Knaus (Munich 1918–79)
MGH	*Monumenta Germaniae Historica*
Micheli, *L'Enluminure*	G.L. Micheli, *L'Enluminure du haut moyen âge et les influences irlandaises* (Brussels 1939)
Milkau/Leyh, Handbuch²	Fritz Milkau/Georg Leyh, *Handbuch der Bibliothekswissenschaft*, 2nd ed. (vol. 1 Wiesbaden 1952; 3, 1 ibid. 1955)
Millares Carlo, *Tratado*	Agustín Millares Carlo, *Tratado de paleografía española* (with José Manuel Ruiz Asencio) 1–3; 3rd ed. (Madrid 1983)
Mitteil. hist. Österr. Geschichtsforsch.	*Mitteilungen des Instituts für Österreichische Geschichtsforschung*
Mss. datés, Belgique	François Masai/Martin Wittek (ed.), *Manuscrits datés conservés en Belgique*, 4 vols. to date (Brussels-Ghent 1968 ff.)
Mss. datés, Pays-Bas	Gerard Isaak Lieftinck, *Manuscrits datés conservés dans les Pays-Bas*, 1 vol. to date (Amsterdam 1964)
Münchener Beiträge	*Münchener Beiträge zur Mediävistik und Renaissance-Forschung*
New Pal. Soc.	*The New Palaeographical Society. Facsimiles of Ancient Manuscripts*, ser I–II (ed. E.M. Thompson et al.; London 1903–30)
Nomenclature	*Nomenclature des écritures livresques du IXe au XVIe siècle* (B. Bischoff, G.I. Lieftinck, G. Battelli) (Paris 1954)
Nordenfalk, *Das frühe Mittelalter*	Carl Nordenfalk in André Grabar/Carl Nordenfalk, *Das frühe Mittelalter vom vierten bis zum elften Jahrhundert* (Die großen Jahrhunderte der Malerei (Geneva 1957)
Die romanische Malerei	idem in André Grabar/Carl Nordenfalk, *Die romanische Malerei vom 11. bis zum 13. Jahrhundert* (Geneva 1958)
Zierbuchstaben	*Die spätantiken Zierbuchstaben*. Text and plates (Stockholm 1970)
Paläographie 1981	*Paläographie 1981*. Colloquium du comité International de Paléographie, Munich, 15–18 Sept. 1981 (Proceedings, ed. by G. Silagi). Münchner Beiträge 32 (Munich 1982)
Pal. Soc.	*The Palaeographical Society, Facsimiles of Manuscripts and Inscriptions*, ser I–II (ed. E.A. Bond et al.; London 1873–94)
Petzet/Glauning, *Deutsche Schrifttafeln*	Erich Petzet/Otto Glauning, *Deutsche Schrifttafeln des IX. bis XVI. Jahrhunderts aus Handschriften der K. Hof- und Staatsbibliothek (4/5: der Bayerischen Staatsbibliothek) in München, 1–3* (Munich 1910–12), 4/5 (Leipzig 1924–30)
Rev. Bénéd.	*Revue Bénédictine*
s. (I ex.)	saeculi (I exeuntis)

x

Santifaller, *Beiträge*	Leo Santifaller, *Beiträge zur Geschichte der Beschreibstoffe im Mittelalter. 1. Untersuchungen.* Mitteilungen d. Inst. f. Österr. Geschichtsforschung, supplementary volume 16, 1 (Graz-Cologne 1953)
Schramm/Mütherich *Deukmale*	Percy Ernst Schramm/Florentine Mütherich, *Denkmale der deutschen Könige und Kaiser* (Munich 1962)
Seider, *Lat. Pap.*	Richard Seider, *Paläographie der lateinischen Papyri*, 1, 2/1, 2/2 (Stuttgart 1972 ff.)
Settimane	Settimane di Studio del Centro Italiano di Studi sull'Alto Medioevo
Steffens², *Lateinische Paläographie*	Franz Steffens, *Lateinische Paläographie*, 2nd ed. (Berlin 1929)
Stiennon, *Paléographie*	Jacques Stiennon, *Paléographie du Moyen Age* (Paris 1973)
Stud. Mitteil. OSB	*Studien und Mitteilungen zur Geschichte des Benediktinerordens und seiner Zweige*
Thomson, *Bookhands*	S. Harrison Thomson, *Latin Bookhands of the Later Middle Ages 1100–1500* (Cambridge 1969)
Tjäder, *Nichtliter. lat. Pap.*	Jan-Olof Tjäder, *Die nichtliterarischen lateinischen Papyri Italiens aus der Zeit 445–700*, 1 (Lund 1954/5); 2 (Stockholm 1982)
Traube, *Nomina Sacra*	Ludwig Traube, *Nomina Sacra, Versuch einer Geschichte der christlichen Kürzung* (Munich 1907)
Vorl. u. Abh.	*Vorlesungen und Abhandlungen*, 1–3 (Munich 1909–20)
Catal. of dated and datable MSS	*Catalogue of dated and datable manuscripts c. 700–1600 in the Department of Manuscripts in the British Library* (London 1979); *C. of. d. and d. MSS ca. 435–1600 in Oxford Libraries* (ed. Andrew G. Watson; London 1984)
Wattenbach, *Schriftwesen*	Wilhelm Wattenbach, *Das Schriftwesen im Mittelalter*, 3rd enlarged ed. (Leipzig 1896)
Zbl. f. Bw.	*Zentralblatt für Bibliothekswesen*
Zimmermann, *Vorkarol. Min.*	E. Heinrich Zimmermann, *Vorkarolingische Miniaturen.* Text and plates (Berlin 1916)
Z.	*Zeitschrift*
Z. f. d. Alt.	*Zeitschrift für deutsches Altertum*

The publisher wishes to acknowledge the help and good advice of Dr Rosamond McKitterick in helping to prepare the typescript for publication.

Preface

This book grew out of my contribution to Wolfgang Stammler's *Deutsche Philologie im Aufriß* entitled 'Paläographie mit besonderer Berücksichtigung des deutschen Kulturgebiets', in which the concentration was on the Germanic countries. In that essay it was only possible to sketch briefly the evolution of Latin script from Antiquity, and the forms of writing outside the Germanic countries. My suggestion that a new edition might develop these aspects was welcomed by the editor, and the expanded work enabled me to explain my views on controversial questions in the palaeography of Antiquity, and perhaps to bring one or two of them closer to a solution. I am grateful to Dr Ellinor Kahleyss(†) and to Hugo Moser, who inaugurated their series *Grundlagen der Germanistik* with this new volume. I also thank Michael Bernhard for his drawings of Latin abbreviations, and Gabriel Silagi for his help in correcting the proofs of the German editions.

A second, revised German edition (Berlin 1986) contains substantial additions to the notes and bibliography to keep abreast of the constant developments in international research on palaeography. Here Monsignor Leonard E. Boyle's bibliography (*Medieval Latin Palaeography*, Toronto 1984) and the critical surveys by Jan-Olof Tjäder in *Eranos* have proved particularly helpful. A French translation, by Hartmut Atsma and Jean Vezin, has also appeared (Editions Picard, Paris 1985) which included three new figures and twenty-three plates. These plates have also been included in this first English edition, together with facing sample transcriptions.

I must include a word of thanks to the many friends and colleagues who have assisted me over the years by sending me their books and articles, and I want especially to remember those who have died: Francis Wormald, Franco Bartolini, Giorgio Cencetti, Giovanni Muzzioli, Charles Samaran, Jean Mallon, Neil Ker, Albert Bruckner, Otto Pächt, and T. J. Brown. Without their help this book might not have been completed, and would certainly have contained far more gaps.

Introduction

Palaeography acquired its name with the publication in 1708 of *Palaeographia Graeca* by the Maurist Bernard de Montfaucon, a book that dealt so comprehensively with the handwriting and other characteristics of Greek manuscripts that it remained the leading authority on the subject for almost two centuries. The decisive move towards the systematic study of the handwriting of Latin manuscripts had been made somewhat earlier, in 1681, when Jean Mabillon, Montfaucon's older friend and fellow Benedictine, included in Book V of his *De re diplomatica* samples of Latin scripts from the fourth to the fifteenth century, arranged by type of script and century, and so began to reduce the material to order.[1] But whereas Mabillon had seen 'Gothica', 'Langobardica', 'Saxonica', and 'Francogallica' in isolation from one another as national scripts of the Germanic peoples and set them apart from Roman handwriting, it was Scipione Maffei of Verona who recognised that the so-called national scripts were in fact no more than later developments of Roman script. Maffei's division of Latin scripts into majuscule, minuscule, and cursive could have been the most productive point of departure for a genetic history of writing, but though his thesis was accepted in principle, the outstanding palaeographical achievement of the eighteenth century consisted in the diligent collection of all known varieties of Latin handwriting and their arrangement according to a system. This task was accomplished by the Maurist Benedictines Dom Toustain and Dom Tassin in their *Nouveau Traité de Diplomatique* (Paris 1750–65, especially Vol. 3).

In the *Nouveau Traité*, however, and in subsequent publications, palaeography remained in the shadow of diplomatic until well into the nineteenth century, even at a time when – due to the invention of photography and mechanical means of reproduction – the materials for study could be increased at will and were more reliable than before. In addition to providing instruction in

---

1 See also *De re diplomatica*, I 10. Traube traced the history of Latin palaeography in *Vorlesungen u. Abhandlungen* 1; see also Cencetti, *Lineamenti*, 7–17; Foerster, *Abriß²*, 9–36; Stiennon, *Paléographie*, 23–54. For Renaissance views of the history of Latin script cf. E. Casamassima, 'Per una storia delle dottrine paleografiche dall' Umanesimo a Jean Mabillon', *Studi Medievali*, ser 3, 5 (1964) 525–78.

the correct decipherment of old handwriting, the traditional task of palaeography was to provide the means of dating manuscripts. For this purpose various rules of thumb were derived from the examination of characteristic letter forms and of the nature of writing materials.

The breakthrough to the recognition of what script could tell us about history was achieved by Léopold Delisle and by Ludwig Traube, who linked it closely with Latin philology and the study of text transmission. The concept of the scriptorium was discovered, samples of different types of scripts were collected, and Traube laid the foundations of a historical understanding of abbreviations. The greatest work from Traube's school was the *Codices Latini Antiquiores*,[2] edited by E.A. Lowe, in which all Latin literary manuscripts up to AD 800 are described at length and palaeographically assessed.

The realisation that the development of the structural forms of writing was determined by the act of writing itself only appeared later.[3] But this insight was not restricted merely to some modern palaeographers. I remember how, in the late twenties, Rudolf von Heckel, Professor of Diplomatics at the University of Munich – who, along with Paul Lehmann, introduced me to palaeography – taught us that for him cursive writing was the key to changes in scripts through the centuries. He made us understand that the development of 'b with the bow to the left' to 'b with the bow to the right' was a natural process resulting from the dynamics and economy of writing.

In order to achieve a historical understanding of the development of handwriting certain reservations and misgivings about transgressing the boundaries of the discipline, and the difficulty of some materials, had to be overcome: notably the failure to deal with documentary scripts, with the handwriting of the later middle ages, or with papyrology. We know that during some periods the scripts of chanceries – conservative as they often were – and everyday writing influenced and advanced the development of bookhands. The scripts of the Latin papyri – limited in number and mostly fragmentary as they may be – are even more indispensable for our understanding of changes in scripts, since they constitute the only evidence for centuries which are otherwise inaccessible.

The almost simultaneous appearance of two monumental works on the carolingian centre of Tours, one written by E.K. Rand from the viewpoint of the palaeographer (1929), the other by Wilhelm Köhler from the art historian's perspective (1930), showed that students in these two disciplines need to be aware of the developments in each and to take their results into account.

In the course of more recent work many programmatic statements have been

---

2 On the making of this work see T.J. Brown, 'E.A. Lowe and "Codices latini antiquiores" ', *Scrittura e Civiltà* 1 (1977) 177–97.

3 Cencetti, *Lineamenti*, 10, recalls the understanding of the history of letter-forms which is already set out in Wattenbach's account of the stages in the development of letters, W. Wattenbach, *Anleitung zur lateinischen Paläographie* (Leipzig 1866).

formulated, of which I mention here only those by Augusto Campana and Heinrich Fichtenau.[4] But there are still many desiderata. Latin palaeography has two sister disciplines in epigraphy and Greek palaeography. The research of Jean Mallon into the relationship of bookhands to the script of inscriptions has resulted in very valuable insights, but a synthesis of what has been postulated for these three disciplines to the mutual benefit of them all has not yet been achieved to any great degree.

Palaeographical work, of course, goes on. In our own time international co-operation undertakes to solve fundamental problems. Tools are being created which will provide palaeographers with reliable assistance and ease their work. With the aid of technological advances palaeography, which is an art of seeing and comprehending, is in the process of becoming an art of measurement.

In conclusion I should like to say a few words about the intention and purpose of this book. As the title indicates, it is intended to provide an understanding of handwriting and to introduce the reader to the history of script as part of the history of the book in Roman antiquity and in the middle ages. The first part describes the materials used in books and the procedures in book-making. The second part is the history of script itself. The third part, which is neither a history of transmission nor of libraries, tries to sketch the rôle of manuscripts in our cultural history and draws attention to the high-points of book illumination that are an inseparable part of our subject. Every manuscript is unique. Our aim should be to recognise that uniqueness, to consider the manuscript as a historical monument and to be sensitive to its beauty, especially when its script and illumination are of a high aesthetic order.

Our account of the history of writing ends around the year 1500. The later history of handwriting from its medieval roots up to modern times lies beyond the scope of this book. That is a chapter in modern palaeography that still remains to be written.

4 A. Campana, 'Paleografia oggi', *Studi Urbinati di storia, filosofia e letteratura* 41 n.s., 1–2 (1967) 1013–30; H. Fichtenau in a discussion of 'Die historischen Hilfswissenschaften und ihre Bedeutung für die Mediävistik' in *Enzyklopädie der geisteswissenschaftlichen Arbeitsmethoden* (Munich–Vienna 1967) 125–129.

5 Ch. Samaran, Preface to *Codicologica* 1 [Litterae textuales] (Amsterdam 1976) 9 f.

Codicology

Writing materials and writing tools

1. Papyrus

The most important writing material of antiquity until the first centuries of the Christian era was papyrus,[1] which the Greeks had acquired from the Egyptians at a time unknown to us and which the Romans in turn took over from the Greeks. It is made from the vertically ribbed pith of the triangular papyrus stalk. Egypt possessed a virtual monopoly of its production. It was normally used in the form of rolls. To produce a roll pieces measuring on average 25×19 cm were made by laying strips of papyrus side-by-side. Across these strips a second layer was laid at right angles; the two layers were then pressed together. These nearly square pieces were pasted together end to end to form a roll in such a way that all ribs running in the same direction were on the same side. The first piece of a roll is called the 'protocol', the last the 'eschatacol'.

The side with the horizontal ribs was chosen to receive the script because it was easier to write on; it is called the 'recto' side, and forms the inner side of the roll. Writers in antiquity attest to the fact that writing could be washed off papyrus. When the first text had lost its importance or meaning for the owner the verso of many rolls (or parts of rolls) received different texts, frequently in a different language; this is called an 'opistograph'.[2] Rolls containing Latin

---

1 W. Schubart, *Einführung in die Papyruskunde* (Berlin 1918); Battelli, *Lezioni*[3], 28–30; Cencetti, *Lineamenti*, 23–7; idem, *Compendio*, 34–7; Santifaller, *Beiträge*, 25 ff.; H. Hunger, *Geschichte der Textüberlieferung* 1 (Zürich 1964) 30 ff., 43ff.; T.C. Skeat in *The Cambridge History of the Bible* 2 (Cambridge 1969), 54–60; Seider, *Lateinische Papyri* 1; J. Vezin, 'La réalisation matérielle des manuscrits latins pendant le haut Moyen Age', *Codicologica* 2 [Litterae textuales] (Leiden 1978) 17 f. This description follows I.H.S Hendrick's reinterpretation of Pliny's account, 'Pliny, *Historia Naturalis* XIII 74–82 and the manufacture of papyrus', *Z. f. Papyrologie u. Epigraphik* 37 (1984) 121–36. The same results, supported by experiments, were arrived at by Adolf Grohmann, *Arabische Paläographie* 1. Österr. Akad. Wiss., phil.-hist. Kl., Denkschriften 94, 1. Abt. (1967) 76 and 78 (ref. from Jean Vezin). The traditional view of how the two layers were produced from strips may also describe actual practice.

2 Cf. the Livy Epitome, s. III–IV, with a Greek text of Ep. ad Hebr. on the verso, s. IV: CLA II 208; Seider, *Papyri* 2/1, Nr. 34; ChLA V 304; Seider, *Papyri* 2/1, Nr. 11 was used several times for sums and for school exercises in the second and third centuries. Cf. C.H. Roberts, 'The codex', *Proc. Brit. Acad.* 40 (1954) 194.

literary texts have been preserved from Herculaneum[3] – in a charred state – and from Egypt.[4] As early as the second century AD, Egyptian Christians used papyrus in folded sheets for books.[5]

By the fourth century, the use of parchment for books was so widespread in the West that we can speak of a general transition from papyrus to parchment in the book-making process. This was of decisive importance for the preservation of literature because only very few papyrus manuscripts from medieval libraries have survived, since the European climate is inimical to this material.[6] Nonetheless, in the sixth century AD the law codes of Justinian I were distributed from Byzantium in papyrus as well as in parchment manuscripts.[7] One of the latest western papyrus books preserved (c. saec. VII–VIII) is a Luxeuil codex containing works of Augustine, in which interleaved parchment leaves protect the middle and the outside of the gatherings.[8]

The use of papyrus for legal instruments, lengthy charters, and letters, which was very common in antiquity,[9] continued in some western chanceries during the early middle ages.[10] Until the second half of the seventh century charters were still written on papyrus in the chancery of the Merovingian kings. Ravenna and the papal chancery – the latter until the end of the eleventh century – retained the use of papyrus even longer for documents and cartularies. Its name lives on in our word 'paper', the second writing material to come out of the East.

2. Parchment

Parchment is normally prepared in the following way:[11] the skin of the animal is not tanned but soaked in caustic calcium lye. This loosens the hair and removes the fat. Then the skin is cleaned with a sickle-shaped scraping iron and

3 Giovanna Petronio Nicolaj, 'Osservazioni sul canone della capitale', *Miscellanea in memoria di Giorgio Concetti* (Turin 1973) 11 ff. and plates 2–4; CLA III 385–7; Seider *Papyri* 2/1, 2–4.
4 L. Santifaller, 'Über späte Papyrusrollen und frühe Pergamentrollen', in *Speculum Historiale: Festschrift Johannes Spörl* (Freiburg–Munich 1965) 126–128. (A list of the Latin papyri from Egypt). Further items in CLA S (XII), and CLA Addenda.
5 C.H. Roberts in Roberts–T.C. Skeat, *The Birth of the Codex* (Oxford 1983) 45 ff., 54 ff., inclines to the belief that the papyrus book had been invented in Jerusalem or Antioch already before the year AD 100.   6 A catalogue in Tjäder, *Nichtliter. lat. Pap.* 1, 37–42.
7 Cf. Lowe, *Palaeographical Papers* 2, table following p. 470.
8 CLA V 614; Seider, *Papyri* 2/2. Nr. 59; CLA X 1470 and 1471. In many papyrus codices, then later on in paper manuscripts, strips of parchment were inserted in the central fold of the quire to protect the sewing; see the remains of two MSS in CLA X 1470 and 1471; see also CLA Addenda, plate 16a.
9 Bruckner-Marichal, ChLA 1 ff. In Jerome's time letters were still written on papyrus; E. Arns, *La technique du livre d'après Saint Jérôme* (Paris 1953) 27.
10 Santifaller, *Beiträge*, 52 ff.; Tjäder, *Nichtliter. lat. Pap.* 1, 35 ff., 42 ff.
11 Cf. Wattenbach, *Schriftwesen*, 113–39; Batelli, *Lezioni*³, 30–3; Cencetti, *Lineamenti*, 27–30; Santifaller, *Beiträge*, 78 ff.; H. Hunger, *Geschichte der Textüberlieferung*, 34 ff.; G.S. Ivy, *The English Library Before 1700*, ed. F. Wormald, C.E. Wright (London 1958), 33 ff.; Skeat, *Cambr. Hist. Bible* 1, 61 ff.; Stiennon, *Paléographie*, 152–6; R. Reed, *Ancient Skins, Parchment*

sometimes soaked a second time. It is then stretched on a frame to dry. Whether the parchment was further treated, and in what way, differed from country to country and from century to century, and seems to have depended mainly on the nature of the raw material, that is the type of skin used.

The parchment of Greek and Roman manuscripts from antiquity is often very fine; the oldest surviving remains of a Latin parchment manuscript is the *Fragmentum de bellis Macedonicis.*[12] Continental parchment of the carolingian period, usually made from the skin of sheep, is generally smooth. Italian parchment of the later middle ages, for which goatskins were also used, is more or less calcinated, that is it was treated with liquid chalk before drying. Through very careful treatment both sides can become equally white, but even then they are distinguished by their curvature: the flesh side is convex, while the less stretchable hair-side is concave(!), a fact which can be very helpful in the reconstruction of manuscripts that are preserved only in a very fragmentary state.

The writing material of Insular manuscripts, that is manuscripts written by the Irish or Anglo-Saxons, is as a rule different. They mainly used calfskins, which are stronger,[13] and these they usually roughened on both sides with pumice stone, with the result that hair- and flesh-sides became indistinguishable from one another ('vellum'). For special manuscripts, it seems, sheep parchment too was used in England, as for instance in the Echternach Gospels[14] and the Codex Amiatinus (intended for St Peter's in Rome).[15] The Anglo-Saxon missionaries to the continent took with them their kind of parchment and their manner of preparing it, so that these and other characteristic features of their writing techniques are found also in the regions of their missionary activity and

and Leathers (London 1973); idem, *The Nature and Making of Parchment* (Leeds 1975). On preparing transparent parchment for tracing decoration in the fourteenth–fifteenth century see B. Bischoff, *Anecdota Novissima* (Stuttgart 1984). On a different method, which uses holes pierced through the leaf, D. Miner, 'More about medieval pouncing', in *Homage to a Bookman, Essays Written for H.P. Kraus* (Berlin 1967) 87–147 and plate. There is a sequence of pictures illustrating the preparation and utilisation of parchment from Bamberg, Patr. 5, s. XII in F. Dreßler, *Scriptorum opus, Schreibermönche am Werk, Prof. Dr. Otto Meyer zum 65. Geburtstag* (Wiesbaden 1971) 4 and 8 ff.; a further example from the Hamburg Bible of 1255 (Copenhagen, GL. Kgl. 4.2.2°): A.A. Björnbo 'Ein Beitrag zum Werdegang der mittelalterlichen Pergamenthandschriften', *Z. f. Bücherfreunde* 11 (1907) 329 ff. (Foerster, *Abriß²*, 74 ff.). Cf. also J. Vezin, 'Réalisation matérielle', 18 ff. Medieval Allegory: D. Richter, 'Die Allegorie der Pergamentbearbeitung', in *Fachliteratur des Mittelalters, Festschrift für Gerhard Eis* (Stuttgart 1968) 83–92.

12 CLA II² 207; probably around 100. See below p. 66ff.

13 G. Ivy stresses the difficulty of distinguishing between parchment prepared from calves and that prepared from sheep. G.S. Ivy, *English Library Before 1700*, 34. T.J. Brown, 'The distribution and significance of membrane prepared in the Insular manner', in *La paléographie hébraique medievale*, Colloques Internationaux du CNRS 547 (Paris 1974) 127–35. Some of the decorated leaves of the carolingian San Paolo Bible are apparently made of goatskin. For an account of new results using microscopic analysis see Anna di Majo–Carlo Federici–Marco Palma in *Scriptorium* 39 (1985) 3–13, with illustr.   14 CLA V 578.

15 CLA III 299.

influence. Thus, for instance, 'Insular' parchment is the material of the carolingian manuscripts from Fulda and Mainz, and of the Munich 'Heliand', which originated at Corvey.

The slightly roughened surface of parchment prepared from calfskins was particularly suited to colour painting. As early as the ninth century such leaves bearing miniatures were inserted into manuscripts made from sheep parchment. After the carolingian period the use of calf parchment became commonplace. A speciality of the later middle ages is the extremely thin 'virgin' or 'uterine' parchment, which was prepared from the skin of unborn lambs. The quality of the parchment and the care taken in its selection and preparation are a yardstick for the standards of a scriptorium.

However, the acquisition of parchment must be viewed also as an economic problem.[16] For the production of the Codex Amiatinus alone – and it had two sister manuscripts – over 500 sheepskins were required at Wearmouth or Jarrow. In letters of the carolingian period (for example, Hrabanus Maurus, Ep. 26) we find instances in which parchment was sent along with a request that it be used for copies of texts. Entries in some manuscripts of the ninth century indicate the portions of parchment supplied by individual monks or canons.[17] The scriptoria of houses in reduced circumstances sometimes had to use marginal pieces; the Codex Toletanus of the *Etymologiae* is an extreme case: for it pieces of parchment from the neck and shoulders (of the animal skin), often irregularly shaped, had to be pressed into service.[18]

Parchment had hardly reached equality with papyrus in general esteem as a writing material when the late antique love of splendour led to its being dyed a rich purple colour, for use in special books; such luxury was then transferred to biblical codices. A purple manuscript of the gospels is the Codex Argenteus, probably written for Theoderic the Great. Just as the use of purple parchment was cultivated by the Anglo-Saxons, so too fine biblical and liturgical manuscripts of this kind were produced under Charlemagne and his first successor at the court and in other scriptoria. The dark, precious material required luminous, bright colours and therefore only gold and silver were used for the script.[19] Examples of complete purple manuscripts are, for instance, the Godescalc Evangelistary[20] and the Coronation Gospels of the German emperors, now among the imperial treasures in Vienna;[21] both date from the time of Charlemagne. In other manuscripts only single purple leaves were inserted.[22] It is

16 Lesne, *Livres*, 325 ff.
17 This is what the notes on pages 64 and 65 of St Gall, Stiftsb, 672 mean when they say 'Hucusque patravit Notker', and 'Abhinc vero . . . hoc totum est in commune patratum'; cf. Bischoff *Mittelalterliche Studien* 2, 35 n. l. In my view the entries 'portio Iotsmari, p. Salvioni' etc. in the Reims MSS, Cambridge, Pembroke College, 308 (f. 299 'portio communis') and Paris, BN, Lat. 12, 132 have the same meaning. (J. Vezin believes that they refer to distribution to scribes; see below p. 43n.31).   18 CLA XI 1638.
19 Purple parchment codices: E. Lesne, *Livres*, 14 ff.   20 CLA V 681.   21 CLA X 1469.
22 CLA V 576.

possible that all genuine purple parchment was imported from Byzantium. Purple leaves also appear in Ottonian and Salian manuscripts, but in these the parchment is not deep-dyed but only painted on the surface.[23] A late comparable example is the Sforza prayer-book on black parchment (Vienna, Nationalbibl. Cod. 1856).[24]

3. Palimpsests

As we have seen, it was possible with papyrus to efface one text and to use the material a second time; this procedure was also followed in the case of parchment manuscripts, with important consequences for the preservation of literary texts.[25] The writing was removed by washing or scraping and the parchment was then ready for re-use; this is called a palimpsest (Greek *palin psao*, 'I smooth over again').[26] In some cases this process was repeated, resulting in a 'double palimpsest'.[27] As a rule, manuscripts treated in this way were either incomplete or else the texts had become worthless, as was the case with manuscripts of the Vetus Latina, liturgical manuscripts (rendered out of date by liturgical reforms), or legal manuscripts (rendered void by prohibitions). In other cases texts were erased because they were written in a language that was no longer understood, as happened with Greek or Gothic works. A chance survivor of this kind is a seventh-century manuscript with some Hebrew texts.[28] Only rarely was the deliberate elimination of a text the primary motive for its effacement, such as might occur, for instance, with the destruction of heretical works.

The chances of recovering the original text vary greatly according to the kind of ink used and the nature of the deletion (which sometimes left only the prickings); they may also depend on whether chemicals were ever used in an attempt to recover the original writing. Chemical reagents can bring good results initially but they destroy the parchment and hamper the chances of success in using modern palimpsest photography, which does no harm to the parchment and which is usually the best means of decipherment.[29]

---

23 On purple dyed pages which use *murex* cf. H. Roosen-Runge, *Farbgebung und Technik frühmittelalterlicher Buchmalerei* (Berlin 1967) 2, 25 ff.; on painting with vegetable folium, ibid. 2, 34 ff.   24 E. Trenkler, *Das schwarze Gebetbuch* (Vienna 1948).

25 Fr. Mone, *De libris palimpsestis tam latinis quam graecis* (Karlsruhe 1855); Wattenbach, *Schriftwesen*, 300 ff.; an important bibliography by A. Dold in *Colligere fragmenta, Festschrift Alban Dold* (Beuron 1952) ix–xx.

26 There is a detailed recipe which prescribed bleaching writing in milk in Wattenbach, *Schriftwesen*, 303.   27 CLA II 166 f.; VII 955 ff., 968 ff.

28 Lowe, *Palaeographical Papers* 2, 517 ff. Latin palimpsests in the East: Arabic: CLA III 294 and 306; VIII 1036; Coptic: II 205 f.; XI 1651; Syrian: II 166 f. Cf. also G. Cavallo, 'La produzione di manoscritti greci in Occidente tra età tardoantica e alto medioevo', *Scrittura e Civiltà* 1 (1977) 111–31 with plate. The Latin palimpsests prior to c. 800 are listed by Lowe, *Palaeographical Papers* 2, 480–519; further examples in CLA Addenda.

29 See also B. Bischoff, 'Der Fronto-Palimpsest der Mauriner' *Sitzungsber. Bayer. Akad. Wiss.*, phil.-hist. Kl. 2 (1958) 19.

The most valuable and important western palimpsest manuscripts,[30] whose original scripts date from the fourth (or third?) century to the seventh, with secondary scripts from the seventh and eighth centuries, come from Bobbio, Luxeuil, Fleury, Corbie and St Gall. Amongst them are manuscripts of Cicero (*De re publica* and some orations), Plautus, Fronto, and also Ulfilas (U. Carolinus, in Wolfenbüttel, which was discovered by F.A. Knittel around 1756, an epoch-making event in palimpsest research), and the Visigothic Codex Euricianus. The Irish often used scraped parchment, though its palimpsest character is frequently difficult to determine. From the carolingian period on the use of palimpsests was relatively rare, and the deleted texts are mostly liturgical. But there are some surprising exceptions, such as the Old High German palimpsest from the beginning of the ninth century: it is an abbreviated version of the Abrogans from Weissenau, now Prague NUB, Lobkowitz MS. 434.[31]

4. Paper

From the thirteenth century on a new oriental writing material, paper ('carta papiri', 'carta bambacis', etc.) appears in the West along with parchment.[32] It was a Chinese invention of the second century AD, but it was only in AD 751 that it came to be produced outside China, by Chinese prisoners of war at Samarkand, whence it spread slowly throughout the muslim world. In the twelfth century the existence of a paper mill is attested in Xativa near Valencia, which was still under Arab rule. A century later paper production began in Christian Spain, at Fabiano in Italy (where it still flourishes), and around 1340 at Troyes in France. In Germany the first paper mill was founded in 1390 by Ulman Stromer, a Nürnberg patrician and merchant, with the help of Italian workers.

At first Arab paper was used in the West. Although mandates on paper emanating from the chancery of Frederick II have come down to us, in 1231 he prohibited the use of paper for notarial instruments. Its use in the chanceries was therefore mainly restricted to drafts, registers, minutes, etc. The earliest paper manuscript of German origin is the register of the dean of the cathedral in Passau, Albert Beham, dated 1246/47 (Clm 2574b).[33] The earliest paper is

---

30 J. Benton, 'Nouvelles recherches sur le déchiffrement des textes effacés, grattés ou lavés', *Acad. d. inscript. et belles-lettres*, Comptes rendus (1978) 580–94, with illustr.; idem, 'Digital image-processing applied to the photography of manuscripts', *Scriptorium* 33 (1979) 40–55 with plates 9–13; Ch. Samaran, in *Miscellanea codicologica F. Masai dicata MCMLXXIX* 2 (Ghent 1979) 597–599. This work supersedes É. Chatelain, *Les palimpsestes latins* (Paris 1903) in all respects.   31 Baesecke, *Lichtdrucke*, 36–8.
32 F. Hoyer/ H.H. Bockwitz, *Einführung in die Papierkunde* (Leipzig 1941); Wattenbach, *Schriftwesen*, 139–149; Santifaller, *Beiträge*, 116–52; Cencetti, *Lineamenti*, 30–3; H. Hunger, *Geschichte der Textüberlieferung*, 38 ff.; Foerster, *Aribß²*, 57 ff.; Stiennon, *Paléographie*, 156–8; J. Vezin, 'Réalisation materielle', 22 f.   33 Chroust, *Monumenta* 1 1, 7 and 2, 8.

sometimes thick and soft, sometimes rough and durable. The development of standard measurements in its production has contributed to the standardisation of book sizes.[34] Already before 1300 the custom began of distinguishing paper by the use of watermarks. These trademarks, consisting of a wire outline fastened to the grid of the mould, made many shapes: letters, animals, tools, emblems of all kinds. They are charming in their variety and useful as well, for they enable us in many instances to determine the provenance of the paper and to date a manuscript approximately.[35]

5.   *Wax Tablets*

Wax tablets[36] were used both in antiquity and in the middle ages. They were made by scraping out a shallow bed in a wood or ivory tablet; the bed was then covered with a layer of wax on which letters were scratched with a stylus, whose broad end could be used to remove them again. If two or more tablets were joined together we speak of a diptych, triptych, or polyptych. In antiquity, tablets were probably the most commonly used material for writing on, and examples containing documents, letters and school exercises have been found at many sites dating from Roman times.[37] Tablets are also often represented in sculptures and paintings. Best-known are those found in Pompei and in Transylvania, the latter from the second century AD, the former from the first. Writing with a stylus on wax changes the shapes of the letters considerably, therefore those diptychs are of special interest where we find on the outside of the sealed document, written with a reed pen, and often most likely by the same hand, a copy or summary of the text that is scratched on the wax inside.[38]

Even bare wooden tablets, which could also be joined together to form diptychs, etc., were a common writing material in various regions. They have been found in the most remote corners of the Roman empire: tablets (made perhaps of limewood) bearing accounts and private letters (saec. I ex.) from

34 Dionysius Menger, a Benedictine monk in Regensburg, distinguished between the following sizes of volumes in his library catalogue of 1500–1: 'papirus regalis' (large 2°), 'arcus modus' (2°), 'textpletel' (4°), 'regelpletel' (small 4°, 8°), 'halbregelpletel' (12°); *Mittelalt. Bibliothekskat. Deutschl.* 4, 1, 187.
35 On the study of watermarks: Ch.-M. Briquet, *Les filigranes*² 1–4 (Amsterdam 1968); *Monumenta chartae papyraceae historiam illustrantia* (Hilversum 1950 ff.); G. Piccard, *Die Kronenwasserzeichen*, Findbuch 1 der Wasserzeichenkartei Piccard im HStA Stuttgart, (Stuttgart 1961); idem, *Die Ochsenkopfwasserzeichen* 1–3, Findb. 2, 1–3 (Stuttgart 1966). J. Irigoin, 'La datation par les filigranes du papier, *Codicologica* 5 [Litterae Textuales] (1980) 9–36.
36 Wattenbach, *Schriftwesen*, 51–89; Cencetti, *Lineamenti*, 21–23; Foerster, *Abriß*², 40 ff.
37 R. Marichal, *Scriptorium* 4 (1950) 131 ff.
38 Examples in E. Diehl, *Inscriptiones Latinae* (Bonn 1912) xix–xxvi (from the years 58 and 59); Seider, *Lateinische Papyri*, 1, xii f., Nr. 25 (from the year 128). Cf. G. Cencetti, 'Note paleografiche sulla scrittura dei papiri latini dal I al III secolo D.C.', *Accademia delle Scienze dell' Istituto di Bologna*, Classe di scienze morali, Memorie, ser 5, 1 (1950) 6 f.

Vindolanda, a settlement on Hadrian's Wall in England;[39] another, a deposit of wooden tablets (cedar and oak) bearing agricultural contracts, from south-east Algeria dating from the period of Vandal rule, between AD 493 and AD 496.[40]

From the last centuries of antiquity come the 'consular diptychs', which were presented as gifts by consuls at the beginning of their term of office; these were made of ivory and decorated with bas-reliefs.[41] Such tablets were often used during the middle ages to record litanies or a list of church benefactors, and on some of them the writing can still be seen on the back. Other diptychs were used as book covers for precious manuscripts. Objects similar in outward appearance to the diptychs were also re-utilised in this way, such as the Christian ivory tablets from Ravenna, now in Berlin, and the Barberini ivory polyptych in the Louvre; the former bears an inscribed litany (sixth century) and the latter a long list of names (second half of the seventh century).[42]

During the middle ages wax tablets were in general use.[43] Daily life cannot be imagined without them: students were supposed to carry a diptych at their belt for easy use, while writers used them for rough notes. They were also employed in private correspondence. Above all, medieval accounts were kept to a large extent on wax tablets, and most of the surviving examples served this purpose; even books of wax tablets were formed. In some places the use of wax tablets for accounting continued up to the nineteenth century.[44]

6. Other writing materials and other kinds of writing

Some other forms of writing and some other writing materials have to be mentioned, partly because they are of interest for the history of handwriting

39 Cf. J.D. Thomas, 'New light on early Latin writing: the Vindolanda Tablets', *Scriptorium* 30 (1976) 38–43 with plates. Alan K. Bowman–J. David Thomas and others, *Vindolanda, the Latin writing-tablets*, Brittania Monogr. Ser. 4 (London 1983). Further small tablets were found in Somerset and in Kempten.

40 Chr. Courtois et al., *Tablettes Albertini, Actes privés de l'epoque vandale*, text and plates (Paris 1953); for the script see ibid., 15–62 (Ch. Perrat).

41 R. Delbrück, *Die Konsulardiptychen und verwandte Denkmäler* (Berlin 1929).

42 J. Vezin, 'Une nouvelle lecture de la liste des noms copiée au dos de l'ivoire Barberini', *Bull. Archéol. du Comité des trav. hist. et scientifiques*, n.s. 7 (1971) 19–56, with plates.

43 The rectangular writing tablets from Springmount Bog, Ireland, with texts of the psalms in the earliest type of Irish script (CLA S 1684), may be dated around 600; cf. D. Wright, 'The tablets from Springmount Bog, a key to early Irish palaeography', *Amer. J. Archaeol.* 67 (1963) 219. On the finely-cut diptych from St Maurille, Angers, which has a curved top (s.IX; script c. 1000?) cf. J. Vezin, *Les scriptoria d'Angers au XIe siècle* (Paris 1974) 120 ff. Fourteenth-century writing tablets survive from the Jacobischule in Lübeck; see J. Warncke in *Z. f. Gesch. d. Erziehung u. d. Unterrichts* 2 (1912) 227 ff. with plate. Medieval accounts, Foerster, *Abriß²*, 43.

44 The references in Wattenbach can be greatly augmented; cf. inter alia A Petrucci, *Le tavolette cerate fiorentine di Casa Majorfi* (Rome 1965). On a forgery H. Fichtenau, 'Das Wachstafelbüchlein des Instituts für Österreichische Geschichtsforschung', in F. Brunhölzl and J. Autenreith (edd), *Festschrift Bernhard Bischoff* (Stuttgart 1971) 435–40. On the tallies

(whose development they help to explain in periods where there are gaps in the transmission), partly also because they add to our knowledge of the practical aspects of writing.[45]

Latin graffiti, that is incised inscriptions, have been found in large numbers on walls in Pompeii, close to the tombs of martyrs, and in many other places. The oldest ones date from the time of Sulla and therefore predate the oldest wax tablets and papyri.[46]

In Pompeii excellent examples of capitalis dating from the last years before the destruction of the city can be seen painted with a brush on the walls of houses.[47]

Writing on clay has been preserved both in the form of engraved writing[48] – such as, for instance, the potters' accounts found in Gaul (first century) – and also in the form of writing with ink on ostraca (first to fifth/sixth century).[49]

Latin cursing tables made of lead, with cursive script (both the older and later forms) are preserved from the first century BC to the sixth century AD.[50]

Where slate was available as a natural writing material it too was used. The oldest charters in Visigothic Spain were written in cursive on slate.[51] Examples from both the early and late middle ages come from Ireland;[52] another, a

---

used for accounts (see Wattenbach, *Schriftwesen*, 95 f.) cf. Ch. Johnson (ed.), *The Course of the Exchequer by Richard son of Nigel*, Medieval Classics (London 1950) xliv, 22–4 and plate; K. Menninger, *Zahlwort und Ziffer* 2² (Göttingen 1958) 39–42 with reprod.

45 Wattenbach, *Schriftwesen*, 47 ff (lead), 89 ff. (tile, wood, slate); Stiennon, *Paléographie*, 147 (slate, lead).

46 Charles Petri, art. 'Graffito I', *Reallex. f. Antike u. Christentum* 12 (1983) cols 637–67. Despite its defects the best collection of material from Pompeii is still K. Zangemeister's edition, *Corpus Inscriptionum Latinarum*⁴. On San Sebastiano outside Rome: P. Styger, 'Il monumento apostolico della Via Appia secondo gli ultimi scavi della basilica di S. Sebastiano', *Atti della Pontificia Accademia Romana di archeologia*, ser 2, 13 (Rome 1917) 57 ff. with plate 1 ff.; R. Marichal, 'Paléographie précaroline et papyrologie III', *Scriptorium* 9 (1955) 138.

47 Examples: Mallon, Marichal, Perrat, *Écriture latine*, plate 4; Seider, *Lateinische Papyri* 1, plates 4 (7) and 8 (13).

48 R. Marichal, *Les graffites de la Graufesenque*, Gallia Suppl. 47 (Paris 1988); A. Petrucci, 'Per la storia della scrittura romana: I graffiti di Condatomagos', *Bull. dell'Arch. Pal. Ital.*, ser 3, 1 (1962) 84–132 with 3 plates; *Écriture latine*, plate 6 (7/8).

49 R. Marichal, 'Paléographie précaroline et papyrologie (1) II', *Scriptorium* 5 (1950) 133 f.; idem, 'Les ostraka de Bu. Njem', *Acad. d. inscript. et belles-lettres*, Comptes rendus (1979) 436–52. Seider, *Papyri* 1, plate 1 (2).

50 W.S. Fox, 'The Johns Hopkins Tabellae defixionum', *Supplement to the American Journal of Philology* 33/1, Nr. 129 (1912), with plate; K. Preisendanz, 'Die griechischen und lateinischen Zaubertafeln', *Arch. f. Papyrusforschung* 9 (1930) 11 ff. and 11 (1933) 153 ff.

51 M. Gómez-Moreno, *Documentación goda en pizarra*, R. Academia de la Historia (Madrid 1966); on which cf. M.C. Díaz y Díaz, *Studi Medievali*, ser 3, 7 (1966) 75–107; idem, 'Consideraciones sobre las pizarras visigoticas', in *Paleografía y archivistica. Actas de las I jornadas de metodología aplicada de las ciencias historicas V* (Santiago de Compostela 1976) 23–9.

52 H.C. Lawlor, *The Monastery of St. Mochai of Nendrum* (Belfast 1925) 144 and plate 12; A.J. Bliss, 'The inscribed slates at Smarmore', *Proc. Roy. Ir. Acad.* 64 (C) (1965) with plates 1–4.

benediction, was found at the Cistercian monastery of Vauclair near Laon (c. thirteenth century?).

In Vadstena (Sweden) as well as in Novgorod, birch bark was used as a writing material.[53]

It should be mentioned here in passing that two small, quadrangular wooden rods from Bergen (Norway) have been identified as the verses of two love-songs from the *Carmina Burana* copied in runes.[54]

7. Ink and colours

Already in antiquity different types of ink were known. Some were prepared from soot and gum, some with sepia or with gall nuts and iron vitriol.[55] At a later date the latter type, reacting to a damper atmosphere, has eaten into or even through the fine parchment of late antiquity so that today we see 'little windows' instead of letters.[56] The ink used in manuscripts of the fourth to sixth centuries appears often to have the consistency of lacquer and to have adhered less well to the flesh-side of the parchment than to the hair-side. Its colour varies between clear, deep yellow and olive brown. By the sixth century AD a brown ink was already in use which was prepared from the branches of whitehorn or blackthorn with the addition of wine; the preparation of this ink was described in detail by Theophilus (about AD 1100).[57] The ink could be made darker by adding iron vitriol or soot. From the seventh century onwards, dark brown ink predominated on the continent. During the eighth century ink sometimes has a greenish tinge. The ink of Italian manuscripts is frequently of a greyish or yellowish colour. On the other hand, Irish, Breton, and Anglo-Saxon scribes must have used a different recipe, because they generally use a black or black-brown ink, which they then brought with them to the continent, for instance to Lower Germany and other areas of Anglo-Saxon influence in Germany.

From the late middle ages there are again numerous recipes for ink using combinations of iron vitriol and oak galls mixed with wine, rain-water, or vinegar. The ink produced in this way was usually black or brownish-black in colour, but pale inks too are often found in the later period.

In order to distinguish certain details in a text or manuscript the commonest practice was to write them with brick-red ink (minium, red lead). Already in the oldest western parchment manuscripts, as well as in the peculiar Codex Bezae,[58]

---

53 O. Odenius, 'En notis om björknäver som skrivmaterial i Vadstenakloster under senmedeltiden', *KyrkhistoriskÅrsskrift* (1959) 163–71 with reprod. (see *Scriptorium* 15 (1961) 193).

54 A. Liestøl, 'Runeninschriften von der Bryggen in Bergen (Norwegen)', *Z. f. Archäologie d. Mittelalters* 1 (1973) 129–39.

55 Wattenbach, *Schriftwesen*, 237 ff; Monique Zerdoun Bat-Yehouda, *Les encres noires au moyen âge (jusqu'à 1600)* (Paris 1983).   56 CLA III 345; IV 436 a.b.

57 H. Roosen-Runge, 'Die Tinte des Theophilus', in *Festschrift Luitpold Dussler* (Berlin 1972) 87–112.   58 CLA III 140.

two or three initial lines of a book may be written in red. In explicits, and later in titles, red and black lines frequently alternate. During the early middle ages it is not uncommon to find manuscripts in which the main text is written in red, with the accompanying commentary in black.[59] A unique case is the gospel-book, London, BL, Harl. MS 2795 (saec. IX), from northern France, which is written entirely in red. In some carolingian scriptoria the red ink has a strong blue tinge.

Already in the carolingian period other colours besides bright red were used for display purposes: blue-black in Tours, grey-blue in Lyons and Salzburg, brownish red in Freising. In twelfth–century France there is frequent alternation between red, blue, green, and yellow in titles and small initials, whereas in the thirteenth and fourteenth centuries the alternation between red and blue is very common.

From antiquity we have references to books written in gold, and the luxury of gold and silver writing on purple parchment was adopted by Christians in East and West for the production of gospels and psalters;[60] Saint Jerome, however, sharply denounced this excess in his Prologue to Job. Several different recipes for ink made with gold, silver, or cheaper substitutes have come down to us.[61] There is no evidence for the use of precious inks or purple parchment in Ireland or in Lombard Italy, nor in the Merovingian kingdoms, but the Anglo-Saxons used both (gold writing occurs already in the Lindisfarne Gospels).

The carolingians liked brilliant writing on purple parchment as well as on ordinary parchment, either for complete manuscripts or for occasional display; but they confined its use almost entirely to liturgical manuscripts.[62] Faced with a choice between the precious metals, the carolingians almost always preferred gold or its substitutes. Otto the Great had magnificent copies of his donation to the Roman Church (AD 962) and of the so-called marriage contract of Theophano made in this extravagant style. The tradition of making de luxe manuscripts continued into Salian times. Gold writing is used particularly for the names of saints in calendars, litanies and legendaries. In later times, gold and silver writing becomes rare. John of Troppau, the master of the Golden Gospel of Albrecht III of Austria written in 1368 (Vienna, Nationalbibl., MS 1182) had

59 For red ink in quotations see Lowe, *Palaeographical Papers* 1, 273. Insular scribes, perhaps in order to empty their pens, often added a red stroke to the abbreviation symbol; cf. e.g. CLA II 121, 213, 241, 259, 273; VII 998.

60 See Lowe, ibid. 2, 400. The text of these manuscripts is written in silver, and in CLA III 399, IV 481 and V 616 the Nomina Sacra are in gold, in IV 481 the opening page of each gospel and the Lord's Prayer are also in gold. The Codex Argenteus, in gothic, is written in silver, with the canon numbers in gold.

61 Vera Trost, 'Die Metalltintenrezepte aus der Hs. Aa 20 der Hessischen Landesbibliothek Fulda', in *Diversarum artium studia, Festschrift für Heinz Roosen-Runge zum 70. Geburtstag* (Wiesbaden 1982) 185–208.

62 For the early middle ages see the list in Lesne, *Livres*, 13 ff. In Paris, BN, Lat. 257, s. IX, the words of Christ are regularly written in gold.

amongst his models a display manuscript from the early middle ages.[63] On the other hand, the decoration of initials with gold and silver, later with appliquéd goldleaf, was common practice during the entire middle ages.[64]

Materials and methods of book illumination are described in the collection of recipes of the *Mappae clavicula* (from late antiquity, expanded during the early middle ages); in the so-called *Heraclius* (roughly eleventh-century); in the *Schedula diversarum artium* of the monk Theophilus (about AD 1100), and in others.[65]

8. Writing instruments

For writing with ink, the normal instrument used in antiquity was the reed pen, the calamus.[66] While the reed probably continued to be used in the Mediterranean world at least during the early middle ages, the medieval West otherwise wrote mostly with a quill pen (often still termed a calamus in the sources).[67] Ever since Aldhelm's time, the quill pen was the theme of Latin and Old English riddles amongst the Anglo-Saxons, and the Verona riddle (about AD 800) also refers to the pen.[68] There are some late medieval instructions extant for the cutting of the quill pen, its 'tempering'.[69]

For writing on wax tablets the stylus was used, but it was also frequently employed with parchment for notes of all kinds.[70] Old High German glosses are entered almost undetectably in many manuscripts in this way. Red chalk and, in later times, styluses of soft metal were also used for entering notes.

The equipment of the medieval scribe, who wrote on a sloping desk, consisted of 'chalk, two pumice stones, two ink horns (for black and red ink), a sharp knife, two razors ("novaculas sive rasoria duo") for erasing, a "punctorium", an awl,

63 G. Schmidt, 'Johann von Troppau und die vorromanische Buchmalerei', *Studien zur Buchmalerei und Goldschmiedekunst des Mittelalters. Festschrift für Karl Hermann Usener* (Marburg 1967) 275 ff.

64 Gold leaf was preserved in manuscripts; see the Cologne library catalogue of 833 'Librum S. Augustini, in quo iacebant petulae aureae' (A. Dekker in *Festschrift der 43. Versammlung deutscher Philologen und Schulmänner* (Bonn 1895) 228). Traces of it occur in several manuscripts (CLA IV 484; X 1450); also in Clm 4577, f. 17ʳ, 20ᵛ ff; 75ʳ.

65 Cf. H. Roosen-Runge, *Farbgebung und Technik frühmittelalterlicher Buchmalerei* 1/2 (Berlin 1967). On the 'Mappae clavicula' cf. B. Bischoff, 'Die Überlieferung der technischen Literatur', in *Artigianato e tecnica nella società dell' alto medio evo occidentale*, Settimane 18 (Spoleto 1971) 1, 277 ff.

66 For what follows cf. Wattenbach, *Schriftwesen*, 215 ff.; Cencetti, *Lineamenti*, 33–5.

67 Stiennon, *Paléographie*, 159–61.

68 Cf. P. Rajna, 'Un' indovinello volgare scritto alla fine del secolo VIII o al principio del IX', *Speculum* 3 (1928) 291–313; reprod.: G. Turrini, *Millennium scriptorii Veronensis dal IVᵒ al XVᵒ secolo* (Verona 1967) plate 14. Helga Goebel, *Studien zu den altenglischen Schriftwesen-Rätseln*. Epistemata, Würz. Wiss. Schrift., Reihe Literaturwiss. 7 (1980) (Königshausen).

69 Cf. Wattenbach, *Schriftwesen*, 230 f. The 'Regulae de modo scindendi pennarum' ed. by F. Bech, *Z. f. deut. Philol.* 8 (1877) 348 are particularly detailed.

70 Bischoff, *Mittelalterliche Studien* 1, 88–92.

lead, a straight edge, and a ruling stick'.[71] The 'punctorium' was an instrument for making little pricked markings on the parchment to serve as guides for ruling lines; it consisted of a pair of compasses, though in later times a small wheel with points was also used.[72]

The importance of spectacles (invented about 1285) should not be overlooked, not only for reading, but also for writing.[73]

71 In accordance with the statutes of the Carthusians, cf. Gumbert, *Utrechter Kartäuser*, 308 f.

72 The monk in the well-drawn initial L of Berlin, Staatsbibl. Preuß. Kulturbesitz, MS Theol. Lat. fol. 270 (French, s. XII), f. 224^r seems to be holding a more complicated instrument with the same function: a fully-opened compass from one of whose legs a third movable leg branches out at an acute angle; illustr. infra, plate 14. For literature on the 'punctorium' see p. 21–22.

73 In classical times enlarging lenses were already used. On the use of quartz 'reading stones' in the middle ages and the invention of spectacles see G. Eis, *Vom Werden altdeutscher Dichtung* (Berlin 1962) 41 ff. Medieval evidence for writing with the aid of spectacles in Wattenbach, *Schriftwesen*, 288 f. On the important find of medieval spectacles under the oak floor of the choir of the nunnery at Wienhausen see H. Appuhn, 'Ein denkwürdiger Fund', *Zeiss-Werkzeitschrift* (1958) 27, 1–8 with plates.; idem, 'Das private Andachtsbild im Mittelalter an Hand der Funde im Kloster Wienhausen', *Das Leben in der Stadt des Spätmittelalters*, Sitzungsber. Österr. Akad. Wiss., phil.-hist. Kl., 325 (1977) 162 f. and plates 92 f. Imprints of medieval spectacles have been found both on an early medieval fragment in the Münster University Library and on another in the Gerleve monastery library. On the inside of the front cover of Clm 19717 (psalms, s. XVI^1) a suitably shaped cavity has been fashioned to hold spectacles. (I owe this reference to Frau Dr. H. Spilling.)

The external characteristics of the written heritage

1. The codex

The usual form of book in late antiquity and in the middle ages was the codex, which consisted of simple sheets of papyrus or parchment folded once and sewn together to form quires or gatherings.[1] In origin it was an imitation of wax tablet diptychs and it had a predecessor in the parchment notebook.[2] Martial is the first writer to mention a parchment codex format for a literary work, but he himself clearly preferred the papyrus roll. The terms 'liber', 'volumen', and 'tomus', originally used to designate the papyrus roll, were transferred to the codex after it had become the almost exclusive form of book.[3]

As early as the second century AD, Egyptian Christians were imitating the papyrus codex by making parchment codices, which allowed a more economical use of the writing material than the roll.[4] The size of the gathering varied widely in these first papyrus books, ranging from one bifolium to fifty or more leaves, so that a whole book (such as a gospel) might comprise one gathering. In the age of parchment, this arrangement was still imitated in Irish pocket-gospels of the eighth century, for example in the Codex Bonifatianus 3 at Fulda.[5]

In continental book production, from antiquity until the early middle ages, a regular parchment gathering normally consisted of four double leaves (quaternio). In contrast, the gatherings in most Irish and Anglo-Saxon manuscripts consist of five double leaves (*quinio*, Old Irish *cín*, Anglo-Saxon *cine*). This practice may also have been in imitation of a Roman model, as it is found,

1 Santifaller, *Beiträge*, 162 ff.; Cencetti, *Lineamenti*, 36–42; *Compendio*, 10 f.; G.S. Ivy, in *The English Library before 1700*, ed. F. Wormald, C.E. Wright (London 1958) 38 ff.; J. Vezin, 'La réalisation matérielle des manuscrits latins pendant le haut Moyen Age', *Codicologica* 2 [Litterae textuales] (Leiden 1978) 23 ff. Cf. also the reproductions mentioned on p. 21 n. 11.
2 C.H. Roberts-T.C. Skeat, *The birth of the codex* (Oxford 1983).
3 Santifaller, *Beiträge*, 166 ff. Cf. R. Schieffer, 'Tomus Gregorii papae', *Arch. f. Dipl.* 17 (1971) 169–84.
4 On the question of origins see p. 8, n. 5; T.C. Skeat, *Cambridge History of the Bible* 2 (Cambridge 1969) 65–79. Examples: the Greek Chester Beatty biblical books on papyrus. Cf. also E.G. Turner, *The typology of the early codex* (Philadelphia 1977).   5 See below p. 86.

for instance, in the Bembine Terence.[6] In the later middle ages the number of parchment or paper sheets in a gathering increases.

If flesh-side and hair-side have not been made indistinguishable by scraping with a pumice stone (as is the case with Insular parchment) then one of the rules of orderly book-making is that like pages should face like. On the other hand, some scriptoria in the north of France in the eighth century (for example, the school of Laon),[7] do not follow this rule. In antiquity the flesh-sides normally formed the outside of the gatherings; in the early middle ages, on the other hand, hair-sides faced outwards.

In the middle ages gatherings were formed not only of double leaves but also of large sheets folded several times (which could be carried out in a variety of ways); the gathering had then to be cut along the edges.[8] At the end of the middle ages, and probably already before the invention of printing, it was customary to write books in small format (breviaries, prayer books, school primers) on uncut sheets of eight or sixteen pages – as the discovery of discarded cuttings has shown. In such cases, the arrangement of the pages must have been the same as for a printed sheet (in octavo or quarto).[9] There are indications that this practice of writing on unseparated double leaves, that is, imposition, was followed occasionally even in earlier centuries.[10]

In general, the leaves were ruled when the gatherings were put together. In preparation for the ruling the leaves were pricked to mark the positions of the vertical lines and the spaces between the horizontal ones.[11] There are, however,

---

6 Cf. CLA II, p. vi f.   7 Cf. CLA VI, p. xviii; An exception: CLA VI 766.
8 Cf. L. Gilissen, 'La composition des cahiers, le pliage du parchemin et l'imposition', *Scriptorium* 26 (1972) 3–33 with plates 1–8 and reprod.; idem, *Prolégomènes à la codicologie* (Ghent 1977) 14 ff.; J. Vezin 'Réalisation matérielle', 25 ff.
9 Ch. Samaran, 'Manuscrits "imposés" à la manière typographique', in *Mélanges en l'honneur de M. Fr. Martroye* (Paris 1940) 3–12 with reprod.; idem, 'Nouveaux exemples de manuscrits "imposés à la manière typographique" ', *Comptes-rendus de l'Académie des Inscriptions et Belles-Lettres* (1950) 1–6; G.I. Lieftinck, 'Mediaeval manuscripts with "imposed" sheets', *Het Boek*, ser 3, 34, 210–20 with plate; (on p. 214 there is information on the measurements of elementary schoolbooks which were perhaps copied according to this practice). Ch. Samaran, 'Manuscrits "imposés" et manuscrits non coupés – un nouvel exemple', *Codices manuscripti* 2 (1976) 38–42 with reprod.; Gr. Hövelmann, 'Gaesdonck Ms. 5. Eine unaufgeschnittene Handschrift des 15. Jahrhunderts', *Börsenblatt f. d. deut. Buchhandel*, Frankfurter Ausg., *Aus dem Antiquariat* 18 (1968) 217–22; Gilissen, *Prolégomènes*, 114 ff. Pieter F.J. Obbema, 'Writing on uncut sheets', *Quaerendo* 8 (1978) 337–54, with illustr.; J. Vezin, 'A propos d'un tableau du peintre Hermann tom Ring figurant un scribe transcrivant un livre suivant le procédé de l'imposition', *Bull. Soc. Nat. Antiquaires* 1978/9, 102–6, with illustr.
10 A.L. Doyle, 'Further observations on Durham Cathedral Ms. A. IV. 34' in *Varia Codicologica. Essays presented to G.I. Lieftinck* 1 (Amsterdam 1972) 35–47 with reprod.
11 L.W. Jones, 'Pricking manuscripts: the instruments and their significance', *Speculum* 21 (1946) 389–403; 'Ancient prickings in eighth-century manuscripts', *Scriptorium* 15 (1961) 14–22, with further literature. New methodological suggestions in L. Gilissen, 'Un élément trop peu exploité: la réglure', *Scriptorium* 23 (1969) 150–62; idem, 'Les réglures des manuscrits', *Scrittura e Civiltà* 5 (1981) 231–52.

manuscripts from late antiquity in which only the frame for the writing space was drawn.[12] In antiquity, and in most countries in the middle ages up to the twelfth century, the unfolded sheets (double leaf, bifolium) were pricked and ruled, either individually or in groups of two, or even the whole gathering together.[13] In this way, each individual leaf (folio, half-sheet) shows only one vertical series of prickings (or small slits). In manuscripts up to the sixth century the prickings were frequently inside the writing area; later, they normally appear at the edge of the writing area or at the outer margin. Not infrequently, double tram-lines were drawn to guide the writing of calligraphic initials.[14]

At the beginning of the ninth century, an especially careful antique method of ruling was rediscovered and used in some of the best carolingian schools, such as Tours.[15] This method involved placing one double leaf on top of another with the flesh-sides facing up, ruling them together, and then turning one over so that in the same gathering only homogeneous pages with identical dry-point ruling faced each other, furrows on the flesh-side, ridges on the hair-side.

The Irish and the Anglo-Saxons had their own method: they folded the gatherings of sheets first, then pricked each leaf or half-sheet left and right, that is in both margins.[16]

When double leaves were ruled before folding, the top and bottom lines of both pages were often drawn in one continuous line.[17] From the twelfth century on, lead was frequently used for ruling; from the thirteenth century onwards, ink comes into use.

The economical use of a page of writing, and the impression it makes on the reader, are directly related to the space between the lines, the size of the letters, and the length of the ascenders and descenders.[18] Between the twelfth and the thirteenth centuries, there is a change in so far as the top line was no longer written on but was left blank, in order to serve as a frame.[19] From the thirteenth century on, the sequence of the double leaves in a gathering is frequently

---

12 E.g. CLA III 397a.
13 An exception: the African gospel MS (k), s. IV–V (CLA IV 465).
14 Lowe, *Palaeographical Papers* I, 274; carolingian, e.g. CLA X 1469.
15 On the practice at Corbie cf. T.A.M. Bishop, 'The script of Corbie: a criterion', in *Essays Presented to G.I. Lieftinck* I (Amsterdam 1972) 11 ff. While the scribes (who may have been women) who wrote 'ab' script began each quire with a hair side facing outside, scribes writing caroline minuscule from the time of Maurdramnus to that of Hadoard placed a flesh side outside. Cf. also p. 106 n. 93.
16 E.A. Lowe in CLA II², p. x. The continental system of ruling bifolia was used in England even before the conquest, but when ruling with a stylus or a dry point was replaced by ruling with lead a return to the earlier Insular practice may be observed. See Ker, *English MSS*, 41 ff.
17 The practice of signalling these with double prickings is discussed by Gumbert, *Utrechter Kartäuser*, 153 ff.   18 Ker, *English MSS*, 44 f.
19 N. Ker, 'From "above top line" to "below top line": a change in scribal practice', *Celtica* 5 (1960) 13–16; repr. in A.G. Watson (ed.), *Books, Collectors and Libraries. Studies in the Medieval Heritage* (London 1985) 71–4.

indicated by marks.[20] In some very old manuscripts the first and last pages of a gathering are left blank.[21]

Gatherings were numbered. In Latin manuscripts from the Byzantine East, numbers were placed in the bottom left-hand corner of the first page of each gathering, following Greek usage;[22] whereas in the oldest Latin usage the numbers appear in the bottom right-hand corner of the last page.[23] From the fifth century on, the letters A, B, etc. were also used, often preceded by Q(uat.). In later times the numbers were moved to the centre of the lower margin and were frequently framed. The practice of signing with AX, BU, CT, etc., which is found in two manuscripts from Corbie, following after A–Z, recalls an antique elementary-school exercise.[24]

Other methods of marking the sequence of quires are to use the letters in a name,[25] or a number of points,[26] or even more exotic systems.[27] A further aid for the bookbinder are the catchwords (Reklamanten) written under the last line or word of a gathering, indicating the first word or syllable with which the first page in the next gathering began. This usage is found already in Spain in the tenth century, in France and Italy in the eleventh, and is later found everywhere.[28]

After sporadic earlier occurrences, foliation appears relatively often from the twelfth century on, and from the thirteenth onwards we also encounter pagination or even a continuous counting of columns in both liturgical and other manuscripts. In addition to foliation and pagination, another practice – more obviously intended to serve the purpose of citation – is the numbering of the four columns of an open book in manuscripts with two columns to the page. Even lines were numbered in some scholarly works, but this custom seems to have been restricted to England, and more particularly to Oxford, from the mid thirteenth to the early fourteenth century.[29] Readers as well as copyists used as bookmarks little wheels of parchment with the numbers I to IV (representing the columns); the wheels could be rotated and moved along a thread. Quite a

---

20 Lehmann, *Erforschung* 3, 13; on St Gallen 672, s. IX, cf. Bruckner, *Scriptoria* 3, 116.
21 CLA I 74, 115 and perhaps VI 833.
22 So in the Verona Gaius and in other MSS of eastern origin; cf. Lowe, *Palaeographical Papers* 2, table following p. 470.   23 Lowe, *Palaeographical Papers* 1, 202 and 271 f.
24 H.-I. Marrou, *A History of Education in Antiquity* (pb. New York 1964) 364.
25 CLA IX 1384.   26 In the de luxe MS Tours 22, s. IX.
27 An Italian scribe who copied Vat. Reg. Lat. 1308 in France in the eleventh century numbered the quires with the arabic numerals and their names, which Gerbert had introduced to the West.
28 J. Vezin, 'Observations sur l'emploi des réclames dans les manuscrits latins', *Bibl. Éc. Chartes* 125 (1967) 5–33; idem, 'Codicologie comparée', in *La paléographie hébraïque médiévale*. Coll. internat. du CNRS 547 (Paris 1974) 153–61. For tironian notes as genuine catchwords see Laon 50, s. VIII/IX (CLA VI 763).
29 For the foregoing cf. Lehmann, *Erforschung* 3, 1–59 and 4, 17–19.

number of these have been found dating from the thirteenth to the fifteenth centuries.[30]

2. *Format*

The size of the codex depended not only on the extent of the work(s) which it contained but was related also to the nature of its contents and the purpose of the book, for example, whether it was intended as a de luxe copy, a portable missal, or for refectory reading. The size in turn decisively influenced the type of the script, although there were special traditions for some types of book.[31] What precise format parchment manuscripts took depended on the size of the rectangular area that was available for use after the prepared animal skin had been folded; (in antiquity, and for the most part in the middle ages, this meant sheepskins). The parchment could be folded once or twice or three times, but this natural sequence might be disturbed if wider or narrower proportions, or square books, were preferred. However, later trimming of books often makes it difficult to determine their original formats.[32]

The largest extant antique codices[33] are de luxe copies of works by Virgil and Lucan, and the Florentine codex of the Digests.[34] On the other hand, particularly small formats were known already in Christian antiquity. The smallest extant Latin book from this period, the gospel of St John in Paris, BN, MS Lat. 10,439 (saec. V–VI), 71 × 51 mm (45 × 34 mm, 11 lines) was perhaps worn as an amulet.[35] In the large formats, Bibles in one volume predominate[36] from the

30 Cf. J. Destrez, 'L'outillage des copistes du XIIIe et du XIVe siècles', in *Aus der Geisteswelt des Mittelalters, Festschrift Martin Grabmann* (Münster i. W. 1935) 19–34 with plate; H. Schreiber, 'Cavilla – ein spätmittelalterliches Lesezeichen?', in *Otto Glauning zum 60. Geburtstag* 2 (Leipzig 1938) 97–103 with reprod.; idem in *Zentralbl. f. Bibliothekswesen* 56 (1939) 281 ff. with reprod.   31 See below p. 26.

32 Ker gives some regular sizes of the written space in English manuscripts of the eleventh and twelfth centuries in *English MSS*, 40 f. There is a model for formats (s. XI) in Stuttgart, HB XIV 3, f. 2–3: 'Istud moderatum est secundum modulationem libri qui est de Retinbuch.' See also p. 136.

33 The formats of Roman and early Christian codices are listed by Lowe, *Palaeographical Papers*, 1, 189–95 (writing space) and 253–67.

34 Verg. Augusteus (CLA I 13) c. 425 × 325 mm (c. 250 × 265 mm, 20 lines); Verg. Romanus (I 19) 333 × 332 mm (240 × 250 mm, 18 l.); Verg. Sangallensis (VII 977) (325) × 350 mm (223 × ca. 275 mm, 19 l.); Lucan palimpsest in Naples (III 392) ca. 380 × 360 mm (230 × 180 mm, 15 l.); Digests (III 295) 365 × 320 mm (255–270 × 255 mm, 2 cols of 44 or 45 l.). A Vergil manuscript with only eight lines per page (with wide margins, perhaps for scholia) may once have existed. This would explain the enlarged capital letter which regularly begins every eighth line in the carolingian manuscript Paris, BN, Lat. 7929 (Plate: Chatelain, *Pal. class. lat.*, plate LXVIII).

35 CLA V 600; cf. Bischoff, *Mittelalterliche Studien* 2, 288. An illustrated life of St Margaret 82 × 61 mm, s. XIV, a text considered to have magical properties in relieving labour pains, has a roughly similar format (E.P. Goldschmidt, London, Catal. 39, Nr. 141).

36 A Spanish scriptorium of c. 800 produced bibles and collections of various texts in a very large format (up to 515 × 365 mm) and in three columns: CLA II 195 (and XI, p. 17); XI 1635; XI 1654. For Tours Bibles see p. 208.

seventh century on, that is after the León palimpsest[37] and the Codex Amiatinus[38] (for which the Codex Grandior of Cassiodorus served as a model). On the whole though, the medium folio format is the commonest in early medieval libraries.

Amongst the smaller formats are Irish pocket-gospel books,[39] manuscripts of monastic rules and laws such as the Benedictine rule from Tegernsee,[40] and the manuscript of the Lex Baiuwariorum from Ingolstadt[41] (probably a count's copy), learned notebooks and glossaries such as the palimpsest MS 912 from St Gall[42] and the *Vocabularius Sancti Galli*,[43] and also devotional books.[44] Among later manuscripts the enormous 'Codex Gigas' stands out; it was written in the early thirteenth century by a single scribe in the Bohemian monastery of Podlažice. It contains the bible plus other extensive works by Josephus, Isidore, and others, on 309 leaves in a format of 89.3 × 49 cm (two columns, each of 105–6 lines); it is now in Stockholm.[45]

Towards the later middle ages a more economical way of writing became possible with the use of smaller and narrower letters and less space between the lines, and by increasing the number of lines and the number of abbreviations. In this way the contents of a book could be considerably enlarged while keeping to the same format, and the use of thinner parchment also helped to reduce the thickness of a volume.[46]

A new type of extremely small manuscript was developed for the most important book of all, the bible, which up to this time was normally copied in large folio volumes or (with the inclusion of the commentary) in quarto, divided up into individual books. The 'pocket bibles' which were produced during the thirteenth century in innumerable copies, above all in Paris but also in English and Italian centres, generally have a format of c. 14.5 × 10 cm, with a writing area of c. 9.5–10.5 × 6.5 cm, in two columns of 44–53 lines each. Because only the finest virgin parchment was used, they did not look too bulky, in spite of having four hundred to five hundred leaves.[47]

One of the most monumental German books of the middle ages is the Jena

---

37 CLA XI 1636, 440 × 320 mm (365 × 285 mm) 2 cols of 72–76 lines.

38 CLA III 299, 505 × 340 mm (360–365 × 260 mm) 2 cols of 44 lines. Cf. J.W. Halporn, 'Pandectes, pandecta and the Cassiodorian commentary on the Psalms', *Rev. Bénéd.* 90 (1980) 290–300.

39 P. McGurk, 'The Irish Pocket Gospel Book', *Sacris Erudiri* 8 (1956) 249–70.

40 CLA IX 1322.

41 Collotype facsimile ed. by K. Beyerle (Munich, 1926); cf. Bischoff, *Schreibschulen* 1, 249 f.; *Kalligraphie*, Nr. 19.   42 CLA VII 967a.   43 CLA VII 976.

44 Bischoff, *Schreibschulen* 1, 255 f. (Clm 14,830 and 14,843, both with Isidore, *Synonyma*).

45 A. Friedl, *Codex Gigas* (Prague 1929).

46 N. Ker demonstrated this change with reference to the longest work of Latin patristic literature, in 'The English Manuscripts of the Moralia of Gregory the Great', in *Kunsthistorische Forschungen Otto Pächt zu seinem 70. Geburtstag* (Salzburg 1972) 77–89.

47 Reprod.: *New Pal. Soc.* I, ser 2, plate 217; Crous-Kirchner, *Schriftarten*, Nr. 9; Mazal, *Gotik*, reprod. 4.

Minnesong manuscript from the mid fourteenth century, which measures 56 × 41 cm.[48] In general, the proportion of small format books increases with the centuries. Typical for the later middle ages are, on the one hand, enormous choir books, and on the other, tiny prayer books (8.5 × 6 cm, or smaller).

Also dependent on tradition, fashion and purpose is the relationship of height to width in a book. In classical and early Christian parchment codices two principal types were current: a square format and a tall, narrow rectangular one. The former is relatively frequent amongst early codices (and not only in de luxe manuscripts).[49] Some schools imitated it during the carolingian period, for instance Lorsch and Ferrières. The tall rectangular format sometimes assumes exaggerated proportion, with the height being up to three times the width.[50] The reason for the choice of this format may have been an external one: some liturgical books, such as sacramentaries, psalters, gospels, tropers, sequentiaries, and others, were written in a narrow format because they were to be covered with ivory plates, as is indicated by surviving examples and old inventories. Three manuscripts of this kind are the Bamberg Graduals Lit. 7 (26.6 × 11.1 cm) and Lit. 8 (27.7 × 10.9 cm), each of which was designed to match exactly in outline the arch at the top of the ivory cover,[51] and also the Vita S Liudgeri from Werden (30 × 12.5 cm).[52]

Aesthetic factors could also play a rôle in determining the choice of format, as in those very narrow manuscripts of poetry from the eleventh to the thirteenth centuries in which the text is written in one column.[53] Alternatively, practical reasons may also account for the choice, as was the case with theatrical texts.[54] Late medieval account books are also, as a rule, very narrow, probably by analogy with wax tablets, which were also used for this purpose, but also because they were easier to carry when travelling on horseback.[55] Relatively narrow strips – from margins? – were occasionally used for small oblong books.[56] The

48 *Die Jenaer Liederhandschrift* (Facsimile ed. by K.K. Müller, Jena 1896).
49 See above n. 34. Further in Lowe, see n. 33. For a bibliophile copy of a Cicero speech in uncial, probably once square in shape, s V, ca. 145 × (c. 130 mm) (80 × 80 mm), 17 lines: CLA VIII 1043; Seider, *Papyri* 2/1, Nr. 55.
50 K. Christ, 'In caput quadragesimae', *Zentralbl. f. Bibliothekswesen* 60 (1943/44) 56. The Latin-Anglo-Saxon Psalter Paris, BN, Lat. 8824, s. XI, in two columns, measures c. 526 × 186 mm (Early English Manuscripts in Facsimile 8, Copenhagen 1958); Florence, Laur., Ashb. 1814, Ps.-Hieronymus, Ep., Liber Pontificalis, s. XI, from Poitiers, 455 × 140 mm.
51 Schramm-Mütherich, *Denkmale*, Nr. 118. Cf. K. Weitzmann, 'Die byzantinischen Elfenbeine eines Bamberger Graduale und ihre ursprüngliche Verwendung', in *Studien zur Buchmalerei und Goldschmiedekunst des Mittelalters, Festschrift für Karl Hermann Usener* (Marburg 1967) 11–20.   52 Chroust, *Monumenta* II 23, plate 5.
53 E.g. Chatelain, *Pal. class. lat*, plate 162, Statius, s. XI; plate 92, Ovid s. XII.
54 E.g. the Trier 'Theophilus' 29 × 10.5 cm.
55 Cf. G.S. Ivy, in *English Library before 1700*, on 'Holster Books'.
56 Two carolingian anthologies that have this format are Bremen b 52 and St Gallen 273, c. 128 × 148 mm, and Vatic. Lat. 10,816, 120 × 175 mm; also CLA VII 853, Sedulius, 148 × 166 mm.

study of formats is of interest not only for the history of book-making; it can also tell us something about the function of a book in its time. It was only the age of paper that brought about a greater regularity of formats and proportions.[57]

There are also playful forms of codices, such as, for instance, a twelfth-century circular prayer book from the diocese of Passau, whose German prayers may indicate a woman as its first owner;[58] and the heart-shaped chansonnier of Jean de Montchenu (c. 1460–76).[59] A French prayer book that was written and illuminated for Philip the Good of Burgundy in about 1430 was embedded in the lower half of a binding in the form of a diptych, whose rounded upper parts have devotional pictures on the inside, so that the open book resembles a little house-altar.[60]

3. The layout of the page

The traditional rules of book-making extended also to the layout of the page and the balanced distribution of writing area and margins.[61] In this regard, the striking division of the writing area in a codex into separate columns, which was already frequent in the oldest manuscripts surviving from the fourth century but became the type for the codex, is probably in its origin a legacy of the papyrus age.[62] The division of the text into four narrow columns is found in the fourth (fourth/fifth) century, but only rarely;[63] more frequent is the three-column page. This type of arrangement is found several times in the fifth century (or the fourth and fifth centuries) for classical as well as biblical and patristic texts,[64] but the majority of older codices show a preference for two columns. Writing in long lines is a less common practice in the early period.

It was normal in these earliest manuscripts to enlarge the first letter of every page or of every column, even if they stand in the middle of a word. Hence, an enlarged letter did not necessarily indicate the beginning of a section,[65] as was the case later with initials.[66]

57 Cf. p. 13 n. 34.
58 Paris, BN, Lat 10,526, with 16.7 cm diameter (writing area 13.2–14.7 cm). On the contents cf. V. Leroquais, *Les livres d'heures manuscrits de la Bibliothèque Nationale* 1 (Paris 1927) 314–16. Compare also the 'Codex rotundus' in the Diocesan Museum Hildesheim (a French prayer-book, s. XV). 59 J. Porcher, *Französische Buchmalerei* (Recklinghausen 1959) plate 83.
60 Vienna Lat. 1800; I am grateful to the late Otto Pächt for making photographs available.
61 Later trimming of manuscripts often makes it impossible to study this ratio.
62 Cf. Lowe, *Palaeographical Papers* 1, 201 and 270 f.
63 CLA I 72 (Fronto) and II² 178 (Cyprian), (Seider, *Papyri* 2/2, Nr. 60).
64 CLA III 363; VII 1018; VIII 1028 (Seider, *Papyri* 2/1, Nr. 56) and 1174 (Seider, *Papyri* 2/2, Nr. 61); CLA Addenda 1843. Cf. L. Traube, 'Bamberger Fragmente der vierten Dekade des Livius', *Abh. Bayer. Akad. Wiss.*, 3 Kl. 24/1 (1904) 28 f.
65 The Vergilius Augusteus does follow this practice (CLA I 13) for every page starts with an enlarged ornamental letter in several colours, resembling a decorated initial. See below p. 189.
66 Lowe, *Palaeographical Papers* 1, 196 ff. and 266 ff. Lowe also notes the occasional use of enlarged final letters and discusses the gradual abandonment of this custom. CLA VI 736, a precaroline copy, shows traces of this custom. See also above note 34, end.

The relationship of writing area to page is, of course, dependent on the format. If the format is square, so is the writing area. It may be taken as a rule of thumb that in the majority of early medieval manuscripts of a tall, rectangular format the height of the writing corresponds to the width of the leaf. A set of instructions about the layout of a page with two columns, preserved from the ninth century, shows[67] that more exact rules were sometimes followed, at least in good scriptoria.

Throughout the middle ages the layout of a page either in long lines or in two columns was predominant. An increase in the number of manuscripts with three columns during the carolingian period is restricted to specific texts: the *Liber Glossarum*, and also bibles;[68] Visigothic codices may have provided the models for both.[69] On the other hand, the Utrecht Psalter, written in three columns in capitalis, probably follows an antique model.[70]

Manuscripts which contain a text and, in a different writing area, a commentary, required a special layout of the page. The early medieval method was to write them in two columns side-by-side; the column used for the commentary might have a different width and more lines for a different grade of script. Already in carolingian times manuscripts with one column each for text and commentary respectively are found,[71] but there are also glossed psalters with columns of commentary to the left and right of the text and with double the number of commentary lines to text lines.[72] Williram of Ebersberg (saec. XI) used this design for his Song of Solomon, with a Latin metrical paraphrase in one column and a German translation in the other.[73] In the twelfth-century Lambach Manuscript this complicated system of parallel columns gave way to the simpler method of having the commentary follow the text.[74]

From the twelfth century on the tendency is to unify text and commentary in one solid block of writing, but differentiated by scripts of different sizes. After

---

67 L. Gilissen, *Prolégomènes*, 125 ff.; E.K. Rand, *Studies in the Script of Tours* 2 (Cambridge, Mass. 1934) 87 f. (for which see Gilissen, 216 ff.); J. Vezin, 'Réalisation matérielle', 29 f. A simple rule in Bischoff, *Anecdota* (Stuttgart 1984) 239 f.

68 Both the earliest MS of the 'Liber Glossarum' from Corbie (CLA v 611; vi 743) and later copies (e.g. Clermont Ferrand 240) are written in three columns; three-column Bibles include the earlier Theodulf Bibles, Stuttgart HB II.16 and London, BL, Add 24,142.

69 Cf. CLA xi 1654, the Codex Cavensis (Lowe, *Palaeographical Papers* 1, plates 55–7) and later Spanish bibles.

70 Three-column manuscripts predating the twelfth century are otherwise rare. Examples are Montpellier 160 (Caper, s. IX); St Gallen 1399 a 7 (Venantius Fortunatus, s. IX²); Namur 1 (Aug. in ps., s. IX): Oxford, Bodl., Laud. Lat. 49 (Boeth. in Isag. Porph., etc., s. XI): Paris, BN, Lat. 7993 (Ovid, s. XII); Vienna 12,600 (astronomical and computistical texts, s. XII).

71 A later example: the Tegernsee Psalter s. XI; Chroust, *Monumenta* II 2, plate 4. Cf. C. de Hamel, *Glossed Books of the Bible and the Origin of the Paris Book-Trade* (Cambridge 1984). Cf. also L. Holtz, 'La typologie des manuscrits grammaticaux latins', *Rev. d'hist. textes* 7 (1977) 247–69, with plates.   72 E.g. Frankfurt a. M., Barth. 32, from Fulda, s. IX¹.

73 Petzet-Glauning, plate 15; Chroust, *Monumenta* II 11, plate 6b.

74 G. Swarzenski, *Die Salzburger Buchmalerei* (Leipzig 1908), reprods 413, 417, 420.

various experiments,[75] this goal was achieved to perfection in the two–column university manuscripts of Roman and canon law, in which the commentary encloses the text symmetrically[76] (perhaps following the example of Greek manuscripts with text and commentary). This type of layout was eventually taken over into early printed books ('cum textu incluso').

The writing of rhetorical units 'per cola et commata'[77] is found in early biblical manuscripts and in the Old High German Tatian.[78] Metrical forms too were preserved in writing, unless it happened that they were no longer understood (as was the case with Plautus and Terence). Otfrid and the anonymous author of the Ludwigslied imitated these metrical forms by writing the verses on separate lines. Otherwise, alliterative and rhyming German poems were, as a rule, written like prose prior to the thirteenth century, and verses were indicated only by punctuation marks, if at all.

From the late-eleventh century on, manuscripts of Latin rhythmical poetry occasionally set out the verses on separate lines,[79] and in this the courtly poetry of France probably preceded German poetry, where we encounter it only in the thirteenth century. The attractive three-column layout of a page, relatively frequent in manuscripts of Middle High German and Middle Dutch epic poetry (saec. XIII and XIV), probably follows the example of thirteenth-century manuscripts of French epic poetry as Rudolf of Ems, for instance, must have known them.[80] In three-columned manuscripts of this kind were transmitted the works of Wolfram of Eschenbach, Gottfried of Strasbourg, Rudolf of Ems, Ulrich of Türheim, Henry of Hesler, Henry of Munich, and biblical epics of the Teutonic Order, the Passional, and 'Garin le Loherain'.[81] The layout of these beautiful manuscripts of Middle High German poetry provided the inspiration for the imperial secretary Johannes Ried when he wrote the Ambraser Heldenbuch for Maximilian I.[82]

75 Depending on the extent of text and commentary, short passages of text are often set within the commentary at various points on the page. See e.g. Chroust, *Monumenta* III 13, plate 8 (Petrus Lomb. in ps., 1317–26).

76 This symmetrical layout, spread over two pages of an opening, is already found in a twelfth-century glossed Italian psalter, Florence, Bibl. Laur., S. Croce pl. V dextr. 6.

77 See below p. 169.

78 G. Baesecke, *Der deutsche Abrogans und die Herkunft des deutschen Schrifttums* (Halle 1930) plate 8; Fischer, *Schrifttafeln*, plate 9.

79 H. Van Thiel, *Mittellateinische Texte* (Göttingen 1972) Nr. 10, 22, 23.

80 Cf., e.g., *Recueil de facsimilés a l'usage de l'Ecole des Chartes*, plate 762; *Nouv. sér.*, plate 291. An English example: Oxford, Bodl., Eng. poet. a. 1 (S.C. 3,938–42).

81 Reprod.: *Wolfram von Eschenbach, Parzival, Titurel, Tagelieder, Cgm. 19*, facsimile, transcription: H. Engels, Fr. Dreßler (Stuttgart 1970); Petzet-Glauning, plate 33; *Deutsche Schrifttafeln*, (ibid) 44 (Garin le Loherain); *Deutsche Texte des Mittelalters* 19 (Judith, Daniel, etc) 39 (Ulrich von Türnheim); P. Gichtel, *Die Weltchronik Heinrichs von München in der Runkelsteiner Handschrift* (Munich 1937) Beil. III. To the list given by me in *Paläographie*, col. 390, separatum col. 12 add: Rudolf of Ems, Weltchronik: Berlin, Ms. germ. fol. 1046 and Graz, Landesarchiv (fragm.); Heinrich von Hesler: Marburg, UB (fragm.); Passional: Berlin, Ms. germ. qu. 1722 and Graz, LA (fragm.).

82 Fr. Unterkircher (Introd.), *Ambraser Heldenbuch*, complete facsimile ed. Codices selecti 43 (Graz 1937).

Occasionally, the writing was shaped into particular designs. Cassiodorus, for example, mentions 'Botryonum formulae', cluster-shaped marginal explanations or commentary. The prologues of the biblical books were written in cruciform pattern in a continental Anglo-Saxon gospel from the eighth century,[83] in the Theodulf Bible from Le Puy,[84] and in the Danila Bible.[85] A scribe's whim and fancy could be given full vent when there was not enough text to fill a page, for instance at the end of a manuscript or gathering. In such an event he might complete the text with any kind of symmetrical figure or scribal flourish.[86]

4. Bindings

A normal accessory of a finished book is the binding, which protects the text.[87] The majority of medieval manuscripts do not have their original binding but have been rebound once or even several times. Cassiodorus in his day had devised a model book binding,[88] and five coloured patterns of interlace and braiding in a remarkable single leaf in a Paris manuscript probably served the same purpose.[89] The history of medieval bindings has become known in its essential outlines through the discovery of many early medieval bindings. In all periods three main types of bindings existed simultaneously: de luxe bindings, wooden boards with leather covers, and simple parchment or leather wrappers.

The earliest surviving example of a de luxe binding is the cover of a gospel book in Monza, which was a gift of the Lombard queen Theodolinda. Comparable bindings[90] were made exclusively for the most important liturgical books, using the most precious materials for their decoration: gold, silver, jewels,

---

83 CLA VIII 1195; Lowe, *English Uncial*, plate 16.   84 CLA VI 768.

85 Lowe, *Palaeographical Papers* 1, 340.

86 Lehmann, *Erforschung* 3, 60–6 and plate. This practice was especially popular at Tegernsee in the eleventh century: Christine Elisabeth Eder, *Die Schule des Klosters Tegernsee im frühen Mittelalter im Spiegel der Tegernseer Handschriften*, Stud. Mitteil. OSB 83 (1972) = Münchener Beiträge, Beiheft, 67–9. Decorative layouts are found in the metrical exposition on the Song of Songs by Wilhelm von Weyarn (Clm 17,177 and 6432, s. XII²); Bischoff, *Kalligraphie*, 38 and Nr. 28f.

87 H. Loubier, *Der Bucheinband von seinen Anfängen bis zum Ende des 18. Jahrhunderts*² (Leipzig 1926); H. Schreiber, *Einführung in die Einbandkunde* (Leipzig 1932); in *Reallexikon zur deutschen Kunstgeschichte* 2, col. 1361–84. Some collections of plates: F. Geldner, *Bucheinbände aus elf Jahrhunderten* (Munich 1958); O. Mazal, *Europäische Einbandkunst aus Mittelalter und Neuzeit* (Graz 1971); idem, 'Der mittelalterliche Bucheinband', in *Liber librorum. 5000 Jahre Buchkunst* (Geneva 1973) 342–70; idem, *Romanik* 297–314 and illustr. 83–7; idem, *Gotik*, 191 ff. and reprod. 158–69; E. Ph. Goldschmidt, *Gothic and Renaissance Bookbindings* (London 1928); L. Gilissen, *La reliure occidentale antérieure à 1400 d'après les manuscrits de la Bibliothèque Royale Albert Ier à Bruxelles* (Turnhout 1983).

88 *Institutiones* 1 30.

89 Zimmermann, *Vorkarol. Min.*, plate 113a; C. Nordenfalk, 'Corbie and Cassiodorus, A pattern page bearing on the early history of bookbinding', *Pantheon* 32 (1974) 225–31 (with colour reprod.).

90 Frauke Steenbock, *Der kirchliche Prachteinband im frühen Mittelalter* (Berlin 1965).

pearls, antique gems and cameos, ivory carvings,[91] designs of beaten or molten gold or silver, champlevé enamel work, and engraved or incised silver plaques.

The commonest form of binding comprised a pair of wooden boards covered with leather, frequently reinforced at the corners or in the middle with metal bosses. 'Libri catenati' have a chain fastened to the binding with which the book was attached to its stand. At various times, many workshops decorated the leather covers with characteristic blind tooling stamps: in the ninth and tenth centuries,[92] and in the twelfth and thirteenth,[93] and then again, in new fashions, in the late middle ages, especially in the fifteenth century.[94] These stamps can provide reliable evidence about the history of manuscripts, and the science of book-binding in general has become an important auxiliary discipline in the study of manuscripts.

The art of leather carving is late medieval. Practical book pouches were also designed during this period ('pouch-books', 'libri caudati'). These were bindings for small prayer-books with leather hanging down at the bottom which could be drawn up for carrying them or fastening them to the belt.[95]

The simplest way of protecting a book was to place it in a leather or parchment wrapper. Modest early medieval covers of this kind have been preserved from Fulda[96] – one of them with the title of the book in runes – and from Reichenau. There are some too from the twelfth century.[97] They are frequently used for cartularies, account books, etc. Particularities in the stitching on the back, often protected by stamped leather or horn plates, gave rise to the terms chain-stitching or whip-stitching. Their late medieval designation 'ligaturae more studentium' points to another area where these limp bindings were commonly used.[98]

91 Cf. also p. 14.

92 G.D. Hobson, 'Some early bindings and binders' tools', *The Library* 19 (1938) 215 ff.; Fr. Unterkircher, 'Die Karolingischen Salzburger Einbände in der Österreichischen Nationalbibliothek in Wien', *Libri* 5 (1954) 41–53 with reprod.; E. Kyriss, 'Vorgotische verzierte Einbände der Landesbibliothek Karlsruhe', *Gutenberg-Jahrbuch* (1961) 277–85 with reprod.; idem, 'Vorgotische verzierte Einbände der Stiftsbibliothek St. Gallen', ibid. (1966) 321–30 with reprod.; J. Vezin, 'Les reliures carolingiennes de cuir à décor estampé de la Bibliothèque Nationale de Paris', *Bibl. Éc. Chartes* 128 (1970) 81–112 with reprod.; idem, 'Réalisation matérielle', 36 ff. with reprod.

93 G.D. Hobson, 'Further notes on romanesque bindings', *The Library* 15 (1934) 211 with plate and 19 (1938) 233–49 with plate.

94 A standard work: E. Kyriss, *Verzierte gotische Einbände im altendeutschen Sprachgebiet*, text and 3 vols. of plates (Stuttgart 1951–8); H. Knaus, 'Einbandstempel des XIV. Jahrhunderts', in *Festschrift Ernst Kyriss* (Stuttgart 1961) 55–70 with reprod., ibid. 487–93, *Bibliographie Ernst Kyriss*. 95 Lisl u. H. Alker, *Das Beutelbuch in der bildenden Kunst* (Mainz 1966).

96 P. Lehmann, 'Fuldaer Studien', *Sitzungsber. Bayer. Akad. Wiss.*, phil.-hist. Kl. (1925) 3, 12 ff.; Berthe van Regemorter, 'La reliure souple des manuscrits carolingiens de Fulda', *Scriptorium* 11 (1957) 249–57 and plate 32.

97 H. Knaus, 'Hochmittelalterliche Koperteinbände', *Zentralbl. f. Bibliothekswesen u. Bibliogr.* 8 (1961) 326–37 with reprod.

98 In the St Emmeram catalogue from 1500/01 (*Mittelalt. Bibliothekskat. Deutschl.* 4, I, 187) also 'Wiener pündt'. Cf. H. Alker, 'Wiener Kettenstich- und Langstichbände', *Gutenberg-Jahrbuch* (1965) 368–73 with reprod.

It is important to look at the reinforcement of the binding and, in the case of paper manuscripts, at the parchment guard strips used to protect the stitching. Quite frequently, discarded manuscript fragments were used.[99]

5. *Rotuli and folded books*

Medieval rotuli[100] made of parchment are differentiated from the book 'volumen' of antiquity by the direction of the writing. This was no longer laid out in columns parallel to the long sides; the lines now followed the short sides (as, for instance, in the papyrus documents from Ravenna). Rotuli were used quite extensively in the liturgy; they are attested in episcopal ordines from Rheims, Benevento, York, and Milan.[101] A liturgical parchment roll of the seventh century has been preserved from Ravenna,[102] and the Lorsch litany dates from the time of Louis the German.[103] The Exultet rolls in Beneventan script are remarkable for their pictures, which were shown to the congregation while the deacon was singing the liturgy of Easter eve from a pulpit.[104] The decrees of the Aachen synod of AD 816 were sent to a monastery on a rotulus (the 'Murbach statutes' in Colmar, Arch. dep., 10 C Actes Généraux ladula 12 no. 4).[105] Rotuli were found to be particularly suitable for compendia of biblical history, world and national chronicles, and extended genealogies (in the form of a family tree), which were very common. The roll ('role') has given us the word for the part played by an actor in the theatre. Examples of this type are the roll for the Easter play of Muri (saec. XIII),[106] the Frankfurt director-roll (saec. XIV[1]), and the roll of the fourth guardian of the sepulchre from the south-Italian Easter play (saec. XIV, Sulmona, Arch. Capit.)[107] In Germany the rhymed verse love-

---

99 On lifting pastedowns: A. Dold, in *Festschrift für Wolfgang Stammler* (Berlin 1953) 29 f. G. Eis, 'Von der verlorenen altdeutschen Dichtung', *Vom Werden altdeutscher Dichtung* (Berlin 1962) 7–27 draws on the results of research on fragments; E. Pellegrin, 'Fragmenta et membra disiecta', *Codicologica* 3 [Litterae Textuales] (1980) 70–95.

100 Wattenbach, *Schriftwesen*, 157–174; Santifaller, *Beiträge*, 153–162.

101 N.K. Rasmussen, 'Unité et diversité des pontificaux latins aux VIIIe, IXe et Xe siècles', *Liturgie de l'Église particulière et liturgie de l'Églis universelle* (Rome 1976) 460.

102 CLA III 371 (on which see CLA S 51); now in Milan, Bibl. Ambros., S.P. cassaf. 1.

103 B. Bischoff, *Lorsch im Spiegel seiner Handschriften* (Munich 1974), 45; *Datierte Hss.* 1, plate 1.

104 See p. 111. On Greek liturgical rotuli as a model see G. Cavallo, 'La genesi dei rotoli liturgici beneventani', in *Miscellanea in memoria di Giorgio Cencetti* (Turin 1973) 213–229 with plate; M.L. Wurfbain, 'The Liturgical Rolls of South Italy and their Possible Origin', in *Miniatures, scripts, collections. Essays Presented to G.I. Lieftinck* 4 [Litterae textuales] (Amsterdam 1976) 9–15.

105 The Gorze library catalogue appears to list this in the same way; cf. G. Morin in *Rev. Bénéd.* 22 (1905) 10, line 190 f. A similar item dated ca 813 which is comparable to the 'Annotatio capitulorum synodalium' (MGH Leges III 2, 1, 301 ff.) is the Munich fragment Clm 29555/3.

106 *Das Osterspiel von Muri.* Faksimiledruck der Fragmente mit Rekonstruktion der Pergamentrolle (Basel 1967).

107 See K. Young, *The Drama of the Medieval Church* 1 (Oxford 1933) 701–8; The context has been clarified by the subsequent discovery of the play: M. Inguanez, *Un dramma della passione del secolo XII.* Miscellanea Cassinese 18 (1939).

letter in Munich survives as an example of the rolls of lyrical poetry such as are seen so often in the hands of the poets depicted in Minnesong manuscripts.[108] An example of this type is the poetic dispute 'Ganymede and Helena', which was copied on to a roll measuring 57 cm in length and 6.4 cm in width (saec. XII).[109] Surveying all the other categories of texts that were written on rolls, it seems that pilgrims and other travellers liked to use this handy form, for there are rotuli of the *Mirabilia Romae*,[110] and the *Peregrinationes terrae sanctae*,[111] as well as medical and alchemical rolls,[112] armorial rolls for use by heralds,[113] and guild rolls.

The following items listed in the Nachlaß of Honorius Augustodunensis are probably illustrative materials to be used in school or as models for illustrations: 'Rodale, in quo VII liberales artes depictae. Item rodale, in quo Troianum bellum depictum . . . Item rodale, in quo varia pictura'.[114]

Typical also are the mortuary rolls of the monastic orders: they were sent from one house to another and preserved a record – sometimes extending over several centuries – of deaths and of the names of the monasteries visited, and also their obituary poems.[115] Rolls were also used for records of dues and as inventories of property. In the later middle ages paper rolls were glued together for accounts and dossiers.[116]

Also worth mentioning for their uncommon formats are folded amulets, calendars,[117] and sheets of prayers.[118]

108 Petzet-Glauning, *Deutsche Schrifttafeln*, plate 54. Convincing proof of the accuracy of this representation is furnished by the roll with poems by Reinmar von Zweter (Los Angeles, University of California Research Library, A 1 T 36s); cf. R.H. Rouse, 'Roll and codex', in *Paläographie* (Munich 1981) 107–23, plates 11–14; F.H. Bäuml, R.H. Rouse, 'Roll and codex', *Beitr. z. Gesch. d. Deutsch. Spr. u. Lit.* 105 (1983) 92–213, 313–330.

109 Ingeborg Schröbler, 'Zur Überlieferung des mittellateinischen Gedichtes von "Ganymed und Helena"', in *Unterscheidung und Bewahrung, Festschrift Hermann Kunisch* (Berlin 1961) 321 ff. Wattenbach mentions other literary texts, *Schriftwesen*, 168 f.; N. Ker, *Medieval Manuscripts in British Libraries* 1 (Oxford 1969) 400 f.

110 Manchester, John Rylands Libr, 71; St Gallen 1093; Stuttgart, Hist. 459.

111 Jacques Rosenthal, *Bibliotheca medii aevi manuscripta* 11 (Katalog 90, 1928) Nr. 173.

112 Cgm 174; Kassel, Medic. 8° 11; Bern, Burgerbibl. 803; Göttingen, Deutsches Seminar III, 31.   113 The Zurich heraldic roll, s. XIV, amongst others.

114 Th. Gottlieb, *Mittelalterliche Bibliothekskataloge Österreichs* 1 (Wien 1915) 12. School-texts on rotuli in Gorze: Morin, *Rev. Bénéd.* 22 (1905) line 191 f., 194.

115 L. Kern, 'Sur les rouleaux des morts', *Schweizer Beiträge zur allgemeinen Geschichte* 14 (1956) 139–47; L. Delisle, *Rouleaux des morts du IXe au XVe siècle* (Paris 1866); J. Dufour, 'Les rouleaux des morts', *Codicologica* 3 [Litterae Textuales] (1980) 96–102. The best impression is to be had from the facsimile by L. Delisle, *Rouleau mortuaire du b. Vital, abbé de Savigni* (Paris 1909).

116 L. Santifaller, 'Über Papierrollen als Beschreibstoff', *Mélanges Eugène Tisserant* 5. Studi e Testi 235 (Vatic. 1964) 361–71.

117 A. Pfaff, *Aus alten Kalendern* (Augsburg 1945); *Mss. datés*, Pays-Bas 1, plate 239; *New Pal. Soc.* 11, ser 1, plate 72.

118 Monique Garand, 'Livres de poche médiévaux à Dijon et à Rome', *Scriptorium* 25 (1971) 18 ff. with plates 7/8.

6. Tabulae

The terms 'tabulae' or 'paginae' originally denoted large pieces of parchment (sometimes several sheets sewn together) stretched on a frame or fastened to a wooden tablet. To judge from medieval inventories, they must have been used in the schools[119] for many purposes: elementary instruction in reading, and in the trivium of arithmetic, geometry, and music. From the frequent references to the ABC 'table', we can probably deduce that the school primer of the later middle ages, which had the customary book shape, was also called a 'tabula'.[120] The post-medieval successor to this was the so-called 'horn-book'.

The most important world maps depicted on tabulae are the Hereford map and the Ebstorf map (now destroyed).[121] Many a chronicle of monasteries, monastic orders, or world chronicles also took this form.[122] Religious illustrative material too was contained on such tabulae, as for instance in the schema for the path of salvation entitled *De quinque septenis*,[123] and in the tabula with symmetrically arranged pen-and-ink drawings of the Apocalypse from St Peter's in Salzburg, which originally measured 63.5×63.5 cm (both texts are from the twelfth century). Finally, it may be noted also that in many medieval libraries catalogues inscribed on such tabulae hung on the wall.[124]

7. Charters and letters

In no other area of writing do we find so many peculiar traditions as in that of medieval charters,[125] which had developed from Roman forms of documentation and certification.[126] The papyrus charters from Ravenna occupy a special position as direct descendants of Roman types of charters.[127] In early medieval

119 Cf. e.g., the Gorze library catalogue, s. XI, (in Morin) line 192 ff. and that of Saint-Amand, s. XII, in G. Becker, *Catalogi bibliothecarum antiqui* (Bonn 1885) Nr. 114, 10 ff. Arithmetic: A. Feldham, 'Fraction tables of Hermannus Contractus', *Speculum* 3 (1928) 240 ff. Geometry: a page with ca. 150 figures, s. XII, in Vercelli, Bibl. Capit.

120 Bischoff, *Mittelalterliche Studien* 1, 72 f.

121 Cf. M. Destouches, *Mappemondes A.D. 1200–1500*. Monumenta Cartographica Vetustioris Aevi 1 (Amsterdam 1964) 193 ff.

122 E.g. Berlin, Staatsbibl. Preuß. Kulturbesitz, Lat. fol. 325; cf. Rose Nr. 876. In addition G.H. Gerould, 'Tables in mediaeval churches', *Speculum* 1 (1926) 439 f.; H. Rieckenberg, 'Die Katechismus-Tafel des Nikolaus von Kues in der Lamberti-Kirche zu Hildesheim', *Deutsches Archiv* 39 (1983) 555–81.

123 Jacques Rosenthal, *Bibliotheca medii aevi manuscripta* 1 (Katalog 83, 1925) Nr. 91; now Oxford, Bodl. Libr., Lyell Bequest 84.

124 A summary in P.F.J. Obbema, *Een Deventer Bibliotheekcatalogus van het einde der vijftiende eeuw* 1/2 (Tongern 1973).

125 H. Bresslau–H.W. Klewitz, *Handbuch der Urkundenlehre für Deutschland und Italien*⁴ 1/2 (Berlin 1968/9).

126 I have already mentioned wax diptychs where the text on the inside is not visible because the tablet was sealed, and copies of the text were written on the outside.

127 Tjäder, *Nichtliter. lat. Pap.*

charters, however, not only the formulae but also the external features of antique charters were retained, even when they were now being issued by German officials. A reflection of this was the employment of papyrus in the chanceries of the popes and the Merovingian kings, the use of elongated or enlarged script for emphasis – which was continued, under special circumstances, until the end of the middle ages – as well as the survival of antique types of certification, such as the addition of salutations or a signature written by the issuer's own hand.

The papal chancery[128] retained the use of papyrus until the eleventh century,[129] and sealed its documents with leaden bullae. In the twelfth century, having given up the old script (the curialis, which had been derived from the cursive) in favour of minuscule, the chancery developed a hierarchy of script types and external forms, related to the content of each document: if it was a solemn privilege it was provided with a rota containing signatures and a 'Bene valete' monogram. If it belonged to one of the two classes of simpler documents to which bulls were usually attached, then it was provided with a seal affixed either with a silk cord ('cum filo serico') or with a hemp cord ('cum filo canapis'). The script of the papal chancery documents provided a model also for the secular chanceries.

The chancery of the Merovingian kings used papyrus up to the seventh century, when it was replaced by parchment. The Merovingians were still able to write their own signatures, but by Pippin's time there was substituted for this the simpler practice of completing a cross or adding the final stroke in the monogram of the king's name. Already by this time Merovingian royal documents were being provided with an additional means of certification by the impression of a wax seal.

The external appearance of charters throughout the middle ages was that of a single sheet with writing on only one side. In addition, for those documents which were written in chancery cursive or diplomatic minuscule respectively, the royal chanceries employed simpler forms, derived from letters and private documents, for general correspondence and for legal dispositions. This simplification included even the abandonment of elongated writing. From the Hohenstaufen period on, the make-up of diplomas was graded and two classes of royal letters in particular appear: letters patent ('litterae patentes') and letters close ('litterae clausae').

Very few original private documents have survived from the early medieval period. Only the archives of St Gall, whose original documents begin in AD 744, are a valuable exception. Otherwise the transmission of early medieval private documents is primarily dependent on copies collected in cartularies. These valuable collections were put together from the ninth century on by churches

---

128 L. Schmitz-Kallenberg, 'Papsturkunden', in *Urkundenlehre* 1/2. Grundriß der Geschichtswissenschaft 1/2 (Leipzig-Berlin 1913) 56–116; *Exempla scripturarum* III.
129 See above p. 8.

and monasteries in order to document and protect their property rights, and they were kept continuously up to date, especially during the era of so-called illiteracy (tenth and eleventh centuries). During these years, when the evidence of witnesses was all important, a 'notitia' (a record of individual act) or simply an entry in such a collection, or even in a gospel book, was deemed sufficient in place of a formal document.

New forms of the authenticated and certified document were the chirograph and the private sealed document. In the former, the text of the document was written twice or three times on one page, and between each copy the word CHIROGRAPHUM (or some other word). The parchment was then divided at this point through the word by making either a straight or an indented cut through the word.[130] The chirograph is of Insular origin,[131] (the oldest examples are from England) and its use extended to the continent from the tenth century on. Similar forms of certification were retained down to modern times.

The practice of certifying a document by the addition of a seal, customary for royal documents, can be traced in non-royal documents from the tenth century on, but it is commonest in the twelfth. Under Frederick I the imperial chancery introduced the practice of appending the wax seal with a parchment strip, instead of pressing it onto the document, which had been the normal method for metal seals (bulls) since they were first introduced for diplomas in the ninth century.

In the late middle ages, the notarial instrument is the dominant form alongside the private sealed document. It developed under the influence of Roman and canon law. The document is certified by a notary with his signature and mark (notarial sign), and in Germany a seal is often attached. In comparison with Anglo-Saxon and Provençal, German makes a relatively late appearance, from the thirteenth century, as the language of documents.[132] The oldest private document in German (Wilhelm Nr. 5c) dates from 1238; the oldest royal document in German (Wilhelm Nr. 7) from 1240. However, as late as 1275 the use of the vernacular was still permitted by Conrad von Mure only in certain cases.[133]

Very few original medieval private letters have survived from before the twelfth century.[134] In outward appearance they can scarcely be distinguished

130 Cf. Arndt-Tangl[4], *Schrifttafeln*, 87.   131 Bischoff, *Mittelalterliche Studien* 1, 118 ff.

132 Fr. Wilhelm, *Corpus der altdeutschen Originalurkunden bis zum Jahre 1300* (Lahr 1932 ff.); H. Hirsch in *Mitteil. Inst. Österr. Geschichtsforsch.* 52 (1938) 227 ff.

133 W. Kronbichler, *Die Summa de arte prosandi des Konrad von Mure* (Zürich 1968) 164 f.

134 H. Hoffmann, 'Zur mittelalterlichen Brieftechnik', in *Spiegel der Geschichte, Festgabe für Max Braubach* (Münster/W. 1964) 148 ff.; W. Wache, 'Eine Sammlung von Originalbriefen des XII. Jhs. im Kapitelsarchiv von S. Ambrogio in Mailand', *Mitteil. Inst. Österr. Geschichtsforsch.* 50 (1936) 261 ff. (298–317 with plate 5 f. contain the letters of the Regensburg clerics Paul of Bernried and Gebhard); P. Chaplais, 'The letter from Bishop Wealdhere of London to Archbishop Brihtwold of Canterbury: the earliest original 'letter close' extant in the West', in *Medieval Scribes, Manuscripts & Libraries. Essays Presented to N.R. Ker* (London 1978) 3–23 with plate.

from imperial letters of the Salian period.[135] The earliest examples we have are a papyrus letter of abbot Maginarius of Saint-Denis from 788,[136] a letter on parchment from bishop Wealdhere of London dated 704/5,[137] a letter of bishop Hildegrim of Halberstadt from 876/7, and a letter (perhaps by a student) from the eleventh century.[138]

Letters on parchment were folded and tied;[139] in a later period they might be closed with a thread pulled through them, or with a parchment strip. If the writer possessed a seal, that too could be used. Towards the end of the middle ages paper was more commonly used than parchment.

135 C. Erdmann, 'Untersuchungen zu den Briefen Heinrichs IV.', *Arch. f. Urk.* 16 (1939) 186 ff.
136 For the alleged letter in ChLA II 174 see *Hist. Z.* 187 (1959) 376.
137 ChLA III 185.   138 Bound into Val. Pal. Lat. 57 as f. 173.
139 This was how the propagandising text by Gunther of Cologne addressed to Hincmar was sent; cf. H. Fuhrmann in *Arch. f. Dipl.* 4 (1958) 1 ff. with plate.

Writing and copying

The literary sources have next to nothing to say about the technique of writing.[1] In antiquity, scribes seem to have rested the material usually on the knee,[2] in the middle ages by contrast on a sloping desk. Numerous pictures of scribes[3] (portraits of the evangelists in particular) show the position of the hand for calligraphic writing. The quill is held with three extended or slightly curved fingers ('tres digiti scribunt') and two tucked in, while the hand rests only on the little finger, without any support from the arm.[4] This method of supporting the writing hand – so fundamentally different from modern practice – remained unchanged until the time of the sixteenth century writing masters. The position of the arm, changes in the manipulation of the quill, and besides that the material of the instrument itself (whether reed or feather) and the cut of the quill,[5] all these changed with time and from one to another of the script regions, as the physiological analysis of the script shows. Hence it is difficult to get a clear picture of the interplay of the various factors,[6] and the inferences about the mechanics of writing that can be drawn from the external appearance seem to have only relative validity.[7]

1 For what follows see Wattenbach, *Schriftwesen*, 261–99; Lesne, *Livres*, 336 ff.; Christ-Kern in Milkau-Leyh, *Handbuch*² 3/1, 263 ff.

2 Skeat *Camb. Hist. Bible* 2, 58; Br. M. Metzger *Historical and Literary Studies, Pagan, Jewish, Christian* (Leiden 1968) 123–37, dates the general shift to writing at a desk to the eighth and ninth century, which is probably too late for the West. A scribe with a writing board with two levels (?) on his knees is shown in an eleventh-century French illustration reproduced in J. Vezin, 'La réalisation matérielle des manuscrits latins pendant le haut Moyen Age', *Codicologica* 2 [Litterae textuales] (Leiden 1978) plate 1.

3 J. Prochno, *Das Schreiber- und Dedikationsbild in der deutschen Buchmalerei* 1 (*800–1100*) (Leipzig–Berlin 1929); P. Bloch–H. Schnitzler, *Die ottonische Kölner Malerschule* 2 (Düsseldorf 1970) reprod. 472 ff. portraits of the evangelists s. IX–XI; H. Martin, 'Notes sur les écrivains au travail', *Mélanges offerts à M. Émile Chatelain* (Paris 1910) 535–44.

4 Fichtenau, *Mensch und Schrift*, 58 ff., 166 and note.

5 Late-medieval rules for cutting the pen are devised for writing textura: Wattenbach, *Schriftwesen*, 230 f.

6 Otloh of St Emmeram, recognized as one of the finest calligraphers of the eleventh century, taught himself to write, but he had an incorrect way of holding the pen ('inrecto usu') which he retained all his life (MPL 146, 56 D).

7 Fichtenau is most comprehensive in his treatment of scripts, *Mensch und Schrift* 57 ff. and 75 ff. O. Hurm, *Schriftform und Schreibwerkzeug* (Vienna 1928).

Much can be gleaned from 'probationes pennae' about the methodical procedure of elementary writing instruction[8] in the early middle ages (in which classical practices apparently survive).[9] Once the pupil had learned the entire alphabet, beginning with simple strokes, this was then drilled by copying of mnemonic verses.[10] Not before the later middle ages, however, do we get more detailed information about these didactic methods.[11] Schoolmasters of this period – Master Hugo Spechtshart of Reutlingen and various other anonymous ones – have left detailed descriptions, in verse and in prose, of the common, everyday script:[12] In part they proceed from the breakdown of the letters into various strokes, (*Zerstreuungen*), which are practised one by one. In fact, the mastery both of cursive and textura was widespread.[13] Writing masters used advertisements to attract pupils to their lessons, and these were extended by instruction in alphabets of initial letters, and the commonest abbreviations.[14]

Elementary introductions to the construction and use of abbreviations have survived, the most detailed of which derive perhaps from the circles of the

---

8 Bischoff, *Mittelalterliche Studien* 1, 75–87. On the relationship between minuscule without ligatures and cursive script as stages in teaching writing in the pre-caroline period cf. A. Petrucci, 'Libro, scrittura e scuola', in *La scuola nell'occidente latino dell'alto medioevo.* Settimane 19 (Spoleto 1972) 1, 327 f.

9 A practice sentence using nine elements in ChLA V 304; Seider, *Papyri* 2/1, Nr. 11 e (s. II). In Roman antiquity lines of Vergil were generally used for writing practice; H.-I. Marrou, *History of education in Antiquity* (pb. New York 1964) 365. A. Petrucci, 'Virgilio nella cultura scritta romana', in *Virgilio e noi* (Genoa 1982) 56–8. Evidence from Seneca, Quintilian and church fathers in Wattenbach, *Schriftwesen*, 265.

10 Bischoff, *Mittelalterliche Studien* 1, 79 ff. Instances of classroom terminology which was used in teaching Tironian notes, but probably also for other purposes, in Steffens[2], *Lateinische Paläographie*, xxxii.

11 On St. Hajnal's thesis, that the universities played an important role in the teaching of writing, cf. below p. 138.

12 *Hugo Spechtshart, Forma discendi*: Selections edited by A. Diehl in *Mitteil. d. Ges. f. deut. Erziehungs- und Schulgesch.* 20 (1910) 24 ff. (V 681 ff.); (B. Bischoff), *Ein neuentdeckter Modus scribendi des XV. Jahrhunderts aus der Abtei Melk* (Berlin 1939; English ed.: S.H. Steinberg, *A fifteenth century Modus scribendi from the abbey of Melk* (Cambridge 1940); J. Kašpar, 'Pražský traktát o notule', *Knihtisk a Universiteta Karlova* (Prague 1972) 21–65; there is a simple French writing instruction in Bern 205, s. XV, f 276ᵛ; Françoise Gasparri, 'L'enseignement de l'écriture à la fin du moyen âge: à propos du Tractatus in omnem modum scribendi, Ms. 76 de l'Abbaye de Kremsmünster', *Scrittura e Civiltà* 3 (1979) 243–65; eadem, 'Enseignement et technique de l'écriture du moyen âge à la fin du XVIe siècle', ibid. 7 (1983) 201–22. Advice on how to write evenly ('continuare'), s. XIV/XV, in Bischoff, *Anecdota* (Stuttgart 1984) 237 ff. Other tracts on the alphabet deal with its literal, moral and mystical significance. In the late middle ages some of the commonest abbreviations (especially et, est, con-, not always in the same order) are added in schoolbooks almost as part of the alphabet, so that the sequence of letters continues with them. Cf. Bischoff, *Mittelalterliche Studien* 2, 197; B. Wolpe, 'Florilegium alphabeticum, alphabets in medieval mss.', in *Calligraphy and Palaeography. Essays Presented to Alfred Fairbanks* (London 1965) 69 ff., plate 18 ff.; Gumbert, *Utrechter Kartäuser*, 81 and 135 n. 4.

13 As can be recognised in the script of titles and opening lines.

14 Very instructive writing exercises in textura are preserved in Lucerne Msc Pap. 25 in fol. (flyleaves) (see plate 19 infra), Clm 5900 (offset in the back cover), Wolfenbüttel 404.8 (26) Novi (with enlarged inititals).

Brethren of the Common Life.[15] The writing of scientific books required familiarity with the abbreviations used for the technical terminology.[16]

Training in writing was hard,[17] its result usually a fairly impersonal and typical script (even with display script), for one must realise that, for example, a carolingian scribe had to know how to handle three or four alphabets.[18] This meant not only the forms of the letters but how to achieve something organic with them – something which seldom failed him.[19] In different periods – not only during the Renaissance – individual scribes imitated older scripts as well.[20]

The preliminary stages through which a literary work passed in course of its creation, ranging from notes and rough drafts written on wax tablets and vellum scraps up to the author's fair-copy or that of his secretary, can be sketched here only briefly.[21] It is, however, characteristic of all medieval literature that not only have copies of many works survived from the author's own period and circle, but also occasionally drafts, and more often first recensions (preliminary fair-copies with deletions and expansions) as well as copies revised by the author himself.[22]

15 P. Lehmann, 'Sammlungen und Erörterungen lateinischer Abkürzungen in Altertum und Mittelalter', *Abh. Bayer. Akad. Wiss.*, phil.-hist. Abt., n. F. 3 (1929) 30–5; on text 3 cf. B. Kruitwagen, *Laatmiddeleeuwsche Paleographica, Palaeotypica, Liturgica, Kalendalia, Grammaticalia* (Den Haag 1942) 43 f.   16 Cf. Wattenbach, *Schriftwesen*, 296.

17 Early medieval indications in verse in Bischoff, *Mittelalterliche Studien* 1, 87. P. Riché, 'La formation des scribes dans le monde mérovingien et carolingien', in Riché, *Instruction et la vie religieuse dans le Haut Moyen Age* (London 1981) Nr. XIV.

18 By the ninth century many scribes could also write neumes.

19 One may instance the simultaneous use of Anglo-Saxon and caroline script in England. See below p. 92.

20 C.E. Eder discusses the imitation of Insular minuscule and of charter script at Tegernsee in the eleventh century in *Die Schule des Klosters Tegernsee im frühen Mittelalter im Spiegel der Tegernseer Handschriften, Stud. Mitteil. OSB* 83 (1972) = Münchener Beiträge, Beiheft, 67. Imitations of earlier scripts in the fifteenth century, independently of humanistic scripts, in Reichenbach 1468, copying twelfth-century script (Bischoff *Mittelalterliche Studien* 1, 63 ff. with plate 5) – in Ter Doest 1477 copying a thirteenth-century model (G.I. Lieftinck, MSS. datés, Pays-Bas 1, text, xxviii f., plate 229 f.). See also p. 45. n. 51.

21 For the patristic period the works of St Jerome are most instructive, cf. E. Arns, *La technique du livre d'après Saint Jérôme* (Paris 1953).

22 A survey which needs updating and revising was made by Lehmann, *Erforschung* 1, 359–81. Other contributions to the collecting of autographs of medieval authors are: M.-C. Garand, 'Auteurs latins et autographes des XIe et XIIe siècles', *Scrittura e civiltà* 5 (1981) 77–104, with plate; Fr. Gasparri, 'Textes autographes d'auteurs Victoriens du XIIe siècle', *Scriptorium* 35 (1981) 277–84; G. Ouy, 'Autographes d'auteurs français des XIVe et XVe siècles: leurs utilité pour l'histoire intellectuelle', *Studia Źródłoznawcze*, Commentationes 28 (1983) 69–103, with illustr. See in addition the Vatican MS of the 'Libri Carolini', Ann Freeman, 'Further Studies in the Libri Carolini', *Speculum* 40 (1965) 205 ff. with plate; the various stages in the text of the '*Periphyseon*' of John Scottus (L. Traube, 'Autographe des Iohannes Scottus', *Abh. Bayer. Akad. Wiss.*, phil-phil. u. hist. Kl. 26/1 (Munich 1912) with plates 1–8); the autograph of Thomas à Kempis's '*Imitatio Christi*' (L.M.J. Delaissé, *Le manuscrit autographe de Thomas à Kempis et l'Imitation de Jésus-Christ* (Paris–Brussels 1957); see also p. 186 n. 43 (Cassiodorus?), p. 190 (Gregory the Great?), p. 45 (Alcuin), p. 95 n. 99 (Hrabanus Maurus), p. 63 n. 56 (Walafrid Strabo). For an alphabetical encyclopedia, 5. XIII, see B. Bischoff, *Bibliotheksforum Bayern* 9 (1981) 12ff. Cf. below p. 225 n.9.

Some authors dictated, so that the word 'dictare', which otherwise means 'compose' in the middle ages, also has its present meaning 'dictate'. We are best informed of all about Thomas Aquinas.[23] He had several secretaries available, to whom he could dictate from his written drafts (in 'littera inintelligibilis'), and in later years perhaps only from notes and outlines.

Both literary texts and liturgical manuscripts were copied for the most part in monasteries in the first half of the middle ages, up to the twelfth century. Every well-endowed monastery had a scriptorium[24] and here an important part of the monastic life took place.[25] If a monastery built up a large library or, as in the case of St Martin's at Tours, if it wrote considerable numbers of books for external clients, the community of scribes (and occasionally also nuns) might develop into a kind of living organism which could continue for many years and carry on the scribal style of the school. This then changed with individual scribes and, more perceptibly, with the transition from one generation to another.[26] Pupils of school-going age might also be employed for writing and could, in accordance with their abilities and experience, be led from elementary tasks[27] to higher achievements, up to the level of being able to write liturgical books. For cooperation with book illuminators specially trained calligraphers were required. The average length of a scribe's career would be between ten and twenty years, though some were active for fifty.

The task of copying a book[28] was not infrequently delegated to several scribes[29] by the supervisor of the scriptorium. These either alternated without any regularity or could copy separate gatherings or groups of gatherings

23 A. Dondaine, *Secrétaires de Saint Thomas* (text and plates) (Rome 1956); on p. 207 there are further examples of dictation.

24 In the St Gall ideal plan of c. 820 the scriptorium is on the ground floor of a building adjoining the choir and one of the transepts of the abbey church, under the library; H. Reinhardt, *Der St. Galler Klosterplan* (St Gallen 1952) 11.

25 On scribes and asceticism see Fichtenau, *Mensch und Schrift*, 155 ff. See also the verses of Gerson on writing (below p. 228).

26 For this and what follows cf. Chr. E. Eder, *Die Schule des Klosters Tegernsee*, 11 f., 55 ff., 69 ff. M.-C. Garand, 'Manuscrits monastiques et scriptoria aux XIe et XIIe siècles, travail au scriptorium', *Codicologica* 3 [Litterae Textuales] (1980) 9–45.

27 St Gall MS 8 (Liber Tobiae, s. X) seems to have been copied on parchment as a trial piece by several hands which were not very practised.

28 Cf. in general Ker, *English MSS*, 10 ff.; idem in *Medieval Learning and Literature. Essays Presented to Richard William Hunt* (Oxford 1976) 31–4, 44–7. A request of Irenaeus's for correct copying that was preserved by Jerome was used by Adomnán, *Vita S Columbae* and the Wolfenbüttel MS Weiss. 91, s. IX, f. 159^r, and Würzburg, M. p. th. f. 98, s. XII/XIII, f. 149^v. Late medieval recommendations urge particular accuracy in copying German texts, cf. E. Schröder, 'Vom Abschreiben deutscher Bücher', *Z. f. deut. Alt.* 63 (1926) 128; J. Lechner, *Die spätmittelalterliche Handschriftengeschichte der Benediktinerinnenabtei St. Walburg/ Eichstätt* (Münster i. W. 1937) 89 f.

29 If the different hands in this sort of manuscript are particularly disparate it is probably safe to infer that it was copied in a school to which pupils had come from various different regions; examples: Berlin, Staatsbibl. Preuß. Kulturbesitz, Lat. 4° 690 (apparently from Mainz); Saint-Omer 91.

distributed singly according to a plan; this was particularly the case with long works, or if a speedy production was desired.[30] Scribes often signed their sections.[31] Occasionally the appearance of names, particularly at the opening of a gathering, indicates not the scribe of the manuscript itself but the copyist to whom the respective part was assigned for transcription.[32]

In some manuscripts the teacher has clearly written some lines as a model for the pupils.[33] Work on a manuscript is divided between the scribes and the rubricator (who can also, naturally, be a scribe); he, however, did not always complete his part of the task. If a manuscript has a colophon often only one scribe names himself, even where it is obvious that several scribes have participated in the work. Some manuscripts give indications about the speed of writing – which naturally fluctuates a great deal – by reference either to the time required or to the progress of the work.[34]

In the later middle ages, in which the command of writing increases dramatically, there are many classes of scribes: monks and nuns, new ecclesiastical communities that devote themselves especially to book production, secular clerics, notaries, professional scribes both ecclesiastical and lay, workshops, teachers, students, and pupils all took part in the production of manuscripts.

In the thirteenth and fourteenth centuries the great established universities of Paris, Bologna, Oxford and Naples, and some others, made special provision for the organised and controlled copying of text-books for students through the institution of the 'pecia'.[35] The university had a corrected standard copy of a text

30 As is clearly seen in the Ottonian gospels on purple parchment in the Morgan Library MS 23; cf. Lowe, *Palaeographical Papers* 2, 399–416 with plates 81–4.

31 As in the manuscripts of Augustine copied by the nuns of Chelles s. VIII–IX (Bischoff, *Mittelalterliche Studien* 1, 19 f.); at least 24 of the quires (there were originally 30) in Angers 675 were signed by separate scribes. The manuscript is probably West Frankish; in Vat. Reg. Lat. 762, the Tours copy of the uncial Puteanus of Livy (CLA I 109; E.K. Rand, *Studies in the Script of Tours* 1 (Cambridge, Mass. 1929) 97). These and other examples are listed by J. Vezin, 'La répartition du travail dans les scriptoria carolingiens', *Journal des Savants* (1973) 212–37; but see above p. 10.

32 Examples: CLA VI 709; IX 1288; *Mittelalt. Bibliothekskat. Deutschl.* 4, 1, 108 n. 104. See also p. 10 n. 17 (on 'portio').

33 Dominicus in Clm 6233 (Bischoff, *Schreibschulen* 1², 136; idem, *Kalligraphie*, Nr. 10; Otloh in Clm 14,512 and 14,712 (?) (Bischoff, *Mittelalterliche Studien* 2, 90 f.). First lines in Corbie: T.A.M. Bishop, 'The Script of Corbie: a Criterion', in *Essays Presented to G.I. Lieftinck* 1 (Amsterdam 1972) 11 n. 3. On a writing model cf. Wattenbach, *Schriftwesen*, 187.

34 Wattenbach, *Schriftwesen*, 289 ff.; W.M. Lindsay in *Palaeographia Latina* 2 (1923) 22 f.; 3 (1924) 14; Lesne, *Livres*, 375 ff.

35 J. Destrez, *La Pecia dans les manuscrits universitaires du XIIIe et du XIVe siècle*, text, plates (Paris 1935). Plates 12/13 reproduce a stationarius's copy. Cf. also K. Christ, 'Petia, ein Kapitel mittelalterlicher Buchgeschichte', *Zentralbl. f. Bibliothekswesen* 55 (1938) 1–44; G. Finck-Herrera, 'Une institution du monde médiéval, la pecia', *Revue philosophique de Louvain* 60 (1962) 184–243 (Ital. in Cavallo, *Libri*, 131–65, 284–302). The number of reidentified 'copies' has increased to 82 since 1953, cf. M.D. Chenu-J. Destrez in *Scriptorium* 7 (1953) 68 ff. G. Pollard, 'The pecia system in the medieval universities', in *Medieval Scribes, Manuscripts and Libraries. Essays Presented to N.R. Ker* (London 1978) 145 ff.; A. Brounts, 'Nouvelles précisions sur la pecia', *Scriptorium* 24 (1970) 343–59 (on the consequences for text transmission of following the pecia system, as illustrated by a work of Thomas Aquinas).

prepared, which was then deposited with a *stationarius* it employed, from whom in turn the work could be borrowed in parts ('peciae') for the purpose of recopying. The 'pecia' comprised (with certain local exceptions) two twin-columned double leaves in-folio (c. 31 × 21 cm). The recopying was carried out normally by professional scribes whose work was remunerated according to the number of 'peciae' at a standard rate of pay. The copies would then be checked by the university. The 'exemplars' of texts that were much in demand had to be replaced from time to time. Lists of texts in stock, with details of 'peciae' and prices, have come down to us from Paris, Bologna, Padua, and Florence. In the copies the change of 'peciae' is often noted in the margin. Legal and canonistic texts, and the explanatory apparatus with which they were combined, were copied from different 'peciae' exemplars.

In the fifteenth century the institution went into decline. The oldest German universities also adopted the office of the stationary in their statutes; with them, however, it did not have the significance that it had had in Bologna and elsewhere. Instead, in the later middle ages, the university literature was written predominantly by the students themselves, in part from the dictation of the masters.[36]

The transcribed codex required correction[37] and many late-antique subscriptions are concerned with this process;[38] like 'contuli'-remarks they have been retained in the manuscript transmission. Only rarely is the process explicitly mentioned in the early middle ages; all the more remarkable for that reason is the usage in St Martin's at Tours where, from the mid eighth century, the tironian symbol for 'requisitum(-us) est' is placed at the end of gatherings in many manuscripts.[39]

Many texts have, in the course of transmission, taken on formulaic accessories which can be informative about the transmission itself. Expression is given to the activities of a scribe or redactor in the presentation of the text by additional entries (for example, subscriptions or dedications which are taken over from exemplars into copies).[40] The contents of a book are indicated by a phrase like 'In hoc codice/corpore continentur . . .'; the title often begins with one of innumerable variations of the invocation 'In nomine . . .'; for example, 'In

36 N. Ker, 'Copying an exemplar: two manuscripts of Jerome on Habakuk', in *Miscellanea codicologica F. Masai dicata MCMLXXIX* 1 (Ghent 1979) 203–10. On the copying of an Albertus manuscript by more than 50 scribes at New College, Oxford, shortly after 1480, cf. N. Ker, 'Eton College Ms. 44 and its Exemplar', in *Essays Presented to G.I. Lieftinck* 1 (Amsterdam 1972) 48–60 with plate.

37 For general remarks on correction see Ker, *English MSS*, 50 ff.; idem, in Manuscripts at Oxford: R.W. Hunt memorial exposition (Oxford 1980) with illustr.; W.M. Lindsay *Palaeographia Latina* 2 (1923) 10 ff.; Wattenbach, *Schriftwesen*, 317 ff.

38 See below p. 183–4.

39 The oldest example: CLA VI 762. On Lupus of Ferrières as a corrector cf. Elisabeth Pellegrin, 'Les manuscrits de Loup de Ferrières', *Bibl. Éc. Chartes* 115 (1957) 20 f. Doubtful passages are most often indicated by the use of r or rq̃ ('require') in the margin.

40 See below p. 185.

nomine Dei summi' was especially favoured by the Irish. For the invocation the form 'Christe fave' (XF) occurs,[41] and the group xb-('Christe benedic', with the same meaning) is frequent in Irish manuscripts. A cross is also used, and many Insular scribes begin every gathering or leaf with one. 'INCIPIT' opens a superscription, just as the word 'FINIT' or the ungrammatical 'EXPLICIT' opens a subscription; 'FINIT' is the older of the two and was seemingly preferred by Insular scribes.[42] These formulae were used especially by Insular scribes in arbitrary and bizarre variations (Inc.: occipit, inchoat, etc.; Expl.: explicat, explicuit, etc.).[43] The word 'FELICITER', or something similar, was often added to these.

The term for the table(s) of chapters varies ('capitulatio' being especially common in Spain and Ireland, instead of 'capitula'). Already from early times there is a great variety in the scribe's good wishes for the reader ('Lege cum pace', 'utere c. p.', etc.) and for himself ('Scriptori vita', 'Ora pro scriptore' – often set in a cross-shape, amongst other patterns), and there is a similar variety of expressions of thanks to God for the completion of the work and the closing words of the scribe.

The use of Greek often indicates an Insular path of transmission; Breton formulae contain 'Hisperic' words. Many an Irishman has recorded his mood in marginal comments.[44] In the later middle ages scribes often amused themselves by writing very worldly verses and postscripts.[45]

Only a small number of scribal hands that have come down to us are immediately identifiable from their subscriptions;[46] none the less, certain well-known names are found, from Victor of Capua (541–54) and the Irishman Sedulius (saec. IX med.) up to Thomas à Kempis and Nicholas of Cusa;[47] the traditional identification of 'littera ininielligibilis' with the hand of Thomas Aquinas has been vindicated. Comparison of manuscripts may lead to the identifying and interpreting of unnamed individual scripts as historical witnesses – one of the most fascinating and delicate tasks of palaeography. The definite establishment of the identity of medieval scripts[48] in more than one

---

41 Cf. CLA II, p. xv; W.M. Lindsay in *Palaeographia Latina* 2 (1923) 25 f.

42 Lindsay, ibid., 2 (1923) 5 ff.; 4 (1925) 83 f.

43 Most notably preserved in Paris, Lat. 7498 s. IX; cf. M. Glück, *Priscians Partitiones und ihre Stellung in der spätantiken Schule* (Hildesheim 1967), 88.

44 Ch. Plummer, 'On the colophons and marginalia of Irish scribes', *Proc. Brit. Acad.* 12 (1926) 11–44; W.M. Lindsay in *Palaeographia Latina* 2 (1923) 24 f.

45 Scribal verses: Wattenbach, *Schriftwesen*, 494 ff.; J. Klapper in *Mitteil. d. Schlesischen Ges. f. Volkskunde* 19 (1917) 1 ff.; L. Thorndike in *Speculum* 12 (1937) 268 and 31 (1956) 321–8; A. Dondaine, 'Postscriptum', *Scriptorium* 32 (1978) 54 f. Cf. A. Derolez, 'Observations of the colophons of Humanistic scribes in fifteenth-century Italy', in *Paläographie* (1981) 249–61.

46 These are being collected: Benedictines of Bouveret, *Colophons de manuscrits occidentaux des origines au XVIe siècle* (Freiburg/Schweiz 1965 ff.).   47 Cf. n. 22.

48 Gilissen's book *L'expertise des écritures médiévales*, which sets forth a methodology of description and identification, pays too little attention to the dynamics of writing; cf. the criticisms of E. Poulle in *Bibl. Éc. Chartes* 132 (1974) 101–10. The articles of A. d'Haenens

manuscript, or even the establishment of several different hands within a single codex, can, however, be made rather difficult by the afore-mentioned tendency towards uniformity in the schools, or because of the change in an individual hand, for example, when writing at speed.[49] Scripts can also be substantially altered by the development in a personality[50] or by external conditions. A scribe's hand, transplanted to a different milieu, might take on the basic traits in the style of that new environment.[51] Another reason for change, leading to a steady enlargement of the script,[52] is the deterioration of eyesight brought on by age.

A special situation arose in the case of foreigners, above all Insular scribes in the carolingian empire, or Irish monks who, like Marianus Scotus and his travelling companions, occupied themselves by writing books for the convent at Regensburg; these latter adapted themselves to a continental script.[53] Among the ninth-century Irish teachers Martin of Laon was apparently the most consistent in writing caroline minuscule;[54] others, like Dungal and Iohannes Scotus, seem to have clung to their native script. In the case of Alcuin – whose hand is recognisable in a number of Insular letter forms[55] which he wrote as guides for a Tours copyist – I believe we can conclude that he also assimilated his script to a kind of caroline minuscule, with its appropriate ligatures (*ec, re, ri, ro, rt, st*). But their narrowness, ductus, and Insular forms (like open-*a*, majuscule *T* within words, and *x*) betray their Anglo-Saxon origins.[56]

and E. Ornato in *Scriptorium* 29 (1975) 175 ff. are even further removed from concrete objects. Attempts to apply the results of graphological experience to eleventh-century caroline minuscule are made by W. Schlögl, *Die Unterfertigung deutscher Könige von der Karolingerzeit bis zum Interregnum durch Kreuz und Unterschrift* (Kallmünz 1978) 215 ff.

49 On the problem see Eder, *Die Schule des Klosters Tegernsee*, 13 f.

50 An example is offered by Walafrid Strabo's hand: Bischoff, *Mittelalterliche Studien* 2, 34–51 with plate 2 f. In addition cf. n. 1 ibid and the other instances noted in vol 2, 46 n. 15. On the same problem in a late medieval hand, that of the Wittingau Augustinian Crux of Telcz (ob. c. 1495), see P. Spunar, 'Vyvoj autografu Oldřicha Křize Telče, *Listy filologické* 6 (81, 1958) 220 ff. with reprod.

51 B. Bischoff, 'Die Rolle von Einflüssen in der Schriftgeschichte', in *Paläographie* (1981) 93–103 and plates 3–10. For another example see one of the hands responsible for the inscriptions on the St Gall monastic plan; *Mittelalterliche Studien* 1, 41–9 with plate 3 f.

52 This can be seen in the annal entries by the Regensburg canon Hugo of Lerchenfeld (1167/8–1216) and in the many dated notices of the librarian Bernard Itier of St Martial (s. XIIex–1224). On Lerchenfeld: Bischoff, *Mittelalterliche Studien* 2, 157 f.; on Itier: Marie-Thérèse d'Alverny, 'L'Ecriture de Bernard Itier et son évolution', *Medievalia et Humanistica* 14 (1962), 47 ff. with reprod.; *Mss. datés*, Pays-Bas 1, plate 111.

53 See below p. 89.

54 See below p. 89.

55 Bischoff, *Mittelalterliche Studien* 2, 12 ff. and plate I.

56 It is the script of the three rhythmical poems, transmitted only in Gotha Mbr I. 75, f 20ᵛ–22ʳ, which Wilhelm Meyer established as works 'from Alcuin's circle' in *Nachr. Kgl. Ges. Wiss. Göttingen*, phil.-hist. Kl. 5 (1916), with plate, and which K. Strecker showed to be Alcuin's own work (cf. MGH *Poetae* 4, 903 ff.); plate in CLA VIII 1206.

APPENDIX

Forgeries

A peripheral problem in palaeography is recognising forgeries and texts that have been falsified. The forging of manuscripts[57] of allegedly antique or medieval origin is relatively rare in comparison with the forging of charters, but comes under various guises. There are two motives predominant behind their production: to offer forged texts and promote their authenticity, or to put something on the commercial market. Some forgeries betray themselves by the poor quality of their script, others through blunders; often old parchment is used.

In the eighteenth century Chrysostom Hanthaler, a Cistercian of Lilienfeld, fabricated and penned annals of the monastery allegedly from the thirteenth century.[58] Romantic chauvinism was the motivation around 1820 for Wenzel Hanka in forging the Königinhof and Grünberg manuscripts from which he published his Old Czech songs.[59] The ambition to discover something called forth the forgeries by the many-sided Georg Zappert, his Old High German 'lullaby' (with Hebrew vocalisation) and the 'Conversation-book' of Maximilian, amongst others.[60]

The alleged specimen of handwriting from a 'lost' work of Cornelius Nepos in an uncial palimpsest manuscript was exposed by Ludwig Traube by reference to the inexpertly used facsimile.[61] Uncial fragments of Plautus and Catullus were also produced, the former on purple parchment allegedly of the fourth century,[62] the latter a palimpsest under a Middle

---

57 We deal here only with forged manuscripts which actually exist or whose alleged script has been made available in some form. Material in Wattenbach, *Schriftwesen*, also W. Speyer, *Die literarische Fälschung im heidnischen und christlichen Altertum* (Munich 1971), esp. 315 ff.

58 M. Tangl, 'Die Fälschungen Chrysostomus Hanthalers', *Mitteil. Inst. Österr. Geschichtsforsch.* 19 (1898) 1 ff. with reprod.; Arndt–Tangl⁴, *Schrifttafeln*, plate 30 C.

59 Reprod.: V. Vojtěch, *Rukopisy královédvorský a zelenohorský. Dokumentární fotografie* (Prague 1930). The same and the Vyšehrad song in M. Žunkovič, *Die Handschriften von Grünberg und Königinhof, dazu das Vyšehrad-Lied* (Kremsier 1912). Vgl. Olga Květonová, 'Romantische Handschriftenfälschungen', *Arch. f. Kulturgesch.* 54 (1972) 168–73.

60 H. Fichtenau, 'Die Fälschungen Georg Zapperts', *Mitteil. Inst. Österr. Geschichtsforsch.* 78 (1970) 444–67. Reprod. of the 'Conversation book': *Die Lehrbücher Maximilians I. und die Anfänge der Frakturschrift* (Hamburg 1961) plate 42 f. (plus p. 15 f.) reprod. of the 'Lullaby': G. Zappert, 'Über ein althochdeutsches Schlummerlied', *Sitzungsber. K. Akad. Wiss.*, phil.-hist. Kl. 29 (Vienna 1859).

61 L. Traube, 'Der Anonymus Cortesianus', Paläographische Forschungen 4, *Abh. Bayer. Akad. Wiss.*, 3 Kl. 24/1 (1904) 47–54 with plate 6 f. (also in Traube, *Vorlesungen u. Abhandlungen* 3 (Munich 1920) 273–282 with plate 1 f.).

62 H. Degering, Über ein Bruchstück einer Plautushandschrift des vierten Jahrhunderts', in *Sitzungsber. Preuß. Akad. Wiss.* (1919) 468–76, 497–503 with facs.; É. Chatelain, 'Un

High German animal fable.[63] The remarkable and peculiarly spaced script of an illustrated Juvenal codex was meant to be a late-Gothic textura script, but the miniatures by this very prolific forger (around 1900) were of better quality than the text script.[64]

One of the most celebrated cases of more recent times is the 'Vinland Map', a sensational piece of evidence for the Viking discovery of North America allegedly dating from the time of the council of Basle. However, the uncertainty of the script and of the orthography (*ae* beside *e*) aroused suspicion. The nature of the forgery was finally confirmed by ink analysis.[65] A work in wonderfully subtle imitation of Visigothic script, from c. 1772, which was believed until recently to date from the eleventh century, is now known to be a copy from a printed text of the seventeenth century.[66]

Falsification can come about, for example, by the insertion of miniatures, by the substitution for authentic owners' marks of other ones that are intended to obliterate important details, or by other kinds of tampering that attempt to make the object more interesting.[67]

pretendu fragment de Plaute en onciale du IVe siècle', *Comptes rendus de l'Acad. des Inscriptions et Belles-Lettres* (1922) 223–9.

63 B.L. Ullman in *Classical Philology* 24 (1929) 294–7.

64 Cf. H. Omont, 'Un faux manuscrit de Juvénal orné de miniatures', *Bibl. Éc. Chartes* 75 (1914) 229 f. On the forger see Janet Backhouse, 'The Spanish Forger', in *The Eric George Millar Bequest of Manuscripts and Drawings* (London 1968), 65–71; '*The Spanish Forger*'. Catalogue of an exposition in the Pierpont Morgan Library (New York 1978).

65 R.A. Skelton–Th. E. Marston–G.D. Painter, *The Vinland Map and the Tartar Relation* (New Haven–London 1965); on this cf. Traudl Seifert, 'Anmerkungen zur sog. "Vinland Map"', *Börsenblatt für den Deutschen Buchhandel* (Frankfurter Ausg.), *Aus dem Antiquariat* 1974, Nr. 2, a 53–8. The authenticity of a recently published fragment of a Virgil roll, s. XV, must be doubted, not only because of its peculiarity but also because of the remarkably abbreviated heading; see Jeanne Krochalis, 'A Humanist experiment: Princeton's new Virgil roll', *Princeton Univ. Libr. Chron.* 42 (1981) 178–85, with plate.

66 M.C. Díaz y Díaz, 'El codice "Visigotico" de la Biblioteca Provincial de Toledo, sus problemas literarios', in *Homenaje a Antonio Tovar* (Madrid 1972) 105–14.

67 An entry was added to the colophon of the Leningrad Bede, in our view in the post-medieval period, which might have seemed to be Bede's own autograph; see D.H. Wright and P. Meyvaert in *Rev. Bénéd.* 71 (1961) 265–73 with plates, and 274–86; plate 3 is particularly clear.

The History of Latin Script

Preliminary remarks

Before surveying the history of Latin script it is necessary to refer to several forces and tendencies that fashion and alter writing, things that make this history visible.[1] This should make it simpler to understand the processes at work in writing.

There are two fundamentally different techniques of writing[2] (though certainly with some overlap); I term them the calligraphic and the cursive. The former is in general proper to bookhands, the latter is proper to the whole spectrum of everyday scripts.

The calligraphic technique, for which a broad (and slit) quill is suited, is required for the realisation of script types such as the canonical capitalis,[3] uncial, half-uncial, caroline minuscule, Beneventan script, and the Gothic textura. In these kinds of script the letters have to be constructed from their various elements with either broad or hair strokes and have to be executed technically correctly, that is either towards the body or towards the right, following the limits of the quill-point(s); the quill should not injure the page surface or spill through shaking. These 'constructed' scripts are written with the hand firmly supported on the little finger. In their realisation the sequence of strokes must be followed, that is the 'structure'[4] of the letters – not haphazard but organically and technically determined; this structure also determines the first alterations that appear in cursive writing. The constructed scripts, especially the established script types, preserve the form of the letters. Only exceptionally is there question of 'mutation';[5] this occurs with *g*: at various times the scribes tried to

---

1 Our concern here is with the graphical aspect of the scripts. For other factors which determine the form and the evolution of script, such as the physiology and the psychology of writing, changes in style and culture, political and social conditions, cf. Fichtenau, *Mensch und Schrift*; S. Morison, *Politics and Script* (Oxford 1972); Stiennon, *Paléographie*, 7–18; W. Schlögl, *Die Unterfertigung deutscher Könige von der Karolingerzeit bis zum Interregnum durch Kreuz und Unterschrift* (Kallmünz 1978) 215 ff.

2 Cf. the section on 'Terminologia e principi' in Cencetti, *Lineamenti*, 51–6 (idem, *Compendio*, 14–17).   3 This script was previously called 'capitalis rustica'.

4 'Structure' is used by Gumbert, *Utrechter Kartäuser*, 216, n. 7. I prefer this term to 'ductus', which is more common, but which I would rather reserve for the features of an individual's graphical style.

5 For which see principally Gumbert, *Utrechter Kartäuser*, 216 n. 7, who speaks of 'metanalysis'.

avoid the 3-like right-side of that letter inasmuch as they connected the left-side curve of the head to the lower curve on the right, forming an *s*-shaped line, and the letter was then completed with other strokes.[6] These scripts, however, participate in changes of style and taste that occur.

The other extreme is a script in which the hand moves swiftly over the writing surface without conscious distinction between broad and hair-strokes, often with the use of a finer quill. It is a script which, as far as possible, writes the letters as a unit, without lifting the pen, immediately attaching them in a natural way to their neighbours. The principal consequences that follow from this kind of writing with more rapid, lighter strokes could be described as follows: because they are simplified, the flourishes (for example, the finals in capitalis) drop out. As a result of this more rapid writing the script is, when space allows, elongated by end-strokes up or down (as, for example, in the cauda of the *Q* in the older cursive). Individual strokes that are contiguous to one another or that can be brought together in relative positions are joined (for example, the right-angles of capital *L B D*; the concluding, small inner curve of capital *G* is attached to the lower curve; the addition of the cauda in capitalis *Q* is shifted to the upper end of the oval). Angles are rounded off (for example, the right-angle of *L B D*), and difficult curves are smoothed out (the right-hand side of *B* and *R*). Neighbouring strokes at angles to one another can be written as parallel strokes (in the open-*a* of minuscule cursive; cp. already *E*, *F*, *L* and *M* in the script of wax tablets). Changes can come about as well through altered division or combination of the strokes (change of direction, for example); the best-known instance is the *b*, which in older cursive has the bow towards the left but towards the right in later cursive. Another example is the round-*s* of the later middle ages from which the progenitors of the German final-*s* and the 'reversed'-*s* ('*Rücken-s*') may derive.[7]

The altered division of the letter, especially in ligatures and chains of ligatures, can lead, by contraction of parts of the same or of different letters (on the left-hand side), to a further freer rightward shift in the flow of the writing. Ligatures not only alter some letters (particularly *a* and *t*), they also alter the sequence of strokes by beginning at a different point of departure, as in *p* (for example, *ap*, *ep* – that is, beginning with the bow). Particularly consequential changes are called forth by tracing on the parchment the normally invisible transitional strokes ('*Luftlinien*'), that is the often curved or *s*-shaped path which the quill has to follow in order to reach the neighbouring letters (in ligatures), or to join parts of letters. This is generally used only sparely. In the new Roman cursive it is the regular practice from the fourth century on, above all in the writing of ascenders and in the heads of *e* and *f*. In this way letters can acquire

6 For illustrations see J. Vezin, *Les scriptoria d'Angers au XIe siècle* (Paris 1974) 132. Further examples: CLA VI 840 (s. VIIIex.); Bischoff, *Schreibschulen* I, 52, 55 (c. s. VIII–IX to IX–X). In the late middle ages attempts were made to link the right side of the upper bow to the left side of the lower bow; cf. Gumbert, *Utrechter Kartäuser*, 217 (plate) and below p. 141.

7 Gumbert, *Utrechter Kartäuser*, 24. This form survived in the French 'final s' in the sixteenth and seventeenth centuries.

bodies, as with *a* (in half-uncial) and *e* and *t* in the curialis, or with the loops on the ascenders of Gothic cursive (including the rounded *d*). It is clear from all this that it is in cursive 'flowing' scripts that the decisive changes occur and the new letter forms appear.

The recognition of the growing divergence between the utilitarian script (which was in daily use and which everyone wrote) and the bookhand had an impact, in elevated higher grades of writing, on the life of book-script itself. Attempts were made to narrow the gap between the two types and to introduce into the bookhand the innovations that had become normal on the lower level, in order to catch up with the developments in the letter-forms. This was generally achieved not by the adoption of individual, altered letters into the alphabet of the bookhand[8] but by the accommodation of a certain state of the cursive to the requirements of bookhand. In conformity with the principles of the constructed style, in order to realise a calligraphic script the flowing forms had to be consolidated[9] (contracted) and transformed into bodies made up of patterns of individual strokes, with or without shading. An example: the *g* of pre-caroline cursive was – apart from the tuft – written in one stroke; the consolidation process meant that this was now written with three strokes: the face, back-line, and 'shoe', so that the whole was completed in four strokes. In the same way, letter forms which, in cursive ligatures, had changed markedly, could live on in bookhand in 'consolidated' ligatures (cp. *et*, *nt*). Because in such a process a more-or-less conscious trend towards calligraphy was involved, the desire for legibility could be decisive in the choice of individual functional forms.

In my view, the origin of uncial, the two half-uncial scripts,[10] and of early medieval minuscule can be understood as a renewal of letter-forms taken from cursive script according to the principles just described. I see in this a decisive factor in the history of Roman and early medieval writing. The new kinds of script, whose finished forms excite admiration in the observer, mark the great landmarks in the history of writing. If this development does not come to a standstill with these coined forms it is because, after the learning of the type in class, the script changes in the individual's own handwriting (perhaps imperceptibly);[11] the pupils, when they come to teach, pass on something that differs somewhat from what their teachers taught them.[12]

8 The occasional K-like form of H in late capitalis, for example in the Bembine Terence (CLA I 12), results from the habit of writing the cross stroke and the lower part of the right shaft without a pen-lift.

9 J.-O. Tjäder, 'Der Ursprung der Unzialschrift', *Basler Z. f. Gesch. u. Altertumskunde* (1974) 24 and 34 misunderstood this expression. His term 'stylized' (38) seems too vague.

10 For these two things, and in the same sense, see Tjäder, 38.

11 See above p. 45.

12 Cf. Christine Elisabeth Eder, *Die Schule des Klosters Tegernsee im frühen Mittelalter im Spiegel der Tegernseer Handschriften, Stud. Mitteil. OSB* 83 (1972) = Münchener Beiträge, Beiheft, 11 f.; this insight serves as the starting point for the study of a closed scriptorium. It can also be applied, on a larger scale, to the history of beneventan script or the development of minuscule from the ninth to the twelfth centuries, a period in which no new types appear.

Latin script in antiquity

1. Latin script

The Latin alphabet is a descendant of a western Greek script which was taken
over by the Romans – according to the prevailing view – not directly but through
the mediation of the Etruscans, who had modified it considerably in accordance
with the character of their language.[1] Up to the first century BC it comprised
twenty-one letters (*A* to *X*); then *Y* and *Z* were introduced (originally in order to
write Greek names and foreign words).[2] After an archaic period (seventh to
fourth century BC), when it was written from right to left or in lines of alternating
directions (boustrophedon),[3] the practice of writing from left to right became
the norm. The letters acquired the classical shapes, though *P* (which was derived
from an angular *P* with short right stroke) is often not closed even in the
majuscule script of codices.

In the script of inscriptions, which is the only evidence we have up to the
beginning of the first century BC, certain cursive tendencies are already visible
two centuries before that date.[4] At the time *E* and *F* appear as ‖ and ‖', forms that
are typical of wax-tablet script. In this script, whose best-known monuments,
dating from the mid first and the second century, are the tablets found at
Pompeii and in Transylvania, the normal script (as already with the incised
script ('graffiti') from Sulla's time) is much altered by the dissolving of the
letters into strokes drawn as much as possible in the same direction.[5]

Monumental script was executed for a long time in grooves of equal width. Its
classical construction, with its swelling and narrowing curves, its firmly-based

---

1 Cf. Foerster, *Abriß²*, 106 ff.; B.L. Ullman, *Ancient writing and its influence* (New York 1963)
   32 ff.; H. Jensen, *Die Schrift in Vergangenheit und Gegenwart²* (Berlin 1958) 491 f. Direct
   derivation from Greek script has been proposed anew by St Bassi, *Monumenta Italiae graphica*
   (Cremona 1956/7) 73 ff.
2 G. Perl, '*Y* und *Z* im lateinischen Alphabet', *Philologus* 115 (1971) 196–233.
3 Reprod.: E. Diehl, *Inscriptiones Latinae* (Bonn 1912) vii and plate 1; Bassi, *Monumenta*,
   reprod. 82–4; Steffens², *Lateinische Paläographie*, plate 1.
4 G. Cencetti, 'Ricerche sulla scrittura latina nell'età arcaica. I. Il filone corsivo', *Bull.
   dell' Arch. Pal. Ital.*, n.s. 2/3 (1956/7) 175–205 with plate.
5 Examples in E. Diehl, *Inscriptiones*, xiii ff.; Steffens², *Lateinische Paläographie*, plates 5 and 8;
   Seider, *Lateinische Papyri*, Nr. 25c, 25d; Bassi, *Monumenta*, reprod. 190 ff.

shafts and serifs, is first attested in early imperial times. From the first century BC on there appear, alongside the monumentalis, inscriptions in a less formal, narrower form of alphabet ('scriptura actuaria') with a simple alternation of hair- and broad-strokes and which is best represented by painted inscriptions (for example, the election slogans at Pompeii).[6]

Its counterpart in manuscript writing, perhaps of the same age, is the 'canonical' capitalis of calligraphic Roman manuscripts.[7] One should keep in mind, however, that this agreeable script (undoubtedly cultivated by the Roman book trade) presents what was originally only one form isolated from 'current' script,[8] which then became stylised.

2. *Capitalis*

The oldest handwritten monument of Latin script[9] is the letter of a slave from about the middle of the first century BC.[10] Additional items of more precise date are: an account-list[11] from the time of Augustus and the letters to Macedo;[12] the next most important after that are a legal decision (AD 37–43)[13] and the Berlin papyrus containing the oration of Claudius (probably AD 43–54).[14] Only the first

6 See above p. 28. Plates: *Écriture latine*, Nr. 4; Seider, *Lateinische Papyri* 1, Nr. 7 and 13; Bassi, *Monumenta*, reprod. 184–7. J. Mallon has repeatedly explained and insisted that inscriptions on stone represent the definitive and permanent form of monuments that are constructed in several stages; that is, in successive written versions: visualisation of the text and its 'ordinatio' on stone precede the work of the stonemason. In many articles he has shown that this procedure can be detected by the study of errors and imitations of letter forms in the inscriptions or in the copies of the sketch. They complete the palaeographical documentation from the Roman world; cf. especially his chapter 'Paléographie romaine', in *L'Histoire et ses méthodes* (ed. Ch. Samaran) (Paris 1961) 564 ff., and 'Scriptoria épigraphiques', *Scriptorium* 11 (1957) 177–94.

7 This script is traditionally called 'capitalis rustica' as a poor relation of the 'capitalis quadrata' ('capitalis elegans') used in two manuscripts of Vergil, which imitates the style of inscriptions. This script is distinguished by serifs at the top and base of the letters and by a writing angle of 45–50° (see note 17). It was considered appropriate for elegant calligraphy for many centuries until, after the disappearance of cursive majuscule, it became a type of bookscript like many others, and from the fourth century it was simply described as 'capitalis'. I borrow the term 'canonical capitalis' from G. Cencetti.

8 The expression 'Écriture commune', 'Scrittura usuale' had become current in various works of Mallon and G. Cencetti.

9 For the sections on writing in Antiquity cf. Foerster, *Abriß*[2], 113–35; Cencetti, *Lineamenti*, 60–81; idem, *Compendio*, 19–38; R. Marichal, 'De la capitale romaine à la minuscule', in M. Audin, *Somme typographique* 1 (Paris 1948) 61–96; John, *Latin Paleography*, 7–13; Mallon, *Paléographie romaine*.

10 *Écriture latine*, Nr. 19; Seider, *Lateinische Papyri* 1, Nr. 1; Mallon, *Paléographie romaine*, plate 1, 1.   11 ChLA v 308 (31–8 BC); Mallon, *Paléographie romaine*, plate 2, 1.

12 Seider, *Lateinische Papyri* 1, Nr. 3.4; Mallon, *Paléographie romaine*, plate 3, 2; *Écriture latine*, Nr. 11 (c. 17–14 BC). There is a letter of roughly equal date in Virginia Brown, 'A Latin letter from Oxyrhynchus', *Univ. London Inst. Class. Stud. Bull.* Nr. 17 (1970) 136–43 with plate. The ostraca from El-Fawâchir containing letters are probably to be dated to around the turn of the century; Seider 1, Nr. 2.   13 ChLA v 280.

14 CLA VIII 1038; Steffens[2], *Lateinische Paläographie*, plate 4; *Écriture latine*, Nr. 11; Seider, *Lateinische Papyri*, 1, Nr. 5; Mallon, *Paléographie romaine*, plate 6; ChLA X 418.

Λ B B C D E F G G H

K I I K L L M N O P Q R

S T V U X Y Z Q U R

1. Capitalis

FINES · ISCHYRAN · THEONIS · ET ·

JINES · ISCHYRAN · THEONIS · ET

2. Capitalis and Older Roman cursive from Oxyrhynchus

Λ (A) B C D E F G H

I L M N O P Q R S

T Y X Y Z

3. Capitalis quadrata

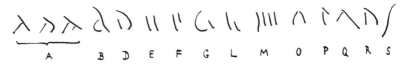

A   B D E F G L M O P Q R S

4. Wax-tablet script

two show the basic Latin alphabet almost unchanged; in the other two, the script has gone over in varying degrees to cursive (with the characteristic letters *B, D, R*). The two directions into which the script has diverged are illustrated in a rare way by the two fragments of a household inventory of AD 47/48 from Oxyrhynchus: one copy of the identical text is written in a bookish capitalis; the other in 'common' script,[15] a cursive.

The first literary Latin papyri can be dated from the time of Augustus until roughly the mid-first century. The oldest is probably the fragment of Cicero's second Verrine oration now in Giessen, written in a skilled cursive;[16] further examples are the Latin papyri from Herculaneum (before AD 79). The script of many of these has the firm canonical form of the book-capitalis; it is written with a relatively broad pen and the writing angle[17] lies at roughly 45°. The feet on *A* and *M* (wavy), on *F* and so on, and the end-strokes above on *N* and *V* are firm; the third stroke of *G* is relatively long and extends somewhat below the line.[18] Simpler, because written without feet (although the *A* does have a sloping middle bar) is the script of the *Carmen de bello Actiaco* dating from between 31 BC and AD 79 and also found at Herculaneum.[19] In other papyri from there the script approaches cursive.[20] The capitalis remained in use as the basic alphabet in public records, for emphasis, and even for whole lists and texts (like the 'Feriale', the list of official feasts of the garrison at Dura-Europos, from AD 225–35); these were mostly written in a ductus lacking contrast between thick and thin strokes and without the features[21] of the canonical script.[22]

---

15 *Écriture latine*, Nr. 9.10; Seider, *Lateinische Papyri*, 1, Nr. 6a, 6b; Mallon, *Paléographie romaine*, plate 5.

16 CLA VIII 1201; Kirchner, *Script. Lat. Libr.*², plate 3b; Mallon, *Paléographie romaine*, plate 4, 1; Seider, *Papyri* 2/1, Nr. 1. A further literary survival from the same era, in capitalis, is the papyrus containing elegiac verses by Cornelius Gallus published by R.D. Anderson–P.J. Parsons–R.G.M. Nisbet, 'Elegiacs by Gallus from Qasr Ibrîm', *J. Roman. Stud.*69 (1979) 125–55 and plates 4–6; CLA Addenda 1817. The authenticity of the find has recently been questioned by Fr. Brunhölzl, 'Der sogenannte Galluspapyrus von Kasr Ibrim', *Codices Manuscripti* 10/2 (1984) 33–40, with illustr.

17 I use the term writing angle (Tjäder's 'Schriftwinkel') in the same way as Tjäder, 'Der 'Ursprung der Unzialschrift' (following D.F. Bright, *The Origin of the Latin Uncial Script* (Diss., Univ. of Cincinnati, 1967) to mean the angle between the widest pen-stroke and the base line.

18 Giovanna Petronio Nicolaj, 'Osservazioni sul canone della capitale libraria romana fra I e III secolo', in *Miscellanea in memoria di Giorgio Cencetti* (Turin 1973) 11 ff. and plates 2 and 3 (2 and 3a and CLA III 387; Seider, *Papyri* 2/1, Nr. 2; 3e and CLA III 386).

19 CLA III 385; Seider, *Papyri* 2/2, Nr. 7. Juxtaposition of a photograph and an earlier engraved facsimile in Mallon, *Paléographie romaine*, plate 4.

20 Cf. G. Petronio Nicolaj, 'Osservazioni', 16 and plate 4; R. Marichal in G.G. Archi and others (edd), *Pauli Sententiarum Fragmentum Leidense* (Leiden 1956) plate 3, 3; Seider, *Papyri*) 2/2, Nr. 7   21 E.g. *Écriture latine*, Nr. 24 (= Seider, *Lateinische Papyri* 1, Nr. 12).

22 Feriale Duranum: ChLA VI 309; G. Petronio Nicolaj, 'Osservazioni', plates 1 and 5 ff.; Seider, *Lateinische Papyri* 1, Nr. 41; Mallon, plate 17, 4. On the script see Mallon, *Paléographie romaine*, 89 ff.

The status of the 'canonical' capitalis as the recognised bookhand remained undisputed up until the late-antique period,[23] although before the fourth century a considerable part of the literature will have circulated in common (cursive) scripts.[24] Although affected by fashions and schools of style – that is, written broader or narrower,[25] more closed or open – it retained its forms basically unchanged throughout the course of its six-hundred year long history.[26] There are few fluctuations in the forms: *B, F, L, Y* were partly extended beyond the two-line band; *F* was occasionally set lower; the final stroke of *G* was sometimes set above the end of the second, sometimes attached to it. In the case of *H*, in some manuscripts (clearly due to the influence of the cursive *h*-form) the upper half of the second shaft was written as a separate, oblique stroke[27] – indeed, the whole letter looks like a *K*.[28] On the other hand, *V* is often written with the left-stroke outswinging, or is also frequently written as a broad letter with vertical shafts (as in uncial). Even in the latest monuments the oblique down-strokes running from left to right remain the broadest,[29] even when the writing angle becomes steeper.

The Gellius palimpsest in Vatican MS Pal. Lat.24[30] may date from about the beginning of the period of western transmission in parchment codices (which probably does not begin before the fourth century). The first relatively well-dated parchment manuscripts are the Vergilius Mediceus revised in AD 494[31] by the consul Turcius Rufius Apronianus Asterius, and the Prudentius owned by Vettius Agorius Basileus, consul for AD 527.[32]

Biblical texts were apparently only rarely written in capitalis;[33] no other Christian prose texts exist in this script. For them clearly uncial or half-uncial were preferred. From the fourth century on a large part too of classical literature

---

23 The gap in transmission between the papyri from Herculaneum and Western parchment codices is bridged by papyrus fragments from Egypt. A list in G. Petronio Nicolaj, 'Osservazioni', 11 n. 28, to which CLA 11² 223 (Seider, *Papyri* 2/1, Nr. 22); and x 1520 must be added. On the uncertainty of dating manuscripts in capitalis, and possible revisions, Petronio Nicolaj, 'Osservazioni', 23 ff.   24 Cf. below p. 62.

25 A collection of examples: C. Zangemeister–W. Wattenbach, *Exempla codicum Latinorum litteris maiusculis scriptorum* (Heidelberg 1876) plates 1–16, and Suppl. (1879) plate 66; in addition: St Bassi, *Monumenta*, reprod. 118 ff. Cf. A. Pratesi, 'Considerazioni su alcuni codici in capitale della Biblioteca Vaticana', in *Mélanges Eugène Tisserant* 7. *Studi e Testi* 237 (Vat. 1964) 243–54 with reprod.

26 The feet of the script of CLA 1 74 (Gellius) are simply turns to the shafts. With slight variations this script was tried for posters (CLA S 1695, 1781).

27 Especially CLA 1 12 and after 112 (Vat. Reg. Lat. 1283a); *Écriture latine*, Nr. 41; Stiennon, *Paléographie*, 191–5.

28 CLA v 571a. These letter-forms were imitated in the ninth century.

29 CLA 1 115 (Seider, *Papyri* 2/1, Nr. 27) is an exception in which an uncial style is discernible.

30 Cf. n. 26.   31 CLA iii 11; Ehrle–Liebaert, *Specimina*, plate 2.

32 CLA v 571a; Seider, *Papyri* 2/2, Nr. 44; *Écriture latine*, Nr. 42; Stiennon, *Paléographie*, 191–5.

33 CLA 11² 118; Seider, *Papyri* 2/2, Nr. 43 (Ev. Ioh.); S 1694; Seider, *Papyri* 2/2, Nr. 42 (Ep. ad Ephes., Greek-Latin).

appears in uncial, though no uncial or half-uncial manuscript of Vergil has survived. On the other hand, Vergil manuscripts were produced in capitalis, both in illustrated copies and in unillustrated bibliophile ones in the largest format.[34]

The highpoint of refinement was reached with the writing of whole codices of Vergil, not in the traditional capitalis but in an imitation of a monumental, inscriptional script ('capitalis quadrata'). The script of the two witnesses (the Vergilius Augusteus,[35] distinguished by its initials for every new page, and the St Gall Vergil)[36] is not a natural one; it demanded a quite different manipulation of the quill.[37] Perhaps due to the importance of capitalis in the tradition of Vergil, the term 'litterae Vergilianae' is attested in the eighth/ninth century for capitals as verse initials.[38] Probably because of their character as Christian epic writers, Prudentius[39] and Sedulius[40] were also copied in capitalis.

With the disintegration of ancient civilisation the de luxe manuscripts disappear and the rôle of capitalis in Roman calligraphy comes to an end.[41] From the fifth century on, capitalis, in combination with uncial, became a distinguishing script used for running-titles and chapter-headings and also for incipits and explicits; for these latter it was often stylised as a monumental script.[42] It was still used for emphasis and for citations from poetry in Spain in Isidore's time.[43] The Anglo-Saxons took up the late-antique use of capitalis; already in Ceolfrid's bible for St Peter's it is employed for colophons and short introductions.[44] A more plentiful use is made of it in the prefaces of further English uncial codices

34 Verg. Vaticanus: CLA I 11; Steffens², plate 10; Ehrle–Liebaert, *Specimina*, plate 2; Kirchner, *Script Lat libr²*, plate 1a. Verg. Romanus: CLA I 19; Steffens², *Lateinische Paläographie*, plate 19; Ehrle–Liebaert, *Specimina*, plate 3; Seider, *Papyri* 2/1, Nr. 29. Verg. Palatinus: CLA I 99; Ehrle–Liebaert, *Specimina*, plate 3.

35 CLA I 13; Steffens², *Lateinische Paläographie*, plate 12; Ehrle–Liebaert, *Specimina*, plate 1; Kirchner, *Script. Lat. libr².*, plate 2, facs.: C. Nordenfalk, *Vergilius Augusteus* (Graz 1976); I cannot agree with Nordenfalk's view that the manuscript was copied around the last third of the fourth century and that its decoration is to be explained by the art of the calligrapher and stonemason Filocalus (see p. 184). I regard a later date as more probable, since the script and its decoration correspond to the state of evolution of decorated initials in the sixth century which Nordenfalk has sketched (note 189); cf. A. Petrucci, 'Per la datazione del Virgilio Augusteo', in *Miscellanea in memoria di Giorgio Cencetti* (Turin 1973) 29–45 ('between 495 and 530').

36 CLA VII 977; Steffens², *Lateinische Paläographie*, plate 12; *Écriture latine*, Nr. 44; Seider, *Papyri* 2/1, Nr. 30.

37 A fragment of a third Vergil codex, CLA X 1569 (Seider, *Papyri* 2/1, Nr. 28), is closer to the script of the Augusteus.

38 Bischoff, *Mittelalterliche Studien* 1, 4 f.; cf. however *Sammelhandschrift Diez. B. Sant. 66* (introd. B. Bischoff) (Graz 1973) 32.   39 CLA V 571a; *Écriture latine*, Nr. 42.

40 CLA IV 447. The portion of the manuscript written in capitalis is trapped in imitation devoid of style; cf. Zangemeister–Wattenbach, *Exempla*, plates 16 and 56.

41 A. Petrucci, 'Scrittura e libro nell'Italia Altomedievale', in *A Giuseppe Ermini* 2 = *Studi Medievali* 10/2 (1969) 177 ff., 205 f.   42 See above p. 60.

43 CLA XI 1631; Millares Carlo, *Tratado*, reprod. 4. Cf. Bischoff, *Mittelalterliche Studien* 1, 173.

44 CLA III 299; Lowe, *English Uncial*, plate 9.

of the eighth century, the Vespasian Psalter[45] and the gospel-book in Paris, BN, Lat. 281 + 298.[46] The capitalis then returns to the continent: in the double-psalter in Vatican, Reg. Lat. 11 (produced in an outstanding north-French scriptorium of around Pippin's time) a mannered uncial is contrasted with an equally mannered variation of capitalis with *K*-shaped *H*.[47] That the prologues to the Vienna coronation gospel[48] and two gospel-books from south-east Germany[49] were likewise distinguished by capitalis was due probably to the imitation of Anglo-Saxon practice.

From the carolingian reform up to the twelfth century capitalis is the rival display script to uncial, or else is mixed with it. In the hierarchy of scripts at the school of Tours it occupies the second highest place. Ninth-century de luxe manuscripts in this script are the Utrecht Psalter,[50] the Leyden Aratus[51] and descriptions within the zodiac miniatures of the London Aratus.[52] The quality of the capitalis can be taken at this time as a measure of the understanding of antique form: thus it appears that Lupus of Fèrrieres, who mastered it, liked to write it himself for titles in some of his codices.

Also included in the spectrum of medieval writing are the monumental capitalis and the ornamentally formed scripts of titles, openings, and colophons, which developed from it with many changes of form and which are often mixed with rounded (uncial) letters. They reveal, according to time and place, many parallels with contemporary epigraphic script, sometimes they take over forms from it. Even the intrusion of Merovingian lapidary script (with extended shafts) is to be found occasionally in manuscripts.[53] The Insular scribes were probably the most extravagant in their use of large ornamental script.[54] In Spanish writing capricious, tall forms are characteristic.[55]

The carolingian reform returned to the style of inscriptions dating from imperial times; a model alphabet of the kind survives from the circle of Einhard. It is apparently the 'antiquarum litterarum . . ., quae maximae sunt et unciales a quibusdam vocari existimantur, . . . mensura descripta' which Lupus sought from Einhard (Ep. 5).[56] Only through the copying of such models can the perfected gigantic forms of, for example, the bible from S. Paolo be explained.[57]

45 D.H. Wright, *The Vespasian Psalter*. Early English Manuscripts in Facsimile 14 (Copenhagen 1967); Lowe, *English Uncial*, plate 27.

46 CLA v 526; Lowe, *English Uncial*, plate 30; *Écriture Latine*, Nr. 45.

47 CLA I 101.   48 CLA x 1469; Koehler, *Karol. Min.* 3, plate 1.

49 CLA IX 1347; Kremsmünster, *Codex millenarius* (*Cod. Mill. Vollständige Faksimile-Ausgabe des Codex Cremifanensis Cim.* 1; introd. W. Neumüller–K. Holter (Graz 1974); Clm 29270/7.

50 Facs.: *Latin Psalter in the University Library of Utrecht* (London 1874); Arndt-Tangl[4], *Schrifttafeln*, plate 33a; St Bassi, *Monumenta*, reprod. 127.

51 Koehler–Mütherich, *Karol. Min.* 4, plate 96.

52 Koehler–Mütherich, ibid., plates 62, 73.   53 CLA v 617; VII 860.

54 See below p. 88. Ogham or the style of runes may have contributed.

55 Millares Carlo, *Tratado* 1, 78, illustr. 49, 87.

56 Reprod.: *Karl der Große, Werk und Wirkung* (Aachen 1965, Catalogue) plate 36, cf. 222 f. (on Bern 250).   57 See *Arch. Pal. Ital.* IV, plates 9, 14 17.

In the eleventh century the coronation-gospels of Vratislav II was written in the Vyšehrad school of Prague entirely in inscription-like capitalis.[58] In other manuscripts of the same atelier only a few display pages are written in this ostentatious style.[59] The title- and closing-pages of some twelfth-century French codices invite comparison with the intricate majuscule of contemporary inscriptions.[60]

With the return to pre-Gothic script and the renewed study of ancient inscriptions on the part of the Humanists, their attention was inevitably directed as well to display scripts. For simple titles and closing-scripts they took over neither uncial nor the canonical capitalis. The decision in the end was in favour of an easily rounded 'Quadrata', but earlier, after many experiments and with the use of Greek models in books and inscriptions, a curious 'early humanistic' capitalis had met with great approval.[61]

3. *Older Roman cursive*

Reference has already been made above to the diverging tendencies in the first hundred years for which we have written witnesses. While the canonical capitalis is already established at that time as the formal bookhand, the everyday Roman script[62] (as the papyri attest), certainly at latest by the Augustan period, is affected by changes that must be compared with the rise of Greek script two centuries earlier; they were to go much farther than in the wax tablets and graffiti inscriptions. If this unstable script is described as 'cursive', because of its fluidity and its 'running' character[63] that encourages the connection of letters, it is not less a generic term for a great diversity in appearances. Despite a good deal of documentation,[64] it can still only be seen in an incomplete and casual way, and it exists in western material up to the fourth century in little more than wooden or wax tablets, 'tabellae defixionum', graffiti, and inscriptions on clay from the western empire.

Roman cursive is divided into two great stages: the older Roman cursive or majuscule (or capitalis-) cursive, and the later or minuscule cursive. The older cursive predominates into the third century, for the first half of which we must

---

58 Facs.: Fr. Kavka–J. Mašín, *Codex Vyšehradensis* (Prague 1970). Cf. P. Spunar, 'Ein Beitrag zur Festlegung des Platzes des Vyšehrader Kodex in der Entwicklung der Schreibkunst Mitteleuropas', *Scriptorium* 23 (1969) 13–23.

59 Reprod.: G. Reimann–H. Büttner, *Mittelalterliche Buchmalerei in Sammlungen volksdemokratischer Länder* (Leipzig 1961) plates 14, 21.

60 P. Deschamps, 'Paléographie des inscriptions de la fin de l'époque mérovingienne aux dernières années du XIIe siècle', *Bulletin monumental* 88 (1929) fig. 32, 49.

61 See below p. 146 f.

62 'Ecriture commune', 'Scrittura usuale', see above p. 55 n. 8.

63 See above concerning 'stretched' script.

64 A collection in R. Marichal, 'L'Écriture latine du Ier au VIIIe siècle: les sources', *Scriptorium* 4 (1950) 119 ff. (for which see ibid., 9 (1955) 128 ff.).

infer the existence of minuscule cursive from the script of the Livy epitome.[65] However, the replacement of one by the other is a very gradual process, which took generations. In the sequence of metamorphoses that this script underwent in different areas of usage, it could in various countries and in changing conditions become the basis for the new calligraphic writing styles: the script of *De bellis Macedonicis*, the uncial, the older and later half-uncials, and the minuscule (up to the carolingian minuscule).[66]

The older cursive[67] was not only used for letters, charters, and public records, but also for literary works,[68] and this has left its traces in their transmission. The most striking new forms called forth by the acceleration of the writing are: *B*: a bow on the left with a long rounded neck above it (*'B à panse à gauche'*); *D*: a bow with a leftward or upward directed shaft above it; *E*: either in a round form or (greatly simplified) a stroke from whose lower end another is drawn obliquely upwards;[69] *H*: whose second shaft loses the upper half; *Q*: a narrow, oblique oval, on whose upper part the long, oblique cauda rests; *R*: usually with a long shaft and a curving stroke over the top. Even in controlled cursives the forms of *A* and *R*, *B* and *D* approach one another; in continuous script the differences between *C*, *P*, and *T* diminish and ligatures make groups of various letters confusingly similar to one another.[70] Among the older witnesses, a broader,

---

65 CLA II² 208; Seider, *Papyri* 2/1, Nr. 34. See below p. 72.

66 The importance of cursive for the development and creation of new letter-forms is stressed by G. Cencetti, 'Note paleografiche sulla scrittura dei papiri latini dal I al III secolo D. C.', *Accademia della scienze dell'Istituto di Bologna*, Classe di scienze morali, Memorie, ser 5 (1951) 3 f.; J.-O. Tjäder, 'Der Ursprung der Unzialschrift', *Basler Z. f. Gesch u. Altertumskunde* (1974) 38; idem, 'Considerazioni e proposte sulla scrittura latina nell'età romana', in *Palaeographica, diplomatica et archivistica, Studia in onore di Giulio Battelli* I (Rome 1979) 31–62; idem, 'Skrift, skrivande och skrivkunnighet i det romerska världsriket', *Kungl. Humanistiska Vetenskaps-Samfundet i Uppsala, Årsbok 1981–2* (Uppsala 1983) 83–126, with illustr.

67 Cf. especially G. Cencetti, 'Note paleografiche', 40 ff. Description of the alphabets and ligatures. The history of the letter-forms of old Roman cursive has recently been comprehensively discussed by E. Casamassima–E. Staraz, 'Varianti e cambio grafico nella scrittura dei papiri latini', *Scrittura e Civiltà* 1 (1977) 9–110 with 4 folding plates. This fundamental article, which came to my notice long after I had finished this manuscript, establishes conclusively that the preconditions for subsequent development consist in a change in the form of cursive and not a change in the writing material which allowed the scribe to turn the page when writing. Cf. J.-O. Tjäder in *Eranos* 75 (1977) 139ff. See also notes 105 and 140.

68 Besides the Cicero papyrus in Gießen (see above n. 16) a historical fragment is also preserved (CLA S 1714; Seider, *Papyri* 2/1, Nr. 12; Mallon, *Paléographie romaine*, plate 10, 1; according to R.W. Hunt and others, *The Survival of Ancient Literature* (Exhibition catalogue, Oxford 1975) Nr. 46, perhaps Cato, Origines, and Gaius (CLA S 1716; Mallon, plate 16, 1; Kirchner, *Script. Lat. Libr²*., plate 3c).

69 On the origin see R. Marichal, 'L'Écriture latine et l'écriture grecque du Ier au Vie siècle', *L'Antiquité classique* 19 (1950) 122.

70 The recognition that numerous Latin literary texts went through a cursive stage during their transmission makes a systematic understanding of corruptions possible; cf. Fr. Brunhölzl, 'Zu den sogenannten codices archetypi der römischen Literatur', in *Festschrift Bernhard Bischoff* (Stuttgart 1971) 16–31; Michaela Zelzer, 'Palaeographische Bemerkungen zur Vorlage der Wiener Liviushandschrift', in *Antidosis, Festschrift für Walther Kraus* (Vienna–Graz–

more upright style seems to stand out that is first attested in an edict of Nero's, and lastly in an act of sale of 166.[71]

From the beginning of the second century on, the script in legal documents as well as in military and civilian administration took on a very uniform character[72] which gradually became set. The earlier known, almost exclusively Egyptian material was essentially enriched by the complete publication of the finds from the stronghold of Dura-Europos on the Euphrates abandoned in 272 (Chartae Latinae VI–IXff.).[73]

As the older cursive fell out of public use, higher officials, however, did not abandon it.[74] Because in the end the imperial chancery raised it in the very narrow oblique form of the 'litterae caelestes' to the status of their exclusive script – it was still so in the fifth century[75] – in 367 a ban was issued on its misuse by other chanceries.[76] Individual letters, among them the *b* (with the bow on the left) lasted longer in the charter script[77] and even in codices not written in calligraphic script.[78]

4. *Later Roman cursive*

The second great stage in the history of Latin cursive, the minuscule cursive, must have been reached already in the third century. The remains from this period are sparse but a clear witness to the change is the imperial decree written between 287 and 304 (PSI 111, with minuscule *b d g p* beside *L* and *N*).[79] In other

Cologne 1972) 487 ff.; eadem, 'Zur Vorlage des Tacitus-Codex Mediceus 68, 2', *Wiener Studien*, n.F. 7 (86, 1973) 185 ff.; eadem, 'Die umschrift lateinischer Texte am Ende der Antike und ihre Bedeutung für die Textkritik', ibid., n.F. 15 (1981) 211–31.

71 Edict: *Écriture Latine*, Nr. 14; Seider, *Lateinische Papyri*, Nr. 8. Contract of 166: Steffens[2], *Lateinische Paläographie*, plate 9; *Écriture latine*, Nr. 25; Seider, *Lateinische Papyri* Nr. 36; ChLA III 200. In addition a codicil from the time of Domitian: Seider, *Lateinische Papyri*, Nr. 11 (and perhaps the writing exercises CLA XI 1646 f.; ChLA V 304, Seider, *Papyri* 2/1, Nr. 11). Cencetti, 'Note paleografiche', 11 f, considers them as members of a group in which he claims to detect the influence of writing on wax tablets.

72 Cencetti, 'Note paleografiche', 16 ff. For a text in similar script see CLA S 1755.

73 There is a resumé of the script types preserved from there in ChLA IX 16–19, with illustr.

74 Cf. Tjäder, *Nichtliter. lat. Pap.*, 119.

75 The textbook example is the papyrus fragments of two imperial rescripts dating from the fifth century in Leiden and Paris; collected in ChLA XVII 657; J. Mallon, 'L'Écriture de la chancellerie impériale romaine', *Acta Salmanticensia, Filosofia y Letras* 4/2 (1948) plate 2; idem, *Paléographie romaine*, plate 26, 4; Steffens[2] *Lateinische Paläographie*, plate 16; Seider, *Papyri* 1, Nr. 60. Cf. R. Marichal, 'L'Écriture de la chancellerie impériale', *Aegyptus* 32 (1952) 336–50. The type seems to have been almost fully developed by the second century; R. Marichal, 'L'écriture latine', 135 f. and plate 6, 6.

76 Tjäder, *Nichtliter. lat. Pap.*, 122 n. 3. The use of majuscule cursive in the 'enlarged opening script' of the Gesta Municipalia is normal. In Ravenna in the sixth century this ultimately developed highly florid forms; cf. Tjäder, ibid., 122 ff. and plate 1, col 3; idem, 'La misteriosa "scrittura grande" di alcuni papiri ravennati', *Studi Romagnoli* 3 (1952) 173–221 with plate.

77 Tjäder, *Nichtliter. lat. Pap.*, 117 ff.

78 CLA III 280 (reprod. 1) and 397a (reprod. 2). Further references in Tjäder, 'Some ancient letter forms in the later Roman cursive and early medieval script of the notarii', *Scrittura e civiltà* 6 (1982) 5–21.   79 Reprod.: Cencetti, 'Note paleografiche', plate 5 (cf. p. 22 f.).

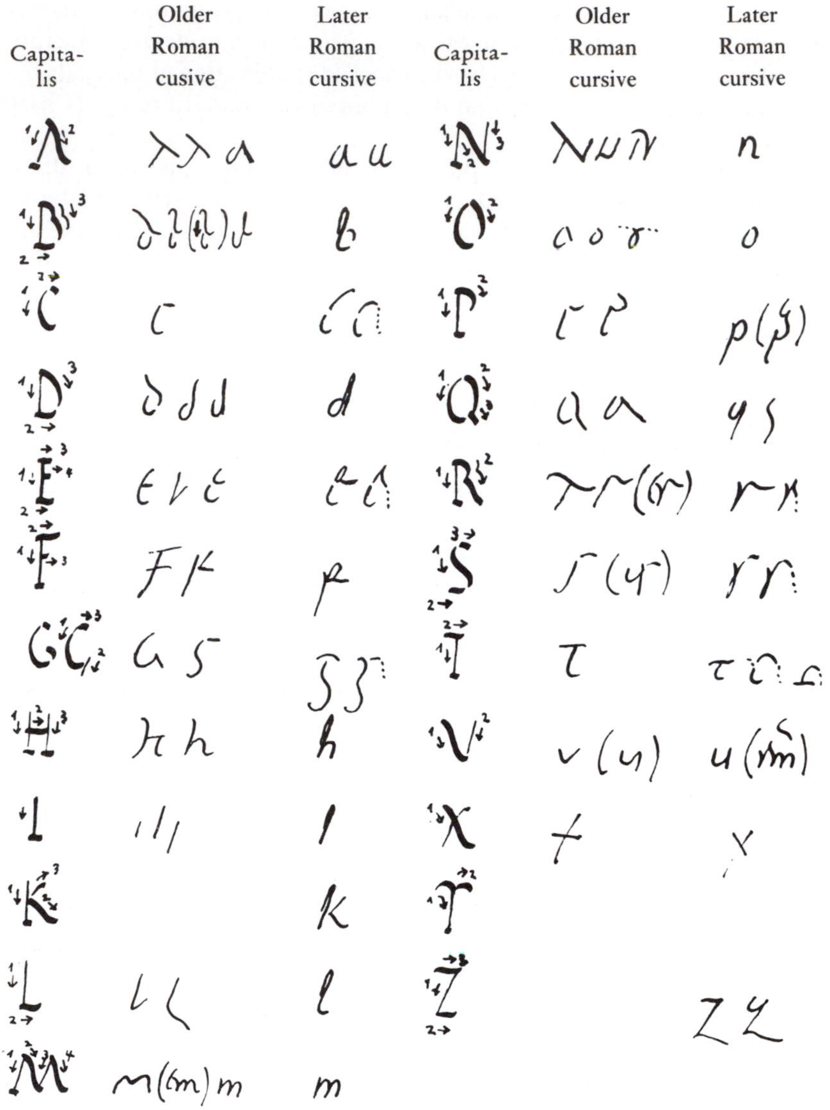

5. Capitalis, older and later Roman cursive

pieces of writing from between 293 and 317–24[80] new forms increasingly appear alongside the old (*a, m, n*) or indeed these have already replaced the earlier ones, as in the signature of 310 in which only the older *b* and *r* are left. The script is now in large part erect, so that ascenders and descenders stand out boldly, and its appearance anticipates the four-line scheme of minuscule. However, vertical and oblique script are still contrasted, the latter for example in salutations and signatures. In increasing measure the ascenders acquire strokes leading up to them. An important novel feature rich in consequences is the materialisation of some necessary joining pen movements; in this way the heads of *e* and *f*, which like the head of *c* rise obliquely above the writing band, become tall, narrow loops. The new forms of cursive minuscule – almost all of which are to be found occasionally in the first and second centuries[81] – can be derived, without a break, from 'cursivised' older script[82] arising from changes of direction, alteration of the arrangement, and writing dynamics.[83] Especially striking, besides the *b*, are: the 'small' *n*;[84] *g* with the larger curve below the line, which in the fourth century, when written as a separate letter, also acquires a flat head-stroke. The oft-discussed *b* with the bow on the right ('*panse à droite*')[85] could have come about if the letter was begun at the upper end and the long neck which the older *b* had was allowed to run into the left edge of its lower bow,[86] and then its lower part was closed.[87]

With this script the structure of Latin letters in principle, reached a final and definite form, and the dual system which still holds good today – majuscule and minuscule – was created. It provided the raw material for new bookhands: the older and later half-uncial and the continental minuscule scripts. The possibility of forming ligatures is heavily exploited,[88] although *u*, unless extended as a

---

80 293: *Écriture latine*, Nr. 30; 310; *Écriture latine*, Nr. 31 and Seider, *Lateinische Papyri*, Nr. 56; 311–21: ChLA v 298; vi–vii 317–24: Steffens[2], *Lateinische Paläographie*, plate 13 and Seider, *Lateinische Papyri* Nr. 51, cf. ChLA iv 253.

81 Tjäder, *Nichtliter. lat. Pap.*, 117 n. 3.   82 See above p. 51 f.

83 Tjäder, *Nichtliter. lat. Pap.*, 95 ff and 118. Not from the rigid forms of official script; Cencetti, 'Note paleografiche', 34 ff., who proposes to seek the milieu in which it originated in private writing.

84 For the metamorphosis of *N* to *n* the Greek parallel is very informative; cf. J.P. Gumbert, 'Structure and forms of the letter *v* in Greek documentary papyri', *Papyrologica Lugduno-Batava* 14 (Leiden 1965) 1–12. On *m* see below p. 68.

85 I refer only to Mallon, *Paléographie romaine*, 41 ff.; R. Marichal, 'Le *B* "à panse droite" dans l'ancienne cursive romaine et les origines du *B* minuscule', in *Studi in onore di Cesare Manaresi* (Milan 1952) 347–63 with plate; A. Petrucci, 'Per la storia della scrittura romana: i graffiti di Condatomagos', *Bull. dell' Arch. Pal. Ital.*, ser 3, 1 (1962) 95 ff., 120; idem, 'Nuove osse vazioni sulle origini della *b* minuscola nella scrittura romana', ibid. 2/3 (1963/4) 55–72 with plate: Tjäder, *Nichtliter. lat. Pap.*, 98 ff (reprod. on p. 101). Cf. also above p. 2.

86 That is, that one 'finished' the left-hand part of the letter; see above, p. 52.

87 Superficially somewhat similar is the capital B evidenced in the Pompeii graffiti, in which the upper part of the double bow is to some extent aligned against the straight shaft of the letter, and to some extent has even disappeared altogether.

88 See the collections in Tjäder, *Nichtliter. lat. Pap.*, 99 ff.

raised flourish, can no longer be ligatured. From the fourth century to the sixth, Greek and Latin cursives produce very similar forms of style[89] and because the identical, or (as with η and *h*, ρ and *p*) the corresponding letters are written in the same way, the bilingual documents frequent in the east can display a fully uniform appearance.[90]

In the fifth century the new cursive is already recognisable even in western charters,[91] and at the latest by this date in corrections and additions to manuscripts and in complete texts.[92] The structure of the script remains the same in the following centuries, despite much variation in appearance, up to about the tenth century.[93]

5. Uncial

The new bookhands of the Roman period originate from the fixing and, where appropriate, the clarifying modification of a state of cursive script by means of 'calligraphic' execution; through this method of writing the forms were consolidated.[94] This may have been due to spontaneous individualistic writing, but it may also be suspected that the script was created by a calligrapher, and in suitable circumstances was then received as a reformed script. At any rate, of the types of script that originated in this way, the uncial, the older and later half-uncial, and the caroline minuscule were successful. These scripts adopted from the changing cursive forms the alterations by which they distanced themselves increasingly from the original alphabet; thus these types mirror the stages of development in cursive.

Early sporadic examples are transmitted from a period of lively literary and professional (above all legal) writing; these are scripts transformed already due to a tendency to cursive and which reappear in consolidated form: a fragment of a juristic papyrus roll in Aberdeen, and the oldest fragment of a Latin parchment codex, *De bellis Macedonicis*, in London.[95] In the Aberdeen papyrus No. 130,[96]

---

89 Cf. R. Marichal, 'L'Écriture latine', 138.

90 An example in Medea Norsa, 'Analogie e coincidenze tra scritture greche e latine nei papiri', in *Miscellanea Giovanni Mercati* 6. Studi e Testi 126 (Vatic. 1946) plate 5 (and 113).

91 The transmission in Ravenna is particularly important; cf. Tjäder, *Nichtliter. lat. Pap.*; ChLA XX–XXII; in addition: Chr. Courtois and others (edd), *Tablettes Albertini, Actes privés de l'époque vandale*, text and plates (Paris 1952).

92 CLA IX 1349 f.; Seider, *Papyri* 2/2, Nr. 52 and 48.

93 Only a few scripts succeeded in drawing through the loop of the *e*, which could lead to a 'modern' connection with the following letter: CLA V 696 (Seider, *Papyri* 2/1, Nr. 68); XI 1628b; Tjäder, *Nichtliter. lat. Pap.*, 104, reprod. 18. Idem, 'Later Roman (Common) script', in *Calames et cahiers, Mélanges de codicologie et de paléographie offerts à Léon Gilissen* (Brussels 1985) 187–97, marks the end of the period of 'New Roman' script in the first half of the seventh century.   94 On this cf. above p. 51.

95 On these fragments, and a portion of an account (s. I?) see also G. Petronio Nicolaj, 'Osservazioni. 17 f. n. 46; J.-O. Tjäder, 'Der Ursprung der Unzialschrift', 31, n. 84.

96 CLA II² 120 ('s. III'), *Écriture latine*, Nr. 53; Seider, *Papyri* 2/2, Nr. 1. Tjäder, ibid. ('wohl

λ c ᴆ ε f h ı ʟ ɰ ɴ

o c a ʀ ʂ ᴛᴛ ᴜ x

6. The script of De bellis Macedonicis

ᴀ ʙ c ᴅ ᴇ f ç h ı

ʟ ɰ ɴ o ᴘ ꭎ ʀ s ᴛ ᴜ

x ʏ z ᴂ œ ᴆ ᴜɴ ᴜɴ ᴜʀ ʏ

7. Uncial (c. fourth to fifth century)

ᴀ ᴆ f ç h ʟ ɰ ᴘ ꭎ

8. Uncial (c. sixth to eighth century)

ʙ ᴘ

9. Eastern (Byzantine) uncial (fifth to sixth century)

written with a strong pressure (saec. II?), the taut letter forms correspond roughly to a kind of cursive attested from c. 60 to 166,[97] especially with *A* and *R* (and in ligature also *ER*), *B* and *D*, *E*, and angular *H*.

The much-discussed fragment of a parchment codex *De bellis Macedonicis*, probably from the period around 100,[98] appears to be controlled to a far greater degree. It is a specimen of an accomplished, stately script with a writing angle of about 50°. Of its letters (*B* is wanting), the reduced *A*, bulging *D*, angular *h*, *M* with three strokes, and *Q* with a narrow head and long, oblique cauda, are all clearly consolidated versions of similar cursive forms, as in Aberdeen 130; *E* (still narrow), *L* and *P* are somewhat rounded at the base; on the other hand *R*, with long vertical shaft and the right-hand part attached to it as in capitalis, is not derived from cursive but is an abritrary form chosen with the intention of preventing confusion with *A*.[99]

The earliest attested new kind of writing that we find in general use is the uncial, which survives in roughly five hundred manuscripts from the fourth century on;[100] its time of origin can only be inferred.[101] Even the new elements in the uncial alphabet were prefigured in majuscule cursive, in which several forms were further developed (by contrast with the state fixed in the *De bellis Macedonicis*). *D*, *h*, and *q* (now upright, with enlarged bow) correspond to the forms in *De bellis Macedonicis*, *E* is round, as in an early stylistic group of the cursive.[102] *U* has two parallel shafts already in a specimen from 131.[103] The *M*, regarded as characteristic of uncial, apparently began originally with a straight shaft to which were added two equal arches one after the other; its later customary twin-arched structure, however, appears already in third-century

---

etwa Mitte des II. Jahrhunderts'). A much later origin – after the Livy Epitome (see p. 72) – is thought possible by G. Cavallo, *Scrittura e civiltà* 4 (1980) 344; however, the points after every word are a frequent occurrence in literary papyri of the first and second centuries. See p. 169 n. 40.   97 See above p. 63.

98 CLA II² 207; *Écriture latine*, Nr. 54; Mallon, *Paléographie romaine*, plate, 10, 2. I think that an Italian provenance can be argued for this fragment.

99 Otherwise it would have looked very like the *A*.

100 Larger collections of reproductions: Zangemeister–Wattenbach, *Exempla*, plates 17–50 and Suppl.; É. Chatelain, *Uncialis Scriptura* (Paris 1901/2) plates 1–60; Bassi, *Monumenta*, reprods 160–83.

101 The secondary literature about the origins of uncial script and the number of attempts at explanation are very large. See the critical survey by J.-O. Tjäder, 'Ursprung', 9–40. Here I am expanding and clarifying the views touched upon in *Paläographie*, col. 400 ff. (separatim col. 22 f.) discussed by Tjäder, 24 f. and 34, who has misunderstood the term 'Verdichtung'. Tjäder considers that uncial arose from capitalis and explains the forms of *D h q* as a 'step down from the canon of classical capitalis' in the first century (p. 29). He notes that the form of *A* with an angle occurs sporadically and that *M*, which in uncial is formed unsymmetrically from three strokes, is supposed to have originated from the capital *M* with twin points of capitalis or early roman cursive, but could not have developed from the *m* of the earliest minuscule script (that is, the *m* with its first stroke as the approach stroke). On the theory that the change in scripts within bookscripts resulted from a change in the writing angle (support incliné) see below note 139. Cf. also E. Casamassima–E. Staraz, 'Varianti e cambio'.

102 See above p. 63 n. 71.   103 *Écriture latine*, Nr. 23.

African inscriptions[104] and in many fourth-century manuscripts.[105] That *A* is written with an angle (instead of the later bow) can be understood from the existence of a form present in the first century.[106] The letters *B* and *R*, which cannot represent consolidated cursive forms, were, I believe, refashioned from capitalis for the sake of clarity,[107] because in cursive they are very like *D* and *A*; this replacement may have been established already in an early bookhand which had transformed the capitalis.[108]

The uncial can confidently be described as majuscule: it is a script confined between two lines.[109] In the oldest manuscripts only *D*, *F*, *h*, *L*, *P*, and *q* slightly exceeded them. Even in later times it retains its weight as against other kinds of scripts.

That the transmission of uncial only begins in the fourth century is probably to be explained by the transition of western book-writing to parchment. Its origin appears to lie in the second century, before models of the later cursive exerted an influence.[110]

As for the technique of writing, uncial follows in the line of capitalis, whose writing angle of 40°–50° some of the oldest uncial codices have clearly preserved,[111] before uncial began to be written with turning of the pen or with a Greek writing angle. It is, however, written broader than capitalis, while the

104 See below n. 112.

105 E.A. Lowe, *Palaeographical Papers* 1, 123 considered the (generally) straight shaft of *M* as one of the distinguishing marks of the earliest uncial. This observation is most clearly confirmed by the 'minuscule-*m*' of the Cicero Palimpsest CLA 1 77 and Codex k of the Gospels (CLA IV 465). Strongly-made straight first strokes are found in CLA II 178 (Seider, *Papyri* 2/2, Nr. 66); IV 485 (Seider, *Papyri* 2/2, Nr. 66); V 562; X 1472, and others which are clearly recognisable such as Cicero, *De re publica* (CLA 1 35; Seider, *Papyri* 2/1, Nr. 52). The dominance of round letter-forms in uncial and the tendency to stylise it make the subsequent adoption of a form which departs from this style (the *M* with a straight first stroke) most unlikely, both in Europe and in Africa. In cursive scripts *M* derived the stroke which leads down to the base of the first point, or which separates the first stroke, from ligatures with a preceding letter, such as e, and this is already visible in the Claudius Papyrus (see n. 14). The letter is already formed with this approach stroke in 131 (*Écriture latine*, Nr. 23) and 167 (ibid., Nr. 26); cf. Tjäder, 'Ursprung'. The conclusions reached by E. Casamassima–E. Staraz, 'Varianti e cambio grafico', 91, are in complete agreement with this account of the development of cursive *M* (which is stylised with round forms in uncial).

106 Cf. besides Tjäder 'Ursprung', 32 f. esp. R. Marichal in *Pauli Sententiarum Fragmentum*, 49 ff. and plate 3.

107 As stated above (n. 101). For a similar view see Schiaparelli (cf. Tjäder, 'Ursprung der Unziale', 19).

108 As is clearly visible in *De bellis Macedonicis*. Cf., however, 68 n. 96 (G. Cavallo).

109 G. Cavallo, *Ricerche sulla maiuscola biblica* (Florence 1967), 124 f., thinks that Greek Bible uncial might have affected this aspect as a model for the earliest uncial.

110 Tjäder, 'Ursprung', 36, assumes 'that uncial was chosen in about the second quarter of the second century AD, as the script for legal literature'. The spur to the success of uncial came from its reception by the book trade.

111 E.g. CLA 1 28 (Scholia Bobiensia) 35; (Seider, *Papyri* 2/1, Nr. 52) (Cicero, *De re p.*); II 283 (Cyprian, Brescia); IV 465 (Evv. cod. k). Lowe describes the peculiarities of the oldest uncial in Lowe, *Palaeographical Papers* 1, 123 ff.

bows (which in the appearance of the writing have few angles left) are roughly circular in shape. It is, in my view, possible to hold that uncial, which in the fourth century was used, alongside capitalis, in perfected form for classical literature, was created and practised in the homeland of Roman calligraphy – Italy.[112] The Christians (who cannot have been its creators) probably gave preference to the new script, though without totally abandoning capitalis for use in biblical manuscripts.[113] The script acquired its name from the fact that Mabillon mistakenly applied to Roman majuscule an expression of Jerome's that was intended for the 'inch-high' letters of de luxe Christian manuscripts.[114]

Examples of the script dated or dateable to the period up to 600 are: a Leningrad codex of 396/7[115] with works of Augustine; the Computus Paschalis of 447 in Berlin;[116] a fragment of the first edition of the Codex Iustinianus dated 529–33,[117] and the oldest manuscripts of the Digests (amongst them the Florence codex) from 533;[118] the Fulda manuscript of Victor of Capua, dating at the latest from 536/7;[119] and the manuscripts from the circle of Gregory the Great (before 604), especially the *Regula pastoralis* at Troyes.[120]

Amongst the examples from the fourth and fifth centuries great stylistic differences already stand out clearly. The script of a North African group that is close to the circle of Augustine[121] is angular. Another consists of unconnected strokes so that only the eye links the letter together.[122] The predominant mode of execution, however, is first that the hair-fine ends of the curves run exactly into one another.[123] In a variant style that was used in Byzantium in the fifth and sixth centuries, and which is known from numerous legal manuscripts, the *B* is twice as high as the other letters and the bow of the *R* is extended down to the line.[124]

In the period leading up to the sixth century the uncial loses spontaneity, the

---

112 The transmission begins too late to offer decisive arguments for the priority of North Africa, which has been supposed. In several north-African third century inscriptions there is an apparent understanding of uncial style, but the elements are a mingling of old letter-forms (e.g. capitalis *M*) and more recent ones (*b*, partly open *r*) see the plate in CLA S, plate 7; S. Morison, *Politics and Script* (Oxford 1972) reprods 46–8.

113 See n. 33.

114 Bischoff, *Mittelalterliche Studien* 1, 4; Tjäder, 'Ursprung', 10 f.; P. Meyvaert, '"Uncial letters": Jerome's meaning of the term', *J. Theol. Stud.*, n.s., 34 (1983) 185–188. See also below p. 184.   115 CLA XI 1613.   116 CLA VIII 1053

117 CLA S, 1713; Seider, *Papyri* 2/2, Nr. 34.

118 CLA III 295; Seider, *Papyri* 2/2, Nr. 25.   119 CLA VIII 1196.   120 CLA VI 838.

121 Cf. CLA S, plate 1b.c, II, III, va. Besides CLA XI 1613 the k MS of the gospels and several MSS containing the works of Cyprian belong to that category.

122 CLA I 57; Seider, *Papyri* 2/1, Nr. 54 (Livy).

123 E.g. CLA IV 467 (gospels, before 371?).

124 Lowe, *Palaeographical Papers* 2, 466–74 with plates 108–13. According to G. Cavallo(-Fr. Magistrale), 'Libri e scritture del diritto nell'età di Giustiniano', in *Il mondo del diritto nell'epoca giustinianea* (1985) 43–58, the script which had become almost canonical in the transmission of the Justinian law codes arose in this context, but preserved an archaic character: the *R*-form continues that of the older half-uncial.

writing angle turns to 90°, and the script is enlarged, fitting now between a four-line band: *D*, *h*, and *L* rise higher, *F* and *P* (whose bow is enlarged) are set lower, like the *q*, and the cauda of *G* is markedly elongated.[125] In the hands of calligraphers the Italian sixth-century uncial acquires fine forks at the end of horizontal lines and small upper bows.[126] Later the script is changed and often transformed by tags on the ascenders and small triangles hanging from the horizontals.

The script everywhere diffused on the continent was also transplanted to large areas of England by the Roman mission of Gregory the Great and his followers, and there it was even used for charters.[127] In the Northumbrian centre of Wearmouth-Jarrow, home of the Codex Amiatinus,[128] for whose text script the finest Roman uncial served as a model, an unornamented, usually smaller-written type was contrasted with this ('capitula type'). The John's Gospel in Stonyhurst College[129] is written in this script, while the carolingian school of Amiens adopted it as one of its models.[130]

The continental uncial was, generally speaking, more crudely written in the pre-carolingian centuries. On the other hand, when, here and there in France before the carolingian reform, uncial was again practised calligraphically,[131] it seems to have been under English influence. Thus was prepared its adoption in the carolingian repertory of scripts. Its use in entire manuscripts was confined to gospels and some liturgical books; otherwise it was used (often mixed with capitalis) generally as display script and for the initial letters of sentences. In the hierarchy of scripts at Tours it stood between capitalis and half-uncial. It is remarkable that in the Theodulf manuscripts, instead of uncial *q*, *Q* is used. The uncial in de luxe manuscripts of late carolingian[132] and Ottonian times[133] is more artificial and lifeless.

In some regions of Italy, in Rome and Lucca for example, uncial remained in continuous use as a text hand into the early ninth century.[134] Uncial became an

125 A. Petrucci, 'Scrittura e libro', with plate 193 ff.
126 A. Petrucci, 'L'Onciale romana', *Studi Medievali*, ser 3, 12 (1971) 75–134 with plates; he connects the origin of these decorative letter-forms with the decoration of the script of the inscriptions from Rome. See also Bischoff, *Mittelalterliche Studien* 2, 331.
127 Lowe, *English Uncial*, on which see Bischoff, *Mittelalterliche Studien* 2, 328 ff.; D.H. Wright, 'Some Notes on English Uncial', *Traditio* 17 (1961) 441–56 with 6 plates. The charters are also in ChLA III 182, 183, 187.   128 CLA III 299.   129 CLA II² 260.
130 Cf. CLA VI 821; X 1579.   131 E.g. CLA V 670 (Gregory of Tours).
132 Like that of the Codex Aureus of the gospels, copied for Charles the Bald in 870. Facs.: G. Leidinger, *Der Codex Aureus der Bayerischen Staatsbibliothek in München* (Munich 1921–31).
133 Cf. Lowe, *Palaeographical Papers* 2, 399–416 and plates 81–7 ('display uncial', again with *Q* instead of *q*).
134 The Anthologia Salmasiana (s. VIII ex.) is an example; CLA V 593; Maddalena Spallone. 'Il Par. Lat. 10,318 (Salmasiano)', *It. Med. e Um.* 25 (1982) 1–71, with illustr. The survival of uncial as a Latin script in Sardinia after the Arab occupation (to 1077) is probably the last vestige of this tradition; a twelfth-century charter is shown in F.A. Ugolini, *Atlante paleografico romanzo* 1 (Turin 1942) plate 26.

element of Romanesque and Gothic title-script and was used also for the initials of sentences as well as in Gothic inscriptional majuscule, above all with the letters *A*, *D*, and *E*, *h*, *M*, and *U*.

6. The older (eastern) half-uncial (the script of the Livy epitome and of related MSS)

Under this term[135] a further 'calligraphisization' from the cursive (that is from the New Roman cursive) can be described which is represented by a number of examples almost exclusively of Egyptian provenance (though not by any means necessarily of Egyptian origin); they date from the third to the fifth century. This script – the first minuscule – appears either in upright or in decidedly right-slanting form. Despite slight divergences in the use of the letters, it has a uniform character in both registers. In what follows we shall describe the upright form,[136] whose best-known example is the Livy Epitome, a papyrus roll from the first half of the third century. In the slanted variety the forms are alike; they have the same relationship to the line and are slanted consistently towards the right. The script arose from a minuscule cursive of whose style we have no witness, and the alphabet (generally with *b d h*[137] and *l* having ascenders, *f p q* and *r* having descenders) is enclosed within four lines; yet ascenders and descenders are relatively short. A symptom of great age[138] in the script is that the ascenders show no sign of being club-shaped. The left part of the *a* is either a sharp angle or a small loop; the *d*, which is now vertical, ends with the shaft on the line; *l* often swings under the line; *m* in several manuscripts has the uncial form; the shoulder stroke of *r* (derived from the rippled upper stroke of cursive *r*) is bent step-like; *s* is usually majuscule (an upright form of the *s* stands with a slim foot on the line); the shaft of *t* is straight; above all the *b* appears in the form common to all later

135 Others are: 'archaic half-uncial', 'bd-uncial'. The term 'roman minuscule', which fits the historical development 'minuscola romana', 'minuscule primitive' has failed to gain acceptance. The name half-uncial 'semionciale' has been in use since the eighteenth century.

136 I would include fewer witnesses to the script than does R. Marichal in *Pauli Sententiarum Fragmentum*, 26 ff. where a list is given. Besides the Livy Epitome (CLA ii² 208; *Écriture latine*, Nr. 46; Steffens² *Lateinische Paläographie*, plate 10; Seider, *Papyri* 2/1, Nr. 34; *Paléographie romaine*, plate 17, 1 and 3; Kirchner, *Script. Lat. Libr.²*, plate 4c). I would include CLA ii² 247; Seider, *Papyri* 2/1, Nr. 36 (Livy), CLA S 1677; Seider, *Papyri* 2/1, Nr. 35 (Greek-Latin letter formulary), CLA ii² 227 and iii 367 (Vergil, Aen. with Greek translation; Mallon, *Paléographie romaine*, plate 19, 1) and the legal fragments CLA viii 1033 (also *Écriture latine*, Nr. 47; Mallon, *Paléographie romaine*, plate 19, 2; Seider, *papyri* 2/2, Nr. 14) and x 1577; The latter are remains of parchment codices and the Vergil fragments of a papyrus codex, the remainder are rolls. Cf. also Br. Breveglieri, 'Materiali per lo studio della scrittura minuscola Latina i papiri letterari', *Scrittura e Civiltà* 7 (1983) 5–49, with illustr.; included here are Latin citations in Greek texts.

137 In several manuscripts with the upright and the slanting form *H* is capital; see Marichal, *Pauli Sententiarum Fragmentum*, 46.

138 This is also confirmed by the less formal minuscule portions in a military list of 242–4 (ChLA v 281).

hands, with the bow to the right.[139] Apart from the new (minuscule) letters, the writing angle is a principal characteristic: here the verticals receive the full breadth of the pen,[140] as in the contemporary Greek 'bible uncial'.[141]

The slanting type, which likewise is used as a text hand, may be an imitation of the slanting Greek script. The items in relatively taut slanted script,[142] among them the *Fragmentum de formula Fabiana*,[143] come (with the exception of a Latin–Greek Vergil)[144] from pre-Justinian Roman law.[145] If the rest of the papyrus and parchment fragments were included[146] (though in part later and

---

139 'Panse à droite'. On the origin of this letter see above p. 65 f.

140 The writing angle has been much discussed in attempts to situate the script of the Livy Epitome in the direct genealogy of Latin bookscript, or the development of uncial. In canonical capitalis the widest stroke slants to the left; if it is the vertical stroke – as in Greek script – this may result from a different position of the arm relative to the body, or from the use of a pen cut slanting to the right. But it can also be achieved, somewhat mechanically, if the written surface is turned to the left. When canonical capitalis arose the writing material was papyrus rolls which had to be held roughly parallel to the body if a large portion had to be unrolled. But the pages of the codex, the more modern form of the book, could be turned and held at an angle to the torso of the scribe. This gave rise to the hypothesis that the script of the Livy Epitome owes its particular form to the altered position of the writing material, which not only altered the writing angle, but also made it easier to transform the letter-forms towards uncial forms. This hypothesis is utilised in the following works with varying degress of emphasis: Marichal, 'L'Écriture latine', 126 ff.; idem, in *Pauli Sententiarum Fragmentum*, 35 f.; Mallon, *Paléographie romaine*, 81 ff.; Ch. Perrat, in 'Relazioni', *X Congresso Internazionale di Scienze Storiche 1955*, 1 (Florence 1955) 370 ff. The new writing angle of the Epitome script, which has justifiably been compared to the angle of Greek bible uncial, cannot be explained by reference to the change from roll to codex because the large number of instances of the development of Greek bible uncial date from the period of the roll; cf. C.H. Roberts, 'The codex', *Proc. Brit. Acad.* 40 (1954) 197 and idem, *Greek Literary Hands, 350 B.C.–A.D. 400* (Oxford 1956) xvi, n. 3; G. Cavallo, *Ricerche sulla maiuscola biblica* (Florence 1967) 42 f. n; cf., however, idem, 'Problemi inerenti all'angolo di scrittura alla luce di un nuovo papiro greco: PSI Od. 5', *Scrittura e Civiltà* 4 (1980), 337–44 (on variations). E. Casamassima and E. Staraz, 'Varianti e cambio grafico', 73 ff., also attribute a merely secondary role to the influence of 'papier incliné' on letter forms. See also the following note.

141 In contrast very many of the oldest western Latin uncial manuscripts are written with the same diagonal pen angle as the *Fragmentum de bellis Macedonicis* and canonical capitalis; see p. 66. Uncial of an eastern, Byzantine type (Lowe, *Palaeographical papers* 2, 466–74 with plates 108–13) almost exclusively reveal a Greek pen angle from their first appearance (in the Verona Gaius).

142 Reprod.: e.g. W. Schubart, *Griechische Paläographie* (Munich 1966) reprod. 97–9; G. Cavallo, *Richerche*, plates 107–111; R. Marichal, 'L'Écriture latine', plate 5, 3 (cf. p. 132 f.). If this script is written with pressure the right-slanting shafts are heavy, as in their Greek counterparts. The slanting script created by the Goths is an analagous development.

143 CLA VIII 1042; *Écriture latine*, Nr. 48; Steffens², *Lateinsiche Paläographie*, plate 14.

144 CLA III 306.

145 CLA II 248 (Seider, *Papyri* 2/2, Nr. 13); VIII 1039, 1041, 1042; X 1527 (Seider, *Papyri* 2/2, Nr. 8); XI 1657 (Seider, *Papyri* 2/2, Nr. 10).

146 See the additional items listed by Marichal, *Pauli Sententiarum Fragmentum*, 26 ff. Variants: *n* as well as *N*, and curved *t*, can be found for instance in the oldest Latin liturgical papyrus (CLA S 1720; Mallon, *Paléographie romaine*, plate 20, Kirchner, *Script. Lat. Libr.*², plate 4b; Seider, *Papyri* 2/2. Nr. 53); there are some cursive features in CLA II² 210, Seider, *Papyri* 2/1, Nr. 50 (Cicero, Speeches, in tiny script).

ʎ (ɑ) b c d e ꜰ ɢ h (H) ı Ʉ m

m N O P ꟼ ꝗ ⋔ ⋏ ꞩ ꞅ T U X Y Z

10. Older (eastern) half-uncial (script of the Livy epitome)

ʌ *b* *d* ᴄ N ᴨ ꞅ s ᴛ

11. Older (eastern) half-uncial (slanted form)

ɑ ɑ ɑ b c d e ꜰ ꜰ ꝫ ꝫ h ıl

к l m N O p ꝗ r n ꞅ ᴛ u ᵛ

x y z н d

12. Later half-uncial

more carelessly written in 'older half-uncial') the proportion of schoolbooks is increased, including the bilinguals.

That a Greek writing norm (that is, the writing angle) has been taken over in this script, and that the slanting type probably imitates a Greek script, seems to me (together with the Greek element in the texts) to be of decisive importance for the question of the origin of this first minuscule script, which I would suppose to be in the East. Given the very considerable component of legal texts transmitted in this kind of writing, the Latin law school of Berytos (Beirut) probably played a rôle, if not already in its formation then certainly in its use from the third to the fifth century.[147] The Greek–Latin Codex Bezae (four

147 R. Marichal, 'L'Écriture latine et la civilisation occidentale du Ier au XVIe siècle', in *L'Écriture et la psychologie des peuples* (Paris 1963) 214: 'ce n'est pas du côté de l'Afrique qu'il faudrait regarder pour voir apparaître la minuscule, c'est au Levant, vers Beyrouth, métropole des études juridiques', having regard to the old name of the script, 'litterae Africanae' (on which see below p. 76). On the law school of Beirut Cf. L. Wenger, *Die Quellen des römischen Rechts*, Österr. Akad' Wiss., Denkschriften 2 (Vienna 1953) 619 ff.

gospels, Acts)[148] and the Seneca manuscript written by a certain Nicianus[149] – two further calligraphic witnesses to this kind of script – also fit into the Greek framework.[150] In the Florentine manuscript of the Digest originating from Byzantium c. 533, the vertical form of the older half-uncial is the script of the introductory decrees.

In the West this script apparently had no great resonance as a bookhand. In support of this view one can point also to its absence from the combination of several scripts in western manuscripts.[151] African inscriptions of the third century, as well as isolated examples from Greece and Italy,[152] show familiarity with individual minuscule letters (*b d f h m r s*) within mixed alphabets. In the fourth century they appear more often, above all in inscriptions of poor quality, also in Rome.[153]

An example with half-uncial *b* and *d* is the Codex Claromontanus (Pauline Epistles, saec. V),[154] a bilingual uncial with western traits. A Codex Theodosianus[155] from Spain and the bilingual Laudianus (Acts, saec. VI–VII, written probably in Sardinia)[156] have only *b* alongside uncial *d*. In my view the Epitome script should be excluded from the development process of the script in the West that leads to uncial and later to half-uncial.[157]

7. *Later half-uncial*

While late Roman cursive in the fourth century emphasises the lateral connection of letters, strengthened by the regular development of the ligature system, another development is the fact that, besides the letters with ascenders, *I*-longa, *s*, and the tall heads of *e c* (*f*) in ligatures extend above the middle writing-band, and as a new descender there appears a rounded *g* capped by either a flat or curved stroke; certain joining strokes and the approach strokes of the ascenders are written in the same movement. It was probably on such a basis that there came into existence in the West the current scripts that were flatter in proportion and that made moderate use of ligatures. These appear in some important late

---

148 CLA II², 140: has a majuscule *R* (with a final stroke on the lower left) broad *S*; uncial *M*. The Greek additions (on f. 285 ff) reveal that the manuscript was used for a long time in an area where Greek was spoken, before it reached Lyon.   149 CLA I 69.
150 CLA III 295; Seider, *Papyri* 2/2, Nr. 25. Here the slanted type still appears in marginalia.
151 See below p. 77–78.
152 Cf., e.g. Ae. Hübner, *Exempla scripturae epigraphicae latinae* (Berlin 1885) Nr. 1146 ff.
153 Cf. Steffens², *Lateinische Paläographie*, plate 11b.
154 CLA V 521 (South-Italian provenance is presumed).
155 CLA I 46 (palimpsest), 's. VII' (?); on the provenance of the upper script cf. CLA XI 1637.
156 CLA II² 251.
157 On marginalia in slanting *bd*-uncial in western MSS see below p. 78. They lack the specifically stiff character of eastern script, as do the analogous variants which the Spanish calligrapher Danila used for the chapter headings in the Codex Cavensis (s. IX); cf. Lowe, *Palaeographical Papers* 1, 338 and plate 55. On the name 'litterae Africanae', which is to be identified with half-uncial, see below p. 86 n. 23.

antique grammatical schoolbooks (Probus, Claudius Sacerdos, etc.)[158] and chiefly in scholia[159] and marginalia;[160] in all cases, in monuments of the fourth and fifth centuries. If one compares these scripts with the later half-uncial, the designation 'cursive half-uncial' seems permitted, although the former is perhaps to be set later in the history of the script's development.[161]

The later half-uncial,[162] which rose to be a bookhand of late antiquity and of the early middle ages, and which in general consists in isolated letters, likewise has its origin in the developed later cursive, which in the 'cursive half-uncial' had already approached book script. Its characteristic letters (by contrast with the older eastern half-uncial) are: *a* in general rounded, in the beginning open and full, then closed and convex on top; the usually long *f* often with a low-lying tongue; the flat-topped *g* bent under the line, curved s-like or with a protruding crest; and *l* that rests on the line; short *r* (often with a curved low shoulder stroke) and short *s*; *t* with a shaft that is sickle-shaped and arched to the right; almost without exception (by contrast with the later cursive) the *N* is retained.[163] Often *u* is written v-shaped suprascript after *q*. The consolidation of the ascenders, which has become usual in cursive, gives it a club-shape. There is often a certain propensity to ligature with *e*, and in earlier examples *rI* and *tI* occur. The script preserved these ligatures and the thickened ascenders from its cursive origin, which was completely independent of the older half-uncial. The lesser degree of standardisation in the organised book-trade probably explains why in some otherwise half-uncial alphabets uncial *d*, *G*, *M*, or *R* are used.[164]

The designation 'litterae Africanae' is transmitted as the old name of this script[165] and points to its African origin. We have to acknowledge its historical accuracy, but we can no longer illustrate it with examples that exceed in age those of possible European origin. One of the oldest western half-uncial

158 In Naples and Turin, from Bobbio: CLA III, 397a, 398 (Seider, *Papyri* 2/1, Nr. 66); IV 462. In addition see CLA III 289 (Seider, *Papyri* 2/1, Nr. 62) and *Écriture latine*, Nr. 51.

159 E.g. in the Terentius Bembinus; CLA I 12; Seider, *Papyri* 2/1, Nr. 26 and *Écriture latine*, Nr. 41.

160 E.g. the report by Maximus Arianus on Ulfilas; R. Gryson-L. Gilissen. *Les scolies ariennes du Parisinus 8907*. Armarium codicum insignium 1 (Turnhout 1980); CLA V, 572 and *Écriture latine*, Nr. 50. In addition CLA I, 117 and *Écriture latine*, Nr. 55; CLA III 280; IV 484 (Seider, *Papyri* 2/2, Nr. 68); IV 491 (Seider, *Papyri* 2/2, Nr. 67); VIII 1174.

161 The unfortunate name 'quarter-uncial' (Lowe in CLA IV, p. xvi; idem, *Handwriting*² (Rome 1969) 19) should be avoided.

162 E.A. Lowe, 'A hand-list of half-uncial manuscripts', in *Miscellanea Francesco Ehrle* 4. Studi e Testi 40 (Rome 1924) 34–61: Chatelain, *Uncialis scriptura*, plates 61–100.

163 To avoid possible confusion with *r*?

164 The Visigoth Danila took as his model a half-uncial with uncial *G* in the ninth century; Lowe, *Palaeographical papers* 1, plate 57.

165 Bischoff, *Mittelalterliche Studien* 1, 2 ff. It may have reached the Irish from Spain, and they preserved its name. The only pertinent examples are the *Fragmentum de Manichaeis* (CLA V 680; 's. V–VII'?; which has an archaic *g*) and the Hilary manuscript dated to the fourteenth year of the Vandal king Thransamund. I would use the term for a minuscule script, but not for the earlier eastern half-uncial of the 'Epitome' and similar scripts, as Mallon does; see also p. 72.

manuscripts is the St Gall codex of the Vulgate gospels (Σ), which may emanate from the circle of Jerome's friends.[166] The oldest dateable ones are the Verona *Didascalia apostolorum* (before 486), with *f* and *g* on the line;[167] the Hilarius Basilicanus D. 182,[168] corrected in Cagliari in 509/10 by the circle of African bishops exiled to Sardinia; and the Sulpicius Severus written by the lector of the Veronese church, Ursicinus, in 517.[169] Half-uncial was probably brought to Ireland already in the fifth century by the Christian mission and refashioned there into the Insular script with an expanded alphabet.

On the whole, half-uncial was much less widely diffused than uncial, although it survived in Italy,[170] Spain, and France in the pre-carolingian centuries, and indeed there seem to have been centres (and times) where it was preferred as a bookhand; such was the case in the Severinus monastery in Naples under Eugippius (first half of the sixth century),[171] Verona,[172] and Ravenna.[173] it also seems to have been written occasionally in the south of England.[174]

In France the Corbie 'Leutchar-type' of the mid–eighth century is still a degenerate half-uncial.[175] Around the same time half-uncial was being written at Tours[176] in unsystematic mixture with uncial, half-cursive, and minuscule. But even Tours, before the end of the century, had stylised first minuscule and then the half-uncial after minuscule, and adopted it for use in prefaces, opening lines, etc., in a hierarchy of scripts lasting roughly three generations.[177] For a short time St Germain-des-Prés,[178] St Denis(?), St Amand (with Salzburg),[179] and Fulda all followed this usage. Finally, its influence (apart from imitations) is to be seen in various places in the ninth century, for example in Freising, in a minuscule that achieves an enhanced effect through small finials and additions.[180]

Outside the system of the received writing types stand those (mostly small)

166 CLA VII 984; Seider, *Papyri* 2/2, Nr. 54. Cf. Bischoff, *Mittelalterliche Studien* I, 101–11.

167 CLA IV 508.

168 CLA I Ia; Steffens[2], *Lateinische Paläographie*, plate 20; *Écriture latine*, Nr. 62; Seider, *Papyri* 2/2 Nr. 62.

169 CLA IV 494; Kirchner, *Script. Lat. libr.*[2], plate 10; E. Carusi–W.M. Lindsay, *Monumenti Paleografici Veronesi* i (Rome 1929) plates 1–5; G. Turrini, *Millennium scriptorii Veronensis dal IV° al XV° secolo* (Verona 1967) plate 6.

170 Cf. the statistics in A. Petrucci, 'Scrittura e libro nell'Italia altomedievale', 208 f.

171 CLA I 16; III 374a; VIII 1031. The exclusive attribution to this scriptorium is mistaken; cf. M. Palma, *Scriptorium* 39 (1985) 8.

172 CLA IV 476, 478 etc.; Carusi–Lindsay, *Monumenti*, 1; G. Turrini, *Millennium*, plates 11, 12.

173 CLA IV 410a.b, 412; VIII 1107; IX 43 (Nr. 41) and the sixth-century litany on the ivory in Berlin showing the Virgin: (W.F. Volbach, *Frühchristliche Kunst* (Munich 1958) reprod. 225); CLA Addenda 1856.   174 CLA II 237; perhaps also VI 740.

175 CLA VI, p. xxiv.

176 E.K. Rand, *Studies in the script of Tours* 2 (Cambridge, Mass. 1934) 21 ff.

177 Rand, *Studies* 1 (ibid., 1929).

178 CLA X 1581; Bischoff, *Schreibschulen* 1, plate 4b.

179 CLA IX 1247; X 1463, 1478, 1489; Bischoff, *Schreibschulen* 2, 56.

180 Bischoff, *Schreibschulen* 1, plate 4b.

scripts that appear in marginalia, corrections, and subscriptions of late antique manuscripts.[181] Some are to be seen as personal usages and combinations of uncial or half-uncial forms, occasionally with a tendency towards cursive.[182] In the case of most of the slanted marginal scripts, the fact that they belong to known types, and their nimble and even elegant script, presuppose some training, although hardly any of them occur in a lengthy continuous text; they represent a personal script of the educated for private use.[183] Depending on their elements, they are either pure uncial[184] or uncial (with regular *A*, *M*, *R*, etc.) having minuscule *b* and *d*.[185] These scripts may have come into existence through familiarity with the slanted form of the older half-uncial[186] or slanted Greek script. They disappear with the end of classical education. The marginalia of several fifth- and sixth-century manuscripts show use of the 'notae antiquae' outside the area of the normal bookhands.[187]

8. Combinations of various scripts

Almost from the beginning of the western tradition, in the Latin book manuscripts, scripts other than the main text script were used as well as the use of minium (red lead) and often a combination of both, in order to bring out the contrast between the material in the margin, headings, etc. and the main text.

The fact that in the oldest codices the closing formula (colophon) was more important than the opening of the book can be explained by reference to the papyrus roll, in which the title stood on the innermost and best-protected part at the end of the text. The emphasis on the EXPLICIT could be expressed in a variety of ways:[188] through setting apart and wider spacing of the script, above all by enlargement of the writing. Lines and even words could be alternately written in black or red, and simple decorations could be set (in the same colours or in monochrome) between or around the generously spaced lines, so that not infrequently frames came into existence; fishbone patterns, spirals, and leaves

---

181 A.R. Natale, 'Marginalia: la scrittura della glossa dal V al IX secolo', in *Studi in onore di mons. Carlo Castiglioni* (Milan 1957) 615–30 with plate; A. Petrucci, 'Scrittura e libro', 179 ff. Cf. also above p. 76.

182 Chiefly uncial: CLA I 30; chiefly half-uncial: CLA I 12, Seider, *Papyri* 2/1, Nr. 26 (Terentius Bembinus) 45, 110; IV 498; VIII 1174; similar, but slanting I 27; III 296; IV 489a; XI 1629.   183 Petrucci, 'Scrittura e libro', 180 f.

184 Several in Lowe, CLA IV, p. xvii; among the others CLA VIII 1196 (Victor of Capua); X 1507 (Dulcitius in the Vienna papyrus codex of Hilary).

185 CLA II² 233a (The Oxford Chronicle of Jerome, the richest witness, cf. the facsimile by J.K. Fotheringham, Oxford 1905); V 571a (Vettius Agorius Basilius); IX 1374 (Agrimensores, where this script is frequently used for compressed line-ends or for runovers).

186 See above p. 73. It occurs still in marginalia in the Florence manuscript of the Digests.

187 Cf. W.M. Lindsay, in *Zentralbl. f. Bibliothekswesen* 29 (1912) 57, and idem, *Notae Latinae* (Cambridge 1915) xiii f.

188 Lowe, *Palaeographical papers* I, 272.

are frequent.[189] At least from the fifth century on, the optional use of another kind of script had arisen as one of the possible means of emphasis: with uncial as the text script, capitalis or capitalis quadrata often appears; with half-uncial, uncial is used;[190] in some manuscripts several kinds of scripts appear with that purpose.[191] Only exceptionally is the principle of opting for an 'older' script abandoned.[192] Between two books of a work a short incipit is connected with the explicit.[193]

The emphasis of the opening was generally restricted at first to writing the first three or four lines or even the first only in red. Insofar as, in Western manuscripts,[194] titles appear from the late fifth century on, they are at first written in a small script in the upper margin of the first page[195] in the same script as the running titles, which likewise could be in a script other than that of the text. The graphical and artistic elaboration of the opening pages took place at the end of antiquity in connection with the development of the initials.[196]

An innovation by contrast with the treatment of the roll is the introduction of running titles into codices; it goes back to the time of the oldest western examples.[197] The names of authors and the book-titles, for the most part abbreviated and in smaller script, are distributed in such a way in the centre of the upper margin of the left- and right-hand side of the opened book that they were to be read as one; in some fifth- and sixth-century manuscripts they stand only on every second opening, and that on the flesh-side.[198] As with the EXPLICIT/INCIPIT, so the running titles are one of the places in which, from the late fifth century on, the use of a second script is practised; for example, the capitalis with uncial, or the uncial with half-uncial text script.[199]

On occasion citations are written as intrusions in another kind of script,[200] and in the Florentine codex of the Digests the publication decrees were prefixed in older half-uncial.[201] Additions of this kind were continued in various ways in the

---

189 Cf. Nordenfalk, *Zierbuchstaben*, 110 ff. and fig. 30.
190 CLA v 658; vii 984; iv 509 (also Capitalis).
191 For instance the half-uncial manuscripts from Eugippius's monastery have both types of capitalis and uncial (CLA iii 374a; viii 1031). In manuscripts in earlier eastern half-uncial, titles are copied in capitalis; CLA viii 1033; x 1527.
192 CLA vi 800 half-uncial (with uncial for text script); cf. also CLA ii 126.
193 Reprod.: e.g. R. Beer, *Monumenta palaeographica Vindobonensia* 2 (Leipzig 1910), plates 36–8; Zimmerman, *Vorkarol. Min.*, plate 1b, 2. A richly varied use of a range of scripts, excluding half-uncial, is found in the codex Arcerianus of the Agrimensores, which is also important for the development of decorated initials; see the facsimile: H. Butzmann, *Corpus Agrimensorum Romanorum* (Leiden 1970).
194 The title in capitalis between ornaments in the Leningrad Augustine manuscript of 396–7 is especially noteworthy; plate in Almut Mutzenbecher, 'Codex Leningrad Q. v. I.3', *Sacris Erudiri* 18 (1967/8) at p. 416.
195 Thus, e.g., in CLA vi 735; viii 1196; x 1491; xi 1614.   196 See below p. 189 f.
197 Lowe, *Palaeographical papers* 1, 199 ff. and 270.   198 Lowe, ibid., 1, 270.
199 Lowe, ibid.
200 P. McGurk, 'Citation marks in early Latin manuscripts', *Scriptorium* 15 (1961) 6 f.
201 See p. 71. f. Cf. also Lowe, *Palaeographical papers* 2, 450–8 and plate 101 f., on the script of the salutation and dating formulae in papal letters in the earliest manuscripts of Bede.

following centuries both for grading of texts and for enlivening the appearance of the script.[202]

9. Tachygraphy

A survey of the kinds of Latin writing in antiquity would be incomplete without mention of shorthand, which, from Cicero to Gregory the Great, was an important ancillary tool in political and literary life and in the practice of law. What first comes to mind in this regard are the tironian notes.[203] The name covers the many layers of material that we have in the *Commentarii notarum tironianarum* (CNT),[204] a list of roughly 13,000 signs with their explanations, and in examples of their practical use as shorthand in many early medieval manuscripts and charters.

According to a credible statement by Isidore of Seville, M. Tullius Tiro, a freedman of Cicero's, was the inventor of a basic corpus of signs that made writing from dictation easier for him. Other personalities of the first century BC and of the first century AD developed and expanded the system, amongst them Seneca (probably the philosopher). To the *Commentarii* that have been transmitted to us special lists of signs for names and concepts were added subsequently (among them Christian ones, which must belong to the latest additions, perhaps from the fourth century). The tachygraphic signs consist mainly in greatly reduced letter forms which show sometimes more capital, sometimes more cursive origin. For the word signs either the initial letter suffices or individual letters[205] are selected and combined in multi-shaped symbols. A great flexibility is achieved in the system by its grammatical structure: the flexion of nouns and conjugation of verbs is indicated in such a way that the fixed word sign (radical) has ending signs (auxiliaries) attached to it in various positions. In the *Commentarii* a large number of syllable signs too are preserved; with these personal names could be written, for example in charters. Still unexplained, however, is the relationship of the *Notae tironianae* to another system, of which half-a-dozen similarly constructed word signs are preserved (beginning with a very unusual *m* form, written in a very firm ductus in one column of a Latin–Greek papyrus lexicon (probably saec. IV).[206]

202 Cf. p. 206.
203 É. Chatelain, *Introduction à la lecture des notes tironiennes* (Paris 1910; repr. New York, n.d.); Chr. Johnen, *Geschichte der Stenographie* I (Berlin 1911); A. Mentz, 'Die Tironischen Noten', *Arch. f. Urk.* 16 (1939) 287–384 and 17 (1942) 155–303; also Berlin 1944 (very subjective, in part with speculative resolutions); H. Boge, *Griechische Tachygraphie und Tironische Noten* (Berlin 1973); Cencetti, *Lineamenti*, 376–89.   204 Ed. by W. Schmitz (Leipzig 1893).
205 Recognition of these 'letters' makes it possible to decipher the notes using the key in U. Fr. Kopp, *Palaeographia critica* 2 (Mannheim 1817); reprint, entitled *Lexicon Tironianum* (Osnabrück 1965); G. Costamagna–M.F. Baroni–L. Zagni, *Notae Tironianae quae in lexicis et in chartis reperiuntur novo discimine ordinatae*, Fonti e Studi del Corpus Membranarum Italicarum, ser 2, Fonti Medievali 10 (Rome 1983).   206 CLA v 699.

The use of tironian notes survived in the chanceries of the Merovingians and Carolingians, but they were progressively garbled until in early carolingian times they became known once more in their correct form by the careful copying of a late antique exemplar[207]|of the *Commentarii*.[208] They were now learned and used in many carolingian schools, though much more rarely in Germany than in France. A reworking of the system was undertaken which ordered the signs or words of the lexicon in a way that made the task of learning them easier (the Berne notes). In the same way learning was simplified by relating the signs to simpler, more familiar ones.[209]|Psalters with tironian notes also served to help the instruction in their use. After the ninth century knowledge of the notes soon declined and in the eleventh century it died out altogether.[210]

In Italy, and perhaps also in Spain, the simpler method of syllabic tachygraphy was preferred which could be expanded by using signs for more common words. It appears in the early middle ages in various guises between which there may exist connections.[211] Two different lists of notes have come down in Spanish manuscripts, one in Madrid (a copy, saec. XVI), the other in the Escorial (saec. XI); a further syllabic list (without explanations) is attested by entries in two codices (probably eighth-century).[212] Two systems can be distinguished in their use:[213]|the older appears in some manuscripts from Bobbio and in charters of the seventh and eighth centuries. The later is used not only in many Italian notarial documents of the eighth to the eleventh century from Genoa, Novara, Pavia, and other cities, but also in the papal curia. Gerbert, when Pope Sylvester II, himself wrote with this syllabic tachygraphy.[214]

It should be mentioned by way of appendix that in the twelfth and thirteenth centuries, stimulated at first by some knowledge of tironian notes, several

---

207 Which may have come from Rome; cf. Traube, *Vorlesungen u. Abhandlungen* 3 (Munich 1920) 197 f.

208 This must be what is meant by the reference in the 'Admonitio generalis' of 789 (72) 'Notas... bene emendate'; A. Boretius (ed), *Capitularia regum Francorum* 1 (Hannover 1883) 60.

209 P. Legendre, *Un manuel tironien du Xe siècle* (Paris 1905); the classroom terminology also in Steffens², *Lateinische Paläographie*, xxxii.

210 In the twelfth century a scholar augmented excerpts from a lexicon with notes of his own invention in Oxford, Balliol College, 306, f. 5r.

211 Johnen, *Geschichte der Stenographie* 1, 230 ff. The 'Notae Matritenses' are also in J. López de Toro, *Abreviaturas Hispanicas* (Madrid 1957) xlviii–liv.

212 In Autun 107, f. 78r/77v (reprod. in R.P. Robinson, *Manuscripts 27 (S. 29) and 107 (S. 129) of the Municipal Library of Autun*, Memoirs of the American Academy in Rome 16 (1939) plate 48, 3 and 4; Geneva, MS Lat. 16, f. 53r (CLA VII, p. 15); the system is possibly used also in Paris, BN, Lat. 9550, f. 32r, 38r, 78r (CLA V 589).

213 L. Schiaparelli, 'Tachigrafia sillabica latina in Italia', *Bolletino della Accademia Italiana di Stenografia* 4 (1948) 1 ff.; Mentz, 'Die Tironischen Noten', 115 ff. and 221 f.; G. Costamagna, 'La tachigrafia dei papiri latini medioevali italiani', *Bull. dell' Arch. Pal. Ital.* n.s. 2/3 (1956/7) 213–220.

214 G. Costamagna, *Il sistema tachigrafico sillabico usato dai notai medioevali italiani (sec. VIII–XI), Regole fondamentali* (Genoa 1953).

attempts were made to devise new shorthand scripts, the oldest definitely in England; they worked with quite arbitrary basic signs which have some connection with 'Greek' and 'Chaldaean' numbers.[215]

215 A. Mentz, *Zwei Stenographiesysteme des späteren Mittelalters* = separate publ. of the *Korrespondenzblatt* 57 (Dresden 1912); Johnen, *Geschichte der Stenographie*, 247 ff. Cf. also below p. 176.

Latin handwriting in the middle ages

1. The Latin script in Ireland

The history of Insular script[1] – by this term we understand the Irish, the other Celtic scripts, and the Anglo-Saxon together – must begin with the conversion of the Irish to Christianity in the fifth century and their entry into the Latin church in the late patristic period. Latin writing established itself in Ireland, introduced by Christianity, and thereby expanded for the first time beyond the frontiers of the Imperium Romanum. The script that Palladius, Patrick, and others brought to Ireland would have been an uncomplicated one.

The series of surviving monuments of Latin script by definitely Irish hands (with which later developments in Ireland can be connected) begins probably not before the end of the sixth century, that is to say, a century and a half after Patrick.[2] These are: the wax tablets with psalter texts, from Springmount bog,[3] and the Codex Usserianus I (Old Latin gospels)[4] that are closely related to one another;[5] the Orosius (probably written in Bobbio c. 614);[6] the psalter of St

1 L. Bieler, 'Insular palaeography, present state and problems', *Scriptorium* 3 (1949) 267–94; Cencetti, *Lineamenti*, 86–93; idem, *Compendio*, 42–5; John, *Latin Paleography*, 13–16; T.J. Brown, 'The Irish element in the Insular system of scripts to circa A.D. 850', in H. Löwe (ed.), *Die Iren und Europa im früheren Mittelalter* 1 (Stuttgart 1982) 101–19. Cf. Also Lowe, CLA II², p. xv–xx.

2 It seems doubtful whether L. Schiaparelli was correct to date to the sixth century the inscriptions which he discusses in *Arch. stor. ital.* 74/2 (1916) 21. D.H. Wright lists the manuscripts which predate the third quarter of the seventh century in A. Dold–L. Eizenhöfer, *Das irische Palimpsestsakramentar im Clm 14429 der Staatsbibliothek München*, Texte und Arbeiten 53/54 (Beuron 1964) 35* f., in an order which depends on their decoration. The list has been significantly enlarged by the recently discovered Rufinus fragment formerly in the Folger Shakespeare Library, Washington, now in Trinity College, Dublin (CLA Addenda 1864). J.-O. Tjäder in *Eranos* 78 (1980) 74, and T.J. Brown, 'The Irish element', 102 f. point out the possibility of provincial Roman influences.

3 CLA S 1684; D. Wright, 'The tablets from Springmount Bog: a key to early Irish palaeography', *Amer. J. Archaeol.* 67 (1963) 219.   4 CLA II 271.

5 Are these the earliest surviving Irish manuscripts? In my view the question of the date of the upper script of the Plautus palimpsest in Milan (Libri Regum) dated by Lowe in CLA III 344a 'saec. VI²' (though he corrected it to VII in *Palaeographical papers* 2, 485) has not been satisfactorily resolved.   6 CLA III 328. For Bobbio see below p. 191 ff.

Columba (Cathach);[7] the St Gall Isidore fragment;[8] gospel fragments in Durham A II 10 and others,[9] and the Munich palimpsest sacramentary.[10]

The stages of the script in this series from three-quarters of a century proceed from a script that is very close to an Italian half-uncial (still with *e* ligatures and *tI*) through scripts with angular features, with the gradual introduction of alternative forms (uncial *D, R, S,* and minuscule *n*) into half-uncial, and (with the development of spatula-shaped terminals) leading to an almost fully rounded type of the half-uncial (without the ligatures of cursive origin).[11]

The Anglo-Saxons became acquainted with this style of script not only through the activities of Irish missionaries in Northumbria (after AD 634) but also because numerous Anglo-Saxons spent many years in Ireland, leading to the emergence of a Hiberno-Saxon calligraphy and book-art in which the respective contributions are blurred.[12] The rise of monastic schools in Ireland in the seventh century probably contributed as well to a transformation of the script – the development of Insular minuscule.[13]

In two codices that, exceptionally, are dateable – the antiphonary produced at Bangor in northern Ireland between 680 and 692 (Milan, Biblioteca Ambrosiana, MS C 5 Inf)[14] and the Adomnán codex written in Iona before 713 (Schaffhausen, Stadtsbibliothek, MS Gen 1)[15] – the medium-sized script is written somewhat narrower and less compactly. Their script shows *a* tightly closed at the top, and straight *s* descending below the line, with a reduction in the use of alternative forms; the shafts end for the most part blunt or narrowing. Two observations suggest that these (modified) scripts are not stages in the development towards minuscule, but rather that they were influenced by a minuscule that had already been perfected:[16] in the antiphonary some letters on the last lines already have the sharp extended points, and *m* occurs at line-end already turned sideways; and in Adomnán a large part of the repertoire of Irish abbreviations that characterises the minuscule is already present. Fully devel-

---

7 CLA II² 266.   8 CLA VII 995.

9 CLA II² 149; cf. C. Nordenfalk, 'Before the Book of Durrow', *Acta Archaeologica* 18 (1947) 159–72.   10 CLA IX 1298; cf. n. 2.

11 On the term 'Insular majuscule' used for this script cf. E.A. Lowe, CLA II², p. xv f.

12 For the historical problems relating to the early history of Echternach, see below p. 93 n. 76.

13 F. Masai's thesis in *Essai sur les origines de la miniature dite irlandaise* (Brussels–Antwerp 1947), that only Insular minuscule was Irish, but half-uncial and decoration were Anglo-Saxon in origin, has been proved untenable. L. Bieler, 'Insular palaeography', 273 f., sees Irish minuscule not as an adaptation of half-uncial but as a new creation drawing on cursive half uncial ('quarter-uncial', cf. p. 76 n. 161).

14 CLA III 311; Facs.: F.E. Warren, *The Antiphonary of Bangor* (London 1893); samples of the script in this and the following MSS can be found together in CLA II², p. xvii.

15 CLA VII 998.

16 The last eleven lines of a column of Durham A II 10 exhibit the oldest flourished minuscule (with short *s*); plate in Nordenfalk, 'Before the Book of Durrow', 161 (reduced). Capriciously florid script is also encountered in later Insular MSS, e.g. in the Book of Armagh, f. 103 (see plate 8, infra).

α b c ꝺ d e ꝼ ᵹ h ı

 l m ꜧ n o p q ꞃ n s

ꞃ ꞇ u x ꝼ z

13. Insular half-uncial

a u b c d ꝺ e ꝼ ᵹ h ı

l l m n o p q ꞃ r ꞇ u x

ꝼ z ᵬ ᵯ ᵲ ꝺ ᵹ

14. Insular minuscule

ꝯb ꝓl ꝼ ꝫ

15. Insular cursive

oped Irish minuscule is a versatile, mostly very angular script, often with sharp spatulate finials and often with claw-like ductus, which is produced by a special way of holding the pen. It is often written minutely and was particularly well adapted to glossing in Irish or in Latin, of which the Irish were so fond. Beside the closed *a* an open *a* with two horns is used, beside *d* narrow round *d*; *r* occasionally reaches below the line. Typical of this script are the ligatures in which the following letters hang below the line: *-a, -i (-is, -io), -o, -u (-um), -s, -t* amongst others. In ligatures with *e*: *er, es, et*, amongst others, the *e* is often written like an oblique 8 or even like a shallow *s*;[17] *st* is mostly left unligatured.

The economy of this script was enhanced by a thoroughgoing system of abbreviations[18] which contains 'notae antiquae' (suspensions), contractions developed systematically by the Irish themselves, and the following sigla: ⱶ = *autem*; ɔ = *con*; ∞ = *contra*; ꝫ = *eius*; ⱶ = *enim*; ÷ = *est*; ⁊ = *et*. The Irish probably knew one or more lists of notae from which ɔ could have derived; this is also tironian, as are also *et* and the h-shaped *a* (from *autem*). The tachygraphic derivation of *eius, enim, est* is uncertain;[19] *eius* is a reversed *e* rather than derived from tironian *eius*; ⱶ could have been formed by analogy with the fence-like *M* of Insular ornamental capitals. In ꝑ = *per* the *p* has an added tuft like ⱶ = *autem*, and was probably modelled on it.[20]

The oldest examples of the small Irish minuscule are a number of pocket-gospels.[21] A compressed, angular type with *R* (instead of *r*) seems to have been only a local Irish experiment of the period around 800.[22]

The most noticeable stylistic peculiarity of almost all Insular scripts, whether half-uncial or minuscule, is the triangular terminals of the ascenders, a decorative element that is repeated on the shafts of *i, u, f, p, r*, the first shafts of *m* and *n*, and the shafts of *N* and *R*, and which is also favoured in the triangular terminals of the horizontal strokes on round *d*, half-uncial *g*, and *t*. Because the short ascenders of half-uncial often end almost horizontally, and as those of *l* and *b* are also curved, imparting a more compact appearance to the line, and since the upper edge of the median letters is dominated by the flat triangular terminals, this script with some justice acquired the name 'litterae tunsae' ('shorn script') from the Irish themselves.[23] The triangular tips of the ascenders derive from the now reduced approach strokes which in the wax tablets and in the Usserianus I are still clearly to be seen. As in these cases, they could be and often were written with a short turn of the pen against the direction of the writing (leftwards, then rightwards into the path of the shaft); with round *d, g, t* this was done with a light upward left stroke then obliquely down to the horizontal. In many manuscripts, however, the easier method of adding a separate, angular stroke to the shaft or horizontal was preferred.

17 Examples in CLA II 270, 275, 277; Lindsay, *Early Irish minuscule*; idem, 'Irish Cursive Script', *Z. celt. Philol.* 9 (1913) 301–8 with plate.

18 An almost identical repertoire of abbreviations was probably received by the Anglo-Saxons from the Irish, together with minuscule, before 665; cf. W.M. Lindsay, *Early Irish Minuscule* (Oxford 1910) 3 f. (CLA VII 998) with idem, *Notae latinae*, 498–500.

19 Lindsay, *Notae latinae*, 498–500.

20 Lindsay, in *Zentralbl. f. Bibliothekswesen* 29 (1912) 58, stresses that the Irish may be credited with the invention of some of these.

21 CLA II² 267, 275–7; VIII 1196; cf. P. McGurk, 'The Irish Pocket Gospel Book', *Sacris Erudiri* 8 (1956) 249–70.

22 CLA II² 268; VIII 1118 (on which see G. Mac Niocaill in *Scriptorium* 15 (1961) 228 ff.).

23 Cf. Bischoff, *Mittelalterliche Studien* I, 2 f. The Irish commentary on Jerome's *Prol. in Iob*: (in half-uncial) 'Sunt et Africanae, quae tunsae appellantur, quas in usu frequenti habemus.'

The Irish did not use standard uncial or capitalis. Their interest in Greek, however, lasted through the centuries, and this found expression also in their script: in the transliteration of words and formulae, in the substitution of ψ for *ps*, and in the use of the spiritus asper (ⱶ) for *h*, and also in the restoration of the Greek spelling to the nomina sacra xᴘ͡c and ι͞н͡c.[24]

It seems possible to speak of a common inheritance which the Irish created at latest, it appears, by the seventh century and which they passed on wherever Insular script was practised. To it belong the two-stage system of script (half-uncial with the alternating forms, and minuscule); their characteristic style, determined by the triangular, spatulate terminals; a peculiar stylisation of decorative capitals;[25] peculiarities of book-production: use of Insular membrane,[26] black ink, their own method of ruling, a basic stock of abbreviations, the tendency to go over to a lower grade of script at page-ends; enlarged and then rapidly diminishing script at the beginning of passages; the triangular construction of the groups of initials; and initials surrounded by red dots. Common Insular also is the frequent substitution of *s* and *ss*; other orthographical peculiarities are Irish, if not exclusively so: false aspiration (especially *ch* for *h*), *-ís* for *-iis*, *y* for *i* or *e*; specifically Irish is *-iens* instead of *-ens*. So also the indifference to proper word-division (for example, *diceba-nt*, *M-artha*) is not confined to Ireland.

The mature, well-rounded Insular half-uncial, which c. 700 was written so magnificently in the Anglo-Saxon Book of Lindisfarne and its relatives, was also used, with more or less success, in Ireland for liturgical and biblical manuscripts, occasionally in combination with minuscule.[27] Probably in the late-eighth century – when the Irish ornamental repertoire had opened up to new possibilities – the arts of Irish writing and painting present themselves at their sovereign best in the Book of Kells, which, although considerably later, stands comparison with the greatest achievements in Anglo-Saxon book illumination and is itself under the Northumbrian influence of the Lindisfarne tradition.[28]

24 Lindsay, *Early Irish minuscule*, 4, 23, 29 f.; Bischoff *Mittelalterliche Studien* 2, 256.

25 This enlarged script, which together with decorated initials belongs to the repertoire of decoration, consists of letters drawn from capitalis, uncial and half-uncial that are, for the most part, written in a slim and angular way, or have altered their form still more, like *g* (Zimmermann, *Vorkar. Min.*, plates 179, 181), *l* (ibid, 246, 255; CLA II 277), *V* (Zimmermann, *Vorkar. Min.*, 218, 221, 246), *O* (a lozenge between two horizontal brackets; Zimmermann, *Vorkar. Min.*, 217 f., 223, 258) and especially *M*, which is constructed like a gate from three ascenders and one or two cross-strokes. Greek π can replace *P* (ibid., 201, 218, 221, 259; and this may even stand for *Rho* in X̄I, ibid., 219 and 254c).

26 In the untrimmed codex Basel F III 15d (CLA VII 847, s. VIII) written on thick vellum, the upper outer corners are round, the lower ones round or tongue shaped (see plate).

27 See e.g. the Turin gospel palimpsest (CLA IV 466; in addition the newly discovered fragments, cf. CLA Addenda 359, see below 200) and the fragment in Colmar (VI 757, with initials), Munich (S 1797, now Clm 29300/2) and St Gallen (VII 980, 988, 991); J. Duft–P. Meyer, *Die irischen Miniaturen der Stiftsbibliothek St. Gallen* (Olten 1953).

28 CLA II² 274; Facs.: E.H. Alton–P. Meyer, *Evangeliorum quattuor codex Cennanensis*, 3 vols (Bern 1951). Cf. T.J. Brown, 'Northumbria and the Book of Kells', *Anglo-Saxon England* I (1972) 219–46.

Here the well-rounded half-uncial, which is very closely integrated with the decoration, is magnificently written, and not infrequently at line-ends it is varied in very fanciful ways;[29] while on ornamental pages the Irish decorative capitals appear.

Half-uncial and minuscule were used side-by-side in Ireland for several centuries, the former principally for gospel books and psalters;[30] in the older *Liber hymnorum* it is used for the Latin hymns,[31] while in the double-psalter of Rouen (saec. X) it is contrasted with a script closer to minuscule. From the twelfth century on only the by now extremely pointed minuscule remains in use.[32]

The Irish script produced some innovations even in post-carolingian times, like the abbreviation $\bar{f}$ for *for*. Some Latin abbreviations were also used in an Irish context for the Irish equivalents, like ⁊ = *ocus* and, especially remarkable, *q* with cross-stroke (Latin *quia*) for the preposition ('for', 'since') and for this group of letters in any combination.[33]

When used for Irish (which was sometimes also written in Gothic script)[34] the pointed minuscule survived into modern times;[35] it also determined the printing fonts for Irish.

During the sixth century the Irish undertook missionary activity from the island monastery of Iona (Hy, off the western coast of Scotland) to the Picts, and from the first half of the seventh century to the northern Anglo-Saxons. Of those who went to the continent, many saw in exile a pious undertaking, others became teachers. As a result of all this they became the 'teachers of the middle ages', not least through their script. After Columbanus (†615), who founded monasteries at Luxeuil in Burgundy and at Bobbio in the Lombard kingdom, near Piacenza, his pupil Gallus, at the site of whose cell the monastery of St Gall later grew up, and Furseus (†c. 649), whose memory lived on in 'Perrona Scottorum' in Picardy, others followed who visited the burial places of their holy countrymen and sometimes even settled there. In Bobbio, where, after the founding generation had died out, the Irish were only a small minority, in the seventh and eighth centuries manuscripts were still being written in Irish script, some of them with

29 *Codex Cennanensis*, introd., plate 5.
30 CLA II², 231, 272; Zimmermann, *Vorkar. Min.*, plates 210, 212.
31 L. Bieler, 'The Irish Book of Hymns', *Scriptorium* 2 (1948) 177 ff. and plate 24.
32 Cf. the gospel book copied by Maelbrigte in Armagh in 1138; Steffens², *Lateinische Paläographie*, plate 83a; Zimmermann, *Vorkar. Min.*, 216b.
33 Bieler, 'Insular palaeography', 187.
34 The succession of thirty-nine hands from c. 1100 to 1321 in the Annals of Inisfallen is especially instructive (Facsimile ed. R.I. Best–E. MacNeill, Dublin 1933); in the thirteenth century even scribes writing gothic cursive use the symbol for *ar*.
35 L. Bieler describes the stages in *Scriptorium* 3 (1949) 283 ff. as 'formation' (eleventh and twelfth centuries), 'standardisation' (thirteenth to sixteenth centuries), 'fossilisation' (from the seventeenth century).

an obviously diminishing grasp of the true style.[36] Several Bobbio manuscripts in north-Italian script reveal the Irish influence in their abbreviations.[37]

The contribution of Irish scholars to carolingian culture is attested by the autographs of Dungal, Sedulius Scottus, Iohannes Scottus, and Martin of Laon (though Martin, as a teacher in a carolingian school, clearly used only a blunt caroline minuscule).[38] In the tenth and eleventh centuries too the Irish migration to the continent had not quite ceased, but because the newcomers mostly adapted their script to their environment many of their manuscripts undoubtedly remain to be identified. However, in the Verdun MS. 51, for example, and with Marianus, founder of the Regensburg '*Schottenkloster*' (1076) who used the native script only for remarks in Irish,[39] the Irish substratum is unmistakeable.

Unquestionably dependent on Ireland is the handwriting of Wales and Cornwall, two Celtic areas in which Insular script was written at least until the tenth century, and with whose scribal practices the pre-caroline practice of Brittany is closely connected. No trace of late Roman script has survived, which was presumably in use among the Celts of Britain in the fifth century, the century when they were pushed westwards and over the sea to Brittany. Rather, the oldest surviving witness that can be produced, the epitaph of king Catamanus of Gwynedd from c. 625,[40] shows a mixture of half-uncial with forms of *a* and *m* that reappear in the Irish-Northumbrian decorative capitals. Probably of Welsh origin are the gospels of St Chad,[41] written in the style of the great gospel books, and the gospels in Hereford cathedral,[42] written in a less formal half-uncial (both from the eighth century). To judge from the surviving manuscripts from Welsh and Cornish scriptoria of the ninth and tenth centuries – amongst them some with Welsh or Cornish texts or glosses – the Celtic Britons were then in possession both of a half-uncial similar to the Irish as well as of pointed and round minuscule.[43] The latter type was still practised in the late eleventh century at St David's.

36 See e.g. CLA III 350, 361; IV 441, 444; cf. P. Collura, *La precarolina e la carolina a Bobbio* (Milan 1943; repr. Florence 1965) 87 ff., A.R. Natale, *Arte e imitazione della scrittura insulare in codici Bobbiesi* (Milan 1950). The Irish style of emphasising is copied in CLA III 365.

37 CLA III 353, 388, 403; IV 439.

38 Bischoff, *Mittelalterliche Studien* 3, 39–54. Cf. J.J. Contreni, *Codex Laudunensis 468*. Armarium codicum insignium 3 (Turnhout 1984) 19 f.; *Paläographie* (1981) plate 6 (Laon 444, f. 299ᵛ, not Laon 468). On St Gall's role in spreading Irish scribal habits cf. p. 119 and 212.

39 Cf. Chroust, *Monumenta*, I 10, 1. Irish script from the autograph of the chronicle of the recluse Marianus Scotus: Ehrle–Liebaert, *Specimina*, plate 23. See *Bayer. Akad. Wiss.*, phil.-hist. Kl. (1929) 1, 13 f.

40 Cf. V.E. Nash-Williams, *The Early Christian Monuments of Wales* (Cardiff 1950) 55 and 57, reprod. 21 and plate VII.   41 CLA II² 159, with ornamental capitalis.

42 CLA II² 157.

43 W.M. Lindsay, *Early Welsh Script*. St Andrews University Publications 10 (Oxford 1912). Some examples of 'Welsh symptoms' on p. 40.

The Celts who in the fifth and sixth centuries occupied Brittany were a part of the Celtic British peoples that were driven, under pressure from the Germanic conquest, overseas. Amongst these the Insular foundations of their script are documented only in a few codices in Insular half-uncial and pointed minuscule from the eighth and ninth centuries, before the Breton scriptoria surrendered completely to caroline minuscule in the ninth century.[44] The Breton substratum also contributed, probably, to the formation of the hybrid continental-Celtic scripts of Fleury (especially Berne 207).[45]

2. *Anglo-Saxon script*

In the development of English writing[46] the direction was given by Irish missionaries who converted the northern Anglo-Saxons to Christianity; amongst them was Aidan, who in 634 founded the monastery of Lindisfarne on a small island off the Northumbrian coast. For a whole generation – until the withdrawal of the Irish after the synod of Whitby in 664 – the north of England stood under the stamp of the Irish church; and in this period the Anglo-Saxons also obtained the common Insular heritage of script which they were able to develop in their own way in the two stages of half-uncial and minuscule. They were made familiar also with the Irish habits of preparing and decorating manuscripts.[47] They received half-uncial in a state in which the angular quality of the early Irish half-uncial had almost vanished,[48] and also in the already well-rounded type with four fully integrated double forms (uncial *d*, *R*, *S*, and minuscule *-n*). The minuscule had two styles, one blunt with *s* extending below the line, and the other whose shafts, resting on the line, end with sharp points, as do those that extend below the line (*f*, the last shaft of final *-m*, *p*, *q*, *r*, *s*). Furthermore, the Anglo-Saxons took over a moderate stock of abbreviations which were slightly adapted by them:[49] the most important of the new abbrevia-

---

44 Half-uncial: gospel book of St Gatien, s. VIII (CLA v, 684), with ornamental capitals, and Sedulius (Orleans 302, s. IX); minuscule: Latin Breton texts in Leiden, s. IX (plate: L. Fleuriot, *Dictionnaire des gloses en Vieux Breton* (Paris 1964) plate 2). Celtic abbreviations are a distinctive group until the tenth century; cf. W.M. Lindsay, 'Breton scriptoria: their Latin abbreviation-symbols', *Zentralbl. f. Bibliothekswesen* 29 (1912) 264–72. The connection with England seems to have left reciprocal traces: in the mid tenth century at the latest, the Breton Eutyches (Oxford, Bodl. Libr., Auct. F.3.32, f. 1–9) was in Glastonbury (R.W. Hunt, *Saint Dunstan's classbook from Glastonbury* (Amsterdam 1961) p. v f.); in the Annals of Redon (probably 919) besides Insular g, the wynn-rune and thorn (ð) are used (Bischoff, *Anecdota* (Stuttgart 1984) 104.   45 CLA v 568; cf. also IX 1380.
46 Cf. the literature cited in n. 1. See also T.J. Brown, 'Late Antique and early Anglo-Saxon books', in *Manuscripts at Oxford: R.W. Hunt memorial exhibition* (Oxford 1980) 9–14.
47 Cf. above p. 87 f. The task of distinguishing Irish and Anglo-Saxon elements is often very difficult; cf. T.J. Brown, *Codex Lindisfarnensis*, 68f. with plate 15a.
48 Only in the Book of Durrow are traces of this feature to be found; CLA II² 273; Facs.: A.A. Luce–G.O. Simms, P. Meyer, L. Bieler (edd), *Evangeliorum quattuor codex Durmachanus*, 2 vols (Olten–Lausanne 1960).   49 See above p. 86; Lindsay, *Notae Latinae*, 498–500.

tions was *t* with a downstroke through the bar for *-tur*. For writing in Anglo-Saxon the rune ᵽ (wynn, for Old English *w*) and þ (thorn) were taken over into the alphabet, the latter as an equivalent of the round *d* with oblique top-stroke, as well as for the voiced and voiceless fricatives.

At the beginning of the tradition stand four gospel manuscripts that are among the most important works of Anglo-Saxon illumination. In the Irish-Northumbrian style which they represent in their decoration, the Irish impulse and the experiences of Anglo-Saxon artistic craftsmanship are amalgamated. The Book of Durrow, which is regarded as the oldest Northumbrian gospel book (c. 670),[50] is written in what is still a slightly angular half-uncial; the 'interpretationes' on f 124[r] are partly in a script closer to minuscule.[51] Of the three others dating from c. 700, the Book of Lindisfarne (named after its place of origin),[52] the fragmentary Durham A. II. 17 (f. 2–102),[53] and the Codex Epternacensis in Paris,[54] the first two are written entirely in majestic half-uncial; the Epternacensis on the other hand (which is apparently by the same hand that wrote Durham A. II. 17, and which begins in the same script) is written mostly in a no less imposing blunt minuscule.[55] The use of pointed minuscule in colophons of the Codex Epternacensis,[56] and in the last lines on some pages of the roughly contemporary Cologne Canones MS 213,[57] indicates the simultaneous existence of these three fully-developed kinds of script.[58] On these three levels (half-uncial, blunt minuscule, pointed to cursive minuscule)[59] the development of Anglo-Saxon script basically proceeds in the eighth century through various mixtures (of the forms *a*, *d*, *n*, *r*, *s*, *t*) innumerable transitional forms and variations of style, leading to a fluctuating general appearance. A specifically English variant of half-uncial is a compressed, at times even with letters half as broad as they are high.[60] Northumbrian minuscule is represented by, for example, the codices of Bede's *Historia ecclesiastica* of 737 and 746.[61]

The Anglo-Saxon script spread in the course of the eighth century from the

---

50 See n. 48.   51 Reprods of this page also in CLA II² 273 (olim f. 116[r]).

52 CLA II² 187; Facs.: T.D. Kendrick, T.J. Brown and others (eds), *Evangeliorum quattuor codex Lindisfarnensis*, 2 vols (Olten–Lausanne 1956–60).

53 CLA II² 149; Chr. D. Verey and others (edd), *The Durham Gospels, together with fragments of a gospel book in uncial, Durham Cathedral Library MS A. II. 17*, Early Engl. MSS Facs 20 (Copenhagen 1980). Cf. T.J. Brown in *Codex Lindisfarnensis*, 89 ff.

54 CLA V 578. Cf. T.J. Brown, ibid.

55 There are fragments of two further gospels in half-uncial in CLA II² and IX 1335. There is a collection of other Northumbrian groups in Brown, ibid, 90 ff.

56 Cf. *Codex Lindisfarnensis*, plates 12 and 14.   57 CLA VIII 1163, see the reprods.

58 In these and other English manuscripts Irish ornamental capitalis appears (cf. n. 25); cf. Brown, ibid, 75 ff.

59 Especially cursive: CLA II² 184; Kirchner, *Script. Lat. libr.²*, plate 20. For a south-west English group see above p. 85 (illustr. 15).

60 CLA II² 138; in addition 194b and further instances ('compressed majuscule').

61 CLA II 139 and XI 1621; both reproduced in full: *Early English MSS* 2 (Copenhagen 1952) and 9 (1959).

north southwards (perhaps also from south-west England), and supplanted the uncial that had been introduced by the Roman missionaries to England and which had an important stronghold even in the double monastery of Wearmouth-Jarrow in Northumbria.[62] The half-uncial and the minuscule, which is amply attested in the southern kingdoms as a charter script too,[63] acquired new styles during this process. In general it can be said that the southern script (of Kent and Mercia) was weaker in style and that this style declines altogether in the course of the eighth century, and instead there appears a tendency towards bizarre and precious traits.

From south-west England comes a very versatile minuscule with cursive traces, especially in the flat *s*-shaped *e*[64] which is also found in the circle of Boniface. The history of the development of Anglo-Saxon script in the eighth century is to be completed by reference to the large production of the Anglo-Saxon foundations on the continent.[65]

In England examples of Anglo-Saxon half-uncial are only exceptionally attested after the eighth century, although the script was still being used even in the tenth.[66] The minuscule continued to be used for manuscripts and charters, and among the stylisations which it underwent[67] there occurs a very heavy, upright angular type ('square minuscule'), which was cultivated in some scriptoria into the eleventh century.[68] But from the tenth century, when caroline minuscule spread from France, writing takes on a double face: Latin is written in common minuscule which is more or less Insular in ductus, but for Anglo-Saxon (for example, names in charters) scribes pass over immediately to the national script.[69] A reflex of that is seen in the Old High German parts of the Ottonian and Salian 'Cambridge Songs', whose manuscript was written in England.[70] Anglo-Saxon script was written until beyond the mid-twelfth century; and even when the use of common minuscule for English became customary, the Anglo-Saxon additional letter ð was retained until the twelfth century, the runes

---

62 See p. 71 f.   63 ChLA III and IV.

64 See above p. 110. W.M. Lindsay, *Early Irish Minuscule*, 10 f.; Boniface MSS: CLA VIII 1196 and S 1806. Perhaps this type can be explained by means of Irish connections.

65 See below p. 93 ff.

66 *Liber vitae ecclesiae Dunelmensis* (c. 840); Facs.: Surtees Society 1923; *Pal. Soc* I, plate 238; T.J. Brown, *The Durham Ritual*. Early English MSS in Facsimile 16 (Copenhagen 1969) (s. X[1]).

67 F. Wormald, 'The Insular script in late tenth century English Latin manuscripts', *Atti del X Congresso Internazionale di Scienze Storiche* (Rome 1955) 160–4.

68 Examples: *Pal. Soc.* I, plates 71, 72, 188, 189; *New Pal. Soc.* I, plate 164; Steffens[2], *Lateinische Paläographie*, plate 71a; T.A.M. Bishop, *English Caroline Minuscule* (Oxford 1971) plate 3, reprod. 5. On the script see Bishop in *Trans. Cambr. Bibliograph. Soc.* 4/3 (1966) 246 f.

69 Latin and Anglo-Saxon calligraphy by the same hand s.x[2] and XI in Ker, *Catal. of MSS*, plates 2–4 (cf. xxv ff.) and in Bishop, *English Caroline Minuscule*, plates 20 and 24. Names: W. Keller, *Angelsächsische Paläographie* (Berlin 1906) plate 10; Bishop, ibid., plate 15.

70 Facs.: K. Breul, *The Cambridge Songs* (Cambridge 1915); K. Strecker, *Die Cambridger Lieder* (Berlin 1926) with reprod.

þ and ƕ into the fourteenth and fifteenth respectively.[71] From Anglo-Saxon 3 there now developed a new 3-shaped sign used for various fricatives (yogh), while the caroline-Gothic *g* denoted a plosive stop.[72]

The material for the earlier history of English script is considerably enriched by the transmission in Germany. The great differences of style within the Anglo-Saxon script in England in the eighth century can also be traced in the German foundations of the Anglo-Saxons and in their area of influence. In the monastery of Echternach (founded 698) throughout the eighth century Northumbrian scribal art was alive on German soil:[73] until roughly the mid eighth century half-uncial and minuscule appear side-by-side.[74] The Northumbrian script character disappears only with the latest Anglo-Saxon writings from Echternach.[75]

An almost distinct area of Anglo-Saxon influence and Anglo-Saxon script was established in Germany by the activities of Boniface and his pupils, as well as by the monks and nuns who followed them. It stretched from Main-Franken over Hesse and Westphalia. Just as Boniface and Lul had come from southern England, so the script that took root here has a southern English stamp. Nonetheless, many English manuscripts from various regions reached the monastery of Fulda,[76] (founded in 744), just as did the older Italian manuscripts that had passed through England, amongst them Victor of Capua's codex with the gospel harmony of Tatian (with explanations in cursive Anglo-Saxon minuscule that may be, in part, in Boniface's own hand).[77] It is possible, however, that the oldest surviving manuscript of Bonifaces's grammar[78] was written in Fulda itself.

In the region of Würzburg, whose transmission can be more easily studied and whose Anglo-Saxon script stems from the same root, it can be seen how the

71 A succession of Anglo-Saxon hands from c. 900 to 1070 is found in the Parker Chronicle; facsimile: R. Flower–H. Smith, *The Parker Chronicle and Laws* (London 1941).

72 These three signs were also taken over in the earlier script of Norway and Iceland, which developed chiefly under English influence; cf. H. Spehr, *Der Ursprung der isländischen Schrift und ihre Weiterbildung bis zur Mitte des XIII. Jahrhunderts* (Halle/S. 1929); D.A. Seip. *Palaeografi B, Norge og Island* (*Nordisk Kultur* 28) (Stockholm–Oslo–Copenhagen 1954). Hr. Benediktsson, *Early Icelandic script as Illustrated in Vernacular Texts from the Twelfth and Thirteenth Centuries* (Reykjavik 1965) 18–54. For information about these signs I thank H. Gneuss.

73 For Irish involvement in the early Echternach scriptorium see D. Ó Cróinín, 'Rath Melsigi, Willibrord, and the earliest Echternach manuscripts', *Peritia* 3 (1984) 17–42, with 3 plates.

74 T.J. Brown in *Codex Lindisfarnensis*, 90 f. Minuscule: CLA v 584 (= Paris, BN, Lat. 9526!) 588, 605, 606b.

75 Paris, BN, Lat. 9525: Zimmermann, *Vorkarol. Min.*, plate 262, and Lat. 9565, both s. IX in.

76 Reprod: G. Baesecke, *Der Vocabularius Sti. Galli in der angelsächsischen Mission* (Halle 1933) plates 13–15; CLA vii 844 and 848; viii 1134, 1138, 1140, 1143.

77 CLA viii 1196; Steffens², *Lateinische Paläographie*, plate 21a; H. Köllner, *Die illuminierten Hss. der Hessischen Landesbibliothek Fulda*, 1, Bildband (Stuttgart 1976) reprod. 3. Cf. on this M.B. Parkes, 'The handwriting of St. Boniface: a reassessment of the problems', *Beitr. Gesch. d. deutsch. Sprache u. Lit.* 98 (Tübingen 1976) 161–79.   78 CLA S 1803.

writing of the founders was followed by unskilled imitations of the half-uncial and minuscule that must be ascribed to their German pupils, until the last generation to use Insular script fixed its style at the beginning of the ninth century.[79] Women too wrote here.

What has survived of Anglo-Saxon writings from the late eighth century and the early ninth from Hersfeld,[80] Fritzlar,[81] Amorbach,[82] Mainz,[83] and finally Werden[84] all show the southern English tradition of this missionary area. In Regensburg too,[85] and in Freising,[86] Salzburg,[87] Lorsch[88] and St Gall,[89] scribes trained in Anglo-Saxon script were active in the later eighth or early ninth century, although none of these scriptoria had an exclusively Anglo-Saxon appearance. The last phases of the Anglo-Saxon script in Hesse and in the Main region, from the period when no fresh support was arriving from England, are relatively clearly recognisable. Shortly before and about 800 the script is mostly straight with long descenders, often somewhat listless.[90] In this script are written the Saxon baptism vows and the Basel recipes, both from Fulda.[91] From about 820 on, Fulda is the only stronghold of Anglo-Saxon script in Germany. Among the last witnesses to half-uncial are the Frankfurt psalter,[92] a monumental manuscript of Hrabanus's Matthew commentary (probably 822)[93] and several lines of the Frankish baptism vow.[94] The minuscule takes on finally a somewhat stiff and often nail-shaped appearance.[95] In the Fulda cartulary the script changes in 828 to caroline minuscule;[96] scribes writing an Anglo-Saxon

79 B. Bischoff–J. Hofmann, *Libri Sancti Kyliani* (Würzburg 1952) 6 ff.

80 CLA VIII 1225 f.   81 CLA VIII 1133.   82 Arndt-Tangl[4], *Schrifttafeln*, plate 41.

83 W.M. Lindsay in *Palaeographia Latina* 4 (1925) plate 4; CLA IX 1400.

84 Chroust, *Monumenta* 2, 22, plates 6–8 (8b a hybrid type, crossed with Continental cursive); R. Drögereit, *Werden und der Heliand* (Essen 1951) plates 1–10, 16a.b.; perhaps also from Werden is Cologne, Dombibl. 106: Arndt-Tangl[4], *Schrifttafeln*, plates 39/40 and L.W. Jones, *The Script of Cologne from Hildebald to Hermann* (Cambridge, Mass. 1932) plates 40–42 (cf. M. Coens, *Recueil d'études bollandiennes* (Brussels 1963) 139 ff.).

85 CLA IX 1289a, 1307. Bischoff, *Kalligraphie* Nr. 1.

86 CLA IX 1253, 1263, 1283. Bischoff, *Kalligraphie* Nr. 6.   87 CLA X 1500.

88 CLA I 79; S 1749. In several manuscripts the opening lines were copied in Anglo-Saxon half-uncial; see B. Bischoff, *Lorsch im Spiegel seiner Handschriften* (Munich 1974) 25 and plate 6.

89 CLA VII 910.

90 E.g. CLA I 90, 97; II 146; Chroust, *Monumenta* 2, 22, plate 6 (also with half-uncial) and 7. For what follows see Herrad Spilling, 'Angelsächsische Schrift in Fulda', in A. Brall (ed.), *Von der Klosterbibliothek zur Landesbibliothek* (Stuttgart 1978) 47–98.

91 Baptism oaths: J.H. Gallée, *Altsächsische Sprachdenkmäler* (Leiden 1895) plate 11; Koennecke, *Bilderatlas*, 8. Recipes: Enneccerus, *Die ältesten deutschen Sprachdenkmäler* (Frankfurt/M. 1897) plate 17.

92 G. Swarzenski–Rosy Schilling, *Die illuminierten Handschriften und Einzelminiaturen des Mittelalters und der Renaissance in Frankfurter Besitz* (Frankfurt/M. 1929) plate 2.

93 Fragments in the Stadtarchiv Hann. Münden; I owe my knowledge of these to Ludwig Denecke.   94 Fischer, *Schrifttafeln*, plate 8.

95 E.g. Chroust, *Monumenta* 5, plate 6; Steffens[2], *Lateinische Paläographie*, plate 54b.

96 Steffens[2], *Lateinische Paläographie*, plate 54a; E. Heydenreich, *Das älteste Fuldaer Cartular* (Leipzig 1899) plate 2.

script are still involved in the Gellius manuscript of 838 and in Hrabanus's Ezekiel commentary c. 842 (Wolfenbüttel, Cod. Weissenb. 84 and 92).[97] After Hrabanus's era (†856) – he himself wrote a somewhat mixed Anglo-Saxon minuscule[98] – the script died out in Fulda very rapidly. The Anglo-Saxon tradition of book-making and its disciplined writing technique had a noticeable effect, both in Germany in the ninth century and in England in the tenth and eleventh, on the caroline minuscule that replaced it.[99]

Partly, no doubt, because the Anglo-Saxon missionaries were the first to write in German, partly also doubtless due to conscious borrowing from Anglo-Saxon handwriting, the Anglo-Saxon phonetic symbols made their way into German writing and were used in several monuments: ᵽ for *w* in the Hildebrandslied[100] (from Fulda); ʋ for *w* in the Lex Salica (from Mainz, to judge by the script)[101] and in the Leipzig glosses;[102] and finally đ in the Lex Salica and in the Cotton, Vatican, and formerly Prague, now Berlin, copies of the Heliand.[103] Based on the latter sign is the *b* with cross-stroke in the Vatican and Cotton Heliand. From an Anglo-Saxon source also comes the ꝫ (Latin *et*, Anglo-Saxon *ond*) for *enti*, and the writing of *ga-* by means of a runic X with horizontal cross-stroke in the Wessobrunn prayer (from the diocese of Augsburg, probably from the monastery of Staffelsee).[104] The latter occurs also in the glosses in London, British Library, MS Arundel 393.[105] Finally, the earliest tentative attempt at an OHG accent-system is to be seen in the imitation of the earlier Insular general usage of the acute accent as a mark of length.[106]

97 G.I. Lieftinck, 'Le Ms. d'Aulu-Gelle à Leeuwarden exécuté à Fulda en 836', *Bull. dell' Arch. Pal. Ital.*, n.s. 1 (1955) 11–17 with plates 1–4. H. Butzmann, 'Der Ezechiel-Kommentar des Hrabanus Maurus und seine älteste Handschrift', *Bibliothek und Wissenschaft* 1 (1964) 1–22 with plate 1. A scribe schooled by the English writes a few lines on f. 7ᵛ of Basel, F III 15e, even after the mid ninth century.

98 Reprod.: Butzmann, 'Ezechiel-Kommentar des Hrabanus', 20 f. and plates 9/10 (corrections by 'x'). There are further autograph additions by Hrabanus in the Vatican MS of the *De laudibus sanctae crucis* (MS Reg. Lat. 124). His hand was also to be seen in the now lost fragment of an antiphonarius missae formerly at Kassel (Kl. Gamber, *Codices Liturgici Latini Antiquiores*, Nr. 1323).   99 See below p. 117.

100 Enneccerus, *Die ältesten deutschen Sprachdenkmäler*, plates 1–4; Fischer, *Schrifttafeln*, plate 12 f.

101 Koennecke, *Bilderatlas*, 9; *Karl der Große, Werk und Wirkung* (Exhibition catal., Aachen 1965), plate 34.   102 Arndt-Tangl⁴, *Schrifttafeln*, plate 49.

103 Numerous examples of all the manuscripts can be found in Burkhard Taeger, *Der Heliand, Ausgewählte Abbildungen zur Überlieferung*, Litterae 103 (Göppingen 1985). R. Priebsch, *The Heliand Ms. Cotton Caligula A. VII in the British Museum* (Oxford 1925); Gallée, *Altsächsische Sprachdenkmäler*, plate 1b, 1c, 10b, 17a.

104 Enneccerus, *Sprachdenkmäler*, plates 9/10; Petzet-Glauning, *Deutsche Schrifttafeln*, plate 1; Fischer, *Schrifttafeln*, plate 14; There is a full facsimile of the manuscript by C.v. Kraus (Munich 1922); Ute Schwab, *Die Sternrune im Wessobrunner Gebet* (Amsterdam 1974) reprod. 4.   105 Schwab, ibid., reprods 6, 7A, 7B.

106 This is already present in the Pa manuscript of the Abrogans, a calligraphic manuscript from the region of Regensburg; Baesecke, *Lichtdrucke*, plates 1–20. On the MS see B. Bischoff in *Frühmittelalterliche Studien* 5 (1971) 120 f.

3. Visigothic (Mozarabic) script and Sinai script

In seventh-century Spain,[1] which was freed from religious dissension after the conversion of the Arian Visigoths to Catholicism in 589, there still existed a flourishing Romano-German culture which, in the literary field, conserved late-patristic features. Here even capitalis[2] existed in use alongside uncial and half-uncial,[3] and later Roman cursive of the sixth and seventh centuries is preserved in numerous charters, on slate tablets,[4] and in several parchment fragments of diplomas.[5] As a result of the Arab conquest, from 711 on the country was divided into two zones of separate cultural development, though they still communicated with one another. The Christians who lived under Arab rule are called Mozarabs, and the Visigothic script used by them is called Mozarabic.

The new Visigothic minuscule that appears from the early eighth century on in Spanish manuscripts, and which remained the characteristic script of Spain into the early twelfth century (with the exception of Catalonia), and which indeed in some places was still used even in the thirteenth century,[6] appeared not just as a calligraphic counterpart of the preceding cursive[7] but is probably to be seen in other contexts as well. Its oldest monuments are the Visigothic orationale written before 732 in Tarragona, now Verona, Biblioteca Capitolare, LXXXIX (84),[8] and Autun, Bibliothèque municipale, MS 27 (5. 29), f. 63–76, which is probably even older.[9] The script in these has the following characteristics which basically retain their validity until this particular type dies out: it is slanted towards the left (or vertical); the distinctive letters are: open *a* made with two identical horns (similar to *u*); straight *d* and narrow uncial *d* side-by-side; narrow

---

1 For what follows cf. Z. García Villada, *Paleografía española* (Madrid 1923); A. Millares Carlo, *Tratado de paleografía española*[3] 1–3 (Madrid 1983); Vol. 1, 323–42 contains an index of Visigothic MSS. A.C. Floriano Cumbreño, *Paleografía y diplomática españolas* (Oviedo 1946); Cencetti, *Lineamenti*, 134–58; idem, *Compendio*, 60–3; John, *Latin paleography*, 16 f. Reprod.: P. Ewald–G. Loewe, *Exempla scripturae visigoticae* (Heidelberg 1883); Ch. U. Clark, *Collectanea Hispanica* (Paris 1920); A. Canellas, *Exempla scripturarum Latinarum* 2 (Saragossa 1966); Anscari M. Mundó, 'Para una historia de la escritura visigotica', in *Bivium, Homenaje a Manuel Cecilio Díaz y Díaz* (Madrid 1983) 175–96, with illustr.

2 Spanish half-uncial generally uses half-uncial *g*: CLA I 111 (s. VII); V 587 (s. VI), 592 (s. VII); VI 727a (s. VII ex.); 729 (s. VI–VII); XI 1636 (s. VII); this last also has uncial *G*.

3 In the manuscript of Isidore, *De natura rerum* (Escorial R. II.18, s. VII[1]; CLA XI 1631) from southern Spain, the poems and other passages are copied in capitalis (Millares Carlo, *Tratado*, plate 4). 4 See the literature cited on p. 15.

5 A.M. Mundó, *Los diplomas visigodos originales en pergamino* (Diss. typed, Barcelona 1970).

6 A. Mundó, 'La datación de los códices litúrgicos visigóticos toledanos', *Hispania Sacra* 18 (1965) 1-25; J. Janini-J. Serrano, *Manuscritos litúrgicos de la Biblioteca Nacional* (Madrid 1969) 133 ff. and plate 14 date MS 10110 'saec. XIII–XIV'.

7 Only the last slate tablet, copied after the reception of the new style (M. Gómez-Moreno, *Documentación goda en pizarra*, R. Academia de la Historia (Madrid 1966) 95 ff. and reprod. 53) shows uncial *G* in its cursive.

8 CLA IV 515; R.P. Robinson, *Manuscripts 27 (S. 29) and 107 (S. 129) of the Municipal Library of Autun*. Memoirs of the American Academy in Rome 16 (1939) 74 ff. and plates 63–7.

9 CLA III 728; Robinson, *Manuscripts of Autun*, 23 ff. and plates 28–39.

uncial *g* with long descender; short *i* and *I*-longa (in specific usages); *r* at the ends of words with an upturned shoulder-stroke; *t* whose bar begins with a bow drawn down to the line, which then connects with the upper end of the shaft precisely, as in Rhaetian and Beneventan script; besides *u* there often appears a superior pointed *v*. Ligatures are especially common with *e*, *f*, *r* and cursive *t* (also for example *eG*, *rG*); a special form is *it* (high *T* with bar looped down to the left).[10] Among the abbreviations with special signs are *-b* and *-g* with high-set *s* (or semi-colon, for *-bus* and *-que*) and the p (otherwise commonly used for *pro*) with the eye added on the left of the shaft, for *per* (along with the usual abbreviation). In the contractions the groups *nsr*, *nsi*, etc. (and *nri*, etc.), and the preference for consonantal groups ('Hebraicised') like ihrslm (Ierusalem), srhl or srl (Israel), nmn (nomen), pptr (propter) are characteristic; above the *m*-stroke there usually stands a dot (later also with the other abbreviations).[11]

It can be no mere fortuitous coincidence that almost all these characteristics (differing only in the case of the closed-*a*, the looped form of *t* in ligatures without the crest, the *m*-stroke with dot above and below, or with point) also appear in the script in two or three liturgical manuscripts, possibly late-ninth and tenth-century, that came to light some years ago in the library of the monastery of St Catherine on Mount Sinai.[12] A third Sinai manuscript[13] is written in a very slanted cursive but one that nevertheless exhibits comparable traits. Because in other details these manuscripts display familiarity with peculiarities of Greek and perhaps Syrian book-production, their original environment has been thought to be possibly the cosmopolitan Christianity of Palestine.[14] It is not unlikely, however, that there existed on Sinai a local Latin tradition which was a remnant of the Christian culture of North Africa,[15] particularly since the calendar accompanying the Sinai psalter may reproduce the local festal calendar from the period shortly before the Arab conquest.[16] As a result of this conquest the cultural situation in Spain changed as well, because in the seventh century considerable emigration from North Africa to Spain must

---

10 The use of *I*-longa at the beginning of a word is general (except before letters with ascenders), and as a semi-vowel; from the late tenth century assibilated *ti* is rendered by *tj* (plate 15, penultimate ligature); cf. Lowe, *Palaeographical Papers* 1, 9 f., 59 ff.

11 In addition there are peculiarities of Spanish orthography: substitution of *b* and *v*, *b* and *f*, *v* and *f*; *qu* for *c*; aphaeresis: *Srael* instead of *Israel* etc.

12 Lowe, *Palaeographical Papers* 2, 427–40, 520–74 and plates 89–94, 120, 124–7. Cf. A. Février, 'Évolution de formes de l'écriture en Afrique du Nord à la fin de l'Antiquité et durant le Haut Moyen Age', *Accademia dei Lincei, Quaderno* 105 (Rome 1968). Facs.: M. Althauer, *Psalterium Latinum Hierosolymitanum. Eine frühmittelalterliche lateinische Handschrift Sin. Ms. no. 5* (Cologne-Vienna 1978). Further Latin writings were found in the Sinai monastery in 1975 (L. Politis, *Scriptorium* 34 (1980) 7); details of the find are still awaited.

13 Lowe, *Palaeographical Papers*, 2, 520 ff. and plates 121–3, 126.

14 Lowe, *Palaeographical Papers*, 2, 428 ff.

15 My hypothesis of a north-African origin for the half uncial Passiones (CLA vi 825) in K. Gamber, *Codices liturgici Latini antiquiores* 1² (Freiburg/Schw. 1968) 54 remains uncertain.

16 J. Gribomont in *Analecta Bollandiana* 75 (1957) 132.

16. Spanish (Visigothic) minuscule

17. Sinai minuscule

18. Spanish (Visigothic) cursive

have taken place;[17] this may have brought with it the minuscule that may have originated in the first half of that century. This explanation of the indisputable relationship between the Sinai[18] and Spanish minuscules offers the possibility of a new approach to the problem of the origin of the Visigothic minuscule; whereas it had been looked upon exclusively as a derivation from purely Spanish antecedents.[19]

17 As resulted from the settlement of African monks at Servitanum; cf. P. Riché, *Education and culture in the barbarian west* (Colombia, S. Carolina 1976) 298.
18 Which shows the presence of this script also in the East.
19 As L. Schiaparelli attempted to do in 'Intorno all'origine della scrittura visigotica', *Arch. stor. ital.*, ser 7, 12 (1930) 165–207.

Equally early, that is still in the seventh and the early eighth century, various Visigothic varieties of minuscule cursive must have arisen,[20] one of which appears in many manuscripts until the eleventh century and sporadically later for marginalia and brief texts, often together with Arabic marginal notes.[21] This typical Mozarabic-Visigothic cursive is markedly inclined towards the left and heavily ligatured; of the unconnected forms especially noteworthy are ε-shaped *a*; the four letters *c*, *d*, *e*, *f* that often begin with additional strokes on the left either on or above the line; the *p* whose bow often stands left of the shaft; *u* often as a vertical *s*-line; *x* with horizontal second stroke.[22]

In Spain the number 40 is written as a cursive connection with an X that has a small angle attached above on the right; instead of *M* (for 1,000) a *T* is often written with a top-stroke on the left curving down towards the shaft. Display script is almost exclusively an enlarged, narrow, often arbitrarily handled capitalis.[23] Nevertheless, in the ninth century, Danila, the scribe of the three-columned bible of La Cava, mastered capitalis, uncial, half-uncial, a slanting half-uncial with uncial admixture, and minuscule, all with equal elegance.[24]

The Visigothic minuscule dominated not only in the northern kingdoms but remained also the script of the Mozarabic Christians living under Arab rule.[25] Especially in the monasteries of Asturia (Albares, Albelda, Cardeña, San Milan de Cogolla, Silos, Valeranica, etc.) in several manuscripts from roughly 900 the place, date and name of the scribe, and of other participants, have been preserved.[26] In these cases the reckoning is by the 'Spanish era', which antedates the Christian reckoning by thirty-eight years. In the south, bilingual codices were written, such as the Pauline letters[27] and a Latin–Arabic glossary.[28]

20 A. Millares Carlo, *Consideraciónes sobre la escritura visigótica cursiva* (León 1973). There is a particularly rounded script in Autun 27, f. 63ʳ and 63ᵛ; CLA VI 728; Robinson, *Manuscripts of Autun*, 9 f., 51 f. and plates 27/28; Mundó, *Los diplomas visigodos*, 94, dated it c. 700.

21 This seems still to be developing in the Veronensis f. 1ʳ, 2ʳ and 2ᵛ (Robinson, *Manuscripts of Autun*, 38, and plates 63–5).

22 Schiaparelli, 'Scrittura visigotica', 18 ff., suggested that the script was formed under the influence of Arabic scripts. Robinson, *Manuscripts of Autun*, 39 f. (plate 68 ff.) lists a number of manuscripts with marginalia; CLA IV 372 f.; XI 1638. There are scarcely any links with the cursive of visigothic charters (including Catalan charters); plates in Robinson, *Manuscripts of Autun*, plates 71–3 (text, p. 40, 80 f.); Millares Carlo, *Tratado*, plates 108–130. It is close to the capricious 'scriptura filiformis' used for titles and colophons (E.g. Ewald–Loewe, *Exempla scripturae Visigothicae*, plate 35); compare the script of the 'Libro de los testamentos' of Oviedo (c. 1126) in J. Dominguez–Bordoña, *Die spanische Buchmalerei vom 7. bis zum 17. Jahrhundert* (Munich–Florence 1930) I, plate 75.

23 Millares Carlo, *Tratado* I, 78 and plates 49, 87.

24 Lowe, *Palaeographical Papers* I, 335–41 with plates 55–7.

25 On the contact between these areas cf. M.C. Díaz y Díaz, 'La circulation des manuscrits dans la Péninsule Ibérique du VIIIe au XIe siècle', *Cahiers de civilisation médiévale* 12 (1969) 219–241, 383–92.

26 Cf. the collection in Ch. U. Clark, *Collectanea*, 66 ff. M.C. Díaz y Díaz, *Libros y librerias en la Rioja altomedieval* (Logroño 1979); idem, *Códices visigóticos en la monarquía leonesa* (León 1983).   27 Ehrle–Liebaert, *Specimina*, plate 25.

28 P. Sj. van Koningsveld, *The Latin–Arabic Glossary of the Leiden University Library* (Leiden 1977).

Apart from in the above-mentioned manuscripts, subscriptions or other explicit indications of provenance or date of origin are rare.[29] However, the style of script, together with the marginalia and book decoration,[30] provide clues for its localisation.[31] In general the southern scripts are broader and lower, in the early centuries supple and delicate,[32] even if they are more solid.[33] In the twelfth century, however, they are hard and rigid.[34] The northern scripts are generally slimmer with even taller ascenders. By and by the writing pressure eases off and the ascenders become stick-shaped. M. Gómez-Morena,[35] on the basis of book decoration, has suggested the attribution of the manuscripts from the ninth to the eleventh centuries to four centres: Andalusia, Toledo, León, and Castille.

Until the early ninth century the Visigothic script was also written north of the Pyrenees.[36] but simultaneously the caroline minuscule advanced as far as Catalonia, where it was practised especially in the monastery of Ripoll.[37] The Reconquista had already begun when Cluniac influence and the imposition of the Roman liturgy under Gregory VII (which pushed out the old Mozarabic liturgy) reduced even further the area in which the already weakened Visigothic script[38] remained alive. At a León council of 1090 the copying of liturgical texts in Visigothic script was forbidden[39] and its general use came to an end in the twelfth century.[40]

4. The development towards minuscule in Francia and Italy

Uncial, half-uncial and cursive remained as the vital forms of script that late antiquity had bequeathed to the German kingdoms which had arisen within the frontiers of the empire, the first two as bookhands, the third principally as a chancery script[41] and an everyday hand. Uncial and half-uncial, which had long

29 The rules listed by E.A. Lowe in *Studia palaeographica* (1910) (now in *Palaeographical Papers*
   1, 2–65) for dating by means of *ti*- ligatures have proved to be too general in their formulation.
30 Including decorated initials with large interlace knots and distinctive human and animal
   forms.
31 Cf. the lists in A.M. Mundó, 'El Commicus palimsest Paris Lat. 2269', in *Liturgica I, Cardinal
   I.A. Schuster in memoriam* (Montserrat 1956) 173 ff.
32 In Spain the reed too was sometimes used for writing.
33 From Cordoba e.g. León, Cat. 22: Díaz y Díaz, 'La circulation', plate 1; from Toledo perhaps
   came the large three-columned codices like Escorial and I 14 inter alia (see CLA XI 1635).
34 Cf. Mundó, 'La datación'.
35 *Iglesias mozárabes* 1 (Madrid 1919) 355–64; cf. Cencetti, *Lineamenti*, 149 ff.
36 CLA XI 1630; Montpellier, Bibl. de la Ville, 5 and 6 (under Visigothic influence). For
   Visigothic script in Lyons see S. Tafel, 'The Lyons scriptorium', *Palaeographia Latina* 4
   (1925) 64; CLA VI 774c. On Lucca see below p. 103.
37 J. Dominguez-Bordoña, *Die spanische Buchmalerei* 1, plates 40, 43 AB, shows small catalan
   minuscule of the early eleventh century with 'half-uncial' *a* and two forms of *d*.
38 Some scribes take over caroline letter forms; see below p. 126.
39 See below p. 126.   40 See Mundó, 'La datación'.
41 Carolingian sources transmit the names '(litterae) longariae, quae Graece sirmata dicuntur',
   'epistularis' and the incomprehensible 'Iactiaca' for chancery cursive (references below
   p. 211, n. 68): on 'litterae longariae' cf. O. Kresten in *Scriptorium* 24 (1970) 312.

since lost their spontaneity, were in part transmitted in calligraphic form, and in other cases they lost their quality, so that on occasions they appear well-nigh deformed.[42]

The cursive, which is now more extensively visible in the West, developed its forms in many directions. We deal first with Italy. The Ravenna papyri testify to the continuity of their narrow, slanted, later Roman cursive up until 700.[43] But one item from the Ravenna archiepiscopal chancery in the mid-seventh century shows an upright, rounded, elegantly curved script[44] which is clearly imitating a style used in Byzantine imperial charters.[45] From the stylisation of this script, used by one of the highest ecclesiastical offices in Italy, it could be concluded that the curialis that is related to it – the special script of the Roman curia – had already by the seventh century developed its bulging rounded form;[46] it appears first in St Gall, Stiftsbibliothek, MS 1394 (between 731 and 741) and then in a letter of Hadrian I dated 788. It is particularly characterised by its broad omega-like *a* (ω), the *e* and *t* which are completely closed as a result of the simultaneous writing of the joining-strokes, the high-rearing *q*,[47] and several ligatures. This script remained relatively unchanged into the late tenth century. The notaries in the city of Rome also wrote a similar cursive. Shortly before 1000 a second phase of this style begins in which minuscule elements enter into the curialis, the ligatures lose their suppleness, and the general impression becomes more rigid and cramped. The last documents in this 'later curialis' date from the years 1121 and 1123. It is possible to compare with this curialis of Ravenna and Rome the upright, curved script of the early medieval chancery of the archbishops of Naples.[48]

Elsewhere, the field of Italian cursives[49] seems rich in individual, tempera-

---

42 Uncial: CLA II 203; III 314, 369; IV 470, 483, 503; VIII 1061; Half-uncial: CLA IV 502; V 653 (mixed with uncial: the Bobbio Missal).   43 Tjäder, *Nichtliter. lat. Pap.*

44 Tjäder, ibid., Nr. 44; plates 142–7.

45 K. Brandi, 'Der byzantinische Kaiserbrief aus St. Denis und die Schrift der frühmittelalterlichen Kanzleien', *Arch. f. Urk.* 1 (1908) 65 ff.

46 P. Rabikauskas, *Die römische Kuriale in der päpstlichen Kanzlei*, Miscellanea Historiae Pontificiae 20 (Rome 1958); the St Gall entry is on p. 44; Cencetti *Lineamenti*, 110–14, idem, *Compendio*, 53 f. In addition J.-O. Tjäder, 'Le origini della scrittura curiale romana', in *Bull. dell'Arch. Pal. Ital.*, ser 3, 2/3 (1963/4) 8–54; reprods, e.g. in Steffens², *Lateinische Paläographie*, plate 58.

47 Tjäder, 'Scrittura curiale romana', 11–32, believes that this developed from the fusion of *q* and a *u* ligature placed above it (*qu*) which was then used to represent *q* on its own.

48 A. Gallo, 'La scrittura curiale napoletana', *Bull. dell'Ist. Stor. Ital.* n. 45 (1929) 17–112; Iole Mazzoleni, *Esempi e scritture cancelleresche, curiali e minuscole* (Naples 1957) plate 4/5; V. Federici, *La scrittura delle cancellerie italiane dal secolo XII al XVII* (Rome 1934) plate 22; A. Petrucci, *Notarii, Documenti per la storia del notariato italiano* (Milan 1958) plate 10. The Roman curialis was imitated in Terracina; cf. Attilio de Luca, 'La scrittura curiale di Terracina', *Scrittura e Civiltà* 6 (1982) 117–88, with plates.

49 Cencetti, *Lineamenti*, 107 ff.; idem, *Compendio*, 52 ff. Some samples of the script (along with later ones) in F. Bartoloni, 'La nomenclatura delle scritture documentarie', in *X Congresso Internazionale di Scienze Storiche* (Rome 1955) Relazioni 1, 434–43.

mental forms, often full of irregular capriciousness, whether it be in the charters
of the Lombard kings (from the early eighth century),[50] or in those of the urban
notaries. They range between compressed, forms on the one hand slanting[51] to
left or right, that are occasionally extremely pointed, and on the other quite
loose, weak forms.[52] It was possible, however, to demonstrate from an analysis of
the transmission from Lucca (saec. VIII–IX[1]) that a local school tradition
existed there. Many lay people too of middle and upper rank were adept in this
script. Their mastery extends from being able to write ordinary separated letters
to practised cursive flowing scripts.[53] The construction of the ligature *tz* in the
north-Italian cursive is perhaps a trace of Longobard influence on the script.[54] A
fundamental change in this notarial cursive gradually comes about when the
connected character (the proper expression of the cursive type) disappears, and
the script dissolves into greatly altered individual letters and small ligatures
which can appear grotesque and unreadable. In Naples, Amalfi, and Sorrento it
lives on in this form, until its use was banned by Frederick II in 1231.[55]

If in seventh- and eighth-century Italy cursive was used for books – with a
certain reserve,[56] to judge by the transmission – it is significant that it then in
general took on more set forms than in the charters. Examples of such scripts
survive from Bobbio[57] and Vercelli.[58] In Bobbio, where in the same manuscripts
Irish and cursive minuscule are written side-by-side,[59] Irish influence had
apparently a moderate impact on the cursive, while it appeared also in the
abbreviations.[60] However, a Merovingian influence was also at work there,
probably from Luxeuil.[61] At various places in eighth-century Italy scribes
created stylised half-cursive[62] and plentifully ligatured minuscule scripts,

---

50 G. Bonelli, *Codice paleografico lombardo* (Milan 1908); *Arch. Pal. Ital.* 3 and 12, fasc. 56; A.R.
    Natale, *Il Museo diplomatico dell' Archivio di Stato di Milano* 1, 1/2 (Milan 1971).

51 E.g. *Arch. Pal. Ital.* 3, plate 8 (920).   52 An example: Bonelli, *Codice*, plate 16 (774).

53 A. Petrucci, 'Scrittura e libro nella Tuscia altomedievale (secoli VII–IX)', in *Atti del 5°
    Congresso internazionale di studi sull' alto medioevo* (Spoleto 1973) 627–43 with 12 plates; idem,
    'Libro, scrittura e scuola', in *La scuola nell' occidente latino dell' alto medioevo*, Settimane 19
    (Spoleto 1972) 1, 313–37 with 6 plates; cf. also idem, 'Il codice No. 490 della Biblioteca
    Capitolare di Lucca: un problema di storia della cultura medievale ancora da risolvere', in
    Actum Luce 2 (1973) 159–75.

54 L. Schiaparelli, 'Note paleografiche e diplomatiche', *Arch. stor. Ital.* 87 (1927) ser 7, 11, 3 ff.
    Lombard manuscripts occasionally write *tz* to signify a vocalized or palatalized *z* in Latin
    ('Eliphatz': CLA 1 55; 'Tzeno' etc.).   55 Cf. Steffens², *Lateinische Paläographie*, ix.

56 The Milan Josephus papyrus, s. VI, is written in new roman cursive: CLA III 304; Seider,
    Papyri 2/1, Nr. 67; Steffens², *Lateinische Paläographie*, plate 23a.b.

57 CLA III 323b, 334, 353, 388, 403; IV 439, 444.   58 CLA III 322.

59 CLA III 334, 350; IV 444.

60 L. Schiaparelli, *Influenze straniere nella scrittura italiana dei secoli VIII e IX*. Studi e Testi 47
    (Rome 1927) 15 ff.

61 Schiaparelli, *Influenze*, 30 ff.; CLA III 323b; IV 444; I 39 and IX 1386; A.R. Natale, 'Influenze
    merovingiche e studi calligrafici nello scriptorium di Bobbio', in *Miscellanea G. Galbiati* 2.
    Fontes Ambrosiani 26 (Milan 1951) 1 ff. and plate 1.

62 E.g. CLA IV 512 (Insular influence?) 492 and 508 (both Luxeuil influenced), all three perhaps
    come from Verona; Schiaparelli, *Influenze*, 17 ff. and plate 2, and 25 ff. and plates 3/4.

among them some of somewhat precious character.[63] Just how varied the rhythm of the development could be is shown by the chaotic picture of the scripts that appear in MS 490 in the Cathedral Library at Lucca (c. 800): uncial, half-cursive, visigothic-influenced script and other mixtures.[64] While caroline minuscule later ousted all the scripts from northern and central Italy,[65] an early rounded minuscule of that kind led to the genesis of the Beneventan script.[66]

In Francia[67] a continuous evolution of the cursive is manifested in the charter script of the Merovingians (preserved from 625)[68] and of the Carolingians, which ends in France in the tenth century and in Germany already around the mid-ninth. Merovingian chancery cursive, a form of later Roman cursive, is narrow, steep, and compressed, and its convoluted letters and ligatures are not easily decipherable. The habit of using an elongated and enlarged script for individual sections of text (especially the first lines), which gradually becomes a fixed practice, passed from this script into many later charter hands. Other non-literary remains from the seventh century are the list of names on the back of the Barberini ivory[69] and, from the second half of the century, the census lists from St Martin's at Tours.[70] In addition, some of the entries in margins and on flyleaves of manuscripts are written in current script, not in bookhand.[71] These are in a language with distinct Romance forms. An almost invariable sign of Merovingian cursive is the *b* that sends out a connecting-stroke to the right;[72] a second recurrent distinctive feature is the ligature *ex* in which the tongue of the *e* is drawn down to the line, from where it continues at a pointed angle upwards the right-hand stroke of the *x*.[73]

63 From Novara: CLA III 406; VIII 1110; cf. E. Cau, 'Scrittura e cultura a Novara (secoli VIII–X)', *Ricerche Medievali* 6/9 (1971–4), 12 ff. and plate 5 f. From Vercelli: CLA IV 469.

64 CLA III 303a–f; L. Schiaparelli, *Il codice 490 della biblioteca capitolare di Lucca e la scuola scrittoria Lucchese (secoli VIII–IX)*, Studi e Testi 36 (Rome 1924); cf. A. Petrucci, 'Il Codice No. 490'.

65 Cf. also B. Pagnin, 'Formazione della scrittura carolina italiana', *Atti del Congresso internazionale di storia del diritto* 1 (Milan 1951) 245–66.

66 Cf. CLA III 381 and IV 420b.

67 Cencetti, *Lineamenti*, 93–106; idem, *Compendio*, 45 ff.

68 Ph. Lauer–Ch. Samaran, *Les diplômes originaux des Mérovingiens* (Paris 1908); ChLA XIII–XIV.

69 J. Vezin, 'Une nouvelle lecture de la liste de noms copiée au dos de l'ivoire Barberini', *Bull. archéol. Comité des travaux hist. et scientifiques*, n.s. 7 (1971) 19–53.

70 P. Gasnault–J. Vezin, *Documents comptables de Saint-Martin de Tours à l'époque mérovingienne*, Collection de documents inédits sur l'histoire de France (Paris 1975), with complete facs.; ChLA XVIII 659, and see plate 10 infra; on the paleography see J. Vezin, *Documents*, 159 ff.; J.-O. Tjäder in *Eranos* 75 (1977) 149 f, 159 ff.

71 *Theodosiani libri XVI*, edd. Th. Mommsen–P.M. Meyer, *Tabulae* (Berlin 1905) plate 5; E.A. Lowe, *Codices Lugdunenses Antiquissimi* (Lyon 1924) plates 5, 11, 17, 19; Robinson, *MSS 27 (S. 29) and 107 (129)*, plates 42 (1), 55 (2).

72 J. Vezin, 'Le *b* en ligature à droite dans les écritures du VIIe et du VIIIe siècles', *Journal des Savants* (1971) 261–86; J.-O. Tjäder, 'L'origine della *b* merovingica', in *Miscellanea in memoria di Giorgio Cencetti* (Turin 1973) 47–79 with reprod.

73 Already in the Avitus-Papyrus (s. VI); Steffens², *Lateinische Paläographie*, plate 24, line 3, J. Vezin in Gasnault–Vezin, *Documents*, 183 (1st form); in a Bobbio scribe: CLA III 324 (upper script).

In Francia too the cursive was drawn upon as a bookhand; the earliest extant example is the papyrus codex containing the homilies of bishop Avitus of Vienne, from the sixth century.[74] Here again it is noteworthy that the script in books generally takes on a more solid, more disciplined form (semi-cursive) than in the charters.[75] Two recurring features have characteristic significance: the script is either consciously stylised (usually including a large stock of ligatures) or, if it loses something of its élan and rapidity, it increasingly disintegrates into individual letters.

In Italy and France not only do bookhands of smaller proportions derive from the cursives, but there also come into existence new individual forms corresponding to the general tendencies: in this development analogy is partly at work, and in part new differentiations appear. In ligatures the top-stroke (flat at first) of *g* or *t* from the tip of the vertical can reach the following letter with an extra curve or crest towards the right.[76] On the other hand, the flat top-stroke of the letter *g*, when isolated or when in ligatures to the left, can be divided so that the left half continues below the line in two curves, whereas on the right only a tuft remains, which can again be attached to ligatures.[77] In this way the last new minuscule letter form is fashioned, the *g* with the round head.[78]

In cases where fixed writing patterns come into being, their fate is directly related to the continuity and level of organisation in the writing schools. Thus in an active scriptorium a calligraphic script which ultimately acquired a special polish in the hands of an individual artist can retain its normative value over generations. A stylised half-cursive of such type is the slender, somewhat leftward-leaning so-called Luxeuil type, named after the monastery founded AD 590 in the southern Vosges by the Irishman Columbanus.[79] This type, in which the *g*- and *t*- ligatures with crests stand out in the script, is attested from before AD 700 until the time of Boniface. A lengthy marginal addition in the best-known representative, the 'Luxeuil lectionary',[80] which is written in closely related but not regularised cursive, can actually provide an idea of the material from which it was constructed. In Luxeuil it was used with uncial (occasionally half-uncial) and very slim ornamented capitals (amongst them lozenge-shaped *o*) for dis-

---

74 CLA v 573; see previous n.
75 But even the New Testament was copied in a very undisciplined cursive (CLA v 679).
76 On this and what follows see the variant ways of forming the same ligature in Gasnault–Vezin, *Documents*, 184 f. (*ge, gi, gn, go*) and 188 (*te, ti, tr, tu*). The Avitus-Papyrus (note 74) also has the forms with the extra curve.
77 Cf. also Tjäder, *Nichtliter. lat. Pap.* 1, 105 (G 2–4).
78 In the *t* of Visigothic, Rhaetian, and Beneventan script the left part of the head-stroke has been transformed into a large bow.
79 CLA vi, p. xv ff.; Lowe, *Palaeographical Papers* 2, 389–98 and plate 74 ff. Further reprods: Zimmermann, *Vorkarol. Min.*, plates 45, 48 ff.; P. Salmon, *Le lectionnaire de Luxeuil.* Collectanea biblica Latina 9 (Vatic. 1952) 2; Steffens², *Lateinische Paläographie*, plate 25 (1).
80 CLA v 579; E.K. Rand, *Studies in the Script of Tours* 2 (Cambridge, Mass. 1934) plate 34; Salmon, *Lectionnaire de Luxeuil*, plate 21a.

quam

19. Luxeuil type

20. *ab*-type

21. *az*-type

play.[81] The type may also have been wider spread, or may have provided the stimulus towards similar formations, through the numerous daughter houses of Luxeuil, whose scribal art was held in great esteem.[82] One of the oldest manuscripts of the Corbie school, Paris, BN, lat. 17655,[83] was begun by a Luxeuil hand, and instances like Berne, Burgerbibliothek, MS. 199 (gospels),[84] and Hannover, Kestner-Museum, MS. Cul. I 48 (Ps. Hieronimus)[85] betray the

81 The style of the old decorative script held out in Luxeuil (which was destroyed by the Saracens in 732) until the time when caroline minuscule had long been written there; cf. CLA I 10; V 702.
82 A Gregory codex was written for bishop Desiderius of Ivrea (c. s. VII ex.); CLA III 300.
83 CLA V 671; Lowe, *Palaeographical Papers* 2, 381–8 with plate 71.   84 CLA VII 859.
85 CLA S 1700.

influence of the type; this can be recognised also in Bobbio and probably in several Veronese manuscripts as well.[86] Without a doubt the Luxeuil type was drawn upon as a model in the creation of a rougher writing style that was practised in the second half of the eighth century in Laon, probably in the nuns' convent of S Mariae and S Iohannis; this is called '*az*-type' after two of its distinctive letter forms.[87]

The transmission from Corbie (founded c. AD 660 on the Somme), which goes back to and even beyond c. AD 700, gives the impression that here – by contrast with the mother foundation Luxeuil – the route from the early half-cursive to the perfected caroline minuscule leads via an unclear succession of style groups which to some extent are not sharply distinguished one from another. The earliest Corbie manuscripts are written in semi-cursive.[88] In the eighth century late half-uncial with uncial *G* exists there in the so-called 'Leutchar type' (c. AD 765),[89] as well as minuscule that is still almost half-uncial, in which occasionally the peculiar features of the older half-cursive breaks through,[90] or which can develop into a kind of writing that is influenced by Insular ductus ('eN-type').[91]

Corbie, which from its foundation was closely connected with the royal court, is also the principal theatre for a peculiarly anachronistic movement in the prehistory of the carolingian reform whereby an adaptation of a pure charter hand was practised as a bookhand, but this was restricted to very few centres. It appears first in the mid-eighth century.[92] This script, constructed by borrowing from the script of the royal chancery, became at Corbie the *ab*-type that was practised there alongside the early carolingian 'Maurdramnus minuscule' beyond the turn of the century.[93] A similar script, the '*b*-type', distinguished above all by its use of the cc-*a*, was written at the end of the eighth century as a transitory type in Chelles, the convent ruled by Charlemagne's sister Gisela.[94] The script occupies a position at Chelles between the uncial (which is distin-

86 See above p. 102. This remark does not apply to the palimpsest MS XL (38) written in unfalsified type; CLA IV 497.

87 CLA VI, p. xviii. Reprod: Zimmermann, *Vorkarol. Min.*, plate 144 ff.

88 CLA V 624 ff., 671.   89 CLA VI, p. xxiii f.   90 E.g. CLA V 556.

91 CLA VI, p. xxv. Cf. also CLA V 648.

92 In St Gallen 214, of north-east French origin; CLA VII 924; Steffens², *Lateinische Paläographie*, plate 29 (2).

93 CLA VI, p. xxv f. The last dateable example, perhaps not copied at Corbie, is Geneva, Lat. 139, c. 830. It has been suggested that the ab-script was not written at St Pierre de Corbie but in a nearby nunnery; cf. H. Vanderhoven–F. Masai–P.B. Corbett, *Regula Magistri*. Les publications de Scriptorium 3 (Brussels, etc. 1953) 37; J. Vezin, 'La réalisation matérielle des manuscrits latins pendant le haut moyen âge', *Codicologica* 2 [Litterae textuales] (Leiden 1978) 27 n. 72; T.A.M. Bishop, 'The prototype of Liber glossarum', in *Medieval scribes, manuscripts & libraries. Essays presented to N.R. Ker* (London 1978) 69 ff. The problem needs further clarification.

94 Bischoff, *Mittelalterliche Studien* 1, 31; CLA VI, p. xxi f. cf., e.g. CLA VI 791 and 792. Noteworthy is the high number of authenticating strips in b-type found beneath the church of St André in Chelles: ChLA XVIII 669.

guished amongst other things by the trapezoid-shaped *N*) and the minuscule of the nuns Girbalda, Gislildis, and their fellow sisters.

These 'types' and stylised half-cursives accompany the early minuscule that ultimately distinguished itself decisively from the half-uncial through its proportions and its forms of *g* and *n*; although they bring the development forward step by step, nevertheless, through their conservatism, they were destined to be no more than dying offshoots. The later uniformity of the minuscule – a general term for alphabets of a basically similar type but formed differently as far as their details were concerned – probably had the ground prepared for it wherever calligraphic skill was less developed, wherever the less dynamic and perhaps more deliberate script becomes simpler, and where the habit of forming ligatures becomes less frequent. Such phenomena could extend themselves all the more as the level of literacy declined in this age. Our manuscript transmission before the last third of the eighth century is too sparse to provide an adequate conception of the range of script types that once existed[95] or to provide an idea of the simultaneous, gradual spread of the minuscule that had worked itself free from the cursive.[96] Only Tours and St Gall, by virtue of the material they have preserved, provide an insight into the organic development, by means of consolidating and simplifying, from half-cursive to caroline minuscule, a development whose course does not end in fixed 'types' and which is not interrupted by short-lived experiments.[97] But a distinct minuscule is also attested from other early manuscripts like the Gundohinus Gospel of AD 754 (from 'Vosevio')[98] and parts of Berne, Burgerbibliothek, MS 611.[99]

In Tours, where the steps in the clarification of the script can be followed, even the uncial *a* that is characteristic of caroline minuscule already appears alongside round *d* and *G* by the mid-century;[100] where it was used, it could recommend itself because of its clarity (by contrast with cc-*a*).

In the important Alemannic transit area that was able to mediate between Frankish and Italian tendencies, and which itself occupies an intermediate position, the charters of St Gall and the Breisgau are written already in a nascent

---

95 As in the types mentioned above p. 104 f.

96 A further form of minuscule must have become established in the seventh century, probably in Africa. See p. 97.

97 The last stage in this transformation can probably be seen at Novara in the late eighth century; cf. plates 4–7 in E. Cau, 'Scrittura e cultura a Novara'.

98 CLA VI 716; Steffens², *Lateinische Paläographie*, plate 37. Vosevio is located near Laon by B. Merlette, 'Écoles et bibliothèques, à Laon, du déclin de l'antiquité au développement de l'université', *Actes du 95e Congrès National des Sociétés Savantes*, Section de philologie et d'histoire jusqu'à 1610, I (Paris 1975) 26 f. Consequently the minuscule letter forms in the subscription of the chancellor Maginarius dated 769 (illustrated by L. Schiaparelli in *Arch. Stor. Ital.*, ser 7, 5 (1926) 17–19; Cencetti, *Lineamenti* 181) belong in a broader development.

99 CLA V 604 and VII, 9 f.

100 E.K. Rand, *Studies in the Script of Tours* 2 (Cambridge, Mass. 1934); CLA VI, p. xxvii ff. On uncial *a* cf. Bischoff, *Mittelalterliche Studien* I, 13 f. (CLA VIII 1157; X 1571).

minuscule as early as AD 750 to 760.[101] Around AD 760 the somewhat clumsy hand of the assiduous scribe Winithar[102] begins to appear in manuscripts and in one charter. In a charter of AD 758[103] the characteristic form of the round 'Alemannic minuscule' is already discernible, which appears in perfected form in the slightly younger St Gall MS 44.[104] These minuscule scripts can apparently slip into cursive.[105] On the whole, however, the early Alemannic minuscule is already so advanced that it can hold its own basically unaltered in the face of competition from the caroline minuscule until AD 830.[106] In Bavaria the manuscript evidence begins first c. AD 770, but with a minuscule already so developed that hardly any earlier clearly cursive forms can be supposed, and around the same time a pure Italian (probably Veronese) minuscule exerted its influence in Regensburg.[107]

The ground gained by the early minuscule was at the expense of half-uncial, which was less used in those places where uncial had not been retained. A mixture of genera through adoption of the cursive elements or minuscule letters into the half-uncial seems to have happened rarely in the eighth century; there are examples from Verona and Tours.[108] Steps that led to the gradually emerging awareness of the goal of a bookhand free from the cursive appeared in many places;[109] and in spite of the great variety of its styles of script the pre-carolingian period too prepared the ground for the harmonisation of writing that culminated in the new standardisation of the carolingian epoch. From the individual monasteries local scripts were spread through daughter foundations or through the exchange of monks; the regularisation of the canonical and monastic rules, the appointment of bishops, the organisation of the palace school, and the increasing means of communication in the early carolingian period were able to complete this process.

In order to account for the origin of the 'caroline minuscule' (which is primarily a generic term for a situation that was reached as a result of related tendencies and changes of forms) it was not necessary to postulate either 'direct descent from the half-uncial'[110] or a harking back to the highly disparate forms

---

101 Cf. ChLA I 46, 48, 50 ff.
102 761: ChLA I 57; Steffens², *Lateinische Paläographie*, plate 43a; Chroust, *Monumenta* 1, 14, plate 1 f.; CLA VII 893a; Bruckner, *Scriptoria* 2, plate 2a; Kirchner, *Script. Lat. libr.*², plate 35b. In Winithar's script too uncial *a* and *d* predominate.   103 ChLA I 51.
104 Chroust, *Monumenta* 1, 14, plate 3; Bruckner, *Scriptoria* 2, plate 1.
105 Cf. e.g. Bruckner, *Scriptoria* 2, plate 10a.   106 Ibid., passim.
107 Bischoff, *Schreibschulen* 1, 60 ff. and 172 ff.
108 Verona: CLA IV 502; Tours: Rand, *Studies* 2, plate 23 ff.; CLA V 682.
109 H. Steinacker, 'Zum Liber Diurnus und zur Frage nach dem Ursprung der Frühminuskel', *Miscellanea Francesco Ehrle* 4. Studi e Testi 40 (Rome 1924) 105–76.
110 E.A. Lowe in CLA VI, p. xii. The view expressed there (and in Bischoff, *Paläographie*, col. 413; offprint, col. 35) that the Maurdramnus type, the earliest calligraphic caroline minuscule, is the transformation of half-uncial resulting from the substitution of the crucial letters, is invalid. The Maurdramnus scribe in Berlin, Theol. Lat. fol. 354 (CLA VIII 1067a.b.) was

of older and later half-uncial from the fifth and sixth centuries, which in part are attested only from the East and from Africa, but which are reckoned to have disappeared almost without trace from the libraries of the West.[111]

5.   *Beneventan*

The Beneventana, the vigorous south-Italian script that developed from a rounded, richly-ligatured Italian minuscule of pre-carolingian type, was a distinctive script that lasted five hundred years from the late eighth century to the thirteenth.[112] Its chief centres were Beneventum, Bari, and Monte Cassino, which had been reconstructed after the Lombard destruction of AD 717 or 718, and whose monks, expelled because of a second destruction by the Saracens, fled in AD 883 first to Teano, later to Capua, to return finally in AD 949. The situation of the scripts in southern Italy for the greater part of the eighth century is unknown; but a very great similarity between early script from Nonantola (near Modena), which until well into the ninth century cultivated its own rounded and specifically ligatured script, and that from Monte Cassino makes it plausible to suggest that there existed a relationship of dependence; because the Nonantola script is one of a number of rounded north-Italian scripts of the eighth/ninth century the type may have passed from there to Monte Cassino.[113]

The spread of the Beneventan script type, which developed its characteristic features in the south, also made such advances in Campania that the transmission from there (perhaps with the exception of Naples)[114] seems already in the ninth century to be exclusively Beneventan. The area in which the script was written eventually bounded by a roughly north-south line from Chieti to the

trying to supply the gap of a half-uncial manuscript in an appropriate script. Lowe repeats his thesis of half-uncial origin in CLA VIII p. x.

111   This was G. Cencetti's theory in 'Postilla nuova a un problema paleografico vecchio: l'origine della minuscola "carolina"', *Nova Historia* 7 (1955) 1–24, esp. p. 15 ff.; idem, *Lineamenti*, 183–9; idem, *Compendio*, 67 f.

112   E.A. Lowe, *The Beneventan Script* (Oxford 1914); second ed. prepared and enlarged by Virginia Brown 1, 2. Sussidi Eruditi 33 (Rome 1980); E.A. Lowe, *Scriptura Beneventana* 1/2 (Oxford 1929); Cencetti, *Lineamenti*, 126–34; *Compendio*, 58–60; G. Cavallo, 'Struttura e articolazione della minuscola beneventana libraria tra i secoli X–XII', *Studi Medievali*, ser 3, 11 (1970) 343–68; idem, 'Aspetti della produzione libraria nell'Italia meridionale longobarda', in Cavallo, *Libri*, 99–129, 270–84; F. Newton, 'Beneventan scribes and subscriptions', *The Bookmark* 43 (Chapel Hill 1973) 1–35.

113   G. Cencetti, 'Scriptoria e scritture nel monachesimo benedettino', *Il monachesimo nell'alto medioevo e la formazione della civiltà occidentale*, Settimane 4 (Spoleto 1957) 206–11; here historical arguments are also presented. G. Cavallo ('Struttura', 344 n. 5) considers that influence in the opposite direction should not be ruled out; M. Palma, 'Nonantola e il Sud, Contributo alla storia della scrittura libraria nell'Italia dell'ottavo secolo', *Scrittura e civiltà* 3 (1979) 77–88, with 9 plates; idem, 'Alle origini del "tipo di Nonantola": nuove testimonianze meridionali', ibid. 7 (1983) 141–9, with 8 plates.

114   The manuscripts Naples, Bibl. Naz., Lat. 4 (earlier Vienna 750) and XVI.A.9, both in caroline minuscule, appear to come from there.

Gulf of Gaeta. The script was common there also in more cursive versions as a charter hand.[115]

The Beneventan tends from the beginning to rounded and flowing forms with delicate, moderately bold strokes. The bases of the shafts are slightly turned to the right. From the tenth century on it attains its distinctive character. The cc-*a* is closed like *oc*; *c* is frequently two-tiered; the *e*, whose large bow is replaced by two bows, is regularly so; the bar of the *t* is divided: its left half consists of a large bow that rests on the line, at the upper end of which the shaft begins, while the right half of the bar is a separate horizontal stroke; the upper and lower halves of the 3-shaped *g* are roughly equal in size. The use of *I*-longa and of the ligatures is subject to certain rules: *I*-longa is used at the beginning of a word (except before the letters with ascenders) and as a semi-vowel; *t* with *j* extending under the line is obligatory for ordinary *ti*, whereas the 8-shaped ligature form with *i* is used for assibilated *ti*.[116] Other distinguishing features are some abbreviations like *ej* with cross-stroke through the *j* (for *eius*) and the punctuation system with the special question-mark.[117]

Within the Beneventan bookscript several local styles develop.[118] Best-known is that of Monte Cassino, which organises what are at first delicate, barely thickened shafts and bows into a refined interplay of short broad strokes: thereby the shafts of *i n u m* are not traced in one movement but are formed each from two slanted, discretely curved rectangles, of which, in the cases of *i*, *n* and *m*, the upper, in *u* the lower is somewhat longer. Bows in which the full pressure of the pen is on the diagonal stroke seem angular in construction; thus closely connected bows can, with slight contact (different from gothic script) appear to grow together. The strong compactness presented by the written line is enhanced by the fact that the horizontals of *e*, *f*, *g*, *r*, *t* can appear like a continuous binding line. This 'mature' style makes its appearance in Monte Cassino in the early eleventh century and reaches its highpoint under the abbots Desiderius (1058–87) and Oderisius (1087–1108). In the twelfth century the form fossilises with exaggerated mannerisms. Through the influence of Monte Cassino this style was imitated in the whole region.

In Bari, probably already in the late tenth century, the more rounded type that came to predominate in Apulia (Bari type) was created, from the same raw material. In this the shafts are not broken, while the stroke remains more even than in Monte Cassino. Among the letters that differ are short *f* and *s*, among the ligatures *fi* with semi-circular shaped *i*; the two-tiered *c* is even more frequently used. Absent from the appearance of the script are the continuous binding lines;

---

115 Reprod: *Arch. Pal. Ital.* 13, Fasc. 58. Cf. A. Gallo, 'Contributo allo studio delle scritture meridionali nell'alto medio evo', *Bull. dell'Istituto Storico Italiano* 47 (1932) 333–50.
116 Cf. Lowe, *Beneventan Script*, 148; Lowe, *Palaeographical Papers* 1, 20 f.
117 See p. 170.   118 Here I follow G. Cavallo, 'Struttura e articolazione'.

above the abbreviation stroke there often stands a point. A certain relationship of form that exists with rounded Greek scripts[119] could be explained by the re-establishment of Greek rule in Bari in AD 871.

A peculiarity of the Beneventan region are liturgical rolls,[120] above all for the Easter vigil ('Exultet rotuli'); out of these the liturgy was sung from the pulpit, in the course of the reading the illustrations that were inserted upside-down in relation to the text were gradually unfurled to face the congregation.[121]

Monte Cassino supported Latin monasticism in Dalmatia, which was con- nected by commercial contacts with southern Italy, and the church of Bari possessed diocesan rights on the opposite coast of the Adriatic. Thus from the tenth to the thirteenth century Beneventan became the regional script in Ragusa, Split, Traù, and Zara, and the remains that survive from there are divided between the two types.[122]

Where it had predominated in Italy the script yielded generally to the gothic in the thirteenth century. All the same, even from the fourteenth to the sixteenth centuries there were still scribes competent in the Beneventan.[123]

The attractive power exerted by Monte Cassino, and its radiation throughout the whole Benedictine world, created connections that have left their mark on the text transmission and, in sporadic cases, on the script as well.[124]

119 Cavallo, 'Struttura', 355, has greatly circumscribed the theories of A. Petrucci, 'Note ed ipotesi sulla origine della scrittura barese', *Bull. dell'Arch. Pal. Ital.*, n.s. 4/5 (1958/9) 111 f. and A. Pratesi, 'Influence della scrittura greca nella formazione della beneventana del tipo di Bari', *La Chiesa Greca in Italia dal'VIII al XIV secolo* (Padua 1973) 1095–1109.

120 See above p. 32

121 Myrtilla Avery, *The Exultet Rolls of South Italy* (Princeton–London–The Hague 1936); H. Belting, *Studien zur beneventanischen Malerei*. Forsch. z. Kungstgesch. u. christl. Archäol. 7 (Wiesbaden 1968), reprods. 201 ff., 246; G. Cavallo, *Rotoli di Exultet dell'Italia Meridionale* (Bari 1973).   122 V. Novak, *Latinska paleografija* (Belgrade 1952) 141–65.

123 M. Inguanez, 'La scrittura Beneventana in codici e documenti dei secoli XIV e XV', *Scritti di paleografia e diplomatica in onore di Vincenzo Federici* (Florence 1945) 309–14 and 8 plates; V. Brown, 'The survival of beneventan script: sixteenth century liturgical codices from Benedictine monasteries in Naples', *Monastica* 1. Scritti raccolti in memoria del XV centenario di S. Benedetto (480–1980), Miscellanea Cassinese 44 (Monte Cassino 1981) 237–355, with illustr.

124 A Beneventan scribe was active at Fleury c. 1000, and his writing gradually lost its characteristic ductus; another (s. XI) in northern France; cf. Lowe, *Palaeographical Papers* 2, 479. A scribe more skilled in Beneventan writes a very personal hybrid minuscule in Clm 15,826 (f. 45 ff., s. XI) cf. Lowe, *Beneventan Script*, 262. Montecassino MS 580 is the work of a scribe accustomed to both beneventan and caroline minuscule; cf. H.M. Willard, 'Cod. Casin. 580 T, Lexicon prosodiacum saec. XI', *Casinensia* 1 (Monte Cassino 1929) 297–304 with plate. In contrast the chronicler Peter the Deacon wrote a careless and undistinguished minuscule, but not, as was earlier thought, a decorative and correct beneventan; cf. P. Meyvaert, 'The autographs of Peter the Deacon', *Bull. John Rylands Library* 38 (1955) 114 ff. with plates. Further evidence for the closeness of the two scripts in S. Tristano, 'Scrittura beneventana e scrittura carolina in manoscritti dell'Italia meridionale', *Scrittura e Civiltà* 3 (1979) 89–150, with 4 plates. The occasional occurrence of Beneventan interrogation signs may imply copying of a Beneventan exemplar; cf. Lowe, *Beneventan Script*, 63 ff. and below 170.

6. *The perfection and triumph of caroline minuscule*

When Charlemagne came to power fully developed minuscule scripts already existed alongside many types of half-cursive in various regions of the Frankish kingdom, and likewise in the Lombard kingdom conquered in AD 744. Some scriptoria like Corbie, with the Maurdramnus type, were in advance of the others in calligraphic discipline. Without any doubt Charlemagne's reform of ecclesiastical Latin culture, which tried to restore the bastardised language, also strengthened the tendency toward discipline, order, and harmony that was present in the script, and it is on the whole probable that the more advanced style and successful solutions found in one monastery were taken over by others as a model in the search for a clearer and more balanced script. Charlemagne loved scholarship and art and at his palace the leading intellects of the kingdom came together; a library was assembled for him, and it is inconceivable that fine scripts and able calligraphers would not have found recognition and encouragement there. On the contrary, from the verse dedications in the de luxe manuscripts written under Charlemagne's eyes by Godescalc and Dagulf (who is praised in turn by his pupil Deodatus)[1] there speaks, besides loyalty, the pride of the artist.

Godescalc wrote his evangelistary between AD 781 and 783 and it appears possible that in the school in which he learned the beautifully harmonious script of his dedicatory verses the teachers of the early carolingian groups of scribes in Lorsch and Metz were also trained.[2] The significant feature of the first phase of carolingian writing, however, is freedom in the formation of the script in local schools.[3] Even the principle of the unitary alphabet, which in the classical scripts was generally respected, is only rarely observed, for example, by some scribes of the Maurdramnus type, in the Theodulf Bibles,[4] and in parts of the Dagulf Psalter.[5] Rather it is a part of the characteristics of a house style in most cases that a special selection of double forms and ligatures was admitted or required. Because they contributed to the clarity of the script, certain improvements were carried out: the general introduction of the small uncial *a* and the clear distinction between the abbreviations for *-ur* and *-us*: *-t²* (*-tur*) and *-t'* (*-tus*); the symbol for *-ur* was probably invented in the palace circle c. AD 800. The use of the question-mark, which immediately took on very varying forms, was first adopted at this period.[6]

1 MGH Poetae 1, 91–5. Godescalc-Evangelistary (781–3): Koehler, *Karol. Min.* 2, Text, 22 ff., plate 1 ff.; Steffens², *Lateinische Paläographie*, plate 45a. Dagulf-Psalter (before 795): Koehler, ibid., text, 42 ff.; plate 31 ff.; R. Beer, *Monumenta palaeographica Vindobonensia* 1 (Leipzig 1910) plate 17 ff.

2 B. Bischoff, *Lorsch im Spiegel seiner Handschriften.* Münchener Beiträge, Beiheft (Munich 1974) 26 f.

3 B. Bischoff, 'Die karolingische Minuskel', *Karl der Große, Werk und Wirkung* (Exhibition catalogue, Aachen 1965) 207–10. In general cf. also Cencetti, *Lineamenti*, 166 ff.; idem, *Compendio*, 66 ff. 4 CLA v 576; vi 768. 5 CLA x 1504. 6 Cf. below p. 170.

22. Beneventan

23. Carolingian minuscule

24. Early gothic

25. The formation of the letters in Gothic 'Textus fractus'

In Charlemagne's time the scripts in use were, on the whole, still lacking in uniformity,[7] especially since distinct 'pre-caroline' regional styles existed particularly in the Lake Constance region, in Chur, and in parts of Italy.[8] The Alemannic style, richly attested from St Gall and Reichenau, and to which Constance too probably contributed, is recognisable by its broad rounded strokes, the frequent ligature of *nt* (within the word), and the more recherché ligatures of letters with *f* (*fr, fu*) retained by some scribes;[9] it was written in masterly fashion by the Reichenau librarian Reginbert (†AD 846).

The beautifully formed Rhaetian script, with its emphasis on the breaking of the shafts and the distinctive *t* with divided bar that also appears in Visigothic and Beneventan script, reaches its highpoint in the sacramentary written for bishop Remedius of Chur (c. AD 800), which is decorated with intricate initials.[10]

At this stage of the consolidation process in caroline minuscule only some of the schools preserving their local style succeeded in attaining to the perfected and simplified, regularised script, while the rest tried to do so, but in principle continued to write their own generally round, bolder, richly ligatured scripts. In the productive scriptorium of Fleury was created a new family of very stylised hybrids of minuscule and Celtic Insular script, under influences that derived from Brittany seemingly shortly before AD 800.[11]

Only from the beginning of the second phase, which dates from AD 810–20, did most scriptoria – even those that had held on to the above-mentioned regional styles – accomplish the decisive changeover to more sober scripts. Such scripts were also written in the atelier and scriptorium of the palace under Louis the Pious.[12] Slimmer, rightward slanting scripts became predominant, and perhaps the influence of Tours, whence in the ninth century beautifully written Bibles and other manuscripts were sent to many other monasteries and churches, is in no small way responsible.[13]

7 B. Bischoff, 'Panorama der Handschriftenüberlieferung aus der Zeit Karls des Großen', *Karl der Große, Lebenswerk und Nachleben* 2 (Düsseldorf 1965) 233–254; repr. in *Mittelalterliche Studien* 3, 39–54. (Italian version in Cavallo, *Libri*, 47–72, 243–64); on which see *Scriptorium* 22 (1968) 306–14.

8 For Italy see below p. 102 f. Other scripts of s. VIII and s. VIII–IX which Batelli, *Lezioni*[3], 164 ff. classifies as 'types' are not clearly enough distinguished. Burgundian scripts of this period, but not only that script, often bow or prolong the ascender of *h* to the left (cf. for example CLA VI 717b, 721; but also, e.g. CLA VII 884, 931, IX 1360).

9 St Gallen: Bruckner, *Scriptoria* 2; Chroust, *Monumenta* I, 19. Reichenau: Chroust, *Monumenta* II, 10, 4 f. and 8 f.; Baesecke, *Lichtdrucke*, plates 31–3. Constance: K. Löffler, 'Zur Frage einer Konstanzer Schreibschule in karolingischer Zeit', *Palaeographia Latina* 5 (1927) 5–27 and plate 1/2.

10 CLA VII 936; Chroust, *Monumenta* I 17, plate 7; Bruckner, *Scriptoria* 1, plate 6f.

11 CLA V 568 and VII, p. 6; O. Homburger, *Die illustrierten Handschriften der Burgerbibliothek Bern* (Bern 1962) plates 9–12 and colour plate 2. In addition CLA IX 1380 and Bern A 91/7 + Paris, BN, Lat. 9332 (cf. Homburger, 40).

12 Cf. B. Bischoff, 'Die Hofbibliothek unter Ludwig dem Frommen', in *Medieval Learning and Literature, Essays presented to Richard William Hunt* (Oxford 1976) 3–22 and plate 1/2; repr. in *Mittelalterliche Studien* 3, 170–86.   13 E. Lesne, *Livres*, 159 ff. Cf. below p. 208.

In northern Italy[14] Verona had already, before AD 800, adopted a very clear, composed script[15] which was then practised even after the time of archdeacon Pacificus (†AD 846), who had 218 volumes written for the library.[16] In other places there predominated around and after 800 still round and richly ligatured scripts with individual forms like *r* with upturned shoulder-stroke[17] but on the whole the reception of the simplified minuscule was completed during the second quarter of the ninth century. In Nonantola, whose round script had perhaps become the prototype of the Beneventan in the eighth century,[18] the local type with tall *e* and pronounced *r* ligatures was retained even longer.[19] In Rome, non-liturgical manuscripts were still being written in uncial in the ninth century; after the middle of the century canon-law manuscripts were produced there[20] (now in minuscule), probably in the circle of the curia.[21]

In explaining how caroline minuscule took root in Italy the influence which the activity of non-Italian personalities brought about can hardly be underestimated: we know about the missions of Dungal[22] in 825 and Hildemar c. 840;[23] it is notable also that a Tours scribe collaborated in the writing of the north-Italian MS, Vercelli, Bibl. Cap., CIV(47),[24] and a Frank collaborated on the Biblioteca Valicelliana Codex A 5, which was written in Rome.[25]

With the change of style the cc-*a* and the ligature *nt* (which is replaced by *NT*) gradually disappear. In some places, for instance in many manuscripts of the school of Tours, the new alphabet without variant forms appears now to be accepted as the ideal. Numerous other schools come close to this ideal at times.

14 Cf. also Pagnin, 'Formazione della scrittura carolina italiana'.

15 CLA VIII 1057 and 1076.

16 Teresa Venturini, *Ricerche paleografiche intorno all'arcidiacono Pacifico di Verona* (Verona 1929); G. Turrini, *Millennium scriptorii Veronensis dal IVo al XVo secolo* (Verona 1967) plates 15–17.

17 Ehrle-Liebaert, *Specimina*, plate 10; Chatelain, *Pal. class. lat.*, plate 168; cf. Bischoff 'Panorama', plate 251.   18 See p. 102.

19 G. Cencetti, 'Scriptoria e scritture nel monachesimo benedettino,' *Settimane* 4 (Spoleto 1957) 206 ff. with plate (also in Cavallo, *Libri*, 73 ff., 264 ff.); *Catal. manoscr. datati* 1, plates 1–3.

20 Rome, Bibl. Vallic. B 25². Cf. also the uncial corrections in Vatic., Reg. Lat. 1040 (CLA I 112).

21 Paola Supino Martini, 'Carolina romana e minuscola romanesca', *Studi Medievali*, ser 3, 15 (1974) 772 ff., 781; Fl. Mütherich, 'Manoscritti romani e miniatura carolingia', *Rome e l'età carolingia* (Rome 1976) 79–86 with reprod. Cf. also Cl. Leonardi, 'Anastasio Bibliotecario e l'ottavo concilio ecumenico', *Studi Medievali*, ser 3, 8 (1967) 59 ff., esp. 102 ff., with plate.

22 Mirella Ferrari, 'In Papia conveniant ad Dungalum', *It. Med. e Um.* 15 (1972) 1 ff.; B. Bischoff, 'Die Bibliothek im Dienst der Schule', *Settimane* 19 (Spoleto 1972) 410 ff. (repr. in *Mittelalterliche Studien* 3, 230 f.); J. Vezin, 'Observations sur l'origine des manuscrits légués par Dungal à Bobbio', in *Paläographie* (1981) 125–44.

23 L. Traube, 'Textgeschichte der Regula S. Benedicti', *Abh. K. Bayer. Akad. Wiss.*, 3 Kl., 21/3 (1898) 640 ff.

24 A. Wilmart, 'Manuscrits de Tours identifiés ou proposés', *Rev. Bénéd.* 45 (1933) 162, believed that the first (turonian) quaternio was sent from Tours as a model (followed by Lesne, *Livres*, 164 and 341 f.); however, the colour of the ink proves the unity of production.

25 Fl. Mütherich, 'Manoscritti romani', 82.

Other scriptoria, in contrast, include variant forms: open-*a* with two points (presumably taken over from Anglo-Saxon script), and uncial *d* and *N* are never banished from the minuscule; French schools (for example Fleury, Auxerre) show a preference for half-uncial *a* in the minuscule. The majuscule forms *s* and *v* also re-establish themselves in the ninth century; *s* at the end of a word, *v* for *u* at the end of a word, and less often at the beginning.

Simultaneously with the perfection of the caroline minuscule the majuscule scripts, which in the early carolingian era still appear partly mixed or greatly distorted, were reformed in accordance with good old models. Tours and several other scriptoria also use half-uncial as a display script.[26]

The early and middle carolingian era is distinguished by its literary culture[27] and calligraphic taste, and until the third quarter of the ninth century and beyond many local styles can be recognised and described (if their transmission is favourable), especially if attention is also paid to the ornamentation. Tours,[28] which retained its style of script almost unchanged, is an exception. The majority of the well-known French schools change their styles in the course of the ninth century, for example, Corbie,[29] Rheims,[30] Lyons,[31] St Denis,[32] St Germain-des-Prés.[33] Fleury[34] and Auxerre (St Germain) seem to have been in very close contact in the middle third of the ninth century, so that their house-styles cannot always be sharply distinguished. St Amand, whence Arn, when he was made bishop of Salzburg (785–821) had summoned scribes,[35] became after the mid century the main centre of the Franco-Saxon style also cultivated at St Bertin and Arras; its script achieves an almost typographic regularity.[36] In contrast, manuscripts of other centres with once great libraries, like St Riquier, have been wholly or almost entirely lost.

26 See above p. 77.   27 Lesne, *Livres*, passim.

28 E.K. Rand, *Studies in the script of Tours* 1/2 (Cambridge, Mass. 1929/1934); Köhler, *Karol. Min.* 1; B. Fischer and A. Bruckner, in *Die Bibel von Moutier-Grandval* (Bern 1971) 50 ff., 99 ff.

29 CLA VI, p. xxiv ff.; Bischoff, *Mittelalterliche Studien* 1, 49–63; T.A.M. Bishop, 'The script of Corbie: a criterion', in *Essays presented to G.I. Lieftinck* 1 (Amsterdam 1972) 9 ff.

30 *Catal. mss. datés* 5, plate 211 (and plate 2 Hautvillers); F.M. Carey, 'The Scriptorium of Rheims during the archbishopric of Hincmar', in *Classical and Mediaeval Studies in honor of Edward Kennard Rand* (New York 1938) 41–60. The very richly attested Rheims script of the second half of the century avoids in a peculiar fashion the strengthening of the ascenders (or else allows them to disappear) and also sets the *a* steeply. The same traits are to be found in the affiliated school which produced the Bible of S. Paolo fuori le mura.

31 *Catal. mss. datés* 5, plate 3; 6, plates 3b, 4, 6 to 8; CLA VI, p. xiv.

32 CLA VI, p. xxvi.

33 B. Bischoff in *Der Stuttgarter Bilderpsalter* 2 (Stuttgart 1968) 21 ff.

34 CLA VI, p. xviii ff.

35 CLA X, p. viii ff.; Bischoff, *Schreibschulen* 2, 61 ff.

36 L. Delisle, *Memoires sur d'anciens sacramentaires* (Paris 1886) plates 6 and 11; *Écr. lat.*, Nr. 82; cf. J. Deshusses, 'Chronologie des grands sacramentaires de Saint-Amand', *Rev. Bén.* 87 (1977) 230–7.

Of the ninth- and early tenth-century Breton manuscripts[37] in caroline script only Orléans, Bibl. Munic., MS 221 (193) – one of the scribes is Junobrus – shows intermingling of the Insular *g*. The Breton script is often conspicuous either for its angular forms or for particularly developed rounding. It can betray itself through Insular abbreviations and, not infrequently, through Breton glosses. Also characteristic are the relatively numerous subscriptions in hisperic Latin, whose other remains have been transmitted principally from Brittany.

In northern Italy the carolingian writing schools of the monasteries of Bobbio[38] and Nonantola,[39] Verona[40] Novara,[41] and several other episcopal cities were especially active.

In Germany the schools of the German-Saxon area: Fulda,[42] Mainz,[43] and Würzburg[44] occupy a special position. Here the caroline minuscule made its entry around the turn of the century. In Würzburg the Insular hand dies out c. AD 820; in Fulda, where occasionally Anglo-Saxon and caroline hands work on the same manuscript,[45] and where abbot Hrabanus himself wrote a hand more Anglo-Saxon than caroline,[46] the Insular script disappeared only after AD 850. The training by the Anglo-Saxons was so lasting in effect that the habit of using their cut of the quill and their way of holding it also gives an unmistakable appearance to the caroline minuscule in Fulda, Mainz, and in part Würzburg.[47] Under this influence the script is erect, occasionally even inclined towards the left, more angular and formed with sharper points and fuller bows than the normal minuscule. The ascenders terminate in wedges; in Mainz they actually

---

37 A number are named by W.M. Lindsay, 'Breton scriptoria: their Latin abbreviation symbols', *Zentralbl. f. Bibliothekswesen* 29 (1912) 264–72; L. Fleuriot, *Dictionnaire des gloses en Vieux Breton* (Paris 1964) 4 ff. and plates 3–8.

38 P. Collura, *La Precarolina e la Carolina a Bobbio*, Fontes Ambrosiani 22 (repr. Florence 1965); C. Cipolla, *Collezione paleografica bobbiese* 1, text, plates (Milan 1907).

39 See above p. 109.   40 See above p. 115.

41 E. Cau, 'Scrittura e cultura a Novara (secoli VIII–X)', *Ricerche Medievali* 6/9 (1971/4) 1–87 and plate.   42 Lehmann, *Erforschung* 1, 213 ff.

43 W.M. Lindsay–P. Lehmann, 'The (early) Mayence scriptorium', *Palaeographia Latina* 4 (1925) 5 ff.

44 B. Bischoff–J. Hofmann, *Libri Sancti Kyliani* (Würzburg 1952).

45 E.g., G.I. Lieftinck, 'Le ms. d'Aulu-Gelle à Leeuwarden exécuté à Fulda en 836', *Bull. dell'Arch. Pal. Ital.*, n.s. 1 (1955) 11–17 and plate.

46 H. Butzmann, 'Der Ezechiel-Kommentar des Hrabanus Maurus und seine älteste Handschrift', *Bibliothek und Wissenschaft* 1 (1964) 20 f. and plates 10 and 11 ('Korrekturen von x'); Herrad Spilling, 'Das Fuldaer Scriptorium zur Zeit des Hrabanus Maurus', in R. Kottje–H. Zimmermann (edd), *Hrabanus Maurus*. Akad. Wiss. u. Lit. Mainz, Abh. d. geistes- u. sozialwiss. Kl., Einzelveröffentlichung 4 (Wiesbaden 1982) 165–91.

47 Examples: *S. Bonifatii et Lulli Epistolae*, ed. by M. Tangl, MGH, *Epp. sel. 1* (Berlin 1916) plate 1 (probably from Fulda) and 3 (from Mainz); B. Bischoff–J. Hofmann, *Libri Sancti Kyliani*, reprod. 5 f. (from Würzburg). Even the Bamberg sacramentary from Fulda dating from after 993 shows unmistakable traces of this Insular tradition (Chroust, *Monumenta* I 22, plate 10); cf. also ibid., II 4, plate 6b (from Echternach).

form small oblong triangles. The shafts that end on the line are in some manuscripts even broken towards the right in characteristic fashion.

In several other German carolingian writing schools a rich transmission provides informative insights into the succession of styles, and the decisive rôle that individual personalities played in the efforts of the scriptorium is often evident. In Cologne,[48] for example, archbishop Hildebald (785–819), in Reichenau the librarian Reginbert,[49] in St Gall amongst other abbots Grimalt (†872) and Hartmut (872–83).[50] In Lorsch, where book production was extensive, the greatest activity took place in the time of Adalung (804–37), who was simultaneously abbot of St Vaast in Arras.[51] In Weissenburg Otfrid, a pupil of Hrabanus, seems to have directed the collecting of bible commentaries which he himself expanded by the additon of marginal commentaries on various books.[52]

In south-east Germany bishops Arbeo (764–84), Hitto (811/12–36), and Anno (854–75) of Freising,[53] Baturich (817–47), bishop of Regensburg and abbot of the monastery of St Emmeram,[54] and the archbishops Arn (785–821), Adalram (821–36), and Liuphram (836–59) of Salzburg[55] spurred on their respective scriptoria. The monastic school of Benedictbeuern can also be mentioned.[56] The Salzburg school is distinguished by the fact that already before Arn's time it had become a centre where west-Frankish script could take root through the activities of French scribes (from St Denis)[57] and did so again when Arn brought with him some scribes from St Amand.[58] Besides these can be distinguished numerous other localised or unlocalised groups.

7. The development of handwriting from the late ninth to the twelfth century

After the demise of 'Insular' scripts in Germany and Brittany the realm of caroline minuscule, both as bookhand and also often as charter-hand, extended from Catalonia to East Saxony and Dalmatia, from Denmark to east of Rome. In southern Italy by contrast the canon of a new style of writing, the Beneventana, developed. The impulses received and the cultural unity on the one hand, and on the other a decline of the inner vitality of the script prevented a new disintegration of writing after the partitions of the empire. In the following centuries caroline minuscule from its broad heartland conquered England as well as

---

48 L.W. Jones, *The Script of Cologne from Hildebald to Hermann* (Cambridge, Mass. 1932). On the 'nuns' manuscripts' (from Chelles) see now Bischoff, *Mittelalterliche Studien* 1, 16–34.

49 See above n. 9; K. Preisendanz, 'Reginbert von der Reichenau', *Heidelberger Jahrbücher* (1952/3) 1 ff. 50 Bruckner, *Scriptoria* 3, 24 ff.; Chroust, *Monumenta* 1, 14 ff.

51 Bischoff, *Lorsch*, 27 ff.

52 W. Kleiber, *Otfrid von Weißenburg* (Bern–Munich 1971) 136 ff., colour plate 2 and plate 30 ff.

53 Bischoff, *Schreibschulen* 1, 58 ff. 54 Bischoff, ibid., 172 ff.

55 Chroust, *Monumenta* 1, 7; Bischoff, ibid., 2, 53–61. 56 Bischoff, ibid. 1, 22 ff.

57 Facsimile: K. Forstner, *Das Verbrüderungsbuch von St. Peter in Salzburg*, Codices selecti 51 (Graz 1974) 21 f. 58 Cf. CLA x, p. viii ff.

Spain, whose inherited scripts were finally driving out the traditional scripts. From Germany this script was exported to the large areas won to Christianity from Salzburg, Regensburg, and Passau, and from Hamburg-Bremen, Magdeburg, and Gnesen.

In German caroline minuscule signs of a deeper transformation of script are already visible in the late ninth century. Up to that time writing was dominated – despite conscious calligraphic stylisations – by free, spontaneous formation; each letter, and each part of a letter, was formed according to its natural function in the whole. This harmonic form now disintegrated.[59] The swing was checked and restricted, the individual parts of the letters were put together in an inflexible and clumsy way, and reconstructed in part according to false analogies. Bows now became claw-shaped (for example in *h*, *m*), other curves were inflated,[60] a gentle curve becomes angular (in *r*), in place of the easy lowering and raising of the pen little additional strokes become visible (for example in *i*, *m*), at the end of a word even horizontal end-strokes were tacked on. The few remaining old cursive ligatures were no longer formed fluently but hesitantly, and misunderstandings of the forms led to imitations, especially *rt* written as *st* with an added horn. The ligature *ct*, whose parts were again separated, called forth inorganic imitation.[61] The impoverishment of the script manifests itself around the same time in the deliberate renunciation of cursive in the German royal chancery.[62]

In southern Germany St Gall appears to take the lead in this development; thanks to its rich holdings it can serve as a model case for the demonstration of the individual processes,[63] especially since, thanks to its influence in the period of reconstruction in south Germany after AD 955, it provided norms and forms.[64] In the St Gall scriptorium various levels of style are observed which can be defined in three grades:[65] calligraphic bookhand, ordinary functional script (for library manuscripts), and school style. This gradation of scripts recalls that achieved in Ireland already in the eighth century. Without a doubt Irish influence is present in the appearance of the two lower grades, in the preparation and composition of abbreviations, and in the introduction of ligatures with attached *i* and open *a* under the line. The possibility for this was provided in St Gall by the activity of the Irish teacher Móengal in the second half of the ninth century.[66] These forms too were widely disseminated.[67]

In the tenth century this stylistic phase, which began in the early ninth

---

59 Cf., e.g., Bruckner, *Scriptoria* 3, plates 19a, 26a, 30a.
60 Natalia Daniel, *Handschriften des zehnten Jahrhunderts aus der Freisinger Dombibliothek*, Münchener Beiträge 11 (1973) 30.   61 Bischoff, *Lorsch*, 47 f.   62 See below p. 126.
63 Bruckner, *Scriptoria* 3; Daniel, *Hss. aus der Freisinger Dombibliothek*, 11 ff.
64 Daniel, ibid., 39 ff.   65 Daniel, ibid., 4 ff. (St. Gallen), 45 f. (Freising).
66 Bruckner, *Scriptoria* 3, 27 ff.; J. Duft in J. Duft–P. Meyer, *Die irischen Miniaturen der Stiftsbibliothek St. Gallen* (Olten 1953) 35 ff.; Daniel, ibid., 31.
67 Daniel, ibid., esp. 55–72 (Freising).

century, continues and in the process the harshness (or at least the irregularity) generally increases. When in the late tenth century the great Ottonian schools of illumination began their activity an adequate script was, for the most part, unavailable. Still, it seems that handwriting from the circle of the Registrum Gregorii Master stands out especially early by its high quality.[68] In some scripts of the late tenth century, and also of the eleventh, the knobby effect achieved by the thickening of the beginnings of *i, n, u, m*, long-*s, f, r*, and *p* determines the impression made by the script, for example in the script of Froumund of Tegernsee[69] and in the Bamberg Apocalypse from Reichenau.[70]

In general, it is only around 1000 and shortly thereafter that what had previously, to a greater or lesser degree, lacked cohesion could be harmonised to form a coherent, smooth script.[71] This script, now fully mastered calligraphically, avoids the extremes of both leanness and fullness, and achieves an element of tension through its tendency towards stretching: a slanting oval is the essential form. In the first half and in the mid-eleventh century this 'slanting oval' style is disseminated over a large part of Germany. It is formed at its most elegant in south Germany by the scribal generation that was growing up in Henry II's time and that was active until the middle of the century.[72]

The calligraphic skill of Otloh, the prolific Regensburg scribe, must have enjoyed an unusual esteem because, besides working for his own monastery of St Emmeram, he also worked for numerous outside prelates and places.[73] This style is the script of the great south-east German schools of illumination of the eleventh/twelfth centuries, the 'Bavarian monastic school', for which a group of outstanding Tegernsee calligraphers[74] wrote numerous texts, and of the

68 Cf. Steffens, *Lateinische Paläographie*, plate 70a (Codex Egberti); Chroust, *Monumenta* II 4, plate 2 (letter collection from Trier); Lowe, *Palaeographical Papers* 2, plate 85, 87.
69 Christine Elisabeth Eder, *Die Schule des Klosters Tegernsee im frühen Mittelalter, Stud. Mitteil. OSB* 83 (1972) = Münchener Beiträge Beiheft, 36 ff.; Chroust, *Monumenta* II 1, plate 6a.
70 Chroust, *Monumenta* I 20, plate 6; also in St. Gallen: ibid. I 16, plate 10 (s. XI²).
71 Cf. the script of Ellinger of Tegernsee; Chroust, *Monumenta* II 1, plate 7; and the treatment by Eder, *Tegernsee*, 55 f., 75 ff. Comparable script from Regensburg: Chroust, *Monumenta* I 3, plate 6. The apparently German scribe of Clm 19,453, f. 118ᵛ–201ᵛ, developed a quite individual strong script probably in the eleventh century: vertical, compressed, with tall final *S* and ligatures of *m* (and other letters) with a pendant *a* or *i*, *NeS*, *NS*, *pS*, *vS*, *vv* (the manuscript was not rubricated; initials and verse capitals were added in the twelfth century).
72 Bischoff, *Kalligraphie*, 34 f. Cf. the Uta-evangelistary from Regensburg: Chroust, *Monumenta* I 3, plate 4; Baltimore, Walters Art Gallery MS 71: (Jacques Rosenthal) *Bibliotheca manuscripta* I (Munich 1925) plate 9 (Nr. 40).
73 See his autograph annotations: *Mittelalt. Bibliothekskat. Deutschl.* 4, 1, 149–51. Samples of Otloh's book-scripts: Chroust, *Monumenta* I 3, plate 7; Arndt-Tangl⁴, *Schrifttafeln* plate 19; Petzet-Glauning, *Deutsche Schrifttafeln* 3; Helga Schauwecker, *Otloh von St. Emmeram* (illustrated excerpt from *Stud. Mitteil. OSB* 74) plates following pp. 48, 96, 112. Bischoff, *Kalligraphie*, 35 and Nr. 25.
74 Eder, *Tegernsee*, 57 f., 65, 92 ff. Reprod: E.F. Bange, *Eine bayerische Malerschule des XI. und XII Jahrhunderts* (Munich 1923) e.g. plates 6, 8, 12, 17 f., 38, 46; Chroust, *Monumenta* II 2, plate 1 f., 4 f.

Salzburg school.[75] Sporadically changing, sometimes sharper, sometimes blunter, this slanting oval type of caroline minuscule lived on in south Germany and Austria up to 1200, and in some cases beyond, undisturbed by the gothic mode encroaching from the west.[76] Meanwhile, west German and north-west German schools in the eleventh century do not appear to have perfected the slanting oval stage to the same degree, if they achieved it at all.[77] A certain similarity with slanting oval style (probably without any genuine connection) exists in the script of the calligrapher Goderannus of Stavelot and Lobbes (c. 1100).[78]

One must not, however, formulate the picture of writing in this century exclusively on the basis of the de luxe codices and the library manuscripts. The vigorous rise of the schools, and the reading and commentary of the bible and school authors often demanded more economic writing, which could be achieved by greatly reducing the space between the lines and by the use of a smaller type of writing for entering glosses, etc. Such a script, in which very many OHG glosses were also written, developed more and more from a simple reduction in the size of the text script and led ultimately to certain divergent forms: for example *a* with lengthened shaft, long-*s* and *f* (which in the text hand only slightly cut through the base line), and especially *r*, which extends far below the line.[79]

I add here further remarks concerning alterations of the caroline minuscule (in Germany) between the late ninth and the twelfth century (before the transition to gothic); these also partly apply to France, England, and Italy.[80] The letters *k* and *z* are multiform and often fit badly into the line; but any attempt to determine the time and place of the individual forms seems hopeless.[81] The *h*,

75 G. Swarzenski, *Die Salzburger Malerei von den ersten Anfängen bis zur Blütezeit des romanischen Stils* (Leipzig 1912).
76 Chroust, *Monumenta* II 13, plate 9 (Melk around 1240); II 3, plate 6 (Tegernsee around 1260).
77 A comparable, though wider and straighter, script from Utrecht (after 1138) in *Mss. datés*, Pays-Bas I plates 69–72. Cologne: P. Bloch–H. Schnitzler, *Die ottonische Kölner Malerschule* I (Düsseldorf 1967), with plates of the script in each MS: a unified style can be traced from no. XIV on. Echternach: samples of script in C. Nordenfalk, *Codex Caesareus Upsaliensis* (Stockholm 1971) fig. 11 f. and 22, and in contrast figs 17–21 and Chroust, *Monumenta* II 5, plates 1/2 and 7.
78 *Mss. datés*, Belgique I, Nr. 2 (plates 3 to 7); L. Gilissen, *L'Expertise des écritures médiévales* (Ghent 1973) plates 2–8; *Catal. dated and datable MSS* I, illustr. 52.
79 Examples: Chroust, *Monumenta* I 3, plate 8 (Othloh; compare I 3, plate 7); Chatelain, *Pal. class. lat.*, plate 157 (= *Nomenclature*, reprod. 2); Bischoff, *Schreibschulen* I, plate 6d).
80 Experience has shown that some traditional rules for dating, the gradual development of the shaft of *a* to the vertical, the closing of both bows of *g* etc., are insufficiently rigid. Lists of such rules, e.g. in K. Löffler, *Einführung in die Handschriftenkunde* (Leipzig 1929) 127 ff.; Foerster, *Abriß²*, 193 ff. In contrast the systematic suggestions given by J. Authenrieth, 'Probleme der Lokalisierung und Datierung von spätkarolingischen Schriften (10. und 11. Jh.)', *Codicologica* 4 [Litterae textuales] (Leiden 1978) 67 ff. For a general study see G. Powitz, 'Datieren und Lokalisieren nach der Schrift', *Bibliothek und Wissenschaft* 10 (1976) 124 ff.
81 Margarete Ziemer, *Datierung und Lokalisierung nach den Schreibformen von k und z im Althochdeutschen* (Diss. Halle 1933).

whose bow already in the ninth century is mostly claw-like in shape, usually extends the bow under the line from the twelfth century on. While N soon disappears from the minuscule, and also the use of open a with two points gradually retreats, round d and v (also frequent in internal position from the eleventh century) are now integral parts of the script. The mostly raised S frequent in final position appears already in the tenth century often in ligature with v. In the upper swing of the round d in the twelfth century the small head of an e is added (de).[82] For the sound w, long expressed by doubling the u-sign (uu, uv, etc.), there appears in the eleventh century the composite form w.[83] As a survivor from cursive writing, the wedge-shaped thickening of the ascenders generally goes out of fashion after the tenth century,[84] after it had already been frequently contracted in button-like fashion or in a way similar to the Insular one, by a triangular addition. From this there develops an open fork in France already before 1050,[85] and in west-German writing c. 1100.[86]

The e caudata ($ę$), which is very frequent even in pre-carolingian times for the diphthong ae, replaces the latter more and more in the tenth and eleventh centuries; the result is an uncertainty as to where ae should rightly be used and where not (often $ęcla$, etc.). In the twelfth century simple e replaces the $ę$. For the German diphthong uo was formed already in the ninth century the grouping of o with an open bow above it,[87] which in the tenth century, particularly in intitial position (in names) becomes the set ligature $ŏ$.[88] in the twelfth century the equivalent $ŭ$ becomes more frequent (occasionally also for the diphthong ou).[89] From roughly 1100 (and in Italy already at the end of the eleventh century) two consecutive i's (for which ij often stands in western manuscripts) acquire strokes ($íí$) to distinguish them from u, a feature which occurs in the case of single i already in the twelfth century.[90]

I mentioned above Irish forms that were apparently disseminated from St Gall. A much more general symptom of Irish influence, which is probably to be traced to the important position of Irish teachers in carolingian education, is the surprisingly frequent use of the spiritus asper instead of h, in corrections but also in text script (for example in the Strasbourg oaths);[91] sometimes it even stands on the line.[92] Less frequent is the spiritus lenis in vocalic initial position, or in the

---

82 E.g. Petzet-Glauning, *Specimina*, plate 20.

83 It is almost attained in the tenth century 'Homiliae Bedas' (s. X): J.H. Gallée, *Altsächsische Sprachdenkmäler*, Facs. (Leiden 1895) plate 3.

84 In Angers the old practice was followed sporadically around 1000 and even later; cf. J. Vezin, *Les scriptoria d'Angers au XIe siècle* (Paris 1974) 134 and plate 1 f., 28 ff.

85 *Catal. mss. datés* 3, plate 18a (Dijon); 5, plate 7a.

86 E.g. Chroust, *Monumenta* II 4, plate 10a, reprod 2; 5, plate 5; 8, plate 6b.

87 Petzet-Glauning, *Specimina*, plate 4.   88 Perhaps inspired by the Greek ɣ ligature.

89 Petzet-Glauning, *Specima*, plate 20.   90 Ibid., plate 20.

91 M. Enneccerus, *Die ältesten deutschen Sprachdenkmäler in Lichtdrucken* (Frankfurt/M. 1897) plates 34–6; Steffens², *Lateinische Paläographie*, plate 69.

92 Clm 14,070c, f. 54; 14,792, f. 60.

suppression of *h*.[93] From the same source stem also the monogrammatic ligatures of *qd* with abbreviation-stroke for *quod*, *quidem*, etc.

In France likewise, roughly from the end of the ninth century, a decline in spontaneity is to be seen which leads to a certain loss of style, though clearly to a much lesser extent than in Germany. The wedge-shape of the ascender here too makes for a short, triangular addition or fork. From major tenth-century scriptoria there are numerous manuscripts, the post-carolingian origin of whose script can only be revealed by a very slight sharpness[94] or harshness,[95] or by a lack of firmness.[96] In the eleventh century the script distances itself still further from carolingian harmony and sureness of execution, but in the individual forms it has for the most part hardly changed at all.[97] A possibly unique phenomenon is the extraordinary close and often successful attachment of the very productive scriptoria of Angers to the carolingian style of St Martin's at Tours in the eleventh century. The most noteworthy novelties in contrast with the model are the differentiation – not exclusive to Angers – of the double sounds ae and oe in the writing of *e* caudata, and a weak or medium punctuation (punctus circumflexus).[98] There are, however, more modern stylisations as well. Amongst these are the narrow, vertical, and above all sharply-drawn script that was written in the circle of Abbo of Fleury (†1004),[99] and an elegant, slanted script used at St Thierry at Rheims in the eleventh century.[100] Into quite a few French manuscripts of the school-style in the tenth and early eleventh century strongly noticeable Irish elements also enter in ligatures and abbreviations, either following Irish exemplars or because of contact with Irishmen.[101] In this

93 F.J.H. Jenkinson, *The Hisperica Famina* (Cambridge 1908) xxv. On Greek-inspired forms of abbreviation see below p. 154.
94 E.g. manuscript Laon 274, close to Rather's Lower Lotharingian circle.
95 E.g. *Pal. Soc.*, ser 2, plate 109/110.
96 Many tenth- and eleventh-century examples in the volumes of the *Catalogue des mss datés* and also in Danielle Gaborit-Chopin, *La décoration des mss. a Saint-Martial de Limoges et en Limousin du IXe au XIIe siècle* (Paris–Geneva 1969); J. Dufour, *La bibliothèque et le scriptorium de Moissac* (Geneva–Paris 1972).
97 Cf. from St Germain-des-Prés (*Catal. mss. datés* 3, plate 16b), Cluny (ibid. 3, plates 18b and 234), Limoges (ibid. 2, plate 18). At Cluny different styles came together, cf. Monique–Cécile Garand, 'Copistes de Cluny au temps de Saint Maieul (948–994)', *Bibl. Éc. Chartes* 136 (1978) 5–36, with 6 plates; eadem, 'Le scriptorium de Cluny carrefour d'influences au XIe siècle: le ms. Paris, BN, Nouv. Acq. Lat. 1548', *Journal des Savants* (1977) 257–83.
98 Cf. J. Vezin, *Les scriptoria d'Angers*, 138 ff.; he discusses the *e* with a tail (for *oe*) and *e* with a pendant 6 (for *oe*); on p. 151 he talks about the 'punctus circumflexus' which became characteristic in Cistercian punctuation. In Paris, BN, Lat. 9431 (after 1096) there is a masterly imitation of a ninth-century script; *Catal. mss. datés* 3, plate 25a.
99 A small sample in J. Kirchner, *Die Phillipps-Handschriften. Beschreibendes Verzeichnis der Miniaturen-Hss. der Preuß. Staatsbibliothek zu Berlin* 1 (Leipzig 1926) 22; cf. Elizabeth Pellegrin, 'Membra disiecta Floriacensia', *Bibl. Éc. Chartes* 117 (1959) 14 f. A further example in Chatelain, *Pal. class. lat.*, plate 22, 1.
100 E.g. Vatic. Reg. Lat. 1504; Copenhagen, Fragm. 19, m. 3.
101 The few possibilities are already fully exploited in a caroline ninth-century addition to Paris, BN, Lat. 1535, f. 151ᵛ f.

way the tendency was encouraged towards economy of writing in the school milieu which can already be observed in ninth-century glosses.[102] With the beginning of gothic writing occasionally the old and the new style can be observed in use side-by-side.[103]

In Provence the problem arose, when writing vernacular texts, of graphically differentiating the *z* sounds; by the attachment of a sickle-shaped cedille on *t* or (round) *d* signs were created in the thirteenth century for *tz* and *dz*.[104]

Caroline minuscule was transplanted to England in the tenth century. Amongst the various contacts with the continent – dynastic ties, contacts with Brittany, and finally the powerful Benedictine reform, which had its leaders above all in archbishop Dunstan of Canterbury and Æthelwold, abbot of Abingdon and later bishop of Winchester – the latter influence was the most lasting. Their *Consuetudines* stand under the influence of Fleury and St Peter's in Ghent, but for English caroline script manuscripts from other schools, such as Corbie and St Amand, probably also served as models.[105] In the process the script was subjected to the stronger English scribal tradition; where caroline and Anglo–Saxon minuscule were written by the same hand, the letter forms they have in common assimilate themselves to the Anglo–Saxon form.[106] Like Anglo–Saxon script, the caroline minuscule was also used for charters.

Various styles stand out rather clearly. For example, the benedictional of Æthelwold[107] is written in a broad, rounded script executed in a large mode especially suitable for imposing manuscripts. The earliest examples of this style come from Winchester and Abingdon. The style at St Augustine's, Canterbury, with its narrower forms, pointed ends of the descenders and of *r*, and other particularities, has taken over in free borrowing more from the Anglo–Saxon minuscule,[108] while for Christ Church a finer script is characteristic.[109] In a second, slightly later style at Christ Church (first half of the eleventh century) the longish rounded script already approaches the earliest Anglo–Norman script, without possessing its firmness.[110] From the late eleventh century and from the twelfth there are manuscripts from England in which Norman and English scribes clearly collaborated.[111]

102 Cf. Vatic. Rossian. 247 (probably from western France, s. X), e.g. f. 199[rv]; Metz 227 (s. XI[1]). Dialectical texts of s. X–XI full of abbreviations (among which -᾿ for est): Paris, BN, Lat. 12,958, f. 1–43.

103 E.g. *Catal. mss. datés* 5, plate 11b (with the archaising script of William of St Thierry, ob. 1148) and 234[v] (from Signy).

104 Cl. Brunel, 'Remarques sur la paléographie des chartes provençales du XIIe siècle', *Bibl. Éc. Chartes* 87 (1926) 347 ff.

105 The imitation was sometimes so successful that, for example, the Psalter, Cambridge, CCC, 411, could be considered French.   106 Cf. plates 2–5 in Ker, *Catal. of MSS.*

107 T.A.M. Bishop, *English Caroline Minuscule* (Oxford 1971) plate X.

108 Ibid., plates IV, V, VII.   109 Ibid., plate VI.   110 Ibid., plates XXII.

111 Ker, *English MSS*, plate 1b, 2/3. Cf. also Bishop, *English Caroline Minuscule*, p. xvi f., on a scribe in the service of Countess Judith of Flanders.

In Norway and Iceland among various influences the English was strong-est.[112] Caroline and gothic minuscule there also retained English runic signs; in Iceland the script had to be extended by the addition of new sound symbols.[113] Likewise þ and ð were taken over in Sweden, the former in Denmark as well; the vowel series in both was extended by the addition of signs for the umlauts ae (ǽ) and oe (ǿ and similar).[114]

In Italian bookhands the lack of stylistic rigour in the post-carolingian period is generally less noticeable than in Germany and France.[115] Many scripts remain more solid, less elongated, and the inclination is less marked; the tendency increases to draw the shafts vertically. Thus is the process prepared that leads to the rotunda. In some scripts the ligature *ri* and the two-tiered cursive *ti* persist into the twelfth century.

All the more striking is the appearance in the eleventh and at the beginning of the twelfth century of a slanting style in Rome and its environs. This also frequently stresses the round bodies of the letters (*o*; the very common round *d*; *g* with closed full bows). Here it is a very general phenomenon that the shafts (including even that of *r*, often extended slightly below the line) are provided with finials, and *i* and the end-stroke of *m* and *n* acquire a horizontal stroke.[116] Terminology used to describe this script varies: 'Farfa style', so-called because it is richly and characteristically attested from the monastery of that name in the Sabine mountains, 'minuscola romana (romanesca)',[117] so-called because it was used in Rome, even in the circle of the curia,[118] and in Subiaco, Tivoli, and other places in central Italy. Attempts have been made to derive this 'romanesca' from the Roman caroline minuscule, which is, however, very poorly documented.[119] Considered from the view-point of the development of German script, it appears rather that it might be explained as being the result of a strong

112 Cf. the literature listed p. 93, n. 73.
113 Cf. the expanded alphabet illustrated in D.A. Seip, *Palaeografi B, Norge og Island. Nordisk Kultur* 28 (Stockholm–Oslo–Copenhagen 1954) 36.
114 J. Brøndum-Neilsen (ed.), *Palaeografi A, Danmark og Sverige. Nordisk Kultur* 28 (Stockholm–Oslo–Copenhagen 1943). Examples of Nordic script in Kirchner, *Script. Goth. libr.*, plates 15, 46a, 61a; *Katal. dat. Hss.*, Sweden, 1, reprods 36, 42, 57, etc.
115 Symptomatic changes from the ninth to the twelfth century are listed by A. Petrucci in *Studi Medievali*, ser 3, 9 (1968) 1115–26.
116 W.M. Lindsay, 'The Farfa type', *Palaeographia Latina* 3 (Oxford 1924) 49–51 with 3 plates (E. Carusi, ibid., 58 f.: a list of MSS); *Arch. Pal. Ital.* 2, plates 4 f., 33–43; 6, plates 93–100; *Catal. manoscr. datati* 1, plates 16–26, 29–32 (with interesting fluctuations); Paola Supino Martini, *Studi Medievali*, ser 3, 15 (1974) 790 ff. with plates 9–11.
117 Batelli, *Lezioni*³, 193.
118 Cf. the Collectio canonum of Deusdedit copied between 1099 and 1118 (Ehrle–Liebaert, *Specimina*, plate 35).
119 P. Supino Martini, 'Carolina romana e minuscola romanesca', 790 ff.; eadem, 'La produzione libraria negli scriptoria delle abbazie di Farfa e di S. Eutizio', in *Il ducato di Spoleto*, Atti del IX congresso internazionale di studi nell'altò medioevo (Spoleto 1983) 581–607.

'superimposition of south-German script on the local minuscule style',[120] whose cause has not yet been studied. But it should probably be seen in connection with the extensive influence of the Alemannic style of initials. In the twelfth century Rome also participates in the production of giant Bibles with their now generally straight, 'reformed' minuscule which is disseminated in northern and central Italy.[121]

In Spain several factors contribute to the introduction of caroline minuscule, above all the expansion of the Cluniacs beyond the Pyrenees and the adoption of the Roman liturgy effected under Gregory VII, which has as a consequence the adoption at the León synod[122] of 1090 of a ban on the use of 'littera Toletana' for ecclesiastical books. There are also late Visigothic manuscripts in which the caroline letters (*a*, *g*, *t*) have penetrated the now listless script.[123] A Lucan (c. saec. XI/XII) was written by a Visigothic scribe and by a caroline one whose Spanish stamp is, however, quite unmistakable.[124]

Regarding the charter hands of the period up to the twelfth century, some remarks have already been made concerning Italy,[125] Spain,[126] and England.[127] In Francia the crowded, elongated Merovingian chancery hand[128] was continued in the Carolingian chancery script, but it had become more uniform, open, and courtly.[129] It was retained in this form by the French royal chancery into the tenth century.[130] In the east-Frankish chancery of Louis the German, however, parallel with the changes in the bookhand,[131] the decisive break with the cursive tradition took place. The changeover can be traced back to the notary Hebarhard, who is attested in the chancery from AD 859. The newly created 'diplomatic minuscule' generally adopted the letter forms of the ordinary book minuscule, but the script none the less acquires a particular composite appearance as a result of the long swung ascenders, the open *a*, long *r*, spiral-like additions to the crests of *c*, *e*, and *p*, and the similar alterations of the long letters,

---

120 Daniel, *Freisinger Dombibliothek*, 41. Plate IX in P. Supino Martini may be compared with a choice of St Gall scripts from the late ninth to the eleventh century in Bruckner, *Scriptoria* 3, plates 26a, 27b.c, 32a–c, 46a.b. The theory has been declared unverifiable by B. Bischoff in *Paläographie* (1981) 102 f.

121 Numerous samples of script in E.B. Garrison, *Studies in the history of medieval Italian painting* 1–4 (Florence 1953–6).

122 A. Hessel, 'Studien zur Ausbreitung der karolingischen Minuskel' 1, *Arch. f. Urk.* 7 (1921) 197–202; A. Millares Carlo, *Tratado* 1, 140–3. Cf. however 123.

123 Cf. Ewald–Loewe, *Exempla*, plate 38 (from 1105); Arndt-Tangl 2⁴, *Schrifttafeln*, plate 37 (a subscription from 1109).

124 H. Foerster, *Mittelalterliche Buch- und Urkundenschriften* (Bern 1946) plate 22a.b.; *New Pal. Soc.*, ser 2, plate 144.　　125 p. 102.　　126 p. 99, n. 22.　　127 p. 92.

128 The elongated script of the king's name was extended to the whole of the first line from Charlemagne's reign.

129 The scribe of the Hammelburger Markbeschreibung tried to imitate this type of script: Chroust, *Monumenta* 1 5, plate 7; Arndt-Tangl, *Schrifttafeln* 3⁴, plate 73; ChLA XII 542.

130 F. Lot–Ph. Lauer, *Diplomata Karolinorum*, 1–9 (Toulouse–Paris 1936–49); for the tenth century see vols 6–8.　　131 Above p. 119.

and also by means of several ligatures and the spiralled abbreviation sign. In the eleventh and twelfth centuries the diploma hand of the chancery acquires a stern solemnity; all around Germany it is imitated in royal charters,[132] and in those of many seculars and ecclesiastics;[133] it even affected the stylisation of 'papal minuscule'[134] in the twelfth century. Under Frederick II it goes out of use.

The emphasising of personal names by the use of majuscule letters, customary in the Salian period but already sporadically before that date, is found both in the diplomas and in, for example, many legendaries that emphasise the names of saints. The script of private charters is initially in general bookhand, partly with occasional spirallings, later in increasingly narrower script, often with long ascenders and descenders.

8. Gothic textura (textualis)

A new style of bookhand[1] makes its appearance in the eleventh century in Belgium and in northern France. In the tenth century the script here still clung basically to the caroline forms, which, however, had become stiffer or sharper and had lost some of their harmony. In the eleventh century the alterations are more clearly visible: elongated or compressed or angular scripts predominate; fine strokes are added at an angle top and bottom and the ascenders are emphasised by spatulate terminals; the shaft of *a* is decidedly upright. The breaking of the shafts[2] already appears in the first half of the eleventh century at St Peter's in Ghent, under the provost and later abbot Wichard (abbot 1034/5–8) and roughly at the same time in northern France; this was a feature which had

---

132 To some extent also in France; cf. Françoise Gasparri, *L'Écriture des actes de Louis VI, Louis VII et Philippe Auguste* (Geneva–Paris 1973).

133 Some scribes surpassed themselves in exaggerating the mesh-like flourish on the *s* and the §-like extension of *g*; numerous examples in J. Stiennon, *L'écriture diplomatique dans le diocèse de Liège du XIe au milieu du XIIIe siècle* (Paris 1960); idem, *Paléographie*, 104–7; idem, 'Le rôle pédagogique du "treillis"', in *Miscellanea codicologica F. Masai dicata MCMLXXIX* 1 (Ghent 1979) 185–188.   134 Which soon became an international model too.

1 J. Kirchner in Crous-Kirchner, *Schriftarten*, 7–25; idem, *Script. Goth. libr.*; Mazal, *Gotik*; Thomson, *Bookhands*; Cencetti, *Lineamenti*, 205 ff.; idem, *Compendio*, 71–9; V.L. Romanova, *Rukopisnaya kniga i goticheskoe pis'mo v Francii v XIII–XIV vv* (Moscow 1975). On the gothic system of scripts: G.I. Lieftinck, in *Nomenclature*, 15–32; idem in *Mss. datés*, Pays-Bas 1, texts, p. xiv ff. (with some changes in terminology); the system depends chiefly on Dutch fourteenth- and fifteenth-century MSS. In a new and simplified form it is used by J.P. Gumbert, 'A Proposal for a Cartesian Nomenclature', in *Miniatures, Scripts, Collections. Essays presented to G.I. Lieftinck* [*Litterae textuales 4*] (Amsterdam 1975) 45–52 (an attempt to define gothic scripts according to the letter-forms of a long *s* or *f* and according to the presence or absence of bows); idem, 'Nomenklatur als Gradnetz. Ein Versuch an spätmittelalterlichen Schriftformen', *Codices manuscripti* 1 (1975) 122–5 (as before).

2 It has not yet been sufficiently clarified whether it could depend on 'Insular influences' (J. Boussard) or an analogical formation of a technical and stylistical kind; cf. J. Boussard, 'Influences insulaires dans la formation de l'écriture gothique', *Scriptorium* 5 (1951) 238–64. On the fundamentally different form and function of broken shafts in Beneventan see above p. 110.

also been widely disseminated in Insular and Insular-influenced scripts of the eighth and ninth centuries, as well as in later English scripts. The Ghent type of this fractured script, with short shafts and almost square proportions in *n* and *u*, had only a short lifespan.[3] In contrast, the oblong, fractured north-French script[4] was a creation of wider consequence. In England this Norman script encountered a caroline minuscule that had been amalgamated with English writing technique. The Norman script gained there in dignity, harmony, and density, as for instance in the type practised shortly before 1100 at Christ Church Canterbury, the seat of the primate.[5] If in the twelfth century western early gothic script takes on, besides the compactness, a certain fullness and suppleness, then this is because an English component is at work.[6]

The most striking features of this north-French script and of all later gothic textura[7] – by comparison with caroline minuscule and the predominant German script of the eleventh – are the extension and the vertical alignment of all shafts, including the shaft of *a*. Just as essential, even for the basic appearance of gothic script, is the fact that (with the exception of *g*, *j*, *p*, *q*, *y*, and the bow of the *h*, whose point touches the line or cuts through it) all letters, including *f* and long-*s*, stand on the line. It is one of the principles of the gothic transformation that all vertical shafts standing on the line are handled in the same way, that is either broken or provided with connecting strokes. The kinds of shafts in early French and English gothic are generally dictated by a clear norm: *i*, the shafts of *u*, *r*, and *p*, and the leading (first) shafts of *m* and *n* are on the upper end constructed like ascenders, that is with forks, often very pronounced. The following shafts of *m* and *n* are attached with hair-strokes and very frequently broken on the upper third. If the hair-stroke is set at an angle to the broad stroke, pointed arcades, comparable to the pointed arches in architecture, come about. The forking of the medium (first) shafts, which in Germany too is generally adopted in the course of development toward a gothic script, for example in the Rufinus of 1181 from Trier,[8] is still clearly to be seen in the sumptuously written Bredelar Bible of

3 Cf. A. Verhulst, 'L'activité et la calligraphie du scriptorium de Saint-Pierre-au-Mont-Blandin', *Scriptorium* 11 (1957) 37–49 and plates 5–10; *Mss. datés*, Pays-Bas 1, 88 and plates 44–8.

4 Eleventh-century examples of this script from Mont-St-Michel in J.J.G. Alexander, *Norman illumination at Mont St. Michel 966–1100* (Oxford 1970) plates 2–6; *Catal. mss. datés* 7, plate XXIII. Compare the Carilef Bible in Durham, R.A.B. Mynors, *Durham cathedral manuscripts to the end of the twelfth century* (Oxford 1939) plate 16 f. (with forking of the bases).

5 Ker, *English MSS*, 27 f.

6 This can be seen by comparing the French and English scripts in the mortuary roll of abbot Vitalis of Savigny from 1122–3; Facs.: L. Delisle, *Rouleau mortuaire du B. Vita, abbé de Savigni* (Paris 1909).

7 On the name: C. Wehmer, 'Die Namen der gotischen Buchschriften', *Zentralbl. f. Bibliothekswesen* 49 (1932) 11–34; on the style: Fichtenau, *Mensch und Schrift*, 186 ff.: R. Marichal in 'L'écriture et la psychologie des peuples', *27e Semaine de synthèse* (Paris 1963) 225 ff.

1238.[9] Around the middle of the thirteenth century it is finally replaced by another way of forming the approach strokes, which began in the twelfth century. In contrast with the forked ascenders – which later often acquire only a light decorative stroke – there appears already in the twelfth century the tendency, in the case of the medium length shafts (minims), to contract the forking of the addition to form lozenge-shaped reinforcement.[10] The constructive sense of the gothic era did not cease until the clearest solution had been found for the relationship between the predominating straight stroke and the oblique parts; the latter became lozenges placed on their lower corner, or, in the case of attached shafts, rectangles, or in this case too, squares.

In order to produce rows of shafts all constructed in the same way, it was often necessary to suppress the hair-strokes, and the 'quadrangles' touch each other at the points.[11] According as the shafts were broken either above and below or just above, the writing-masters called the script 'textus fractus' ('t. quadratus') or 'textus semifractus ('t. semiquadratus'). As well as that, however, the simple approach with short hair-stroke continued in use, including for the first shafts. The textura without shaft-breaking was called 'rotunda' by the Dutch and German writing-masters.[12] The oblique approach strokes are mostly slanted;[13] only sporadically in early gothic scripts is the attempt made to restructure them into horizontal basic strokes. Much more often *i, m, n, r,* etc. are cut off flat on the line. For this script the name 'textus praecisus' is later attested. Especially favoured in England, it was occasionally used also in Germany.[14] In a particular precursor of the later biting bow fusions, *bb* and *pp* are often so combined that the second shaft cuts the first bow.[15] Breaking, stretching, and the identical handling of all shafts that stand on the line appear as symptoms of the tranformation to gothic from the eleventh century, and where they work together one can speak of 'primitive gothic' script in order to express the formal difference by comparison with the carolingian script.[16]

The Italian route towards gothic is different and it leads to another form. Many Italian scripts remained erect but were lower (*n* and *m* are more or less square). The tendency towards heavier, vertical and round script, which perhaps has to do with a change in the cut of the pen, makes its appearance early in the twelfth century in Tuscany, later in Rome, and then determines the script

8 Steffens[2], *Lateinische Paläographie*, plate 86; Chroust, *Monumenta* II 6, plate 2.
9 Chroust, *Monumenta* II 24, plate 2.
10 This development can be traced in the English episcopal professions from 1138 to 1180 in Ker, *English MSS*, plate 18 f.
11 E.g. Petzet-Glauning, *Deutsche Schrifttafeln*, plate 48.
12 These styles, which also occur intermingled, are discussed by W. Oeser, 'Das *a* als Grundlage für Schriftvarianten in der gotischen Buchschrift', *Scriptorium* 25 (1971) 25–45 with plates 10–12; cf. below p. 208.   13 E.g. Rufinus of 1181.
14 E.g. in the Antiphonary of Leubus c. 1280–90, in E. Kloos, *Die schlesische Buchmalerei des Mittelalters* (Berlin 1942) plate 29 ff.
15 E.g. Chroust, *Monumenta* I 22, plates 2a and 3.   16 B. Bischoff in *Nomenclature*, 7–14.

type of the widely diffused and influential giant Bibles.[17] In this calligraphy only the last shafts of *n* and *m* (beside *i* and *u*) tend to end in a turn towards the right,[18] in the remaining cases the shaft of *h* and likewise *r* are, by contrast, set broadly on the line; *f* too and long-*s* (often extending somewhat below the line) and the descenders end broad; this canon remains constant. Missing is the forking of the shafts, but their tops can be somewhat thickened. For both reasons formation of the squares on the upper and lower ends of the medium lengths did not come about. The angle that comes into being with the attachment of the second strokes of *n* and *m* is broader. Round *d* and round *s* (at word end) were widespread; round *r* after *o* becomes the rule. The *z*, which in Italy too did not always fit comfortably into the writing line, acquires a new ç-like form, which in Italy, however, has no particular phonetic value.[19] The tironian *et*, which takes on a curving form, replaces the ligature. Thus was created the basic writing appearance of the 'rotunda', which lasted for centuries – only the biting connections were lacking.[20]

Perfected gothic textura acquires its characteristic appearance with the later appearance of 'biting' connections, which were formed according to the rules discovered by Wilhelm Meyer.[21] The rules state: (1) If two adjacent letters have bows facing one another (for example *be*, *oc*, *po*) then they are set so close that the bows partially overlap. But wherever the bows of the textura are changed into straight strokes, there the letters share the vertical parts of the transformed bows; (2) In order to avoid as far as possible the meeting of bow and straight stroke, the 'round' *r* from the old ligature *or* is also attached to the letters with bows: *b*, round *d*, *h*, *p*, *v*, *y*. These rules were taken over into the gothic textura, both the western and German types as well as the Italian, at the beginning of the thirteenth century. Their origin and purpose, in relation to the aesthetic of the gothic script, are to achieve as uniform an image as possible for the script. In the utilisation and application of the biting connectives the scribes behave in very varying ways, but the rules influence the choice of letter forms, whether long or round *d*, whether *u* or *v*, and in the Jena chansonnier[22] even whether *i* or *y* are used. The rules remained in force up to the period of early printing.[23]

Non-Italian textura allows, in its strictest forms,[24] no round strokes whatsoever, but breaks up even the bows into fractured, angular compounded strokes.

---

17 Cf. above p. 125.

18 B. Pagnin, *Le origini della scrittura gotica padovana* (Padua 1933) plates 2–4.

19 Cf. Lehmann, *Erforschung* 4, 4 ff.

20 A. Petrucci in *Studi Medievali*, ser 3, 9 (1968) 1123 f.

21 W. Meyer, 'Die Buchstabenverbindungen der sogenannten gotischen Schrift', *Abh. Kgl. Ges. Wiss. Göttingen*, phil.-hist. Kl., n.F. 1/6 (1897). A striking English name for the phenomenon is 'biting'.   22 Meyer, 93 ff.

23 R. Juchhoff, 'Das Fortleben mittalterlicher Schreibgewohnheiten in den Druckschriften des XV. Jhs., 1', *Beiträge zur Inkunabelkunde*, n.F. 1 (Leipzig 1935) 65–77.

24 E.g. Degering, *Schrift*, plate 95.

By contrast with the narrow gothic textura scripts, whose formation took place in France and England, and which spread throughout the whole Latin West (with the exception of Italy[25] and southern France), the Italian textura retained the broad, regulated character that, in combination with the biting, justifies the name 'rotunda'.[26] Also a rotunda is the 'littera Bononiensis' in which, at Bologna, the university literature of Roman and canon law was copied by professional scribes. It was written with very narrow space between the lines and many abbreviations; it was very economical and yet very clear.[27] Types approaching the rotunda were also written in southern France in the thirteenth and fourteenth centuries.[28] Such types are also attested from Spain.[29] After the humanistic script had come into fashion the rotunda gradually lost its impact, though in Italy its position as the script for legal literature and for liturgical books survived longer.[30]

The reception of gothic script in Germany was facilitated by the fact that German scholars were accustomed to seeing France as the home of higher learning, and they frequented the schools there. In this way sporadic western writing features had perhaps already been introduced (for example a bow-shaped abbreviation-stroke).[31] The allure of the French schools was inherited by the university of Paris. The expansion too of the strongly centralised Cistercian order, which in France was characterised by a book production with very uniform script and decor, facilitated the transition to gothic. However, one can speak only with reservation of a typically 'Cistercian' script in Germany

25 Northern textura was written in Norman southern Italy; see H. Buchthal, 'A school of miniature painting in Norman Sicily', in *Late Classical and Mediaeval Studies in Honor of Albert Mathias Friend Jr.* (Princeton 1955) 312–39 and plates.

26 E.g. Steffens[2], *Lateinische Paläographie*, plate 101; Kirchner, *Script. Goth. libr.*, plate 23; Thomson, *Bookhands*, plate 75; *Arch. Pal. Ital.* II, plate 54 (A. Petrucci, *La Scrittura di Francesco Petrarca*, plate 19).

27 B. Pagnin, 'La "littera bononiensis"', *Atti del R. Istituto Veneto di Scienze, Lettere e Arti* 93/2 (Venice 1934) 1593–1665; Reprod: e.g. J. Destrez, *La Pecia dans les manuscrits universitaires du XIIIe et du XIVe siècle* (Paris 1935) plates 22–6; Steffens[2], *Lateinische Paläographie*, 106; Ehrle–Liebaert, *Specimina*, plate 43 f. Knowledge of regional and local styles of script may have been used in the lists of books of Cardinal Guala Bichieri (†1227) preserved in his will; as well as 'Littera Anglicana' and 'bona littera antiqua Aretina'. Cf. A. Hessel–W. Bulst, 'Kardinal Guala Bichieri und seine Bibliothek', *Hist. Vierteljahrschrift* 27 (1932) 781 ff. B. Pagnin, 'La "littera bononiensis"' is reprinted in *Ricerche Medievali* 10–12 (Pavia 1975–7) 93–168 with plate.

28 Cf. E. Monaci, *Facsimili di antichi manoscritti* (Rome 1881) plate 1 f.; *Musée des Archives Départementales, Recueil de fac-simile* (Paris 1878) Nr. 90, 108, 112; *Catal. mss. datés* 6, plate 26 ff., 42a; Stiennon, *Paléographie*, 257; Kirchner, *Script. Lat. libr.*[2], plate 42.

29 Thomson, *Bookhands*, plate 128 (1416).

30 The gradual shift in the use of both scripts can be observed in the library of the Dukes of Milan; cf. Elisabeth Pellegrin, *La bibliothèque des Visconti et des Sforza ducs de Milan, Supplément* (Florence–Paris 1969). Among the scribes who worked for Ferdinand of Naples only the Bohemian Wenceslaus Crispus wrote rotunda, for instance when he copied Thomas Aquinas; see T. de Marinis, *La Biblioteca Napoletana dei re d'Aragona* I (Milan 1947) 63 f.

31 E.g. Chroust, *Monumenta* II 20, 5 from Hildesheim 1103.

a b c d e f g h i k l m n

o p q r ſ s t u v w x y z

œ oz ꝑ

26. Gothic textura

ab cd ef gh ik ſ mn o pq rſ ꞇt üv ꝡxyʒ

27. Bastarda (German)

a b c d e f g h i l m n o

p q r ſ (s) t u v x y z œ ct &

28. Humanistic minuscule

a f g ſ minus

29. Humanistic cursive

1 ?ᒿ2 ᖯʒ 84 4 6 ᴧ7 8 9 ɵo

30. Arabic numbers

132

because the numerous south–German and Austrian Cistercian monasteries generally clung to the slanted oval script of these regions.[32] In contrast with the western orientation of German writing practice, an influence of the round Italian gothic script is only exceptionally to be perceived there.[33]

In western Germany the slightly more angular writing character facilitated the adoption of gothic script. A look at the school of St Mathias in Trier as an example allows us to see how, after already distinctively elongated but still unsure scripts of the first half of the twelfth century,[34] a strong, straight, steep script follows with consistent observance of the steep approach and finishing strokes (in the case of *f* and long-*s* as well);[35] in a hand of 1234[36] fracturing and biting are fully realised. Thus the symptoms of gothic appear in stages. An approximation of it comes about hesitantly, after 1150, in the Bamberg school.[37] In other regions where script development offered fewer gothic elements to start from, above all in southern Bavaria and Austria, the adoption of gothic script may have resulted for the most part in a sharp break with tradition. But even here in the late twelfth and early thirteenth centuries there are transitional forms, stiff and occasionally even prickly scripts.[38] In the course of the thirteenth century the textura script becomes filled with vitality and vigour.[39]

While it is a general feature of the northern gothic script that the stretched shafts and the interconnecting bows result in dense, block-like word units in which the individual letter seems to be absorbed into the word shape, this striving for closedness is entirely lacking in many scripts of German texts from the thirteenth and early fourteenth centuries. Small scripts above all, with the use of a broad 3-shaped *z* and the *v* that begins with a bulging swing at every place in the word,[40] combine a very loose distribution of letters, whereas other German hands do not depart at all from the normal image of the textura.[41] The difference is probably to be traced chiefly to the fact that some of the scribes were already used mainly to German texts, others (principally monastic?) mainly used to Latin texts.[42]

The high tide of the textura in Germany was reached in the thirteenth and

---

32 Cf. for instance, a typical Cistercian school like Heiligenkreuz: Chroust, *Monumenta* II 14 and 15.

33 Cf. Chroust, *Monumenta* I 21, plate 4 (Bamberg); II 14, plate 9b (Heiligenkreuz c. 1230); E. Kloos, *Die schlesische Buchmalerei*, plates 49 f., 52 ff. (from Silesia around 1320); more frequent in south Germany in the fifteenth century: Kirchner, *Script. Goth. libr.*, plate 36 (1472).   34 Chroust, *Monumenta* II 5, plate 8a from 1126; 5, plate 9, after 1131.

35 Ibid. II 6, plate 2 from 1181.   36 Ibid. II 6, plate 6a.   37 Ibid. I 21/22.

38 E.g. Chroust, *Monumenta* I 17, plate 10 (St Gallen); II 3, plates 2 and 5a (Tegernsee); III 4, plate 3/4 (Weingarten); similarly Petzet-Glauning, *Deutsche Schrifttafeln*, plate 21 (Augsburg?).

39 An example is the Carmina Burana from the first half of the thirteenth century. Facsimile edition ed. B. Bischoff (Munich 1967).

40 E.g. Petzet-Glauning, *Deutsche Schrifttafeln*, plates 26b and 36.   41 Ibid., plate 26a.

42 See the juxtaposition in Crous–Kirchner, *Schriftarten*, reprods 12 and 13.

fourteenth centuries, though the script in the fourteenth takes on an embellished, over-elaborate, or even knotty character. Thus the *t* at word-end acquires a long decorative stroke, and neighbouring ascenders are connected by a hairstroke. A special variety of textura in which the upper quadrangles begin with finely curving points like small flames appears to have been based principally in the area of south-east Germany. Austrian scripts display this phenomenon sporadically already c. 1300.[43] These flame-like squares became the hallmark of a regional style in Bohemia, Silesia, and Poland under Charles IV and Wenceslas, but also lasting into the fifteenth century.[44]

In contrast with this mannerism in the north-west of the empire, a sober and heavy textura in two grades is used in Holland and Germany among the Brethren of the Common Life and the Augustinians of the Windesheim congregation, both of which, from the last quarter of the fourteenth century, developed an extraordinarily active book production. The two grades are textus quadratus (with squares on both shaft ends), and textus rotundus (without these), both principally for liturgical books. In some missals only the canon of the mass is written in enlarged quadrangular script.[45] As a third grade is added the 'bastarda' c. 1425.

In the fifteenth century the large textura, which now often appears somewhat sober and box-shaped, seems to be restricted more and more to liturgical manuscripts of large format and to the elementary schoolbooks – those areas in which early printing continues the tradition. Amongst the factors that contributed to its decline, besides the appearance of bastarda scripts, is probably also the increasing use of paper, which was little suited to the writing of this script; in paper manuscripts it is often restricted to the opening words. Textura with pronounced quadrangles is, however, the first kind of script in which the fontcutters of the early printing era achieved a mastery.

Besides the formal types, the 'textuales formatae',[46] according to which the history of textura has been sketched in the foregoing, this script comprises from the thirteenth century, in contrast with the 'gothic cursive' and its stilted variants, a broad gamut of less formal, mostly smaller scripts, 'textuales', down to forms that verge on charter and letter scripts (for example the script of the

---

43 Chroust, *Monumenta* II 12, plate 7b; 13, plate 4.

44 Reprod.: J.V. Schlosser, 'Die Bilderhss. König Wenzels I.,' *Jahrb. der Kunsthistorischen Sammlungen d. Allerh. Kaiserhauses* 14 (1893) 214–317; J. Krasa, *Rukopisy Václava IV* (Prague 1971); the de luxe Jerome office by Iohannes of Saaz from 1404: Chroust, *Monumenta* III 16, plate 9/10; on Silesia see E. Kloos, *Die schlesische Buchmalerei*, reprods 89 f., 93 ff., 144 f., 203, etc.; Mazal *Gotik*, reprod. 8–13.

45 W. Oeser, 'Die Brüder des gemeinsamen Lebens in Münster als Bücherschreiber', *Arch. f. Gesch. d. Buchwesens* 5 (1964) 255 f.

46 Cf. G.I. Lieftinck in *Nomenclature*, 32; in his system for the fourteenth and fifteenth centuries (Gumbert, *Utrechter Kartäuser*, 204 f.) textualis, defined on p. 204, is distinguished by the following levels; 'T formata', 'T. libraria', 'T. currens'.

Munich *Tristan* and the Munich *Parzival* manuscript G).[47] The great majority of manuscripts are written in these scripts. In England, towards the end of the twelfth century, the grade of script used for text was not only separated from the smaller, slightly modified one used for commentary, as before, but the character of both scripts was more strictly differentiated. But the smaller glossing script too, for its part, rose to become a text hand.[48] A descent in style is also frequent between a text hand and the corresponding glosses and commentary. In the smaller grades the script connects rounding and fracturing or slurring; in these scripts the forms of *c* and *t* often become one. The heavily abbreviated university script of the thirteenth and fourteenth centuries in Paris and Oxford is, for example, generally a simplified textura,[49] and even more, its refined descendant type, the tiny though clearly legible 'pearl-script' that was created in the thirteenth century for pocket copies of the Vulgate and the New Testament.[50]

The letter forms of the textura[51] undergo only a few changes, several of which have already been mentioned. At the end of the thirteenth century the *a* takes on a two-tiered form through a bending of the shaft – as was the case in many places with the cursive – and this is especially pronounced in the fourteenth century. On the other hand, the line of the bow in *a* on the left is often drawn as a straight line and the letter divided in the middle ('box-*a*').[52] In place of the stroke on the *i* the dotted *i* appears from the fourteenth century on. The *r*, from the twelfth century, acquires a flourish, and in the twelfth and thirteenth centuries the shoulder-stroke is often separated from the stem. The *z* has various striking forms in German manuscripts, for example with three bows,[53] and in the *Carmina Burana* partly the ç-like form which became the norm in the southern Romania.[54] *W* is frequently written for vv, for example *wlt*. The suprascript vowels *o* and *e* in umlaut and diphthongs show the tendency in the fourteenth century to simplify into mere strokes, and are finally replaced by ᵛ and groups of points, to which the modern *u*-bow and the small umlaut point go back.[55]

The capitals (the initials, not the coloured 'Lombards') give up their simple majuscule forms and change in accordance with the same principles as ruled the large letters of the charter hands and cursive, by doubling of strokes, sinew-like

47 Petzet-Glauning, *Deutsche Schrifttafeln*, plate 32 f.; facs.: *Wolfram von Eschenbach, Parzival, Titurel, Tagelieder*, Cgm *19*, transcription H. Engels, Fr. Dreßler (Stuttgart 1970).
48 Ker, *English MSS*, 2 f.
49 The distinctions between 'scriptura Parisiensis' and 'scriptura Oxoniensis' (see Cencetti, *Lineamenti*, 220 f., and *Compendio*, 76 f.) need further investigation.
50 Reprod.: *New Pal. Soc.*, ser 1, 2, plate 217 copied from four exemplars; Crous–Kirchner, *Schriftarten*, reprod 9; Degering, *Schrift*, plate 81; *Exempla scripturarum* 1, plate 11; Mazal, *Gotik*, reprod. 4.   51 Cf. Gumbert, *Utrechter Kartäuser*, 215 ff.
52 E.g. Crous–Kirchner, *Schriftarten*, reprod. 49; cf. Gumbert, 226.
53 Examples: Koennecke, *Bilderatlas*, 37; Petzet–Glauning, *Deutsche Schrifttafeln*, plates 42b and 48.   54 See above n. 19.
55 Petzet–Glauning, *Deutsche Schrifttafeln*, plates 37, 39, etc. and vol 5, index.

flourishes, and attached small teeth.[56] Many scribes master several minuscule styles and in the subscription they often reveal their proficiency in a different kind of script.[57]

Before the fifteenth century, a regular book trade did not exist in Germany, and hence no development of types resulting from it. Nevertheless, through use and purpose, certain conventions came into vogue relating kind of script, book type, and content, and these were retained for centuries. Large textura was used not only for missals in folio or imposing psalters, but in the most solemn proportions also for pontificals, canons of the mass,[58] and breviaries of moderate size, and also in Bibles, homiliaries, in books for monastic refectory reading,[59] martyrologies, anniversaria, etc. In law codes and statute books the use of large formats and textura attests to the importance of the decrees;[60] for that reason the stately charter affirming the Magdeburg Law for Breslau (12. X. 1283)[61] exceptionally is written in textura. That manuscripts of German poetry were relatively frequently laid out in large formats and large textura[62] indicates already in external appearance what worth was attached to these books by their patrons.

A very different area of preference for the use of regular textura up to the fifteenth century are – despite their smallness, 8o and under – breviaries, books of hours, and books of private edification, and hence also manuscripts of the German mystics.[63] Finally, children learned reading and Latin with large textura, for their schoolbooks and copies of Donatus (in 4o) were written in this script.

9. Gothic cursive and bastarda

The second great genre of bookhand in the gothic period is the (book-)cursive;[64] the name suggests a parallel with the earlier history of script, but this should not be understood too strictly in its technical sense. The opposition textura–cursive

---

56 See below p. 141 for this.

57 Examples: *Catal. mss. datés* 1, plate 174 (subscription by the self-confident English scribe Manerius, s. XII ex, in charter script); ibid. 2, plate 44a (1321, notary script), 52b (1342–52, as previous), 55b (1356, stylized notary script); ibid. 3, plate 101a (1332, almost bastarda); *Mss. datés*, Belgique 1, plate 30 (1236, ornamental script); *Katal. dat. Hss.*, Österreich 1 reprod. 46 (1247, as previous); Mazal, *Gotik*, reprod. 6 (c. 1300, as previous).

58 Cf. Bruckner, *Scriptoria* 1, plate 38b; Degering, *Schrift*, plate 95; both with only 12 lines per page.

59 E.g. Arndt-Tangl⁴, *Schrifttafeln*, 62 (Legenda aurea); Petzet-Glauning, *Deutsche Schrifttafeln*, plate 55 (*Legenda aurea* in German); Arndt-Tangl⁴, *Schrifttafeln* plate 64 (Gregory's 'Dialogi').

60 Arndt-Tangl⁴, *Schrifttafeln*, plate 28 ('Golden bull'); MSS of the *Sachsenspiegel* and of eastern German laws.   61 Chroust, *Monumenta* III 12, plate 7/8.

62 E.g. the Jena Songbook; the Manesse MS; Petzet-Glauning, *Deutsche Schrifttafeln*, plate 39, 40, etc.

63 E.g. Petzet-Glauning, plates 49b, 50; Bruckner, *Scriptoria* 4, plate 38d; *Deutsche Texte des Mittelalters* 18 (Berlin 1910) plate; *Mss. datés*, Belgique, 1, Nr. 58.

64 Literature p. 163. Mazal, *Gotik*, 40 f.

is also not yet firmly established at the beginning of this new genre, the borderline is still fluid, and at the end of the middle ages there are again hybrid forms of various kinds.[65]

By the term 'cursive' is understood the new script that developed when book- and charter-hands were reduced to simpler forms. The term can be used from the end of the twelfth century; and, beginning with the most careless script of drafts, there can be included in this everything below the grade of what can just about still be called a bookhand, and everything below the grade of the formal charter hands that are close to bookhand, scripts that in addition have long-*s* and *f* extended below the line. The script as a bookhand owes a lot to the charter hand, and the history of the later charter hands runs for three hundred years within or along its borders. Hence we must cast an eye on that first.

When the papal chancery gave up the (later) curialis, following a transition period under Honorius II, it formed the papal minuscule after the model of the diplomatic minuscule of imperial charters. This remained the curial script up to the fifteenth century – though naturally with certain stylistic modifications – and depended in its execution on set rules according to the nature of the document.[66] The medium shafts of its text script are more delicate than those of the model, the ascenders are partly devoid of their flourishes. In this the imperial and other chanceries gradually followed the curia, into whose scripts modest, more cursive letter and register scripts also penetrate in the thirteenth century.[67]

In this field too new tendencies first manifest themselves outside Germany. The charters of the Anglo-Norman kings were written in simple minuscule which, in the hands of busy scribes, already achieves an extreme of cursive writing (with round *d* closed above)[68] in the mid-twelfth century. Phenomena that are present in pronounced fashion with these 'scriptores regis' can be observed more generally from the end of the twelfth century in many of the scripts used by notaries: the same inclination towards the left that can almost lead to an appearance resembling garlands, whereby the possibility is regained[69] of writing letters like *u*, *n*, *m* in one stroke. Besides these there appears – as in

65 I have previously called the script by the late medieval name of 'Notula' (*Paläographie*, col. 482 ff. or offprint col. 50); the texts of scripts so described by fifteenth-century writing masters suggest that they were used for teaching scripts for letters. Consequently it seems too restricted.

66 A. Brackmann, *Papsturkunden* (Leipzig–Berlin 1914); *Exempla scripturarum* III. Both these collections contain examples of the 'Scrittura bollatica' ('Littera Sancti Petri') used by the curia from the late sixteenth century to 1878, a caricature of a script; cf. Steffens[2], *Lateinische Paläographie*, on plate 125; Th. Frenz, 'Littera Sancti Petri, zur Schrift der neuzeitlichen Papsturkunden 1550–1878', *Arch. f. Dipl.* 24 (1978) 483–515.

67 Compare the two styles in two different copies of the same charter of Frederick II in Arndt-Tangl[4], *Schrifttafeln*, plate 88. For France: Françoise Gasparri, *L'écriture des actes de Louis VI, Louis VII et Philippe Auguste* (Geneva–Paris 1973) 116.

68 T.A.M. Bishop, *Scriptores regis* (Oxford 1961), e.g. plate 19b; an enlargement in Ch. Johnson–H. Jenkinson, *English Court Hand A.D. 1066 to 1500* (Oxford 1915), frontisp.

69 See also a Genoese register of 1154–64 in V. Federici, *La scrittura delle cancellerie italiane dal secolo XI al XVII* (Rome 1934) plate 33.

earlier charter and glossing hands – the use of long-*s* and *f* extending below the line, and in part also the use of *r* and round *s*, and the bending of these and other descenders that occasionally leads to loops.[70] In addition to these features there is the fact that word-ends, including those with *m* and *n*, are frequently closed with a downward rounding, and finally the forks on the ascenders are dropped – in sum, a simplification of the letter forms.

In these fundamental features scholarly hands,[71] register hands,[72] and the majority of letter hands are closely related to one another from the end of the twelfth century and in the thirteenth. Even the script of literary texts sporadically approaches this character.[73] A further opportunity of forming loops was provided by the ascenders of *b*, round *d*, *h*, and *l*, which in charter hands open with a curve from the right; here the tendency was to start the pen further down for the upward swing that was necessary to reach the peak. In more cursive writing these curves could be closed. The possibilities of this kind of writing are, however, not always used in equal measure; frequently the same hand wrote some of the letters without lifting the pen, while it combined the others.[74] Indeed, in one and the same document the same letters are written sometimes cursively and sometimes composed of separate strokes.[75]

The continental charter script of the thirteenth century was for the most part dominated by European trends that partly imitate the stately and gracious script of the curia and partly are diffused from France. The explanation of the fact that in Hungary, Poland, and Sweden the same letter forms existed as in France is probably that notaries in the schools of the *Ars dictandi*, for example in Orléans or Bologna, were trained in these forms.[76] Charters in the hands of the famous

---

70 Early examples: *Exempla scripturarum* I, plates 6 and 8; II, plates 7 (from 1209) and 34.

71 E.g. Robert Grosseteste (Thomson, *Bookhands*, plate 89); Albertus Magnus (Thomson, plate 38; Kirchner, *Script Lat. libr.²*, plate 44b; H. van Thiel, *Mittellateinische Texte* (Göttingen 1972) Nr. 26; H. Ostlender, 'Die Autographe Alberts des Großen', in *Studia Albertina, Festschrift für Bernhard Geyer* (Münster 1952) 1–21 with 4 plates; Petrus of Limoges († 1306) (Madeleine Mabille in *Scriptorium* 24 (1970) 45–7 and plates 10–13). Marginal notes written in pen or lead in university manuscripts are often as rough as this. The cursive script used by Thomas Aquinas goes even further and in his notes it dissolves into unconnected strokes or strokes linking different words (Steffens², *Lateinsiche Paläographie*, plate 98; Thomson, *Bookhands*, plate 64; *Exempla scripturarum* I, plate 14; A. Dondaine, *Secrétaires de Saint Thomas* (Rome 1956) plates 1 f., 9, 11, 30 ff., 36 ff.; P.-M. Gils in *Scriptorium* 24 (1970) 44 f. with plate 9.) Another example of extremely cursive script is in Paris, BN, Lat. 15,652; reprod: M.-D. Chenu, 'Maîtres et bacheliers de l'université de Paris vers 1240', in *Études d'histoire littéraire et doctrinale du XIIIe siècle*, ser 1 (Paris–Ottawa 1932) 11–39; see plate 17 infra.

72 Steffens², *Lateinische Paläographie*, plates 90 (Hugo of Ostia) and 92 (Frederick II, with the beginnings of sling formation); Arndt-Tangl⁴, *Schrifttafeln*, plate 26 (Albert Beham) and Chroust, *Monumenta* I 1, plates 7 and 2, plate 8 (the same). See also n. 69.

73 Cf. the hand of the Munich Tristan manuscript mentioned above, and manuscript G of Parzival; Petzet-Glauning, *Deutsche Schrifttafeln*, plates 32 and 33.

74 Cf. e.g. *u* and *n/m* in Arndt-Tangl⁴, *Schrifttafeln*, plate 92 from 1288.

75 Chroust, *Monumenta* II 17, plate 7a and 7b from 1287 and 1282.

76 St. Hajnal paid special attention to this phenomenon, but his attempt to prove that a special training in writing at the universities was its cause has not succeeded for Paris. Cf. St. Hajnal, *Vergleichende Schriftproben zur Entwicklung und Verbreitung der Schrift im 12.–13.*

thirteenth-century Bolognese teachers of the *Ars notaria*, Rolandinus and Salatiel, are also preserved.[77]

There are also charters that diverge from the majority in having strong scripts of the textura kind, though with elongated *s* and *f* and other characteristics of charter hands.[78] These became more rare towards the early fourteenth century. In the German charter hands, despite great differences in the local traditions of the numerous chanceries, various styles prevail at different times and it is the imperial chancery that, in part, sets the tone. In the second half of the thirteenth century the tendency towards a much lower model predominates: the delicate script is low and broad. Already at the end of the century this preference for the horizontal disappears and in the fourteenth century the thin descenders often dangle like threads. In the imperial chancery the development of the script proceeds towards the elaborate and artificial; it reaches a highpoint under Louis the Bavarian,[79] in whose time the bows of the ascenders are fractured into pointed angles and are excessively heavily shaded. Under Charles IV the script becomes simpler and the model of the Avignon chancery gains in influence. In the fifteenth century the special character of the charter scripts becomes weaker, particularly as a consequence of the diffusion of models taught by masters for charter and book production. An extreme level of cursive writing is reached in the low, coiled draft script of the chanceries which makes its appearance already in Sigismund's time,[80] and which spread rapidly in the second third of the fifteenth century.[81] Here the forms of the later German (current) script make their appearance (e.g. *d*, *e*, *x*).[82]

Jahrhundert (Budapest–Leipzig–Milan 1943); idem in *Scriptorium* 6 (1952) 177–95; idem, *L'Enseignement de l'écriture aux universités médiévales*², ed. by L. Mezey (Budapest 1959).

77 G. Orlandelli, 'Ricerche sulla origine della "littera Bononiensis": scritture documentarie bolognesi del sec. XII', *Bull. dell'Arch. Pal. Ital.*, n.s. 2/3 (1956/7) plate 6.

78 Cf., e.g., Steffens², *Lateinische Paläographie*, plate 93.

79 Christa Wrede, *Leonhard von München, der Meister der Prunkurkunden Kaiser Ludwigs des Bayern* (Kallmunz 1980), with plates; Arndt-Tangl⁴, *Schrifttafeln*, plate 94. Compare the similar script in plate 27 and even Enikel's Textura (Petzet-Glauning, *Deutsche Schrifttafeln*, plate 40). The stylisation in the 1331 charter of Edward III is comparable: *New Pal. Soc.* 1, ser 2, plate 198.   80 Chroust, *Monumenta* 1 13, plate 3.

81 Chroust, *Monumenta* 1 24, plate 7: Nürnberg 1449.

82 For France cf. L.I. Kiseleva, *Gotičeskij kursiv XIII–XV vv.* (Leningrad 1974); E. Poulle, *Paléographie des écritures cursives en France du XVe au XVIIe siècle* (Geneva 1966), with 32 plates; V.N. Malov, *Proiskhoždenie sovremennogo pisma* (Moskow 1975). M. Prou, *Manuel de paléographie*, Facs. (Paris 1904) plates 32/2 (1367) 35 (1401), shows the extremely cursive scripts of parliamentary decisions. See the complete facsimile of the *Registrum autographum priorum collegii Sorbonae*. Umbrae codicum occidentalium 3 (Amsterdam 1960): 1431–85. In Italy a particular cursive was developed from the script of notaries in the fourteenth and fifteenth centuries which had the form of the 'Mercantesca', which was used chiefly for mercantile records and correspondence. Cf. *Arch. Pal. Ital.* 1, plates 22–6; Cf. Cencetti, *Lineamenti*, 232 f.; G. Orlandelli, 'Osservazioni sulla scrittura mercantesca nei secoli XIV e XV', *Studi Filangieri* 1 (1959) 445–60; R. Marichal in *Storia d'Italia* 5 (I documenti) 2 (Turin 1973) 1288. Examples of Spanish cursive which by the fifteenth century had developed very flourished features ('cursiva cortesana' and 'cursiva procesal') e.g. in Millares Carlo, *Tratado*, plates 290, 315 f., 319 ff., etc.; A. Canellas, *Exempla scripturarum Latinarum* 2 (Saragossa 1966) plate 67.

The last creation that comes from the cradle of the late-medieval imperial chancery is the fractura, an oblong chancery script with slightly flamed rectangles, spindle-shaped *s* and *f*, and majuscules that have the 'elephant trunk' as a special ornament.[83] Display and text script in charters from the chancery of Frederick III show elements of the later script, and in 'prefractura' and textura the chancery scribe Wolfgang Spitzweg wrote two schoolbooks for Prince Maximilian I,[84] who subsequently showed a special preference for the perfected fractura. Such a script was already in use in his chancery around 1500[85] and through the bibliophile printings of the emperor, the prayerbook of 1513[86] and the 'Teuerdank' of 1517[87] – for whose font the imperial secretary Vincenz Rockner wrote the 'sample' – it rapidly attained popularity.

Already in the late thirteenth century the writing practice of the schools, the universities, and literature brought about a transition to smooth cursive that was fond of loops. This could be written rapidly and is similar to charter hand but has fewer extravagant ascenders and less pronounced curves, and is also often written on very crammed lines.[88] Early examples in which the use of cursive characteristics is still in part inconsistent come from the years 1273 (Lorraine),[89] 1277 (Germany: 'Wernherus scripsit'),[90] 'before 1281' (Belval, in the Ardennes),[91] 1282 (Oxford?),[92] and 1289 (Paris).[93] The rapid influx of the simpler, more or less cursive scripts in the area of bookhand was facilitated by the changes in teaching methods brought about by the universities and city schools, by the intensification of pastoral care through the new orders and the secular clergy, and by the growth of vernacular literatures, which found their public also among the laity.

With the fourteenth century, writing practice for books shifts on a wide front to cursive; paper and cursive go together in this period.[94] The writing of loops

---

83 A. Hessel, 'Die Schrift der Reichskanzlei seit dem Interregnum und die Entstehung der Fraktur', *Nachr. Göttinger Ges. Wiss.*, phil.-hist. Kl. (1937) 43–59. The form of *a* in Fraktur, with the upper compartment narrower than the lower, was already present in many cursive and bastarda scripts; see above p.135. See also P. Zahn, 'Nürnberger kalligraphische Fraktur 1493–1513 in Handschriften aus dem Besitz des Kirchenmeisters Sebald Schreyer', in *Festschrift für Peter Acht* (Kallmünz 1976) 295–304 with plate.

84 H. Fichtenau, *Die Lehrbücher Maximilians I. und die Anfänge der Frakturschrift* (Hamburg 1961), esp. 34 ff. and plates 12–16, 31–7; Mazal, *Gotik*, reprod. 38.

85 Reprod. in C. Wehmer, 'Augsburger Schreiber aus der Frühzeit des Buchdrucks', *Beiträge zur Inkunabelkunde*, n.F. 2 (1938) 164.   86 Crous-Kirchner, *Schriftarten*, reprod. 81.

87 Ibid., reprod. 82.

88 The levels of 'cursiva' in Lieftinck's system (Gumbert, *Utrechter Kartäuser*, 204 f.) are 'cursiva formata', 'c. libraria', 'c. currens'.   89 *Catal. mss. datés* 5, plate 25a.

90 H. Grauert, 'Magister Heinrich der Poet in Würzburg und die römische Kurie', *Abh. K. Bayer. Akad. Wiss.*, phil.-hist. Kl. 27 1/2 (1912) plate 2 (partly in Bischoff, *Paläographie*, col. 449/450; offprint col. 71 f.).   91 *Catal. mss. datés* 5, plate 29a.

92 Thomson, *Bookhands*, plate 94.

93 Ibid., plate 13. On plate 67 (marginalia) there is a contemporaneous Italian example; cf. plate 72.

94 Examples, e.g. in Schum, *Exempla codicum Amplonianorum Erfurtensium*; Petzet-Glauning, *Deutsche Schrifttafeln*, plate 5 f.

becomes general also in book cursive, the changes in the letter forms are the same as in charter hand, but the script is more modest than that of the chanceries and the differences in style are less pronounced. Around the turn of the fourteenth century to the fifteenth the book cursives in Germany collapse,[95] and round loops are now written. A result is the possibility of confusing *b* and *v*, *lb* and *w*. Modest book cursives persist also in the fifteenth century,[96] and are used, when they needed them, by scribes who learned a bastarda.[97] The script of the city administration[98] and of urban book-keeping is a simple cursive.[99]

With the widespread use of this script, with the steady increase of written communication and the growth of registries, with the immense scribal activity in the universities and in the religious orders, it was inevitable that changes should come about also in the manner of fashioning the letters, whereby either the quill remained on the paper, or simpler constructions were tried.[100] Besides the loops-and-slings-formation some others should be mentioned. Some have influence on the textura, like the two-compartment *a* created by the formation and closing of an upper bow common in the more fluent cursive of the thirteenth century, and which frequently survives in the fourteenth. It is then gradually replaced by an *a* closed with a slight point at the top, or bluntly closed due to a break of the right shaft. Various changes in direction are to be observed in the case of *q*: in the cursive of abbot Iohannes von Viktring's draft[101] the right upper and left lower halves are joined in one movement; in the fifteenth century the descender is frequently drawn up again with a swing so that it closes the letter flat on top and at the same time adds a tuft.[102] Other changes in direction follow in the fifteenth century with round *s*: it consists in a shaft or bow on the left side and a flat 3 on the right ('reverse *s*')[103] or it is written from below upwards.[104] A new ligature comes into being with *sz*. The large letters (initials), which are variants of old majuscule and minuscule forms, have changed drastically since the thirteenth

95 In charters, e.g., already in Chroust, *Monumenta* II 17, plate 10b from 1362 and 18, plate 1a from 1360.

96 E.g. Crous-Kirchner, *Schriftarten*, reprods 33, 37, 42, etc.; Th. Frenz, 'Gotische Gebrauchschriften des 15. Jahrhunderts: Untersuchungen zur Schrift lateinisch-deutscher Glossare am Beispiel des "Vocabularius Ex quo"', *Codices Manuscripti* 7 (1981) 14–30, with plates.

97 Cf. the two scripts used by the chronicler Andreas of Regensburg: Chroust, *Monumenta* I 6, plate 6.

98 R. Thommen, *Schriftproben aus Basler Handschriften des XIV.–XVI. Jahrhunderts*, 2nd enlarged ed. (Berlin 1908); A. Largiadèr, *Handschriftenproben aus den Zürcher Steuerbüchern des XIV. und XV. Jahrhunderts* (Zürich 1952). Numerous specimens from registry manuscripts in Bruckner, *Scriptoria* I/7, 10–12.

99 Reprod: Fr. Bastian, *Das Runtingerbuch 1383–1407*, I (Munich 1944) 240, 256, 264, 328 etc.; C. Wehmer, *Mainzer Probedrucke in der Type des sogenannten astronomischen Kalenders für 1448* (Munich 1948) plates 6, 10–12 (debit book of a Mainz tailor, end of the fourteenth century). 100 Cf. Gumbert, *Utrechter Kartäuser*, 242.

101 Arndt-Tangl⁴, *Schrifttafeln*, plate 27. Otherwise attested also in the fourteenth century: Petzet-Glauning, *Deutsche Schrifttafeln*, plates 35, cols 1, 9; 44; 52; 53.

102 E.g. Crous-Kirchner, *Schriftarten*, reprod. 42.

103 Gumbert, *Utrechter Kartäuser*, 227. 104 Gumbert, reprod. 33.

century through sinew-like ornamental strokes, doubling of strokes, and loop-formation, occasionally even to the point of illegibility.[105] From the late four-teenth century there appear fashionable approach-strokes in the form of a horn or the 'elephant trunk'.

In England, with the transition of cursive to book script, the *r* which is long and attenuated and whose right stroke usually touches the following letter without any intermediate element is taken over as a traditional element of the English chancery script. To the 'anglicana'[106] belongs the two-compartment *a*; a favoured form of the *e* is a circle in which a little tail hangs down. In the early period of this script the ascents of *b*, *h*, *k*, and *l* that are provided on the right with loops frequently acquire a forking through adding of a horn towards the left.[107] In calligraphic execution ('anglicana formata') it can approach a bastarda in appearance.[108] In the fifteenth century, under continental influence, a simpler austere cursive with a single-compartment *a* appears that is joined at an acute angle,[109] the 'secretary hand', which likewise allows a higher stylisation.[110]

In Spain a stylised charter hand, 'letra de privilegios', developed in the thirteenth century, is taken over towards the end of that century almost unchanged as a bookhand, 'redonda de libros'.[111] It is an upright script written with broad quill which allows the doubled ascenders and the long leftward-inclined stem of the regularly-used uncial *d* to appear club-shaped, and which emphasises the extremely long abbreviation strokes.[112]

The gap between cursive and textura was bridged mainly by means of the bastarda scripts,[113] whose name – despite all the variety in their actual appear-ance – allows one to say that they combine peculiarities of two genres of script.[114] The use of this historical name should respect this definition.[115]

---

105 F. Uhlhorn, *Die Großbuchstaben der sog. gotischen Schrift mit besonderer Berücksichtigung der Hildesheimer Stadtschreiber* (Leipzig 1924) offprint from *Z.f. Buchkunde*; W. Heinemeyer, 'Studien zur Geschichte der gotischen Urkundenschrift', *Arch.f. Dipl.*, Beiheft 4/2, enlarged ed. (1982); Peter Langhof, 'Triebkräfte und Entwicklungstendenzen der gotischen kursiven Urkundenschriften im Gebiet der deutschen Ostexpansion im Spätmittelalter', *Jb.f. Gesch. d. Feudalismus* 3 (1979) 87–109, with illustr.

106 M.B. Parkes, *English cursive book hands 1250–1500* (Oxford 1969) xiv ff. North German examples of the form of e, Chroust, *Monumenta* III 6, 6 (Brandenburg Chancery 1319); III 20, 5a (Lübeck 1345).   107 Parkes, xv.   108 See below p. 143.   109 Parkes, xvii f.
110 See below p. 144.   111 Cencetti, *Lineamenti*, 244 and 253 f.
112 Examples in Kirchner, *Script. Goth. libr.*, plate 53; Millares Carlo, *Tratado*, illustr. 273; E. Monaci, *Facsimili di antichi manoscritti*, plates 6, 97.

113 Lieftinck now calls these '(littera) Hybrida' for his earlier usage of (*Mss. datés*, Pays-Bas 1, texts, xv ff.), (*Nomenclature*, 32). Here too the three levels 'H formata', 'H. libraria' 'H. currens' are possible (Gumbert, *Utrechter Kartäuser*, 204 f.). In Italy the name is used for a chancery cursive, not a bookscript.

114 The above mentioned forceful charter hands (see note 78) developed according to the 'Bastarda' principle in the thirteenth century. For a use of this sort of stilted script s. XIII² as a bookscript: Bruckner, *Scriptoria* 5, plate 41 b (Einsiedeln 355; Martinus Polonus).

115 C. Wehmer, 'Die Namen der gotischen Buchschriften', *Zentralbl. f. Bibliothekswesen* 49 (1932) 230 ff.

Various trends led to a bridging of the gap between textura and the cursives – originally the expression of a contrast – that came about in the fourteenth and fifteenth centuries in multifarious ways. In Italy a stylish notarial script found approval as the script for literary works; this is evidenced by the codices of the *Divina commedia* belonging to the group of 'Dante del cento'.[116] Nor are examples completely lacking in Germany in the fourteenth century: those that can be mentioned are the fair copy of Iohannes of Viktring (c. 1342),[117] Rudolf of Ems in Pal. Germ. 146,[118] the Berlin *Parzival* fragment,[119] and the miscellany in Munich, Bay. Staatsbibl., Cgm 717.[120] The cursives themselves tended towards the textura[121] when they were consciously written with the purpose of making a stately impression. This could be achieved through solidification of the stroke and a stretching of the medium lengths. In the two highest grades of the above-mentioned English scripts even the shafts could be fractured. Most bastarda scripts use the simple *a* of the cursive.

The best known bastarda is that affected fifteenth-century script styled from the French chancery cursive, mostly inclined slightly towards the right with or without loops, which is written with bold contrasting or hair- and broad-strokes and separately appended shafts of *n* and *m*, the last ones, within the word, being mostly fractured and arched slightly inwards. It acquires an elegant prickly character ('Bourgouignonne') through its pointed descenders, through its forms of *t* and *st*, and through small points of *e*, *g*, and *s*. Used mainly for French texts, it becomes the court hand par excellence under Philip the Good and Charles the Bold, but was also much used in France into the sixteenth century.[122] It affects the scripts of England and the Low Countries. Of the two English bastarda, the 'bastarda anglicana', which appears already in the mid-fourteenth century,[123] still retains the two-tiered *a* up to 1500, while the later 'bastard secretary' comes more under the influence of the French 'lettre bâtarde'.[124]

A Dutch and Lower German bastarda that was also written by the monks of Windesheim and the Brethren of the Common Life, and which was so designated by them, dispensed with the loops and is mostly heavier and blunter like

---

116 E.g. Steffens[2], *Lateinische Paläographie*, plate 103; Kirchner, *Script. Goth. libr.*, plate 39. Further instances in *Arch. Pal. Ital.* 10, facs. 69. Cf. Cencetti, *Lineamenti*, 247 f.

117 Arndt-Tangl[4], *Schrifttafeln*, plate 27.

118 *Deutsche texte des Mittelalters* 20 (Berlin 1915) plate.   119 Degering, *Schrift*, plate 92.

120 Petzet-Glauning, *Deutsche Schrifttafeln*, plate 56.

121 By contrast a 'Textus praecisus' with hairlines which approach bows used to finish off certain letters could be employed for the ritual for the coronation of Edward II, *Pal. Soc.*, ser 2, plate 196.

122 Cf. e.g. Lieftinck, *Nomenclature*, fig. 25; *Catal. mss. datés* 1 (many examples from 1426, plate 88b, to 1543, plate 166a); *Mss. datés, Pays-Bas* 1, plates 269 ff.; Fr. Winkler, *Die flämische Buchmalerei des XV. und XVI. Jahrhunderts* (Leipzig 1925); O. Pächt–Dagmar Thoss, 'Französische Schule 1', *Österr. Akad. Wiss.*, phil.-hist. Kl., Denkschriften 118 (Wien 1974); Mazal, *Gotik*, reprod. 24. A precursor: Kirchner, *Script. Goth. libr.*, plate 49 (1406).

123 Parkes, *English cursive bookhands*, xvii f., xxiii f. and plate 7/8.

124 Ibid., xxi f. and plate 14/15.

the scripts there on the whole; it was created around 1425.[125] The numerous scripts from other regions of Germany that are designated as bastarda in the literature[126] are very diverse, some with, others without loops, some with regular approach-strokes on the shafts, others written to a large extent without lifting the pen. Nonetheless the early printing press, when it chose bastarda for German texts, was able to base its samples on some regional scripts.

The Czech bastardas, which have their roots in the fourteenth century[127] and with which the somewhat later Polish types can be compared, have a relatively narrow area of variation, upright or almost upright, with somewhat broad stroke, written mostly with slings. In strict calligraphic forms with stressed fracturing, this script, which the printers took over as a model, was used until well into the sixteenth century in liturgical manuscripts. Through Jan Hus's *Orthographia Bohemica* a path was indicated towards a unified and simplified spelling of the Czech sounds by means of diacritics.[128]

In German writing practice, forms of the gotico-antiqua make their entry around the mid-fifteenth century.[129] Half a century later printing undermined the living tradition of medieval bookhands.[130]

In contrast with the writing practice of the fourteenth century, that of the fifteenth presents a bewildering wealth of forms and types. Textura script are graded in accordance with the degree of fracturing the shaft, and lower scripts are varied by stretching and enlarging, through suppression of the loops, through fractured or rounded stylisation, and in many other ways. This multiplicity of types, if not produced by the professional writing-masters was at least increased by them and they devised a nomenclature for it. One of their number, Wolfgang Fugger, in the sixteenth century remarked that 'they make the script bend, curve, mangle, hang, behead, and walk on stilts'.[131] Advertisement sheets from writing-masters and teachers, with samples of types and their names, are

---

125 Lieftinck, *Nomenclature*, reprod. 26; Gumbert, *Utrechter Kartäuser*, 204 and reprods 142–50; Crous-Kirchner, *Schriftarten*, reprods 45 f., 48 (written in Vadstena), 49–51; 59; Kirchner, *Script. Goth. libr.*, plates 60a, 62.

126 J. Kirchner, in Crous-Kirchner, *Schriftarten*, 19 ff. and reprods 31–44; Mazal, *Gotik*, 42 f., and reprods 25–32.

127 P. Spunar, 'Genese české bastardy a její vztah k českým prvotiskům', *Listy filológické* 3 (78, 1955) 34–51 with reprods; idem, 'L'évolution et la fonction de la bâtarde en Bohême et en Pologne', *Studia źródło znawcze* 6 (1961) 1–19 with reprods; J. Pražák, 'Puvod české bastardy', *Studie o rukopisy* 20 (1980) 93–118. Fr. Muzika, *Die schöne Schrift in der Entwicklung des lateinischen Alphabets* 1 (Hanau 1965) plates 104–10; A. Gieysztor, *Zarys dziejów pisma łacińskiego* (Warsaw 1973) plates 27 and 29; Wł. Semkowicz, *Paleografia Łaciński* (Krakow 1951) reprods 125, 127, 129. *Katal. dat. Hss.*, Österreich 4, reprods 94, 206, 297.   128 J. Schröpfer, *Hussens Traktat 'Orthographia Bohemica'* (Wiesbaden 1968).

129 See below p. 148.

130 See the remarkable artificial bastarda used by a nun at Ulm in 1496; Crous-Kirchner, *Schriftarten*, reprod. 36.

131 *Ein nutzlich und wolgegründt Formular* (Nürnberg 1553; repr. Munich-Pullach 1967) f.k IV[v].

preserved from roughly 1400 on from Germany and France;[132] for example, that of Johannes Hagen from Lower Saxony contains, besides four kinds of textura, 'notula simplex', 'notula acuta', 'notula fracturarum', 'notula conclavata', another kind of notula, 'separatus', 'bastardus', and a transitional script.[133] The Augsburg Benedictine Leonhard Wagner, who dedicated to Maximilian a collection of one-hundred old, contemporary, and fantastically varied script samples with in part equally fanciful names, surpassed all the writing-masters of his time.[134]

10. Humanistic script

When, at the very end of the fourteenth century, Coluccio Salutati and, with a wider audience, Poggio Bracciolini inaugurated a new era in the history of writing with the imitation of early medieval minuscule, a stimulus that went back to Petrarch brought forth its first fruits.[1] Petrarch's numerous autographs, which show sometimes a chancery script and sometimes a business hand, partly a gothic bookhand, and especially frequently its lower grade, a glossing script, display a striving after loosening and naturalness in the script that frees it from the bold gothic.[2] He himself expressed his displeasure with the 'litterae

132 B. Kruitwagen, *Laatmiddeleeuwsche Palaeographica, Palaeotypica, Liturgica, Kalendalia, Grammaticalia* (The Hague 1942) 1–116; the writing-master's page of Hermann Strepel from 1447 also in *Mss. datés*, Pays-Bas 1, plate 366/367); C. Wehmer, 'Die Schreib-meisterblätter des späten Mittelalters', in *Miscellanea Giovanni Mercati* 6. Studi e Testi 126 (Vatic. 1946) 147–61; H. Steinberg, 'Medieval writing-masters', *The Library*, ser 2, 22 (1942) 1 ff. with reprod.; M. Steinmann, 'Ein mittelalterliches Schriftmusterblatt', *Arch. f. Dipl.* 21 (1975) 450–58 with plate; Herrad Spilling, 'Schreibkünste des späten Mittelalters', *Codices Manuscripti* 4 (1978) 97–119, with illustr.; Françoise Gasparri, 'Note sur l'enseignement de l'écriture aux XVe–XVIe siècles', *Scrittura e Civiltà* 2 (1978) 245–61. On fragments of an English writing master's advertisement sheet with textura scripts for liturgical manuscripts with music see S.J.P. Van Dijk, 'An advertisement sheet of an early fourteenth-century writing master at Oxford', *Scriptorium* 10 (1956) 47–64 with plates 8–11.
133 Crous-Kirchner, *Schriftarten*, reprod. 30.
134 C. Wehmer (ed), *Leonhard Wagner, Proba centum scripturarum*, facsimile ed. (Leipzig 1963).
  1 Batelli, *Lezioni*³, 245 ff.; idem, in *Nomenclature*, 35–44; Cencetti, *Lineamenti*, 258 ff.; idem, *Compendio*, 79 ff.; B.L Ullman, *The Origin and Development of Humanistic Script* (Rome 1960); A.C. De la Mare, *The handwriting of Italian Humanists* 1, fasc. 1 (Oxford 1973); A.J. Fairbank–R.W. Hunt, *Humanistic Script of the Fifteenth and Sixteenth centuries*. Bodleian Picture Book 12 (Oxford 1960); John, *Latin Paleography*, 33–6. Recent research has shifted the origins of humanistic script to the last years of the fourteenth century; Niccoli's share in its development may also be larger than had previously been thought. Cf. Albinia C. De la Mare, 'Humanistic script; the first ten years', in F. Kraft–D. Wuttke (edd), *Das Verhältnis der Humanisten zum Buch*, Deutsche Forschungsgemeinschaft, Kommission für Humanismusforschung, Mitteilung 4, 89–110 with reprod; eadem.–D.F.S. Thomson, 'Poggio's earliest manuscript?', *It. Med. e Um.* 16 (1973) 179–96 with reprod; G. Billanovich, 'Alle origini della scrittura Humanistica: Padova 1261 e Firenze 1397' in *Miscellanea Augusto Campana* 1 (Padua 1981) 125–140 f. (on a transcript written by Poggio when he was 17 which shows transitional features in the script.
  2 A. Petrucci, *La scrittura di Francesco Petrarca*, Studi e Testi 248 (Vatic. 1967).

scholasticae', just as on the other hand he expressed in programmatic words his hopes for worthier, simpler, more agreeable and clearer script. Features of his personal script reappear in the hands of Boccacio and Salutati. Salutati (†1406) was used to chancery script and a 'half-gothic' bookhand, some of whose forms he changed somewhat in the course of the years.[3] He was familiar with their script from early medieval codices, of which he possessed a large number, and it was probably shortly after 1400, while completing an older manuscript of Pliny's letters,[4] that he reintroduced the long final *s* and the lost ligatures *ae* and *e*, as well as *&*, and with this experiment the history of humanistic script begins.

Somewhere between 1400 and 1402 Salutati's pupil Poggio Bracciolini copied the first manuscript modelled on a script from roughly the tenth or eleventh century, somewhat stiff but with a homogeneous ductus. The bitings are abandoned, round *d* and round *s* (the last within the line) are banished, the ligature *&* is taken up anew, and the *æ* ligature is partially restored. Poggio was secretary in various posts, longest of all in the service of the papal curia, and as such he wrote a more formal or cursive traditional chancery script; in this script he also produced the first transcripts of antique texts newly discovered by him. But alongside this his humanistic script achieved greater freedom and harmony and in his Roman period he himself instructed assistants in this new style of script.[5] Among the Italian circles that were open to the humanistic ideal this script became an expression of the new intellectual tendency.

For display script with the humanistica the capitalis was mostly used, modelled on antique inscriptions, and this acquired its final form c. 1454 through Mantegna.[6] But in some humanistic circles, in crude contradiction of the classical ideal, a majuscule much given to variation found favour which in part followed Greek examples and had adopted double-bellied *E*, *H* with a drooping middle stroke, and *M* in the form of a broad *H* with a T-shaped crossbar.[7] As a result of early humanistic currents this script also won great favour in Germany amongst scribes, painters, and stonemasons.[8]

Though devised as an imitation of earlier hands, the humanistic script was

---

3 A. Petrucci, *Il protocollo notarile di Coluccio Salutati (1371–1373)* (Milan 1963) 21 ff.; Braxton Ross, 'Salutati's defeated candidate for Humanistic script', *Scrittura e civiltà* 5 (1981) 187–98.

4 Ullman, *Humanistic Script*, 16 ff. and plate 8/9; *Handwriting*, 37 and plate 8h.

5 For a detailed list of the distinctive features see Th. Frenz, 'Das Eindringen humanistischer Schriftformen in die Urkunden und Akten der päpstlichen Kurie im XV. Jahrhundert', *Arch. f. Dipl.* 19 (1973) 334 ff.

6 Cf. M. Meiss, 'Toward a more comprehensive Renaissance palaeography', *The Art Bulletin* 42 (1960) 97–112, with reprod.

7 An exemplary collection in S. Morison, *Politics and Script* (Oxford 1972) reprod. 174; idem, *Byzantine Elements in Humanistic Script Illustrated from the Aulus Gellius of 1445 in the Newberry Library* (Chicago 1952). An example from 1419: *Mss. datés*, Belgique 2, Nr. 137. A further alphabet with numerous variants in M. Steinmann, 'Die humanistische Schrift und die Anfänge des Humanismus in Basel', *Archiv. f. Dipl.* 22 (1976) 396–437, reprod. 46.

8 R.M. Kloos, *Die Inschriften der Stadt und des Landkreises München*, Die Deutschen Inschriften 5 (Stuttgart 1958) xxiii.

modified by individual scribes with regard to special types that stood somewhat outside the run of early medieval minuscule. Hence the script of Ciriaco of Ancona, meritorious as a collector of inscriptions, is overloaded with forms that were based on early medieval ligatures and abbreviations, on the majuscule of inscriptions, and even on Greek;[9] and Giovano Pontano – scribe of the Wolfenbüttel Tibullus and of the Leyden Tacitus – following a beneventan model, occasionally used in his easy, elegant script high, tightly-belted *e, f, r, s* passing under the line, and several ligatures.[10] Other scribes who held fast to rotunda forms partially adopted humanistic habits, so that mixtures of all levels came into existence (gotico-antiqua). In the end the humanistic antiqua, perfected by important calligraphers like Giovanni Aretino,[11] who was active already before 1410, together with the humanistic cursive conquered practically the whole of Italian book production, with the exception of the liturgical and legal domains.

The humanistic cursive is the personal contribution with which Niccolo Niccoli († 1437), Poggio's friend and a participant in his discoveries, enriched the reform of script. Just a few years after Poggio's decision to make the switch, Niccoli too was in possession of a humanistic script. But by 1423 at the latest (when almost sixty years old) he went over to writing the humanistic reformed alphabet in the fashion of his slanted Italian cursive, with a thin cursive ductus in paper manuscripts.[12] This script too found favour in humanistic circles and was preferred by some, such as Pomponio Leto.[13] The slanted script was written as a finely tuned series of elegant individual letters[14] by the Paduan native Bartolomeo Sanvito, a member of Leto's Roman circle, and in this form it became available for book printing. The Venetian printer Aldus Manutius introduced it in 1501, decades after the humanistica had become the model for the antiqua letters.[15]

9 D. Fava, 'La scrittura libraria di Ciriaco d'Ancona', in *Scritti di paleografia e diplomatica in onore di Vincenzo Federici* (Florence 1945) 295–305 with reprod., and with discussion also of Ciriaco's imitators; J. Wardrop, *The Script of Humanism* (Oxford 1963) 14 f. and plate 8 f.
10 M. Ihm, *Palaeographia Latina* 1, reprod. 20; Ullman, 'Pontano's handwriting and the Leiden manuscript of Tacitus und Suetonius', *It. Med. e Um.* 2 (1959) 328 ff. with reprod.
11 Ullman, *Humanistic Script*, 91 ff., reprods 45–50; Giovanna Nicolaj Petronio, 'Per la soluzione di un enigma: Giovanni Aretino copista, notaio e cancelliere', *Humanistica Lovanensia* 30 (1981) 1–12.
12 Ullman, *Humanistic Script*, 59 ff. and reprods 29–39; *Handwriting*, 50 ff. and plates 10/11; J.L. Butrica, 'A new fragment in Niccoli's formal hand', *Scriptorium* 35 (1981) 290–2 and plates 15/16.
13 J. Wardrop, *The Script of Humanism*, 22 f. and plate 15; Ehrle–Liebaert, *Specima*, plate 50.
14 Wardrop, 19–35 and plates 16–38.
15 Through the introduction of humanistic cursive most gothic chancery scripts were transformed in a process which was slow, and not exempt from setbacks. Florence led the way, and after the Council of Florence the script of the papal secretariat fell under humanist influence, as evidenced by the briefs written in the new script. Cf. P. Herde, 'Die Schrift der Florentiner Behörden in der Frührenaissance (ca. 1400–1460)', *Arch. f. Dipl.* 17 (1971) 302–35; Th. Frenz, 'Das Eindringen humanistischer Schriftformen', ibid. 19 (1973) 287–418 and 20 (1974) 384–506.

At different dates in different regions, the new scripts became known and were copied outside Italy, the antiqua first of all. At the councils of Constance and Basle, which brought the non-Italian participants into contact with humanists like Poggio, it appears that only isolated humanistic initiatives were adopted.[16] Greater perhaps was the influence exercised by Aeneas Sylvius, one of the apostles of humanism at the court of Vienna. However, Petrus of Rosenheim, later prior of Melk, who went to Subiaco in order to familiarise himself with the religious reforms there, returned with the new script as early as 1418,[17] and this was even more the case with the numerous German students who were fascinated by classical studies in Italy and who assimilated their script more or less to the antiqua, for example, the great book collector Hartmann Schedel,[18] and Hieronymus Rotenpeck.[19] Others remained in Italy and earned their living as scribes of the antiqua.[20] In the imperial chancery the humanistic script came into occasional use under Frederick III and Maximilian.[21] Gothic-humanistic mixed scripts also penetrated into Germany and took the place of the bastarda. In the case of the German professional scribe Molitor one can observe how the humanistic taste shows increasingly in his script.[22]

Poggio spent the years 1419–22 in England, though the script initiated by him seems to have attracted attention there for the first time probably somewhat later, thanks to the humanistic inclinations of Duke Humphrey of Gloucester (1390–1447), the 'protector' of Oxford University. Books were written for him in this script in Italy and England. Then members of the Oxford and Cambridge universities brought back the humanistic script and manuscripts after their years of study in Italy.[23]

In France one of the earliest possessors of humanistic manuscripts was Zanone da Castiglione, bishop of Lisieux (1422–32) and of Bayeux (1432–59),

16 On transformations in the script of Johannes Keck, Prior of Tegernsee, Bischoff, *Mittelalterliche Studien* 1, 66 n. 11. An exemplary method is used by M. Steinmann, 'Die humanistische Schrift und die Anfänge des Humanismus in Basel', *Arch. f. Dipl.* 22 (1976) 376–437 with reprod; idem, 'Die lateinische Schrift zwischen Mittelalter und Humanismus', in *Paläographie* (1981) 193–9 and plates 25–7.   17 Chroust, *Monumenta* II 14, plate 1.

18 Chroust, *Monumenta* I 10, plate 10.

19 Ibid., I 10, plate 8. Cf. also the Latin and German script of the Zürich doctor Konrad Türst, in Bischoff, *Paläographie*, col. 449 f., reprod. 9/10 (offprint, col. 71 f.).

20 P. Liebaert in 'L'Italia e l'Arte straniera', *Atti del X Congresso Internazionale di Storia dell'Arte* (Rome 1922) 200–14. Gerardus Helye, Erasmus of Rotterdam's father, wrote a gotico–antiqua script during his activities in Fabriano in 1457/8; cf. G. Avarucci, 'Due codici scritti da "Gerardus Helye" padre di Erasmo', *It. Med. e Um.* 26 (1983) 215–55 and plate 4 f.

21 There are imperial charters in reproductions XI, 26, 28, 30; cf. also Chroust, *Monumenta* I 12, plates 8 and 13, plate 1.

22 Reprod. in C. Wehmer, 'Augsburger Schreiber aus der Frühzeit des Buchdrucks', *Beiträge zur Inkunabelkunde* n.F. 2 (1938) 116 f.

23 Cf. R.W. Hunt, *Duke Humphrey and English Humanism in the fifteenth century* (Exhibition catalogue, Oxford 1970); A.C. De la Mare, 'Humanistic hands in England', in *Manuscripts in Oxford: R.W. Hunt Memorial Exhibition* (Oxford 1980) 93–101.

who was also in contact with Duke Humphrey.[24] The first example written by a Fleming is dated 1439.[25] Spanish humanistic manuscripts are mentioned from the years 1467 and 1469;[26] but a codex of 1452 already shows an almost perfected imitation.[27]

The humanistic cursive became familiar to scholars of Reuchlin's, Sebastian Brant's, and Erasmus's generation; it was an outward sign of the new education and was preferred for Latin. However, even after the turn of the century outstanding humanistically-minded personalities such as Mutian (born in 1471) still wrote Latin in a German school cursive.[28] Luther's early Latin script was mixed.[29] The humanistically-run school contributed to the complete separation of the scripts. In German printing a differentiation according to languages had taken place already in the mid-eighties with the end of the gotico-antiqua; for the rotunda that replaced it was used for Latin, while for German texts, on the other hand, the bastarda and its derivatives were used. The antiqua was disseminated only with the Reformation literature.

24 *Mss. datés* 2, plate 99a. The effect of Italian influence on early French humanism is also shown by Jean de Montreuil's (†1418) conscious attempt to develop a strongly italianising script, no longer gothic, but not yet humanistic; cf. G. Ouy, 'Jean de Montreuil et l'introduction de l'écriture humanistique en France au début du XVe siècle', in *Miniatures, scripts, collections. Essays presented to G.I. Lieftinck* 4 [Litterae textuales] (Amsterdam 1976) 53–61; idem, 'In search of the earliest traces of French Humanism: the evidence from codicology', *The Library Chronicle, Univ. of Pennsylvania* 43 (1978) 3–38, with various examples of the script of Nicolas de Clamanges.   25 *Mss. datés*, Pays-Bas 1, plates 462–4.

26 Millares Carlo, *Tratado* 1, 218.   27 Thomson, *Bookhands*, plate 130; cf. plate 132.

28 G. Mentz, *Handschriften der Reformationszeit* (Bonn 1912) plate 2.   29 ibid., plate 4.

Supplement

1. Abbreviations (Forms and methods of abbreviation in the high and later middle ages)

Latin scribal practice employed abbreviations extensively.[1] Amongst the Romans already in pre-Christian times first names, diurnal signs in calendars, and numerous formulae from official business and especially legal language were abbreviated in inscriptions and otherwise by 'litterae singulares', as well as the syllables *-bus* and *-que*; the grammarian M. Valerius Probus (first century AD) collected and explained these symbols.[2] In the period after Probus, at any rate when Roman tachygraphy was already in use, new abbreviations were fashioned for use in normal script: above all for particles, relative and demonstrative pronouns which could be used for general requirements, and in addition to that very many abbreviations of legal terms.[3] Late antique legal manuscripts of the fourth and fifth centuries such as the Verona Gaius, the fragment of the Formula Fabiana, and the Fragmenta Vaticana show their use.[4]

In these manuscripts the abbreviations consist either of groups of several (usually two) elements – in general the first letters of syllables – or words after which the others are left out (by 'suspension'). In contrast, short or frequent words, final syllables, and also some legal terms are abbreviated by means of various signs or suprascript letters. In a few technical terms the final syllables too could be attached. Abbreviation was indicated mostly by a stroke above, in part also by a crossbar. Examples of simple suspensions are: m', p', t' (*-mus, pos* or *post, -tur*); examples of 'syllabic' suspensions: $\overline{qq}$ (*quoque*); with final syllables: hðe, hðum (*herede, heredum*); examples of superscription: m̊, ṗ, q̇ (*modo, pri-,*

---

1 For what follows see Cencetti, *Lineamenti*, 353 ff.; idem, *Compendio*, 89 ff.
2 M. Valerii Probi *De litteris singularibus fragmentum*, ed. Th. Mommsen in *Grammatici Latini* (Keil) 4, 271 ff.; P.F. Girard, *Textes de droit romain*[5] (Paris 1923) 214–220.
3 L. Wenger, *Die Quellen des römischen Rechts*, Österr. Akad. Wiss., Denkschriften 2 (Vienna 1953) 114 ff.
4 CLA IV 488; VIII 1042; I 45; a collection in Steffens[2], *Lateinische Paläographie*, xxxiv. Cf. also B. Bischoff–D. Nörr, 'Eine unbekannte Konstitution Kaiser Julians', *Abh. Bayer. Akad. Wiss.*, phil.-hist. Kl., n.F. 58 (1963); an exemplar rich in Notae (perhaps fourth-century) was uncomprehendingly copied in the tenth century.

qui); examples of abbreviation with tachygraphic signs: ꝑ , ꜿ (*pro, con*); examples of letters with crossbars; +, ꝑ (*inter, per*); in the case of *enim, nihil, nisi* the letter *N* is written in monogram with *I*, *L*, or *S*. Divergent is e̅e̅ (*esse*). For some abbreviations several variants are attested. Late antique and, in part, already Christian interpolated lists of these and also of others not found in manuscripts are preserved from the eighth and the following centuries.[5] Because in pre-carolingian and carolingian transcripts the use of such abbreviations is sporadically attested also in non-legal texts (Theodore of Mopsuestia's psalm commentary, Augustine's letters and *De musica*; Marius Victorinus's grammar)[6] and since, besides, they appear in manuscripts from various regions (saec. V and VI) in contemporary marginalia,[7] it is better to speak of 'notae antiquae' rather than 'notae iuris'.

The use of the unstable notae and of the ambiguous 'litterae singulares' must have resulted in great uncertainty especially in legal texts concerning the correct reading of a word and so, with the publication of the Codex Theodosianus in AD 438, a ban was issued on the use of 'notae iuris' for official copies. More far-reaching strict prohibitions on 'siglorum captiones et compendiosa aenigmata' were issued in 533 and 534 under Justinian, whose legal codices were to be written 'sine ulla signorum dubietate'.[8] These prohibitions too were restricted to legal books and to the sphere of Roman control. A true continuation of the 'notae antiquae' in the middle ages existed only for a few pronouns, particles, some endings and the words *est, sunt, esse*.

The frequency with which final *M* appeared gave rise to an abbreviation in keeping with the character of the Latin language; it appears already in a single instance in the year 167: the principal shaft of capitalis *A* is struck through at the lower end.[9] In contrast, the abbreviations of -*M* and -*N* that appear first in the fourth century at line-ends, where they served to avoid run-over into the margin, appear to be later imitations of a Greek writing habit, namely the replacement of -*N* at line-end by a horizontal stroke.[10]

5 The oldest of these 'Laterculi Notarum' is in St Gall, Stifstsbibl., 194, s. VII–VIII (CLA vii, 918). Most of the lists were edited by Th. Mommsen, *Grammatici Latini* 4, 277 ff. A further list, with many distinctive features, is in Durham A. IV.19, f. 85ʳ–86ʳ, s. X² (T.J. Brown, *The Durham Ritual*. Early English MSS in Facsimile 16 (Copenhagen 1969) p. 51); the sigla are omitted in the edition: *Rituale Ecclesiae Dunelmensis*. Surtees Society Publ. 140 (1927). For a general view P. Lehmann, 'Sammlungen und Erörterungen lateinischer Abkürzungen in Altertum und Mittelalter', *Abh. Bayer. Akad. Wiss.*, phil.-hist. Abt., n.F. 3 (1929) 6 ff., and *Sitzungsber. Bayer. Akad. Wiss.*, phil.-hist. Kl. (1933) 9, 19–27.

6 CLA iii 326; vi 737; S 1776. Cf. Bischoff–Nörr, 'Eine unbekannte Konstitution', p. 13.

7 Lists in W.M. Lindsay in *Zentralbl. f. Bibliothekswesen* 29 (1912) 57, and idem, *Notae Latinae*, xiii.

8 On these prohibitions cf. Cencetti, *Lineamenti*, 397 ff.; Wenger, *Quellen des römischen Rechts*, 119 f.   9 ChLA iii 204; *Écr. lat.*, plate 26.

10 Lowe, *Palaeographical Papers* 1, 199 and 268 ff. Traube, *Nomina Sacra*, 241 asserts that they were adopted at the same time as the Nomina Sacra. The mark of abbreviation for *M* or *N* was later often differentiated in various ways by the addition of a dot above or below the stroke (or two dots below).

A second tradition of Latin abbreviation technique takes its origin from Christian 'nomina sacra', the abbreviations of terms central to Christian worship: *deus, Iesus, Christus, spiritus, dominus (noster), sanctus*. With the beginning of the transmission of Latin manuscripts of Christian texts, above all the bible, there appear in the fourth century abbreviations by means of 'contraction' that comprise in each case the beginning and end of words for *deus, Iesus, Christus, spriritus* – the first and last with their Christian significance: $\overline{DS}$, $\overline{IHS}$, $\overline{XPS}$, $\overline{SPS}$; by changing in each case the last letter the casus obliqui could be expressed: $\overline{DI}$, $\overline{XPO}$, $\overline{SPM}$, etc. Almost simultaneously $\overline{DMS}$ and $\overline{DNS}$ (*dominus* for *Christus*) appear. $\overline{IHS}$ and $\overline{XPS}$ are half-Greek, and in his last work, *Nomina Sacra*,[11] Ludwig Traube showed that all five words were abbreviated on the model of Greek contractions; these belong to the group of fifteen biblical or theological concepts and names (*David, Israel, Ierusalem*) which in Greek book practice were contracted (where otherwise the 'suspension' is used).[12] Traube sought the origin of the majority of these abbreviations in the writing practice of hellenistic Jews who at first, in order to express the inexpressible tetragram, had created the symbols $\theta\overline{C}$ and $K\overline{C}$ for their Greek versions of the Old Testament, and then added further ones.[13] This theory cannot, however, be sustained after examination of much more extensive material than was available to Traube; nevertheless an initial motivation by means of the tetragram in Jewish-Christian circles (such as in Alexandria) does seem possible.[14] In Latin there was a further step by which the formal connection with $\overline{SPS}$ called forth the important abbreviation $\overline{SCS}$ (instead of the 'syllabic suspension' $\overline{SC}$) and Traube demonstrated how suspended $\overline{N}$ (*noster*) in connection with $\overline{DMS}$, $\overline{DMI}$ or $\overline{DNS}$, $\overline{DNI}$ (for *Christus*) could take on the forms $\overline{NR}$, $\overline{NI}$ and $\overline{NR}$, $\overline{NRI}$.[15] It was inevitable that, the more one receded from the period of pagan-Christian conflict, the more their originally sacral character should fade,[16] so that the abbreviations that had become routine were occasionally used almost unthinkingly for profane things, and $\overline{dns}$ (for *dominus* or *domnus*) finally became general.[17]

From the fifth/sixth century at the latest new contractions came into being. For state and ecclesiastical chanceries the necessity arose of coining abbrevi-

11 L. Traube, *Nomina Sacra*. For important early supplements to Traube's evidence: CLA xi 1613 and S 1782. The Old Latin Gospel MS. k (Traube 138 ff.; CLA iv 465) has a totally different set of symbols (with the Chi-Rho monogram for Christus).

12 There was a parallel development of abbreviations for Nomina Sacra in Coptic, Gothic and Armenian, Traube, 269 ff.

13 The elevated character of the Nomina Sacra can be emphasised by overlining the entire word, written in Greek or Latin; see Traube, 49 ff. and CLA S 1782.

14 A.H.R.E. Paap, *Nomina Sacra in the Greek Papyri of the First Five Centuries A.D.*, Papyrologica Lugduno-Batava 8 (1959).   15 *Nomina Sacra*, 195 ff., and 204 ff.

16 Christian of Stablo's comments about how to write 'Iesus' are an example of scholarly learning. For earlier Irish explanations B. Bischoff, *Mittelalterliche Studien* 1, 259 and 267 (Ps. Hilarius: A. Hamman, MPL Suppl. 3 (Paris 1963) 61).

17 Besides the examples in Traube (idem also in *Vorlesungen u. Abhandlungen* 3, 213 ff. on $\overline{DS}$ and $\overline{DO}$ in the Codex Romanus of Vergil, s. VI) Lindsay, *Notae Latinae*, 396 ff.

ations for ecclesiastical officials (*episcopus, presbyter*, etc.) that could be used in the manuscripts of conciliar decrees and councils. But *omnipotens* also (which stands close to the nomina sacra in concept) was already written in abbreviated form in the sixth century; like the hierarchical terms, it had taken on contracted forms already admitted, amongst them those that were eventually to become the final ones.[18]

The Irish especially (and their pupils the Anglo–Saxons), who took over a selection of notae antiquae and who used several tachygraphic symbols,[19] considerably extended the number of words which could be abbreviated by contraction long before the carolingian period, in part already certainly in the seventh century, for forms of *dico, habeo, nomen, omnis*, amongst others,[19a] and for *saeculum* and *populus*.[20] Arising from these beginnings, and under the influence of the Insular element, a broader development of the medieval contractive system came about; this does not begin on the continent, however, before the eighth century. While now *gloria, gratia, misericordia* and many other words had abbreviations created for them, they were contractions only, just as old suspensions like f̄f̄ (*fratres*) were replaced by contractions (frs). The obviousness of their resolution, which was the characteristic of the ubiquitous model of the nomina sacra, led to this result.[21]

In their use of the abbreviations the great script regions, the Insular, Visigothic, and Italo–Frankish, developed differing traditions in the early middle ages, and within these again smaller units and even some individual scriptoria clung to peculiarities.[22] The full Irish system,[23] is particularly consistent and effective. The Anglo–Saxon is distinguished from it by the use of a smaller number of abbreviations and several peculiar forms (such as *t* with cross-stroke through the bar for *-tur*, alongside *-t'*). It is characteristic of Visigothic abbreviations that the consonants are more regularly, even exclusively retained ('hebraicising writing'). A few examples of the variety of the systems are: *autem*: ħ or aꞁ̄ (Ins.), aūm (Span.), aū or auꞁ̄ (the rest); *nomen*: nō (Ir., genitive nōis),

---

18 *episcopus*: cf. e.g. CLA I 1b, 26, 107; IV 490; VIII 1031, 1162, XI 1631; *presbyter*: VII 724; VIII 1162; *omnipotens*: I, 1b, 41; III 263; IV 438; VI 836; VII 949. An isolated instance of *magister* (MḠR) already in CLA XI 1613 (from the year 396/7).

19 Lindsay, *Early Irish Minuscule Script* (Oxford 1910). 19a Lindsay, *Notae Latinae*, 495–8.

20 Lindsay, *Notae Latinae*, 278; CLA II 2, 152, 177; S 1682.

21 This view contradicts L. Schiaparelli's opinions *Avviamento allo studio delle abbreviature latine nel medio evo* (Florence 1926) 39–41 and Cencetti, *Lineamenti*, 406, 428 f. Both consider the distinctive contractions of 'Notae antiquae' (in part technical legal terms) or the system of forming Tironian notes from notes for the word and signs for its endings (see above p. 80) as the model for the development of the medieval system.

22 Lindsay, *Notae Latinae*, is fundamental. On p. 495 ff. he lists abbreviations from the British Isles (Anglo–Saxon and Irish differences are tabulated on p. 498 ff.), Spain, Italy and other continental regions. Doris Bains, *A Supplement to Notae Latinae* (Cambridge 1936) gives an inadequate account of the period from 850 to 1050, since school books are barely touched on. For Spanish abbreviations (including recent ones) from Baroque collections: J. López de Toro, *Abreviaturas Hispanicas* (Madrid 1957). 23 See above p. 86.

nm̄n (Span.), nōm (the rest); *propter*: *pro* and *per* combined (Ir.), pp̄tr (Span.), pp̄ and others (the rest).

Thus the abbreviations, like the orthography, complete the distinctiveness of the manuscripts, and where they appear outside of their normal areas of use they can be eloquent symptoms of preceding phases in the transmission.[24]

The carolingian reform had a unifying effect here also; wherever the caroline minuscule extended there were hardly any differences. Around AD 800 the new abbreviation ^{2} = *ur* was created, which then quickly spread. It now depended on the dignity of the manuscript to what extent abbreviation could be used. It is found most thoroughly in the school manuscripts where, in the age of flourishing dialectic and intensive grammatical studies (ninth to twelfth centuries) a supply of abbreviations and their usage was established.[25] In contrast with this, however, they are often entirely absent in ostentatious manuscripts, with the exception of nomina sacra. Under learned influence probably propagated by the Irish a 'Greek' writing of nomina sacra gained ground. It was not restricted to IH̄C, XP̄C and the short form x̂, but passed over as well (without any justification) to sp̄c = *spiritus*, tp̄c = *tempus*, ep̄c = *episcopus* (instead of ep̄s), om̄pc = *omnipotens*. There are also gradually developed the ∫ for *er*, *re*, and *r* from the various forms of the abbreviation stroke.

The rapid expansion of the specialist disciplines, whose teaching methods were newly organised in the universities around 1200, in a very short time changed the writing of scientific books through the creation of new abbreviations and symbols for words and terms of frequent occurrence, through greater utilisation of the grammatical structure and of Latin word formation, and through frequent use of suprascript final syllables.[26] The versatility of the abbreviation system was increased; if earlier the scribe had, on the whole, a set, easily learnable supply, now he was given the means of forming abbreviations for himself.[27] The acoustic element stands out more clearly, especially in the abbreviation of *m*, *n*, and *r*, and in the words with *a*.

Among the possibilities available in the late-medieval cursive was that the abbreviation sign already in the thirteenth century was written with a joining stroke starting from the respective letter, and likewise the general abbreviation

---

24 Examples: L. Traube, *Vorlesungen u. Abhandlungen* 3, 114; Lowe, *Palaeographical Papers* 2, 463 f.; CLA S 144 (p. 19) and 1785.

25 This was also aided by the widespread use of glossing.

26 The scribe of the inserted leaves 14 and 17 of the Boethius MS Clm 14,516 (which I date s. XI^2) deftly created new abbreviations of dialectical termini in part by suspension: sp^{ei} (*speciei*), g^a (*genera*), sub^a (*substantia*), d^a (*differentia*), etc.

27 For a summary treatment of the possibilities of abbreviation in this fluid system see p. 157 ff. Serious errors could arise in copying a hastily written manuscript and because of an inadequate command of the subject (discipline). Such errors would not have been possible under the earlier and more fixed system; cf. A. Dondaine, 'Un cas majeur d'utilisation d'un argument paléographique en critique textuelle', *Scriptorium* 21 (1967) 261–76 with fig. and plates 24–7.

stroke.[28] Later (from the end of the fourteenth century) this simple stroke was drawn back from right to left.

In the late middle ages also alphabetical lists of abbreviations and their solutions were compiled, especially as instruments for legal and canonistic studies.[29] The abbreviations used in German texts are almost entirely dependent on the flexible Latin system and, measured by that, they are as a rule only of the simplest kind: *-m, -n, -er* (later also *-r*), *-ur*;[30] omission of *r* (after *p*, amongst other letters, shortened by superscription of the vowel), and several others.[31] Also taken over unchanged from Latin is un̄ (Latin *unde*) for German *unde*, later for *und* (along with v̄, which is rare). The most original are the abbreviations dc, wc for *das/daz, was/waz* (in the Manesse manuscript, though not restricted to Zürich). In the thirteenth century they are occasionally found in south German manuscripts,[32] and frequently in Swiss charters,[33] later mostly *dz* and *wz*. Only sporadically do scribes fashion the German forms of *Iesus* and *Christus* like Latin nomina sacra: for example, the scribe of the OHG Isidore (ihūses, xp̄ist, and xr̄ist, etc.), the Romance language scribe of the Nithard in the Strasbourg oaths (xp̄anes folches), and one manuscript of the Saxon world chronicle.[34]

It is presumably a result of the acoustic principle in abbreviations, together with the ready inclination toward accumulation of consonants, that in German writings of the fifteenth century not seldom *m, n,* or *r* which were already written as letters were doubled unnecessarily by addition of the appropriate abbreviation.[35] In German fifteenth-century cursives the abbreviation sign for *-r-* is regularly linked to the appropriate vowel (for example *facere*: faceé), and the one for *-e-* is drawn up from the elongated last shaft below (for example *wollen*: wolln̄). In the second half of the century the rapid cursive brings forth a new

28 Chroust, *Monumenta* 1 1, plate 7a (the register of Albert Beham 1246/7).
29 Aids for resolving abbreviations: J.L. Walther, *Lexicon diplomaticum* (Göttingen 1747; repr.); A. Cappelli, *Lexicon abbreviaturarum*² (Leipzig 1928); A. Pelzer, *Abréviations latines médiévales*² (Louvain–Paris 1966); M.–H. Laurent, *De abbreviationibus et signis scripturae Gothicae* (Rome 1939); E. Seckel, *Paläographie der juristischen Handschriften des 12. bis 15. und der juristischen Drucke des 15. und 16. Jahrhunderts* = separate print from *Z. Savigny-Stift. Rechtsgesch.* 45, Romanist. Abt. (Weimar 1925); P. Sella, 'Sigle di giuristi medievali, in ispecie dello Studio Bolognese, tratte dai codici vaticani', *L'Archiginnasio, Bull. d. Bibl. Comunale di Bologna* 27 (1932) 177–203; idem, 'Nuove sigle di giuristi medievali', *Studie e memorie per la storia dell'università di Bologna* 12 (1935) 159–75. There are late-medieval lists in Lehmann, 'Sammlungen', 23 ff., 37 ff. On the problem of creating new methods cf. the discussion in *Bull. Inst. Rech. d'Hist. Textes* 14 (1966) 121–38.
30 Only in the Abrogans from St Gall, one of the earliest texts, are the German words copied with a larger range, using n(us)–, –p(re)–, –p(ro)–, –q(ue)–, –s(unt).
31 Cf. e.g. 'Flos und Blancheflor' (Koennecke, *Bilderatlas*, 19).
32 Petzet-Glauning, *Deutsche Schrifttafeln*, plates 37 and 46.
33 Cf. D. Haacke, 'Studien zur Orthographie der deutschsprachigen Originalurkunden', *Beitr. z. Gesch. dt. Spr. u. Lit.* 84 (Tübingen 1962) 184–244; 85 (1963) 147.
34 Degering, *Schrift*, plate 84 (xp̄enheit amongst others).
35 E.g. Chroust, *Monumenta* 1 1, plate 9 from 1435.

abbreviation for the ending *-en* in the form of an energetic downward swing.[36] It
is indicative, however, of the incompleteness of the German abbreviation system
that Stephan Roth and Georg Rörer, when they wrote down Luther's sermons
after hearing them, did so for the most part in an improvised Latin translation.[37]
The familiar German manner of abbreviating frequent words by writing only
the initial letter(s) is frequently attested from the twelfth century on (h. or
heil. = *heilig*; sp. = *spricht*, and so on). Peculiar is a method widespread in the
Alemannic-Bavarian region in the eighth/ninth century of indicating words by
means only of the ending; thus in glosses and in the St Gall Benedictine Rule,
here partly combined with abbreviations of the opening: tin = *truhtin*, ke
ti = *keskrifti*, and k = *keuuisso*.[38] Entirely outside the Latin system stands the
writing of well known phrases or biblical words (to be explained by musical
influence) by means only of the vowels *a e u i a* (*alleluia*); this method is common
in Munich, Bay. Staatsbibl., Clm 18140.[39]

Forms and methods of abbreviation s. XII–XV[39a]

Central- and late-medieval abbreviations too can be divided into syllabic
abbreviations (formed by dropping or doing away with letters), suspensions,
contractions, and abbreviations using special signs. In legal and canonistic
manuscripts the names of glossators or commentators (bul.: Bulgarus; pi. or py.:
Pillius; y: Irnerius, to list just a few) are given usually in the form of suspensions.

Names ending in -en(sis) and -an(us) are suspended in the same way in all
cases, for example Frisingen. Contractions whose endings stand on the line and
which are mostly indicated by strokes above (superscript) can, through inflexion
of the ending, follow the declensions and comparative cases. The number of
more frequently used forms for these contractions is relatively limited, but they
can occur nevertheless in various different forms (which are separated in the
following table section V by /), for example: ecclesia, elimosina. The same
abbreviations can have different meanings, depending on the context and the
subject matter; for example decło: declinatio, or declaratio. Much freer and
more arbitrary are the possibilities provided by superscription of the endings;
cp. section VI. If an abbreviated word contains the symbols for more than one
abbreviation these are to be expanded separately, in accordance with the

36 E.g. Chroust, *Monumenta* 1 1, plate 10.
37 Cf. Chr. Johnen, *Geschichte der Stenographie* 1 (Berlin 1911) 293 ff., with reprod.
38 Baesecke, *Der deutsche Abrogans und die Herkunft des deutschen Schrifttums* (Halle 1930) plates
  1–5.
39 Cf. E. v. Steinmeyer in *Festschrift der Universität Erlangen zur Feier des 80. Geburtstages des
  Prinzregenten Luitpold* 4/1 (Erlangen 1901) 17 ff.
39a Cf. G.G. Meersseman, 'Einige Siglen der mittelalterlichen Logik', *Freiburger Z. f. Philos. u.
  Theol.* 2 (1955) 88 f. Cf. for additional sigla P. Sella, 'Sigle di giuristi medievali, in ispecie dello
  Studio Bolognese, tratte dai codici vaticani,' *L'Archiginnasio, Bull. della Bibl. Communale di
  Bologna* 27 (1932) 177–203; idem, 'Nuove sigle di giuristi medievali', *Studi e memorie per la
  storia dell' Università di Bologna* 12 (1935) 159–75.

appropriate methods; for example ī๖útibłr: i(n)(con)-v(er)tib(i)l(iter),ᵢénox^lis: e(qu)inox(ia)lis(!), rōcina^o3: r(aci)ocina(ci)o(ne)m.

The accompanying survey, which attempts to bring together and to order the most important examples, is divided in the following way: section I, frequently used letter metamorphoses; section II, abbreviations of syllables and letters on the line: (a) general, (b) longer endings, (c) other abbreviations within words; section III, abbreviation of syllables by suprascription of letters; section IV, common abbreviations of particles, pronouns, conjunctions, prepositions; section V, a selection of contractions on the line; section VI, abbreviation by suprascription of endings; section VII, sigla and appendix.

I. In abbreviations, -m is often indicated by a sign in the form of a three, and suprascript open-a by a broad horizontal stroke peaked in two places.

- m: āɪaz, -c̄oez   (anima)m, (–cione)m; cf. IV a) b)

- a: m̃rca   marca; cf. also V end

II. Abbreviations of syllables and letters indicated by a tilde or a straight horizontal line (abbreviations not expanded)

(a) General

-e(-): ᛞ, ᛞτrahɪτ, ᕃaτuſ, m̄a, m̄o (cf. IVa), -n̄,
        (-)r̥º-, -r̥º

- em(-): eoᛞ, quɪᛞ, m̄brɪſ

- en(-): m̄τɪſ, lum̄

- eν, -ɪʀ s. -ʀ

- eτ, -enτ: debɪ/debʒ, maᛞʒ̄ (cf. IVb)

- ɪs(-): no̅ᕃ, vτɪt, venerℓ, ᛞτanτɪa

- ɪτ: dɪc̄, dɪx̄

- m (-): modū, -ē, -ē̃

- n(-): ī, po̅ɪτ (po̅ɪτuſ!)

-ʀ-, -eʀ(-), (-)ʀe(-), -ɪʀ ('`··~~?) :
        ma̋τɪs, pa̋ʀ, c̓τuſ, c̓aτuſ, ᕃτuſ; ℓ̓mo,
        ✗τo (✗/ℳ often: versus); ✗go

- um: c̄, -ᛞ, -n̄, -τ̄; ṙṙ'(rerum); -ʒ/-ʒℓ

- unꞇ : er̄
- ur : ² ∾ ~
- us : ' ⁹ , -ƀꝫ

(-) con-, (-) com-, (co-, - cun-, cum): c̄ɗo, gꞅul,
  gmunıꞅ, ggnıꞇuꞅ, ꞅegɗuꞅ, g

(b) Longer endings

- ıꞇer, -bılıꞇer : uꞇıꞇr, noꞇabꞇr (cf. sıꞇr)
- ıꞇur: legr̄, lıberaꞇ̄a, coꞇr (cf. V d̄r, q̄r)
- ꞇıo (-cıo) : - ꞇ̄o, - c̄o, (Gen.) - c̄oıs, (Acc.) - c̄oem / - c̄om / - c̄o
- ꞇıvus, -a, -um : relaꞇ̄s, - ꞇ̄a , - ꞇ̄m

(c) Other abbreviations within words

Vowels next to l (-e-, -u-, -u-u-):

ꞅlagꞇꞇıꞅ, dupꞇx ; cꞇpa, mꞇꞇa / mꞇa (!) ; ocꞇꞅ

Two adjoining syllables with –i-:

[-mı-] proxı̄, sıꞇr, [-nı-] remıꞅcımı̄, ꞅı̄s, [-mın-] hoı̄ꞅ,
  lūı, ꞅeı̄, [-vı-] ɗı̄ɗımus, ɗı̄nıꞇuꞅ

Two adjoining syllables with -o-:

[-no-] h̄oꞇem (cf. IV m̄o, V h̄o)
- e - (before n) : ınꞇ̄nɗıꞇ (cf. V onꞅū, d̄nɗeꞅ)

A second stroke usually adds an -m (and therefore indicates the accusative)

c̄a (causa), c̄̄a ; r̄oe (raꞇıone), r̄̄oe ; q̄ (quae), q̄̄ (quaedam)

Compare however section V under 'verbum'

III. Syllabic abbreviations by means of suprascript letters (abbreviations not expanded)

(e): nᶜ, pᶜcaτum, aſpᶜtuſ

(ι): ſᶜ (cf. IVb), amᵗτo

(u): q̂ etc. (cf. IVa aᵈð), cᶥ, alιcᵘ

(n): cog̓tuſ, cog̊ſco

(r): [-ra(-)] membᵃ, ĝtuſ, supᵃ (cf. IV exᵃ)
 [-rι-] democ̓tuſ, po̷, f̓gιðuſ, [-ιr(-)] v̇,
 v̇τuſ, c̓culuſ, f̓muſ, [-ru-] cong̓um

(qu): êtr (equalιτer), ėᶜᵉ (equιvoce)

(b,c,g,m,n,r,τ vor a): p̂² (probaτur); vônτ²;
 nêτur; ŷgo, sτôchι; ôτuſ; hôſ;
 τôlιſ, mûrι

IV. Abbreviations of pronouns and particles in constant use

(a)

a̓/aτ̄	autem	g̓/ι²	igitur
aᵟ, aº	aliud, alio	g̊ (cf. VI)	ergo
a̓ð	aliquid	ħ	hec
aꭔ̄	ante	h̓	hoc
apᵟ	apud	hᵘ	hac
aᵗ/aů	aut	h̓/hᶥ	hic
bꭔ̄	bene	h̄c	hunc
c̄/(9)	cum	h̓ι	huiusmodi
c̃c	circa	i̯ᵃ	ita, infra
9̊ᵃ	contra	ιᶥ	ibi
ē	est (cf. VII)	ιꭔ̄	inde
ēe/ėė/eᵉ	esse (cf. VII)	ῑo	ideo
eᵘ	enim (cf. IVb)	ιp̄e, ιpιuſ	ipse, -ius
exᵃ	extra	ιτ̄	item

ʐ/ɀ	et	t/ut	vel
ɀ̄	etiam	m̄g	magis
ṁ	michi	q̊̈/q̊m	quam
ṁ/m̄o (cf. IIa)	modo	q̊ı	quasi
n̄	non	q̊tr	qualiter
n̈ (cf. VI)	nulla	q̇	quid
nb̵	nobis	q̄m	quoniam
n̄c	nunc	qᵐ	quantum
ṅ	nisi	qm̄o	quomodo
nt̵/nᵗ	nichil	qq/qq3/q3	quoque
n̄r	noster	qτ	quot
oīſ, ōe, ōa/o̊̈,	omnis, -e,	q̄ts	quatenus
ō3	-ia, -em	řᵛ	respectu
p̄	prae	ſ/ſm/2ᵐ	secundum
(-)p(-)	per, -par-, -por-	ß/ſt	sed (cf. IVb)
p'/p̄ (cf. VI)	post	s̊ (cf. VI)	supra
ꝑ	pro	ſaτ̄	satis
p̊a	prima, praeterea	ſb̵	sub
pᵐ	primum	ſ'	sibi
p̄p/pp	propter	ſīc	sicut
q̄	qu(a)e	ſn̄	sine
q̿	quaedam	ſp	semper
q̵/q̇	qui	ſr̄	super
q̵/qd̵	quod	ſt	sunt
q̄ (ſeq̄ſ)	quem (sequens)	ſu	sive
qᴿ	quia	ṫ	tibi
⁻q3	-que	τm	tantum
q̇dam	quibusdam	τn	tamen

u̇	ut	un̄	unde
u̧	ubi	uτ ᵐ	utrum

(b)   Special groups

aʒ	apparet	oʒ	oportet
δʒ	debet	pʒ	patet
lʒ	licet	vʒ	videlicet, valet
ꝙlʒ	quodlibet		

Defining words

·ı·	idest	·q·, ·q·δ·	quasi, qu. dicat
·n·/·н·	enim	·ſ·	scilicet

Groups of abbreviated words (compare section VI under gerunds)

eτ ᶜ	et sic	hᵒᵒ	hoc modo
ʒ ᶜⁱⁱˢ	et sic de aliis	ılloᵒ/ıᵒᵒ	illo modo
aᵒᵒ	alio modo	uτʒ	ut patet

V.   Contractions indicated by a tilde or straight horizontal line (selection)

fc̄s, sατısfc̄ıo, affc̄s	factus, satisfactio, affectus
lc̄s, detcabılıs, ınτttcus	lectus, delectabilis, intellectus
rc̄a	recta
retca	relicta
dc̄s	dictus
acc̄ns	accidens
acc̄τs	accusativus
aīa/āa	anima

aп̄s	antecedens
ao̅	actio
bꬲ̄ι / bꬲ̄	beati
ca̅ , ca̅τus	causa, causatus
ca̅ualıs	casualis
co̅ıs	communis
compto	complexio
concupı̅a	concupiscentia
9'enτιa	convenientia
dıffa / dꬲ̄a, dꬲ̄ns	differentia (cf. VI), differens
dıffo	diffinitio
dп̄dē̄s	descendens
dꬲ̄, dᵹ	dicitur, dicendum
dᵹ̄ʃus	diversus
ecꬲ̄e / ecꬲ̄ıe	ecclesie
eta	elementa
etıa / eta	elimosina
etcm	electuarium
ex̄ns	existens
feı̅a	femina
fta	falsa, fallacia, fleuma
fꬲ̄	frater, feria
gta	gloria
gꬲ̄a	gratia
ho̅	homo
hꬲ̄des	heredes
hꬲ̄, hm̄s, hп̄τ, ha̅τ, hꬲ̄e	habet, -emus, -ent, -eat, -ere,
hı̅τατ, hūndaτ, ıhı̅co̅	habitat, habundat, inhibicio

m̄a / m̃a	materia (cf. IIa)
mḡr	magister
m̄ɩa	misericordia, minima
m̄m	matrimonium
m̄r	mater, martyr
nc̄c̄ɩtaſ, ncc̃ɩa	necessitas (!), necessaria (!)
ōnsū	ostensum
or̄o	oratio
paτ̄ɩa	patientia
pc̄c̄m	peccatum
ptes / pľes	plures
pn̄ɩa	penitentia
pn̄ſ	praesens
p̄o	positio
p̄r	pater
pr̄are	praestare
prɩūo	privatio
p̄τaτe	potestate
q̄o, q̄om, q̄r	quaestio, - nem, quaeritur
r̄o, r̄oɩs, r̄om / r̄ōe / r̄ō	ratio, -nis, -nem (cf. VI)
Ꝗndere, rn̄s	respondere, respondens
ſƀa	substantia (cf. VI)
sp̄es, sp̄alɩτer	species, specialiter
sp̄s / sp̄c, sp̄ualɩτer	spiritus, spiritualiter
ſſ'	sensus
ſuḡḡones	suggestiones
v̄m, v̄a	verbum, -a
vtɩſ	universalis

Further contractions with special signs

(͠) gño	generatio
mr̃e, der̃ι	monstrare, demonstrari
nũι	numeri
(ʾ ˵) fḷ	fieri
gṅá	genera
ιτ́m	iterum
nuʳ́	numerus
τέιuſ, τίm, deτέιaɾe	terminus, - um, determinare
(²ᵃ) nἀ	natura (cf. VI)
nuʳ̇, nũ̇ι	numerus, -i
vr̃	videtur

VI. Contractions with suprascript endings

The principal, already applied in the early middle ages, of omitting the middle of the word before the suprascript ending, as in mihi, nunc etc (this includes the signs for -us and -ur), acquired great practical significance in the scholastic period. Almost all the typical word-endings for nouns, adjectives and verbs, as well as those formed by inflection or derivation could be written suprascript. The preceding part of the word was often, (though by no means always) shortened in such a way that one precise expansion is possible: experi[tus] = experimentatus, igno[te] = ignobilitate (expertus, ignote would be impossible). The expansion of these abbreviations was facilitated by the fact that some ways of abbreviating words according to this method were preferred over others, especially for words in frequent use. It is according to this preferred practice that the following list has been compiled. It is set out in the following manner: the suprascript endings (the basic forms and where necessary the oblique cases); examples of these; the preferred abbreviated endings according to this method; expansion of the examples.

Nouns

$$-^a \ (-^e;\ -^{\bar{a}}/-^{ag};\ -^{a\alpha}/-^{\gamma};\ -^{"s};\ -^{as}):$$
(1) foȃ; n̂(cf.IVₐ); p̊; r̂; ŝ(cf.IVₐ); ẙ;
(2) auaɾιᵃ; c̣gᵗ; gᵃ; ðᵃ/ðr̂ᵃ; ēenᵃ; ōιpoᵃ; scιᵃ

-a (1), especially common

$-\text{'}: \ mo\text{'} ; \ \int ylo\text{'} / \int y^{mg}$

-us: modus; sylogismus

$-^{m}(-^{a}): \ ex^{m}, \ ex^{a} \ (cf.IV_{a})$

-um: exemplum, exempla

$-^{\bar{t}}/-^{m} (-^{tu}/-^{\iota}): \ expi^{\bar{t}}$

-tum, -mentum: experimentum

$-^{l9}, -^{la}, -^{lum}: \ ar^{los}; \ p^{la}$

-lus, -la, -lum: articulos; particula

$-^{\alpha}: \ 9^{\alpha}$

-or: commentator (i.e. Averroes)

$-^{o}(-^{o\iota s}/-^{nis}, \ -^{o\iota}/-^{n\iota}, \ -^{oem}/-^{o_3}, \ -^{oes}/-^{es}, \ -^{b_3}):$
$9^{es}; \ \delta^{o}; \ d\bar{\iota}^{o}; \ \mathring{g}(cf. IV); \ in\tilde{cr}na^{o_3}; \ \mathfrak{r}; \ resti^{o}; \ \mathfrak{f}r^{o}$

-sio, -tio, -atio: conclusiones (auch: coniunctiones, complexiones, communes); distinctio; divisio; generatio; incarnationem; ratio (cf. V); restitutio; resurrectio

$-^{do}(-^{nis}, \ -^{ne}/-^{e}): \ b\bar{\tau}\iota^{ne}; \ forti^{do}$

-tudo, -itudo: beatitudine; fortitudo

$-^{s}/-^{as}/-^{tas}(-^{t\iota s}/-^{t\ell}): \ \int uau\iota^{t\bar{e}}; \ uo^{tas}; \ y\text{\dj}p^{t\iota}$

-tas, -itas, -litas, -alitas, -ilitas: suavitatem, voluntas
(also: volubilitas), ydemptitati (ident.)

$-^{n}(-^{ns}): \ r^{n}$

-men: regimen

$-\text{'}(-^{ve}/-^{\iota s}): \ g\text{'}; \ cor^{\iota s}$

-us: genus; corporis

$-^{ma}(-^{ta}): \ s\iota^{ma}$

-ma: sincategorema

$$-^{s}/-^{es}(-^{ei};-^{e}): \text{fff}^{e}$$

-ies: superficie

Adjectives

$$-^{9}, -^{a}, -^{m}: \text{bo}^{9}; \text{merito}^{a}; \text{ma}^{m}$$

-us, -a, -um: bonus; meritoria; manifestum (also: maximum)

$$-^{c9}, -^{ca}, -^{cum}: \text{b\bar{t}\iota}^{ca}/\text{b\bar{\iota}}^{ca}; \text{ca}^{ca}; \text{dya}^{c9}; \text{gra}^{ci}$$

-icus, -ficus, -vocus: beatifica; canonica (also: categorica);
dyabolicus (also: dyalecticus); grammatici

$$-^{v9}/-^{9}, -^{ua}/-^{a}, -^{um}: \text{sen}^{ua}$$

-tivus, -sivus: sensitiva

$$-^{lis}/-^{t}, -^{le}/-^{e}(-^{b}): \text{arti}^{b}; \text{car}^{le}; \text{cor}^{alis}; \text{p}^{le}$$

-lis, -alis, -abilis, -ibilis: artificialibus; carnale; corporalis; possibile

$$-^{re}: \text{p\tau\iota}^{re}$$

-ris: particularis

$$-^{tis}/-^{re}, -^{re}: \text{ce}^{re}$$

-tis, -te: celeste

$$-^{x}: \text{s}^{x}$$

-x: simplex

Adverbs

$$-^{e}: \text{\dot{5}d\bar{c}o}^{e}$$

-e: contradictorie

$$-^{ce}: \text{è}^{ce}$$

-ice, -fice, -voce: equivoce

$$-^{re}: \text{\bar{\imath}me}^{re}$$

-ate: immediate

$-^{ue}$: $\dot{q}^{ue}$

-sive, -tive: quidditative

$-^{\bar{r}}/-^{\dot{t}}/-^{r}$: δup^{r} ; $\tilde{ma}^{r}$; $\mathring{p}^{r}$; $\bar{p}\delta\iota^{\dot{t}}$; $\bar{p}n^{r}$; s^{t}

iter, -nter, -liter, -biliter: dupliciter; materialiter; probabiliter;
predicamentabiliter; presentialiter; similiter

Verbs

$-^{\tau}$: $p^{\tau}(cf. N)$; $\int^{\tau}$

-t: potest; significat

$-^{\iota\tau}/-^{\tau}$: 9^{α} ; δ^{τ} ; $\delta\iota^{\tau}$; $exce^{\tau}$; o^{τ} ; $resti^{\omega}$

-it: convenit (also: contingit); dicit; distinguit; excellit; ostendit;
restituit

$-^{mq}/-^{9}$: $conce^{9}/9^{9}$

-mus: concedimus

$-^{nc}$: $a\ddot{r}^{nc}$

-ant, -ent, -unt: arguunt

$-^{2}/-^{\sim}$: $a^{2}/a\tilde{r}$; 9^{2} ; $\overset{A}{5}r\iota\tilde{a}$; mo^{2} ; $p\tilde{o}$; $\dot{r}\int u\bar{a}^{2}$

-ur: arguitur; conceditur; contrariatur; movetur; ponitur;
reservantur

Participles

$-^{ns}/-^{s}(-^{\tau\ell}, -^{b_{3}})$: $\dot{9}^{ns}$; 9^{ℓ}

-ans, -ens: conveniens; consequentis

$-^{\tau'}, -^{\tau A}, -^{\bar{\tau}}/-^{m}$: $oppos^{m}/oppo^{m}/o^{m}$; $resti^{\tau'}$

-tus, -ta, -tum: oppositum; restitutus

Gerunds and gerundives

$-^{\delta'}, -^{\delta\Delta}, -^{\delta}/-^{m}$: $\bar{o}n^{\delta}$; $satisfa^{\delta o}$; sci^{m} ; $mo^{\delta\iota}$

-dus, -da, -dum; ostendendum; satisfaciendo; sciendum; modus
(etc.) significandi

Symbols

=, =τ, =ᐃ (Tiron. =)	esse (cf. IVa), esset, essentia
÷ / ȝ / ȝ	est (cf. IVa)
ø/øⁿˢ, øᐃ	instans, instantia*
aᵅ ; bᵅ	maior, minor
ff (from Ð)	digesta

Appendix

aⱦ	Aristoteles
bo' (cf. VI)	Boethius
ċſȝ	Crisostomus (Chrysost.)
88	Gregorius
ι°/ιoħ	Iohannes
ιȯ	Ieronimus (Hieronymus)
ιᶜ	Lucas
ιι°	libro
ṁ	Marcus
ṁ	Matthaeus
p̂·ℓ· / p̂e·ℓ·	pecia 4
ph'	philosophus
ꝑιeᵃˢ/ꝑyᵃˢ	Periermenias
p̊p, p̊p	papa, pape
p̊s	psalmo
℞	rubrica, responsorium
·s·	sanctus
for·	Sortes
yᵃˢ	Ipocras (Hippocrates)
yᶜᵉ	yconomice (oecon.)
x̊/x̊, x̊, x̊ane	Christus, -i, Christiane

2 *Punctuation and related matters*

The linguistic organisation of a text in Roman antiquity basically followed the requirements of something that was to be read aloud.[40] As a result, punctuation was expressed in rhetorical units and pauses much more than today, where syntactic division of the sentences is the rule. The means of indicating the rhetorical units varied. The continuous text could be interrupted by spaces of anything from one-half to five letters in length. A second method, writing *per cola et commata*,[41] each unit being written on a new line (which is perhaps still preserved in some carolingian Cicero manuscripts), acquired great importance from the fact that Jerome divided up the text of his Vulgate bible in that way, to facilitate reading in divine service. Many of the oldest manuscripts have retained this division.

Finally the ancient grammarians up to Isidore of Seville – whom numerous medieval authors follow – have left clear and simple instructions for the use of the actual marks: low point (comma) for the short pause; medial point (colon) for the middle pause; high point (periodus) for the end of the sentence.[42] Instead of the clear ancient triad, however, in the early middle ages a large number of combinations of points and virgulas were created and used in bewildering multiplicity. In carolingian times . and ΄ were preferred for the short pause, and ., or .,. for the long one. A number of schools (for example Regensburg, Freising, and western ones like St Amand) pass over to a simplified Isidorian system in the ninth century: lower point for the short pause, high point for the long one; and this is also the prevailing usage in sumptuous liturgical manuscripts of the tenth and eleventh centuries.

The system was extended by the addition of the question mark. Since its first appearance, seemingly in manuscripts in Maurdramnus minuscule and of the Carolingian palace school, this had the clear form of a curving or broken zig-zag sign with musical value. The shapes that it takes are very different from the ninth to the twelfth century; often, however, they agree overall with the contemporary form of the neume Quilisma, which medieval music theoreticians describe as a

---

40 R.W. Müller, *Rhetorische und syntaktische Interpunktion* (Diss. Tübingen 1964); numerous examples are here given from the oldest MSS (for which see J. Moreau-Maréchal in *Scriptorium* 22 (1968) 56 ff.); E. Otha Wingo, *Latin punctuation in the Classical Age* (The Hague 1972). A scribal habit (found also in inscriptions) in the first and second centuries AD in literary texts is the placing of a point after every word, but this is not punctuation in the strict sense.

41 Müller, 28 ff., 70 ff., 141. For the correction of texts written per cola et commata see R. Weber in *Scriptorium* 9 (1955) 57–63.

42 Latin texts on punctuation before the Renaissance are collected by M. Hubert, 'Corpus stigmatologicum minus', *Arch. Lat. medii aevi* 37 (1970) 14–169 (index ibid., 39 (1974) 55–84); cf. G. Silagi, *Deutsches Archiv* 28 (1972) 275. M. Hubert, 'Le vocabulaire de la "ponctuation" aux temps médiévaux', *Arch. Lat. Medii aevi* 38 (1972) 57–166. J. Greidanus, *Beginselen en ontwikkeling van de interpunctie, in't biezonder in der Nederlanden* (Utrecht 1926); J. Moreau-Maréchal, *Scriptorium* 22 (1968).

'quavering and rising tone connective', which emphasises its function as a musical sign.

A distinctive usage developed in the area of the Beneventan script in which a question mark is at first absent at the end of a sentence: the interrogatory character is indicated by a sign similar to a 2 that stands above the interrogative word, in predicate clauses over the words that are decisive for the accent of the sentence. A differentiation according to the category of the interrogatory sentence is also observed by Visigothic writers: they use a circumflex above the last word in a nominal question to contrast with the general question mark.[43] Both Beneventan and Visigothic book production were familiar also with a sign for an assertion: it was similar to a spiritus asper or a circle with a point within it;[44] both are placed above the word in question.

31. Forms of the question mark.

> 1. Carolingian palace school. – 2. Corbie (Maurdramnus period). – 3. Corbie (Hadoard period). – 4. Saint-Amand (s. VIII–IX). – 5. Saint-Denis (s. IX). – 6. Palace school of Charles the Bald. – 7. Bavaria (s. X). – 8. Benediktbeuern (s. IX). – 9. Monte Cassino (from the end of the 9th c.). – 10. Most widespread form.

From the eleventh century to the end of the middle ages there is an important innovation that can be observed at the latest by the end of the eleventh century in western France (Angers): a weak or middle punctuation consisting of a circumflex or a clivis (later a small suprascript [7] or similar) – these are the punctus elevatus, or the punctus circumflexus/flexa.[45] Rapidly diffused, the expanded system (arranged in ascending order . .ˊ.? or . .?.ˊ. .) was taken over by the Cistercian order for books that were read in the refectory; it is an important aid in identifying Cistercian manuscripts of the twelfth and thirteenth centuries. The Dominicans too adopted it for the liturgy. In the later middle ages the system is encountered also (with the partial addition of; or:) among the Carthusians,[46] from whom the *Devotia moderna* took it over. Hence it is used, for example, by

---

43 J. Vezin, 'Le point d'interrogation, un élément de datation et localisation des manuscrits. L'exemple de Saint-Denis au IXe siècle', *Scriptorium* 34 (1980) 181–96, with plate. On the Beneventan practice, which was spread further by copies, and on Spanish usage, see E.A. Loew, *The Beneventan Script* (Oxford 1914) 236 ff. On occurrences of Beneventan practice in England cf. Ker, *English MSS*, 49.

44 Loew, ibid., 270 ff. ('assertion sign'); Millares Carlo, *Tratado* 1, 284 ('signo de admiración').

45 J. Vezin, *Les scriptoria d'Angers au XIe siècle* (Paris 1974) 151 ff.; Ker, *English MSS*, 46 ff. In England there is also a sign of the same value placed on the line.

46 Cf. the texts printed by Ker, *English MSS*, 58 f.; Gumbert, *Utrechter Kartäuser*, 161 ff.; Hubert, 'Corpus stigmatologicum', 161 f.

Thomas à Kempis, who, however, in Dutch texts used only the point.[47] With the rise of humanism new rules of punctuation appear in Italy which the humanistically influenced translators Nicolaus of Wyle and Steinhöwel, amongst others, tried to adapt to German in the same way.[48] The exclamation mark appears first in the sixteenth century.[49]

In antique manuscripts accents stand over long syllables. In the middle ages accents sometimes indicate stressed, sometimes long syllables, and in addition to the acute accent the circumflex appears (chiefly above long syllables), in accordance with ancient teaching.[50] The placing of the acute accent over monosyllables was introduced by the Insular scribes, isolating those syllables as a result, and this became the practice also on the continent. An insular usage also is the writing of the dat./abl. ending -*is* (and -*iis*, which was apparently pronounced as a monosyllable) as -*ís*.[51] At the latest in the early ninth century lie the beginnings of the OHG accent system. Developed by Notker, it became widely disseminated. Its purpose was twofold: partly to regulate stress, partly to preserve the vowel quantities.[52]

Syllable separation by means of a single stroke at the end of a line first comes into use in the eleventh century, by means of a double stroke more generally from the fourteenth.[53] The peculiar usage of Italian and French scribes of the late thirteenth to the fifteenth century, whereby they 'justified' the margins of a column by filling up, where necessary, empty spaces at line-ends with either an expuncted or crossed stroke, goes back ultimately to a Hebrew scribal custom.[54] Likewise the group 7c (*et cetera*) at the end of a text in the later middle ages is generally a mere meaningless closing sign, not an indication that a continuation has been dropped.

To indicate cancellation the underlining or marking by means of suprascript groups of points was more frequent in the case of words than crossing out, and suprascript or subscript points (or both) for individual letters.[55] Otfrid made use of the latter kind in order to indicate graphically the elision of vowels in hiatus in

47 L.M.J. Delaissé, *Le manuscrit autographe de Thomas a Kempis et "l'Imitation de Jésus-Christ"* (Brussels–Paris 1957). Degering, *Schrift*, plate 101; other plates in the edition by M. Pohl.
48 J. Müller, *Quellenschriften zur Geschichte des deutschsprachlichen Unterrichts bis zur Mitte des 16. Jhs.* (Gotha 1882) 7 ff., 14 ff., 277 ff.
49 The advances in organized layout and presentation of scholarly texts in later medieval manuscripts are discussed in M.B. Parkes, 'The influence of the concept of Ordinatio and Compilatio on the development of the book', in *Medieval Learning and Literature. Essays Presented to Richard William Hunt* (Oxford 1976) 115–41 with plates 9–18.
50 Loew, *The Beneventan Script*, 274 ff.   51 Steffens, *Paläographie²*, xv.
52 P. Sievers, *Die Akzente in althochdeutschen und altsächsischen Handschriften* (Berlin 1906). See also Ker, *Catal. of MSS.*, xxxv.
53 Loew, *Beneventan Script*, 277 f.; Ker, *English MSS*, xxxv. Cf. however, already in CLA ix 1302; x 1478; Oxford, Bodl. Libr., Marshall 19 (s. IX in.).
54 Colette Jeudy, 'Signes de fin de ligne et tradition manuscrite', *Scriptorium* 27 (1973) 252–62 (esp. 253 n.); cf. ibid. 28 (1974) 296–8; on Hebrew usage see M. Beit-Arié, *Hebrew Codicology* (Paris 1976) 88.   55 Cf. W.M. Lindsay in *Palaeographia Latina* 3 (1924) 65 f.

his verses.[56] If in the later middle ages a longer passage had to be cancelled or no longer copied, the syllable 'va' was written beside the beginning and 'cat' beside the end (i.e. 'vacat').

In order to supply omissions, symbols ($\downarrow\uparrow$) or certain letters were inserted that originally had local meaning, and these lead from the position of the error in the text to its correction.[57] These letters are partially characteristic of some schools (for example *hl* for Lorsch and Weissenburg). For the purpose of referring to other things, whether glosses or scholia, the Latin and Greek alphabets, runes (as in the Codex Bonifatianus l),[58] and tachygraphic signs were used, and new arbitrary ones created.[59] Inversion is marked, for example, by letters (a c b) or strokes ($-\ \equiv\ =$) above the words, most frequently, however (and not always clearly), by prefixing signs ($\times\times$ amongst others). Of the various methods for indicating citations which connect antiquity and early medieval Latin book production with Greek book practice, a frequently occurring one is the indentation of text (in the oldest manuscripts by one to four letter spaces), without any sign. This usage, however, was abandoned in favour of marking in the margin with signs, first with the classical diple, later with other signs. Writing of the citations in red or in another kind of script can be added.[60] Irish words in a Latin context are occasionally emphasised by distributing accents over them.[61]

Already in antiquity the division of a text into sections could be made clear by use of a horizontal stroke or right angle (⌐). The chapter sign ¶ and the § are medieval transformations of the latter sign.[62] For the syntactic understanding of school texts the Irish and Anglo-Saxons developed systems in which unobtrusive groups of points and strokes, above and below the line, were used.[63]

References to the text were, from the early middle ages, often given in the

---

56 In Old Irish a sound shift is indicated by the use of the punctum above *f, s, n* (lenition); see R. Thurneysen, *Grammar of Old Irish* (Dublin 1946; repr. 1975) 21.
57 Lowe, *Palaeographical Papers* 2, 349–80.
58 Steffens², *Lateinische Paläographie*, plate 21a.
59 Otfrid's arsenal is probably unmatched; see W. Kleiber, *Otfrid von Weißenburg* (Bern–Munich 1971), 391 f.
60 P. McGurk, 'Citation-marks in early Latin manuscripts, *Scriptorium* 15 (1961) 3–13, and plates; Caroline P. Hammond, 'A product of a fifth-century scriptorium preserving conventions used by Rufinus of Aquileia', *J. Theol. Stud.*, n.s., 29 (1978) 366–91. In a sixth-century codex of Augustinus, *De civitate Dei* (CLA v 635) there is a clear attempt to distinguish quotations from Christian and pagan authors by different marks.
61 L. Bieler in *Scriptorium* 8 (1954) 90 f.   62 Lehmann, *Erforschung* 4, 9 ff. and 21.
63 Martje Draak, 'Construe marks in Hiberno-Latin mss,' *Mededelingen d. Kon. Nederl. Akad. Wetenschapen* Afd. Letterkunde, nr. 20, Nr. 10 (1957); eadem, 'The higher teaching of Latin grammar in Ireland during the ninth century', ibid. 30, Nr. 4 (1967); Fr. C. Robinson, 'Syntactical glosses in Latin Mss. of Anglo-Saxon provenance', *Speculum* 48 (1973) 443–75; M. Korhammer, 'Mittelalterliche Konstruktionshilfen und altenglische Wortstellung', *Scriptorium* 34 (1980) 18–58. Continental school manuscripts also use these signs, e.g. the Bern Vergil MS 165 (Chatelain, *Pal. class. lat.*, plate 67).

margin by means of 'nota', from which many permutations of monograms were constructed,[64] some of which can have the value of local symptoms;[65] less frequent is 'D.M.' ('dignum memoria').

The principle of word–division was slowly recognised. In the first century, and also still in the second, points are placed after every word in Roman texts. Later the writing practice switches over to scriptura continua. The need to make the word units recognisable was probably first felt among the Celts and Germans, and the Insular scribes seem to have been the first to aim at that. In carolingian times it is still generally the practice to draw prepositions and other short words towards the following word. From the twelfth century on the division is mostly quite clear.

3. Musical notation

The oldest form of musical notation in the medieval West that goes beyond indication of the intonation in liturgical reading[66] is that presented by the Latin neumes, among whose systems only that which had its origins in Rome finally became the ultimate standard for central Europe. Behind it lies an eastern-Christian basis; it was, however, especially styled in imitation of the Latin grammatical accents ('accent neumes') and was constructed under the influence of Byzantine musical script. The names of more than forty signs in the system are mostly Greek; depending on their forms, they are divided into stroke- and hook-neumes. None of the surviving examples can be dated with certainty to before the ninth century. The oldest known example from Germany comes from Regensburg, from the period c. AD 830;[67] the OHG Petrus-Lied belongs roughly to the early tenth century.[68]

Various regional types of neumes were formed in the early middle ages on the same basis, through varying expressions of form and ways of writing the elements and ligatures.[69] The oldest are the palaeofrankish, attested only in a few monuments ('Notation' 1 and 3). The most important are the German ('Not.' 2),

---

64 A short anthology in E. Cau, 'Scrittura e cultura a Novara (secoli VII-X)', *Ricerche Medievali* 6/9 (1971/4) 58 ff.   65 E.g. for Chartres: CLA x 1582.

66 Cf. the section on punctuation.

67 Reprod.: Bischoff, *Schreibschulen* 1, plate 6d; idem, *Kalligraphie* Nr. 3; *Musik in Geschichte und Gegenwart* 9 (1961) 1625 f.   68 Petzet-Glauning, *Deutsche Schrifttafeln*, plate 9.

69 To understand the varieties see the series of facsimiles edited by the Benedictines of Solesmes from 1889, *Paléographie musicale*; comparative tables are in vols 2 and 3 (1891 f.); in addition see (J. Hourlier), *La notation musicale des chants liturgiques latins* (1963) (cited above under 'Notation'); P. Wagner, *Neumenkunde*[2] (Leipzig 1912); J. Wolf, *Handbuch der Notationskunde* 1 (Leipzig 1913); idem, *Musikalische Schrifttafeln* (1922/3); G.M. Sunyol, *Introduction à la paléographie musicale grégorienne* (Tournai 1935; earlier Catalan ed., Monserrat 1925); Battelli[3], *Lezioni*, 215 ff.; W. Lipphardt in *Musik in Geschichte und Gegenwart* 9 (1961) 1611–28; B. Stäblein, 'Schriftbild der einstimmigen Musik', *Musikgeschichte in Bildern* 3 (Leipzig 1975); Solange Corbin, *Die Neumen* (vol. 1/3 in W. Arlt (ed.), *Paläographie der Musik* (Cologne 1977).

within which the more differentiated St Gall type excels by virtue of the richness of its transmission from the tenth and eleventh centuries ('Not.' 4), and the Metz style, which spread from this old centre of ecclesiastical music and culture to Luxembourg, Belgium, northern France, and also south Germany ('Not.' 16, 17); this shows a noteworthy disintegration into short corrugated separate strokes. In addition there is the Aquitanian style ('Not.' 9, 10) with its centre at St Martial, Limoges. The two latter styles are recognisable by the vertically superimposed writing of falling tone sequences. Other forms belong to Brittany, England, and northern France, Spain, and various parts of Italy.

The most serious disadvantage of the original neumes was that, though they roughly conveyed the movements of the melody, they did not preserve the exact intervals. Numerous ways were suggested for overcoming this difficulty. Hence various sequences of letters were used to indicate the tones, especially in theoretical literature, but also to write down the melodies, for example in the Lieder appended to the 'Minne Regel' of Eberhard Cersne. In a different way, the connection between melody and rhythm was conveyed with letters, which were written along with neumes; Notker the Stammerer informs us of these 'litterae Romanae' in one of his letters.[70]

A solution to the problem of establishing the intervals clearly in the neumes was first found by Guido of Arezzo (eleventh century, first half), after earlier unsuccessful attempts. He transposed the neumes on to a four-line system and also emphasised the c- and f-lines with different colours; through shifting these lines the range of the notes could be varied. The original flexible character of the neumes facilitated their adaptation to the line system. This practical discovery, which in principle still determines present-day musical notation, was taken over already in the twelfth century by German schools such as Reichenau. It was not until the fifteenth century, however, that it was established everywhere. St Gall clung particularly long to the lineless system[71] which long since had declined into coarseness.[72]

Palaeographically viewed, the choral notation on lines developed in the later middle ages in two typical forms: the gothic, which prevailed in the greater part of Germany and in its eastern area of influence, and the romanesque 'roman' square note script. The former is a stylisation of neumes in the sense of gothic textura. The virga, the normal note for the single tone, was written bold and vertical and acquired a little flag; the bows are broken.[73] A late phase is the 'hobnail' script of the fifteenth and sixteenth centuries in which the virgae

---

70 Commentary in P. Wagner, *Neumenkunde*[2] (Leipzig 1912) 233 ff. with reprod.; cf. e.g. Steffens[2], *Lateinische Paläographie*, plate 70b.
71 Reprod., Wagner, 220.
72 Examples also in the Codex Buranus; see the facs.
73 Reprod., Wagner, 337 ff.; O. Hurm, 'Zusammenhang zwischen gotischer Textur und gotischer Choralschrift', *Gutenberg-Jahrbuch* (1973) 37–43.

proceeding to a point are provided with a small rhomboid head.[74] The more complicated ligatures are often avoided entirely.[75]

The square music script has its origins in the later twelfth century in northern France; its form is likewise determined by a gothic stylisation of the stroke-neumes: the emphasis is on the contrast between vertical hair-stroke and squarish block or emphatic point. Already in the thirteenth century this block or point is carefully drawn square with a broad quill. Thus the script arrived at that shape in which it became the dominant romanesque musical script of the late middle ages, extending also to England and the Scandinavian lands. It extended to Germany above all through the liturgical books of the Cistercians, Dominicans, and Franciscans. It is used there also on occasions for notation of secular melodies, for example in the sumptuous Jena song book.[76]

The second deficiency of the neumes, which was shared by the choral notation, was the insufficient expression of the rhythmical or metrical values that it allowed. It was only in connection with the theoretical clarification of the relationship between melody and rhythm in Latin and Romance poetry that Franko of Cologne,[77] a music theoretician, c. 1260 developed, after earlier unsystematic attempts, a strictly regulated scale of note values from the duplex to the semi-brevis, as well as the pause symbols.[78] However, ligatures and conjunctions, the imitations of the more complicated neume forms, were not at all excluded as a result. From around 1300 red music script is used alongside black for contrast in various situations, for example with a change of rhythm or to indicate the smaller values.[79] For simplicity's sake 'white' symbols (i.e. symbols left empty inside) were later used for that purpose. Around the middle of the fifteenth century an exchange of 'black' and 'white', and vice versa, takes place, i.e. the larger (hitherto black) notes – bars, squares, lozenges – were now only written in their outlines, while the smallest (hitherto empty) lozenges were now filled in. The Lochamer song book is one of the earliest examples of this kind.[80]

The gradual perfection of the medieval choral notation had a peculiar reflex on book production. With the clear indication of the intervals a reading of the melody was possible, instead of learning it by heart. This was the presupposition behind the tendency to enlarge church songbooks and their notation so that as

---

74 Reprod., Wagner, 340; J. Wolf, *Handbuch der Notationskunde* 1 (Leipzig 1913) 127.
75 E.g. in Hugo of Montfort: *H. v. M., Gedichte und Lieder*, Facsimilia Heidelbergensia 5 (Wiesbaden 1985); Wolf, *Handbuch*, 1 177.
76 Facs.: K.K. Müller, *Die Jenaer Liederhandschrift* (Jena 1896).
77 H. Besseler, 'Franco von Köln', *Musik in Geschichte und Gegenwart* 4 (1955) 688–98.
78 L. Dittmer–M. Ruhnke, ibid., 9 (1961) 1628–41.
79 E.g. in Oswald of Wolkenstein: Koennecke, *Bilderatlas*, 52.
80 Facs.: K. Ameln, *Locheimer Liederbuch und Fundamentum organisandi des Conrad Paumann* (Kassel 1972).

many as possible could use the one book. Thus the books from the thirteenth century on grow in size, and at the end of the middle ages we meet in large numbers the huge antiphonaries that suffice for a whole choir.

4. Numerals

The Roman number symbols[81] do not differ from the corresponding letters in the older script, and they often retain these forms also within the later cursive (esp. D L V). The same applies to the connection for VI similar to an uncial G and which originated as a ligature in the older cursive and survived until into the eighth century.[82] Visigothic special forms are, for 40: X with a bow open upwards, or an angle on the right upper bough; for 1000: a large T in which the left half of the crossbar is drawn down towards the shaft. In early medieval manuscripts the numbers are set between points in order to stand out; in rare cases suprascript strokes are added (without change of meaning).[83] M is regularly written in majuscule (after the disappearance of the cursive form OO), and this is true also for the rest of the numerals in increasing measure. However, V in caroline script is frequently written U; with ordinals (rarer with cardinals) the endings are very frequently written above. In the later middle ages XX and C are also set high ($vi^{xx} = 120$; $iii^c = 300$, and so on), the former, however, probably only in Romance-speaking areas. Ancient fraction symbols are more studied than used in the middle ages. In the late-medieval period the cross-stroke of the last shaft, or even of V or X, indicates that the last unit is halved.

The Indian-Arabic signs[84] that appear in the tenth century in west-Arabic shape in Latin manuscripts in Spain were used by Gerbert of Rheims for writing on calculating tokens, without the zero and without knowledge of its positional value. The West was made familiar with this first in the twelfth century through the translation of arabic manuals of arithmetic ('Algorismus', named after the mathematician Mohammed ibn Musa al-Kharizmi).[85] The oldest German examples are a Salzburg computus of 1143[86] and a Regensburg manuscript of saec. XII*ex.*[87]

81 For what follows cf. W. Wattenbach, *Anleitung zur lateinischen Paläographie*[4] (Leipzig 1886) 97–105; Steffens[2], *Lateinische Paläographie*, xxxv f., xl; Battelli, *Lezioni*[3], 218 f.; Foerster, *Abriß*[2], 242 ff.

82 Such forms in inscriptions imply that the masons had a draft (ordinatio) written in later Roman cursive; cf. Mallon, *Paléographie romaine*, 124 ff.

83 This survived into the twelfth century, Bruckner, *Scriptoria* 8, 32. For a possible misunderstanding cf. W. Levison, 'Das Werden der Ursula-Legende', *Bonner Jahrbücher* 132 (1928) 39–42.

84 G.F. Hill, *The Development of Arabic Numerals in Europe Exhibited in 64 Tables* (Oxford 1915).

85 K. Vogel (ed), *Mohammed ibn Musa Alchwarizmi's Algorismus, das früheste Lehrbuch zum Rechnen mit indischen Ziffern. Nach der einzigen (lateinischen) Hs. (Cambridge Un. Lib. Ms. Ii. 6.5) in Faks.* (Aalen 1963).

86 Arndt-Tangl[4], *Schrifttafeln*, plate 26a; Mazal, *Romanik*, illustr. 19.

87 Ibid., plate 23b. Cf. also Clm 23, 511 (Euclid, s. XII[2], from Wessobrunn).

The few examples of 'eastern arabic' forms also stem from the twelfth century.[88] In practical usage the numerals were introduced slowly; they were excluded from the realm of finance here and there until into the fifteenth century. Characteristic of the difficulties brought about by their adoption were the mixtures of roman and arabic signs like MCCC7 and the serious errors which the number nought and the sequence of digits caused (21, 31 instead of 12, 13; 101 instead of 11, etc.). The signs 4, 5, and 7 generally take on the forms similar to their present ones only in the late fifteenth century.

Also widely diffused in Germany are the witnesses to a knowledge of a 'Greek' or 'Chaldaean' system in which the one- to four-character numbers are written with one symbol, and at the same time present a link between the medieval and more recent shorthand.[89]

5. Ciphers

The middle ages had a peculiar, playful relationship with ciphers.[90] They were used in many cases in which actual concealment was neither called for nor earnestly intended. German writing practice is especially rich in these. According to the short tract *De inuentione linguarum* (instead of *litterarum*),[91] published by Melchior Goldast under the name of Hrabanus Maurus, Boniface transmitted two systems of cipher in which the vowels *a e i o u* were expressed by points or by the immediately following consonants *b f k p x*; the latter system goes back to antiquity. English examples of the use of this cipher make the tradition plausible. In Germany from the ninth century on countless OHG glosses were written using both systems.[92] Other ciphers use the numerals for the vowels or for the letters, depending on their position in the alphabet. A further source of secret scripts was foreign alphabets, as they occur in the above mentioned tract and, not infrequently, in other manuscript collections: runes (in later manuscripts often designated 'Syrian', 'Arabic', or 'Saracen'(!)),[93] Greek,[94] Hebrew, and the alphabet of the so-called Aethicus Ister. In addition there are freely

---

88 Wilhelm Schum, *Exempla codicum Amplonianorum Erfurtensium* (Berlin 1882) reprod. 13.

89 Bischoff, *Mittelalterliche Studien* 1, 67–73 and plate VI f.; Jaques Sesiano, 'Un système artificiel de numération du Moyen Age', in Menso Folkerts–Uta Lindgren (edd), *Mathematica, Festschrift für Helmut Gericke* (Wiesbaden 1985) 165–96.

90 B. Bischoff, *Übersicht über die nichtdiplomatischen Geheimschriften des Mittelalters* (Vienna 1954; also *in Mitteil. Inst. Österr. Geschichtsforschung* 62 (1954); expanded in *Mittelalterliche Studien* 3, 120–48; the tables are repeated in Stiennon, *Paléographie*, 131 f.); A. Meister, *Die Anfänge der diplomatischen Geheimschrift* (Paderborn 1902).

91 The text is edited by R. Derolez, *Runica Manuscripta, the English Tradition* (Brügge 1954) 349 ff. Plates from several manuscripts in Ute Schwab, *Die Sternrune im Wessobrunner Gebet* (Amsterdam 1973) reprod. 13 (not earlier than s. IX²!) 15 f.

92 E.g. Petzet-Glauning, *Deutsche Schrifttafeln*, plate 12.

93 E.g. Clm 14,436; f. 1, s. XI; reprod. in Derolez, plate 6, Schwab, *Sternrune*, reprod. 12.

94 In which the Greek *M* often has the form)—(, *N* having the form)—.

composed symbol alphabets which may have served for personal use or as ciphers. A favourite method, finally, is the inversion of the word or syllable. The amalgamation of several methods is also found. Ciphers are employed in the later middle ages above all in scribal subscriptions, receipts, and charms, especially of a superstitious nature.

Additional note on abbreviations

The abbreviations ē and ·ē·

Shortly before AD 800, alongside the ancient abbreviation ē (= est), there appears a variant form, e between mid-raised points (·e·), which is not mentioned by W.M. Lindsay, *Notae Latinae*, 69 ff. or 405 ff.

The earliest example (Paris, BN, Lat. 1572, s. VIII[2]; CLA V 530) comes from Tours, where this abbreviation was already firmly established in Alcuin's time. It was disseminated from Tours to early St Denis, Cologne, Metz, St Amand, and Fulda, but seems to be particularly closely linked with places of strong Alcuinian tradition, whereas it was not adopted by such centres as Lorsch, Reichenau, or St Gall. Its appearance in codices of s.IX[1] can, therefore, be decisive as a criterion for localising manuscripts in specific scriptoria.

The Manuscript in Cultural History

Roman and Christian antiquity

With the beginning of the golden age of Roman literature, in the time of Cicero and Caesar, an organised system of book production appears in Rome.[1] The book trade used slaves to make multiple copies of books; at that time the first public libraries were established in Rome. Besides the spread of literature through the book trade the custom may have come about that also in houses of the well-to-do, slaves were engaged in enlarging libraries, and in the same way private copies were certainly produced.

In Herculaneum, destroyed by the eruption of Mount Vesuvius in AD 79, a library has been preserved whose founder (probably L. Calpurnius Piso Caesonius) assembled principally Greek philosophical literature; alongside roughly 1800 Greek papyrus rolls only about thirty Latin ones are attested. On the basis of what has become known in recent times from photographs about the state of the Latin texts – despite the desolate state of the charred rolls – they are written partly in a canonical, partly in a somewhat freer capitalis (as in the *Carmen de bello Actiaco*).[2] That papyrus rolls in canonical capitalis (as in this library) represented a standard form of Latin literary transmission during the first three centuries is confirmed by a few papyri from Egypt, amongst them Sallust (Hist. and Jug.).[3] But the notion of an exclusive or even preponderant transmission of the literary texts in this classical calligraphic form can no longer be maintained. For there exist literary remains that are written in majuscule cursive of various grades, or in newly established book script: Cicero, *De Servio Tullio* (Cato, *Origines?*); Gaius, and *De bellis Macedonicis*, and the transmission of other texts, amongst them Lucretius and Livy (fifth Decade), must have passed through a cursive majuscule stage before, for example, the basis of Lucretius's medieval transmission was reached.[4]

Besides literature proper, the educational system of the first centuries, founded on a selection of authors, is more richly documented, again, however,

---

1 C. Wendel-W. Göber in Milkau-Leyh, *Handbuch* 3/1² (Wiesbaden 1955) 119 ff.; T. Kleberg, *Buchhandel und Verlagswesen in der Antike* (Darmstadt 1967); G. Cavallo (ed.), *Libri, editori e pubblico nel mondo antico* (Rome–Bari 1975).
2 See above p. 57.   3 See above p. 58 n. 23.   4 See above p. 62 n. 70.

only through witnesses from Egypt. Amongst these are bilingual texts (fables, Vergil, Cicero, glossaries) tailored to requirements that remained more relevant in the Greek half of the empire than in the West, where Greek studies were in decline.[5] At the end of the first century Martial is the earliest writer to attest to a new development in book production, namely the parchment codex. Its advantages: easiness of handling and suitability for travel, Martial did not overlook, but against that he preferred the papyrus roll. The oldest surviving remains of a parchment codex, the *Fragmentum de bellis Macedonicis,* is probably almost contemporary with Martial – the sole example of a new calligraphic type. Among the Christians of Egypt the codex form was already in general use in the second century, but as a papyrus book, whereas non-Christian literature admitted it only very hesitantly before the fourth century.[6]

At the time of the conversion to Christianity Rome had twenty-eight libraries within its walls and book production was so well established a line of business that Diocletian, in his price edict, set rates for various qualities of script: for one-hundred lines in 'scriptura optima', twenty-five denarii; for somewhat lesser script, twenty denarii; and for functional script ('scriptura libelli bel tabularum'), ten denarii.[7] The unit of valuation was the normal length of line in a verse of Vergil. The extent of a work is given in these units at the end of some manuscripts (stichometry),[8] and stichometric lists survive for biblical books and for the writings of Cyprian.[9]

In the West the transition in book production to the new book form and to parchment had taken place by the fourth century at the latest. This means that books newly made at that time were, as a rule, written as parchment codices.[10] Indeed this was the case not only with copies of new authors (i.e. above all the patristic writers) but also with ancient literature for which there was a requirement.[11] The rolls disappeared from libraries and the result for classical literature

5 Cf. R. Cavenaile, *Corpus papyrorum Latinarum* (Wiesbaden 1958); R. Seider, *Paläographie der lateinischen Papyri* 1–2/2 (Stuttgart 1972 ff.).
6 Cf. C.H. Roberts and T.C. Skeat, *The Birth of the Codex* (Oxford 1983).
7 S. Lauffer (ed.), *Diocletians Preisedikt,* Texte und Kommentare 5 (Berlin 1971) 120. For a commentary on the prices of books, which are implied by the regulations about bookscript, cf. R. Marichal, in L'Écriture et la psychologie des peuples', *XXIIe Semaine de Synthèse* (Paris 1963) 214 f.
8 These numbers were included in copies; they are frequent in gospel books.
9 Ed. by Th. Mommsen, *Gesammelte Schriften* 7 (Berlin 1909) 286 ff.; another ed. in E.G. Turner, *Studies in Early Church History* (Oxford 1912) 265.
10 Only a few more or less damaged papyrus codices have survived from the early middle ages; they contain Josephus, Avitus, Augustine, Isidore, a Greek-Latin glossary, the Digests, and Hilary (CLA III 304 Seider, *Papyri* 2/1, Nr. 67); V 573 (ibid. 2/2, Nr. 50), 614 (ibid. 2/2, Nr. 59); VII 929 (ibid. 2/2, Nr. 75); VIII 1171; IX 1351 (ibid. 2/2, Nr. 36); X 1507 (ibid. 2/2, Nr. 57), an unidentified fragment (II² 192) and remains of two irregularly written rolls with Nicetas of Remesiana and Evagrius (IX 1349 (Seider 2/2, Nr. 52), 1350 (ibid. 2/2, Nr. 48) – both probably from Ravenna. On the use of papyrus for charters see above p. 8.
11 On the legal literature cf. F. Wieacker, 'Textstufen Klassischer Juristen', *Abh. Akad. Wiss. Göttingen,* phil.-hist. Kl., 3 F., 45 (1960) 93 ff.

was that timely transcription in the new form was what decided the selection that might be transmitted to later centuries. But not even all the works copied on parchment have survived in their former extent.[12] For us the age of western bookhands begins with this changeover. They are represented for the fourth and fifth centuries above all by codices of Italian and North African provenance, for the sixth century by Italian and Gaulish ones.[13]

In the meantime new bookhands had been created or were in process of creation: uncial in the West,[14] older half-uncial in the East (perhaps spread there from the law school at Beirut).[15] In addition there appears, as the last antique fixing of a bookhand, the later half-uncial that is attested from roughly the early fifth century, and which acquired the descriptive name 'litterae africanae', but which was also used in the West.[16]

By the fourth and fifth centuries the fashion may have already arisen of choosing canonical capitalis for some authors such as Vergil, Sallust, and Cicero (Orations),[17] so reflecting a consciousness of Roman tradition; but this kind of script apparently had only slight importance for the multiplication of Christian texts.[18] On the other hand Cicero, Livy, Ovid, Lucan, and Fronto were copied at the same time in uncial.[19]

Numerous subscriptions, that are mostly preserved in medieval copies, give an idea of the life of books of the ancient authors in the last centuries of antiquity.[20] These remarks, which originally were entered in their own hand by the correctors after revision, date from the period of the fourth to the sixth century. Not only private citizens and teachers of rhetoric, but also the highest officials with their literary assistants read and emended their Livy, Vergil, Persius, Martial, Juvenal, and Apuleius in Rome, Ravenna, Barcelona, Constantinople, and on the estate of the Symmachi in Henna (Sicily); and in some entries there is reflected something of the spirit of the pagan reaction in the Theodosian period.[21] The consul Turcius Rufius Apronianus Asterius read and punctuated the Vergilius Mediceus ('legi et distinxi') in his year of office 494, and according to another subscription he preserved the *Carmen Paschale* of Sedulius for

---

12 For example, in the works of Sallust, Cicero, the tenth Decade of Livy, Fronto, etc., which survive only fragmentarily as the lower texts of palimpsests.
13 In the West, classical Greek parchment manuscripts survive only as palimpsests (technical literature and Euripides); cf. Lowe, *Palaeographical Papers* 2, 518 f.
14 See above p. 66 ff. 15 See above p. 72 ff. 16 See above p. 76 ff.
17 Which apparently at some stage received the name 'litterae Vergilianae'; see above p. 59.
18 See above p. 58 f.
19 The rare use of half-uncial for classical texts (CLA I 29; III 305), may result from a lack of interest in them at the end of late Antiquity.
20 O. Jahn, 'Die Subskriptionen in den Handschriften römischer Classiker', *Sitzungsber. Kgl. Sächs. Ges. Wiss.* (1851) 327–72; G. Cavallo, 'La circolazione libraria nell'età di Giustiniano', in G.G. Archi (ed), *L'imperatore Giustiniano, storia e mito* (Milan 1978) 201 ff.
21 H. Bloch in *The Conflict Between Paganism and Christianity in the Fourth Century*, ed. by A. Momigliano (Oxford 1963) 214 ff.

posterity.[22] Vettius Agorius Basilius Mavortius, who was consul in 527 and who later emended his copy of Horace, was the owner of the Paris Prudentius.[23] A monument in which the pagan and Christian traditions encounter one another was created in the richly illustrated Calendar of 354 by the calligrapher Filocalus (well known as a stonemason for pope Damasus) for a distinguished person by the name of Valentinus; a carolingian copy still existed in the seventeenth century.[24]

From the time of Constantine's decree, Christian book production was in a position to develop freely,[25] but already in Diocletian's time Latin biblical manuscripts must have been available in large numbers.[26] A century later Jerome became impassioned about conspicuous luxury in Christian books. He wrote with biting sarcasm about biblical codices of old, badly translated texts: 'veteres libros vel in membranis purpureis auro argentoque descriptos, vel uncialibus, ut vulgo aiunt, litteris onera magis exarata quam codices', i.e. manuscripts made with expensive material and with 'inch-high' letters.[27] He compared this with his own ideal: 'pauperes scidulas et non tam pulchros codices quam emendatos', and one can refer immediately to the plain St Gall gospel manuscript (Σ), saec. V, which stands very close to the text-critic Jerome.[28]

The oldest document of the Christian book trade is the stichometric Indiculus of the books of the Bible and of Cyprian's works which was made somewhere outside Rome, probably at Carthage.[29] A 'statio' (workshop) is twice named in Christian books: in a fifth/sixth-century gospel that of Gaudiosus in Rome is mentioned,[30] and the Laurentian Orosius, saec. VI*med.*, was made in that of the Gothic 'antiquarius' Viliaric in Ravenna.[31]

22 CLA III 296; Jahn, 348 ff.   23 CLA v 571a.

24 H. Stern, *Le calendrier de 354* (Paris 1953).

25 The emperor himself commissioned fifty Greek Bibles for the churches of his new capital. On the symbolic and allegorical meanings attached to the book and to writing in the Christian world cf. A. Petrucci, 'La concezione cristiana del libro fra VI e VII secolo', *Studi Medievali*, ser 3, 14 (1973) 961–84 (and in Cavallo, *Libri*, 3–26, 233–8).

26 B. Fischer in *La Bibbia nell'alto medioevo*, Settimane 10 (Spoleto 1963) 522 f., according to acts of the Diocletian persecution.

27 *Prol. in Iob.* On gold and purple see above p. 17. The Psalterium Lugdunense (CLA vi 772) may give an idea of these inch-high letters. Since Jerome says that books are written (exarata) with them I think it is incorrect to refer 'uncialis' (following a medieval attempt at explanation) to the large decorated initial-like letters of the Vergilius Augusteus (Nordenfalk, *Zierbuchstaben*, 89 ff.); P. Meyvaert, '"Uncial letters": Jerome's meaning of the term', *J. Theol. Stud.*, n.s., 34 (1983) 185–8.

28 CLA vii 984; Seider, *Papyri* 2/2, Nr. 54. P. McGurk, *Latin Gospel Books from A.D. 400 to A.D. 800* (Paris 1961) 99 f.; Bischoff *Mittelalterliche Studien* I, 102 ff. Jerome makes the same contrast in his letter to Laeta (Ep. 107, 12) 'Divinos codices . . ., in quibus non auri et pellis Babyloniae vermiculata pictura, sed ad fidem placeat emendata et erudita distinctio'; cf. Nordenfalk, ibid., 112 ff.   29 See above n. 9.

30 D. De Bruyne, 'Gaudiosus un vieux libraire romain', *Rev. Bénéd.* 30 (1913) 343–5.

31 J.-O. Tjäder, 'Der Codex argenteus in Uppsala und der Buchmeister Viliaric in Ravenna', *Studia Gotica* (Stockholm 1972), 144–64. The MS Paris, BN, Lat. 2235 (CLA v 543) can be ascribed to the same workshop (Nordenfalk, *Zierbuchstaben*, 167 and plate 66a.b).

In the golden age of Latin patristic literature in the fourth and fifth centuries, for the first time in large quantity, copies almost contemporary with the authors themselves survive. It is to be presumed, however, that the dissemination of their works resulted less from the book trade (and not so much either through the propaganda and copying by the authors) as by the endeavours of interested people and through a network of personal connections.[32] Possidius relates in his *Vita Augustini* that the writings of that church Father could be found in reliable exemplars in the library of the church at Hippo, should anyone wish to make a copy.[33]

Subscriptions are also transmitted with Christian texts from the fifth and sixth centuries,[34] and even more often dedications and personal benedictions such as 'lege Ianuariane feliciter in Christo' (Cyprian, letters),[35] 'Tene in Christo felix Domitiana' (Origines, homilies),[36] 'Lege felix Amantia cum tuis in Christo Iesu domino nostro' (Priscillian).[37] Some manuscripts were written for and in the environs of churches: 517 by Ursicinus, lector of the church at Verona, the Martinian works for Tours by Sulpicius Severus,[38] a gospel for archbishop Ecclesius of Ravenna (521–34),[39] 581 the Augustine excerpts by Eugippius for the church of Naples, during a siege of that city.[40] The Hilary codex corrected in Cagliari in 509/10 is in fact a direct biographical document for Fulgentius of Ruspe and the catholic bishops exiled with him to Sardinia.[41]

The transcription of books was, however, laid down as a task from the beginnings of Latin monasticism, in which the book belonged to the foundations of that way of life. This was the case with Martin of Tours, Caesarius of Arles in his nuns' rule, and with Benedict, whose rule presumes the existence of an adequate collection of books in the monastery (especially chapter 48). A monastic scriptorium of the sixth century in which the scribes must have been trained in the uniform use of a stylised half-uncial was Eugippius's foundation at Naples.[42] From here Fulgentius of Ruspe was able to request copies. High praise is accorded the writing monks by Cassiodorus, who in his monastery at Vivarium created a centre for biblical studies; in the *Institutiones* composed for

32 H.-I. Marrou, 'La technique de l'édition a l'époque patristique', *Vigiliae Christianae* 3 (1949) 208 ff.; E. Arns, *La technique du livre d'après Saint Jérôme* (Paris 1953) 137 ff.
33 Cap. 18 (MPL 32, 49). Almut Metzenbecher, 'Codex Leningrad Q. v. I.3 (Corbie)', *Sacris Erudiri* 18 (1967/8) 406–50, rejects the possibility that this codex could be one of these volumes from Hippo because of its faulty text.
34 A. Reifferscheid, *De Latinorum codicum subscriptionibus commentariolum* (Breslau 1872); this collection can be significantly enlarged.   35 Clm 208, s. IX, f. 2ʳ.
36 St Gallen 87, s. IX, P. 125.   37 CLA IX 1431.   38 CLA IV 494.
39 The exemplar of Clm 6212, s. IX; cf. Bischoff, *Schreibschulen* 1, 131.
40 CSEL 9, 1, xxiv ff.   41 CLA I 1a.b; Seider, *Papyri* 2/2, Nr. 62.
42 From this scriptorium come CLA I 16 (Eugippius's own excerpts from Augustine); III 374a (a further subscription of Donatus to Origines *Peri archon* from 562, see Origines, *Werke* 5 (1913) IX); VIII 1031; and probably also VI 810 and 819. On the library see Traube, *Vorlesungen u. Abhandlungen* 108 f. Cf., however, p. 77, n. 170.

this monastery he describes the considerate measures in favour of their work.[43] He had the first known pandects, or full bibles, written in one volume; pictures and tables from his Codex Grandior were copied into the Codex Amiatinus.[44] Until the central middle ages it was now in the monasteries that most manuscripts were written.

Through Theodoric, who wanted to erect a Roman-Gothic organisation in his Italian kingdom, Gothic writings came to Italy,[45] and because the Arian church supported the Gothic rule bilingual books were also written. Examples of such bilingual Gothic-Latin manuscripts are the Wolfenbüttel palimpsest (Ep. ad Rom.)[46] and the Giessen fragment, discovered in Egypt but destroyed in 1945 (Ev. Luc.).[47] The Codex Argenteus of the gospels, written with silver on purple parchment probably for Theodoric himself, has an exact counterpart in the equally sumptuous contemporary Codex Brixianus with Latin text,[48] which must likewise be seen as a monument to this bilateral culture. These three Gothic manuscripts are written in the upright type of this script. A single Latin manuscript of the sixth century contains Gothic marginal comments in slanted script (Verona, Bibl. Cap., MS LI, Maximinus Arianus).[49] Gothic subscriptions in slanted script, among them that of 'Wiljarith bokareis', the stationarius well-known from the Florence Orosius, appear beneath a Ravenna charter of 551.[50] With the end of Gothic rule the Gothic manuscripts in Italy were rendered valueless; what remained of them (with the exception of the Codex Argenteus) became part of that waste material which in the seventh and eighth centuries was re-used in Bobbio.

From the East, where, since the third century, the centres of legal studies lay, first at Beirut then at Byzantium, there came in the sixth century as the last great contribution to Latin writing culture the official dissemination of the Justinian law codes. The Florence codex of the Digests (on parchment), which was in southern Italy at an early date, and the Pommersfelden fragments (from Ravenna?), as well as other fragments on papyrus, are all written in the same type of fully rounded uncial with characteristic B and R; they stand at the end of a richly-attested production of almost exclusively legal codices whose Greek symptoms support the assumption that they originated in Byzantium.[51]

It is probably as an echo of the dogmatic controversies of the patristic period

---

43 Institutiones I 30 (ed. Mynors, 75 f.). On manuscripts from Vivarium and their place in the transmission of texts see P. Courcelle, *Les lettres grecques en occident, de Macrobe a Cassiodore*[2] (Paris 1948) 356 ff.; F. Troncarelli, 'Decora correctio, un codice emendato da Cassiodoro?', *Scrittura e Civiltà* 9 (1985) 1–22, with 4 plates.

44 B. Fischer, 'Codex Amiatinus und Cassiodor', *Biblische Z.*, n.F. 6 (1962) 57–79.

45 A. Petrucci, 'Scrittura e libro nell'Italia altomedievale' in *A. Giuseppe Ermini* (Spoleto 1970) = *Studi Medievali* 10/2 (1969) 188–91. On all the MSS cf. P. Scardigli, *Die Goten, Sprache und Kultur* (Munich 1973).   46 CLA IX 1388.   47 CLA VIII 1200.

48 CLA III 281.   49 CLA IV 504.

50 Facs.: Tjäder, *Nichtliter. lat. Pap.*, plate 120 f.; idem, 'Der Codex Argenteus'.

51 Lowe, *Palaeographical Papers* 2, 466–74.

that not infrequently, on the margins of older theological manuscripts, remarks on the content, either vigorously expressed approbation or contradiction, occasionally also warnings ('caute lege'), were written in by critical readers, usually in slanted uncial or a mixed script.[52] Thus, for example, in the Vienna Hilary papyrus, the words 'inenarrabiliter', 'admirabiliter', 'invicte', and many more are found.[53] Works of the heretics had almost no chance of escaping annihilation[54] unless they either circulated under a pseudonym or were anonymous. The two codices of heretical authors that have come down from early Christian times, the Veronese Maximinus Arianus and the Würzburg Priscillian (or Instantius), may have survived because they were anonymous.[55]

A consequence of the changeover in book production from papyrus to parchment was the rise of book illustration.[56] The history of the illustrated papyrus roll goes back to Egyptian antiquity. In the Roman world it began at least with Varro, whose *Imagines* were illustrated with seven hundred pictures. Specialist and technical literature too required illustration. Illustrations of literary texts, amongst them some in colour, are known from Greek rolls. However, it was only with the reception of parchment into book production that the miniaturists acquired a material which both met the requirements of technical refinement and displayed the full potential of the colours. Thus the manufacture of bibliophile illustrated books could reach a climax between the late-fourth and the early-sixth century. Older pictorial compositions were now fruitful sources for pictures of authors[57] and cycles of illustrations in book painting. Of original Latin illustrated manuscripts from the period two Vergil codices, the Wolfenbüttel Agrimensores manuscript and, in a few fragments, the Quedlinburg manuscript of the Old Latin Book of Kings, are preserved.[58] Our knowledge of what was created at that time can be enlarged from the medieval

52 See above p. 78 f.

53 These opinions, which might be instructive for the study of textual transmission, are preserved also in carolingian and later copies; cf. W.M. Lindsay in *Palaeographia Latina* 3 (1924) 18; V. Rose *Die Meermann-Handschriften*, 15 f. In the same way the views of medieval readers and audiences are preserved in manuscripts, for instance on the *Libri Carolini*.

54 Illustrations of the first ecumenical church councils show heretics in the foreground casting their books into the flames; Chr. Walter, 'Les dessins carolingiens dans un manuscrit de Verceil', *Cahiers archéologiques* 18 (1968) 99 ff. (reprod. 2 f.). Cf. also W. Speyer, 'Büchervernichtung', *Jahrb. f. Antike u. Christentum* 13 (1970), esp. 150 f.

55 CLA IV 504; IX 1431. On Pelagius in Ireland see p. 198.

56 K. Weitzmann, *Ancient Book Illumination* (Cambridge, Mass. 1959); idem, *Spätantike und frühchristliche Buchmalerei* (Munich 1977); Nordenfalk, *Das frühe Mittelalter*, 87–218; cf. also the following general surveys: A. Boeckler, *Abendländische Miniaturen bis zum Ausgang der romanischen Zeit* (Berlin–Leipzig 1930); idem–P. Buberl–H. Wegener, 'Buchmalerei', *Reallexikon deutsch. Kunstgesch.* 2 (Stuttgart–Waldsee 1948) cols 1420–1524; idem–A.A. Schmid in Milkau-Leyh, *Handbuch* I² (Wiesbaden 1952) 249–387.

57 Martial (14, 186) refers to an author portrait on the first leaf of a Vergil MS.

58 CLA I 11 and 19; IX 1374b (Facs.: H. Butzmann, *Corpus Agrimensorum Romanorum* (Leiden 1970); VIII 1069.

copies and adaptations, the picture cycles in Terence[59] and Prudentius,[60] in Aesop's fables,[61] the catalogues of the constellations,[62] and from a Ravenna chronicle.[63] The illustrated specialist literature of late antiquity also, be it botanical, medical,[64] or architectural,[65] was reproduced in the middle ages and could in that way provide the impetus for more independent works.[66] Even such time-bound books as the Calendar of 354[67] and the Notitia dignitatum[68] have enriched medieval illustration. Early Christian Bible-illustrations live on in the pictures of Spanish, carolingian, and Anglo-Saxon manuscripts.

This period enriched western book art in a lasting way with two types of decoration. The concordance tables of Eusebius ('canones'), which Jerome had taken over, were prefixed to the gospels, and instead of being written between simple lines they were laid out in coloured frames set between two columns topped by arches or gables which could be decorated in the most varied manner and to which other motifs could be added (canon tables).[69] In the same way author portraits were created for the witnesses to the Christian message of salvation, the inspired evangelists. A special type is represented by the gospels in Cambridge, Corpus Christi College, MS 286, probably Roman saec. VI, which shows on the portrait page with the evangelist Luke and on a separate page scenes from the life of Christ as in a picture book.[70]

With the transition from papyrus rolls to the parchment codex is connected a decisive change for the whole area of European book production. It was customary in papyrus rolls to distinguish the ending, which was better protected and in which the author and title were named in the closing script (colophon), by means of larger script or through ornamentation. This usage passed over initially also into the codices.[71] But from roughly AD 500 on, if not already before

59 L.W. Jones–C.R. Morey, *The Miniatures of the Manuscripts of Terence Prior to the Thirteenth Century* 1/2 (Princeton 1931); Koehler–Mütherich, *Karol. Min.* 4, text, 85 ff., plates 28–61.

60 R. Stettiner, *Die illustrierten Prudentius-Handschriften*, text vol, plates (Berlin 1905).

61 A. Goldschmidt, *An Early Manuscript of the Aesop Fables of Avianus and Related Manuscripts* (Princeton 1947).

62 Koehler, *Karol. Min.* 3, text, 119 ff., plates 53–60; idem–Mütherich, ibid. 4, plates 62–91.

63 B. Bischoff-W. Köhler, 'Eine illustrierte Ausgabe der spätantiken Ravennater Annalen', in *Medieval Studies in Memory of A. Kingsley Porter* (Cambridge, Mass. 1939) 1, 125–38 (Ital. transl. in *Studi Romagnoli* 3 (1952) 1–17).

64 L. McKinney, *Medical Illustrations in Medieval Manuscripts* (London 1965); R. Herrlinger, *Geschichte der medizinischen Abbildung* 1. *Von der Antike bis um 1600* (Munich 1967).

65 B. Bischoff, 'Die Überlieferung der technischen Literatur', in *Artigianato e tecnica nella società dell'alto medioevo occidentale*, Settimane 18/1 (Spoleto 1971) 275 ff. and plates 1–4; repr. *Mittelalterliche Studien* 3, 277–97, plates 19–22.   66 The same applies to maps.

67 H. Stern, *Le calendrier de 354*; cf. above, p. 184 f.

68 J.J.G. Alexander, 'The illustrated manuscripts of the Notitia Dignitatum', in *Aspects of the Notitia Dignitatum*. BAR Suppl Ser 15 (1976) 11 ff.

69 C. Nordenfalk, *Die spätantiken Kanontafeln* 1/2 (Göteborg 1938).

70 F. Wormald, *The Miniatures in the Gospels of St. Augustine* (Cambridge 1954); repr. in F. Wormald, *Collected Writings* 1 (Oxford 1984) 13–55. For the script cf. A. Petrucci, 'L'onciale romana', *Studi Medievali*, ser 3, 12 (1971) 110 f.

then, the weight of ornamental layout at the end gradually shifted towards the opening, where the author's portrait and, in the gospels, the canon tables had their natural place anyway. Various factors worked together here with varying rhythm. Thus connected with the colophon was a specifically Christian ornament, the cross as staurogram, with Rho-bow on the shoulder, plus alpha and omega.[72] It has already shifted to before the text[73] in the miniature codex of John's gospel.[74] Following the example of the arch-framed canon tables, lists of contents are set under coloured arcades in the sixth century,[75] and from the fifth/sixth century on they also acquire greater emphasis through such formulae as: 'In hoc corpore (codice) continentur. . .'[76]

Even before the end of Christian antiquity the germ of a further, extremely consequential development was set in motion in the field of writing with the initial. As Carl Nordenfalk has shown, decoratively laid out letters provided with ornaments were widespread in various areas of late antique art trade and in the emblematic of Christianity. It had probably been a technical book practice – found in many of the oldest parchment manuscripts – to enlarge the first letters of a page or column, which led to the ornamentation of letters in books and subsequently to the invention of the initial. In the Vergilius Augusteus – probably around AD 500 – a monumental de luxe book that stands apart from other types through its imitation of inscriptional capitalis, every page, following this usage, begins with a large patterned and coloured letter.[77] Probably the first manuscript that shows a considerable number of actual initials with various patterns, especially the A with a fish as the left beam, is the Viliaric Orosius of Ravenna.[78] The fish (and the dolphin) is one of the most important motifs for initials up to the ninth century, along with the bird, which appears at first only as a secondary or peripheral ornament. As with the initials, so also the following letters and the titles could increase in size and acquire more varied forms.[79]

71 See above p. 79 f.   72 Nordenfalk, *Zierbuchstaben*, 63; plate 14, bottom.

73 CLA v 600; Nordenfalk, plate 14, top.

74 The cross is common as a motif in frontispieces and in the centre of Insular carpet pages from the second half of the seventh century; cf. Bischoff, *Mittelalterliche Studien* 2, 288 ff.

75 Zimmermann, *Vorkarol. Min.*, plate 1.

76 L. Traube, 'Enarratio tabularum', in Th. Mommsen–P.M. Meyer, *Theodosiani libri XVI* (Berlin 1905) 2.

77 On the Vergilius Augusteus cf. Nordenfalk, *Zierbuchstaben*, 89 f. Colour facsimile: idem, *Vergilius Augusteus* (Graz 1976). The dating above corresponds to that proposed by A. Petrucci, 'Per la datazione del Virgilio Augusteo', in *Miscellanea in memoria di Giorgio Cencetti* (Turin 1973) in contrast to Nordenfalk, who sees the MS as contemporaneous with Damasus and Jerome.   78 Nordenfalk, *Zierbuchstaben*, plate VIa. 61–5.

79 Cf., e.g. Zimmermann, *Vorkarol. Min.*, plate 41.

The early middle ages

The invasions and the foundation of the Visigothic, Vandal, Frankish, Ostrogothic, and Lombard kingdoms destroyed the unity of the empire and its civilisation;[1] the victorious campaigns of Justinian's commanders in Italy, Africa, and Spain brought about no lasting change in the situation. In north and central Italy only Rome and its environs, and coastal strips, above all Ravenna and Naples, remained outside Lombard rule. There followed a period during which cultural life had to be built up with great effort in the areas overwhelmed and often wasted by the barbarian invasions, as well as in the countries that were newly won over to Roman Christianity. Because Latin was taken over too by the conquerors as the language of religious service, of law, and of administration, sooner or later, along with the transmission from the early church, what remained of the ancient heritage could become fruitful once again.

The bonding force was the church. Of the popes, none did as much as Gregory the Great for the preservation of the unity of the Catholic West through the invigoration of diplomatic and ecclesiastical connections. Because his works were copied in Rome he was able to send manuscripts to queens Theodelinde and Brunhilda, and to the Spanish bishops. At least one authentic original manuscript from his scriptorium is preserved,[2] the *Regula pastoralis* in Troyes 504, written in calligraphic uncial. When bishop Augustine, at the instigation of Gregory, began his work among the Anglo-Saxons that was to have such consequences in the future for western Christendom, the pope sent him 'many books'.[3]

Such production of manuscripts is no longer attested after Gregory. Still, Rome remained important in providing from its accumulated treasures of books

---

1 Cf. on the entire section K. Christ–A. Kern, in Milkau-Leyh, *Handbuch* 3/1², 243–334; P. Riché, *Education and culture in the barbarian west* (Colombia, S. Carolina 1976).

2 CLA VI 838; cf. A. Petrucci, 'L'onciale romana', *Studi Medievali*, ser 3, 12 (1971) 75 ff. with plate 1. According to Richard W. Clement, 'Two contemporary Gregorian editions of Pope Gregory the Great's Regula Pastoralis in Troyes MS 504', *Scriptorium* 39 (1985) 93, at least two of the corrections in that MS can be identified as written in Gregory's own hand.

3 On the 'Augustine gospels', Cambridge, Corpus Christi Coll. 286 (CLA II² 126) see Petrucci, 110 f. and plate 13; also above p. 188.

missionaries like Theodore and Hadrian with the manuscripts necessary for their work, and many book requests from abroad could be answered.[4] For that purpose books were also drawn from Cassiodorus's library at Vivarium, which had found a refuge in the Lateran.[5] In Rome and in Campania Anglo-Saxon book-collectors, of whom Benedict Biscop is the best known,[6] could acquire many of the codices which were preserved, copied and studied in English libraries up to Alcuin's time; others made their way back to the continent. Books still left Rome as papal gifts to Pippin and Charlemagne, and it is a sign of Roman provenance when the oldest entry in curialis script appears in a St Gall manuscript.[7] Rome in these centuries housed a large Greek colony and several popes up to Zacharias (741–52), who translated Gregory's Dialogues into Greek,[8] were Greek. As late as the ninth century one of the scribes of a Roman canon law manuscript can be recognised as a Greek from his ductus.[9] Of the Italian episcopal cities only Verona had been able to preserve manuscript witnesses to an unbroken tradition from the early Christian period.[10]

A distinguished rôle fell to one monastery in precarolingian times: Bobbio, south of Pavia, which was founded in 613 by the Irishman Columbanus.[11] The Irish monks were never at any time in the majority, or even particularly numerous there, and its earliest abbots after Columbanus were Burgundians. But the contact with things Irish that is reflected in the hybrid script of various codices[12] left deep traces on the appearance of the Bobbio book collection. Even in the continental scripts of Bobbio from the eighth century the Insular, Irish abbreviations remained and Irish style had an influence on its Lombard environment; the initials of the fine St Gall manuscript of the *Edictus Rotharii* – typically Lombard and probably written in Pavia – are in part modelled on Irish initials.[13]

---

4 Christ-Kern in Milkau-Leyh, *Handbuch* 3/1², 299 f.

5 P. Courcelle, *Les lettres grecques en occident, de Macrobe à Cassiodore*² (Paris 1948) 356 ff.

6 Beda, *Historia abbatum*, c. 4 and 6.

7 See above p. 101. This is also the probable explanation for the entry in Bamberg Patr. 87 (plate Lowe, *Palaeographical Papers* 1, plate 42).

8 There is a plate of the manuscript of this translation, probably written in Rome in 800, in F. Franchi de' Cavalieri–I. Lietzmann, *Specimina codicum Graecorum* (Bonn 1910) plate 6. See G. Cavallo, 'La produzione di manoscritti greci in Occidente tra età tardoantica e alto medioevo', *Scrittura e Civiltà* 1 (1977) 111–31 with plate.

9 In Düsseldorf E 1 (Cresconius, saec. IX²) on f. 40ᵛ–44ʳ. A Greek scribe wrote a Roman benediction in Latin uncial (c. 800) in the Euchologium Barberini (Vatic. Barb. Gr. 336); cf. A. Wilmart in *Rev. Bénéd.* 45 (1933) 10–19. G. Cavallo, 'Interazione tra scrittura greca e scrittura latina a Roma fra VIII e IX secolo', in *Miscellanea codicologica F. Masai dicata MCMLXXIX* 1 (Ghent 1979) 23–9, plates 6–8.

10 G. Turrini, *Millennium scriptorii Veronensis dal IV⁰ al XV⁰ secolo* (Verona 1967).

11 G. Mercati, 'De fatis bibliothecae monasterii S. Columbani Bobiensis', in *M. Tulli Ciceronis De re publica libri e codice rescripto Vaticano Latino 5757 phototypice expressi* (Vatic. 1934).

12 See above p. 102.

13 Cf. Zimmermann, *Vorkarol. Min.*, plate 13c with CLA III 365; likewise reprod. 6 in A. Dold, *Zur ältesten Handschrift des Edictus Rothari* (Stuttgart 1955).

c. The manuscript in cultural history

Bobbio remained a goal for Irish pilgrims and it was probably these who brought pure Irish manuscripts like the Antiphonary of Bangor (written between 680 and 692) to Bobbio. But many older manuscripts too from Italy, North Africa, and Spain ended up in Bobbio. A large number came probably as waste parchment from disbanded libraries and these – among them classics, heretical works, and apocrypha, Gothic texts and Greek and Hebrew ones – were used in the monastery as palimpsests or, as it seems, given to Luxeuil, with which Bobbio was closely linked, for the same purpose.[14]

Of three codices in which stand the names of abbots: '(Liber) de arca domno Atalani (Bobuleni, Vorgusti)',[15] the first is written in a half-uncial with Insular symptoms, definitely in Bobbio itself and probably before 622. In accordance with the wish of Honorius I, the monastery was to be especially active in combatting the Arianism that was observed by the Lombards, and perhaps it was for that reason that the acta of the councils of Ephesus and Chalcedon, and dogmatic works, were acquired and in part copied here in the eighth century.[16] Bobbio, however, was also a safe retreat for rare grammatical literature in very old manuscripts,[17] and that reflects once again the interest that the Irish in particular had in these texts. In the eighth century Irish and Italian scribes transcribed grammatical works here.[18] Already c. 700 Bobbio brought forth a stylishly executed half-cursive, and around the same time texts were copied in the scriptorium that were quite unusual for the time: Rutilius Namatianus, Sulpiciae Satira, Epigrammata Bobiensia,[19] Iulius Valerius,[20] and the *Liber pontificalis*.[21]

The monastic library was significantly expanded even in the ninth and early tenth century.[22] While Gerbert of Rheims was for a short time abbot at Bobbio he made welcome discoveries. After that the library seems to have been hardly noticed until the fifteenth century. In 1461, after the reforms of the monastery, a large catalogue was compiled and in 1493 a sensational trove of grammatical and late-Roman poetry was discovered.[23] However, it was only the revelation of the palimpsests by Angelo Mai that brought about a realisation of how fortunate was the Bobbio transmission both of manuscripts which it preserved and those which had been palimpsested.

14 See below p. 194.
15 CLA III 365 Jerome; I 36 (Augustine amongst others); IV 438 (Lactantius).
16 CLA I 26; III 321, 334, 361; IV 451.
17 CLA III 397a, 398; IV 462; the Probus-Codex CLA I 117 may also have been preserved through Bobbio.   18 CLA III 394, 396a, 397b, 400.
19 Cf. Mirella Ferrari, 'Spigolature Bobbiesi' *It. Med. e Um.* 19 (1973) 12 f., 15–30 and plate 4.
20 CLA IV 439.
21 CLA III 403. The bibliographies by Jerome and Gennadius (CLA III 391) should also be mentioned.   22 Cf. the catalogue saec. IX in Becker, *Catalogi*, Nr. 32.
23 Mirella Ferrari, 'Le scoperte a Bobbio nel 1493: vicende e fortuna di testi', *It. Med. e Um.* 13 (1970) 139–80.

Of the western lands Spain experienced a late flourishing of Christian antiquity, in the cultural sense, in the seventh century, after the conversion of the Visigoths to Catholicism; synonymous with this are the names of Isidore of Seville and the Toledo archbishops Ildefonsus, Eugenius, and Julian. The mentions of libraries in this period are numerous: the captions composed by Isidore for the various sections in his library are still preserved.

The writing practice of the Iberian peninsula was probably no less varied in the seventh century than that of Italy a century before. The handful of surviving manuscripts no longer reveal much about their centres[24] of origin, but amongst these several monuments possess great significance. Because the oldest Spanish codex of Isidore's *De natura rerum*[25] may date from his own lifetime and from southern Spain, it can possibly convey some idea of what its exemplar looked like, with its alternation of uncial and, for citations, capitalis. The manuscript of the *Liber iudiciorum* preserved in León as a palimpsest[26] may derive from the centre of Visigothic royal power, Toledo, during the time of Reccesuinth. The second León palimpsest, which is written in half-uncial of the seventh century, is the oldest partially-transmitted example of a full bible (pandect) in one volume,[27] older than the Northumbrian Codex Amiatinus. This it surpasses considerably in economy through its format of c. 44×32 cm in almost equal writing area in two columns (36.5×28.5 cm), with 71–76 lines. Also Spanish probably is the Ashburnham Pentateuch, saec. VII, with a series of nineteen richly detailed picture pages of great significance in terms of cultural history.[28]

Christian refugees who had fled to Spain before the Arab conquest of North Africa may perhaps have brought a script which influenced the origin of Visigothic minuscule.[29] Already in the seventh century a large part of Isidore's works were European property; after the catastrophe of 711 a heavy Spanish emigration towards southern France via the Narbonensis and beyond to Lyons and Autun, and besides that to Sardinia and various parts of Italy, helped to disseminate Visigothic manuscripts and script.[30]

The homeland of the oldest surviving manuscripts from the Merovingian kingdom is to be sought in southern Gaul. There the Visigoths and Burgundians, as later the Merovingians, attached themselves to Roman administrative institutions and retained Roman law initially, and it was there that most of the uncial and half-uncial codices of the Codex Theodosianus and the

---

24 Cf. the maps in P. Riché, *Education*, 298 and 354.   25 CLA XI 1631.

26 CLA XI 1637. Since three fragments of legal manuscripts ('Fragmenta Vaticana', Codex Theodosianus, Lex Romana Burgundionum; CLA I 45–7) could be used for a copy of Cassian in a similar uncial, it is possible that they were among those dismembered on Reccesuinth's orders; cf. *Lex Visig.* 2,1,9 (MGH Leges 1, 1, 58).   27 CLA XI 1636.

28 CLA V 693a. Reprod., e.g., in Nordenfalk, *Das frühe Mittelalter*, 102 ff.; K. Weitzmann, *Spätantike und frühchristliche Buchmalerei* (Munich 1977), plates 44–7.

29 Cf. above p. 96 f.   30 See above p. 100 n. 36.

Breviarium Alarici came into existence and were preserved because they were not touched by Justinian's ban.[31]

The tradition of an episcopal chancery in southern France is represented by the important canon law manuscript, Paris, BN, Lat. 12097,[32] which was written around 523 in half-uncial and continued in the same century in uncial, half-uncial, and various formal cursives. Ascetic manuscripts of a cruder kind, such as the Ephrem fragments from Corbie and the Cassian from Autun, could have originated in southern monasteries.[33] Of the great cities of 'Roman' Gaul, Lyons alone preserved in its cathedral library a trove of manuscripts from the fifth century.[34]

The farther north one goes the more important seems the rôle of the monasteries, whose number rose impressively in the seventh and eighth centuries,[35] for the establishment of a new cultural continuity. The mastery of writing, however, also extended in the seventh century to the Merovingian aristocracy,[36] and the kings signed their diplomas themselves. King Chilperich (561–84) even concerned himself, like a second Claudius, with the reform of the alphabet, inserting the letters $\odot$, ψ, Z, $\triangle$, according to the manuscript, (for the sounds w (long-o), ae, the, and wi; cp. the wyn-rune), and promoting their use. We learn this from the sardonic report of Gregory of Tours (*Hist. Franc.* V 44).[37]

Among monasteries of the Merovingian period Luxeuil in Burgundy, founded in 590 by the Irishman Columbanus, and Corbie near Amiens (one of its daughter foundations), occupy a special position by virtue of their transmission. Luxeuil must soon have freed herself outwardly from its Irish patrimony, but it stood in close connection with Bobbio, Columbanus's last foundation, and from there it probably received those remains of Italian manuscripts (Livy, Vergil, Ovid, Pliny, etc). which, as in Bobbio, were palimpsested.[38] In Luxeuil an Augustine codex of 669, the 'Missale Gothicum', and what is probably the latest literary papyrus codex (Aug., Epp., Serm.) were written in uncial and half-uncial.[39] Here in the same seventh century the first perfected book minuscule

31 CLA I 110; V 591; VIII 1064; IX 1324; L. Traube, 'Enarratio tabularum' in Th. Mommsen–P.M. Meyer, *Theodosiani libri XVI* (Berlin 1905). Many of the texts which were palimpsested in BN Lat. 12,161 must also come from southern France (CLA v 625 f., 629: Brev. Alar., Cod. Euric., Fronto).
32 CLA v 619. Manuscripts like these, and also CLA I 110 (with its marginalia) and v 591 (see previous note), and the slightly later MSS of canon law CLA VI 836 (Albi, from 666/7), VIII 1061 and 1162, may explain how a core of Notae was transmitted to the early middle ages for wider use.   33 CLA IV 708 and 724.
34 E.A. Lowe, *Codices Lugdunenses antiquissimi* (Lyon 1924); CLA VI, xiii f. It is hard to establish which manuscripts were autochthonous. The Codex Bezae (CLA II² 140, see above p. 74) is eastern in origin; on Lyon 478 (CLA VI 777) cf. Lowe, *Palaeographical Papers* 2, 466–74.
35 Cf. the maps in Riché, *Education*, 269, 332, 428.   36 Riché, 216 f.
37 Riché, 224 f.; reprod. in Br. Krusch, *Hist. Vierteljahrschrift* 27 (1932) 747.
38 CLA IV 498–501; IX 1377, 1420, 1421, X 1455 (f.).
39 CLA XI 1659; I 106; v 614 (Seider, *Papyri* 2/2, Nr. 59); reprod. also in Lowe, *Palaeographical Papers* 2, plates 74, 78, 77a–c.

known to us was developed,[40] the slim, heavily ligatured 'Luxeuil type'. This was associated with an equally slim distinguishing capitalis.[41]

Corbie, which was founded from Luxeuil,[42] was from the beginning (c. 660) distinguished by its connections with the Merovingian court. A definite example of Corbie-written uncial has not been identified; instead, after the early half-cursive, various styles succeeded one another up to the bizarre 'ab-type' and the exemplary caroline minuscule of the Maurdramnus Bible (c. 772–80).[43] Characteristic marginalia by one reader[44] provide the proof that Corbie around 700 must have possessed older codices from southern France and Italy.[45]

Fleury, another seventh-century foundation, had also acquired a considerable holding of biblical and patristic manuscripts from Italy, to judge from numerous fragments that have survived; these perhaps accompanied the relics of St Benedict from Monte Cassino to the Loire.[46] Here the last manuscript of Sallust's *Historiae* was partially rewritten and partially reutilised as flyleaves.

Of the scriptoria in and around Tours, whose tradition goes back to St Martin's time, the impression to be had from the manuscripts – at least those from the monastery of St Martin in the early eighth century – is that here, despite all the immaturity of the script, a collation of the text regularly followed its transcription, and the books were studied.[47]

On German territory[48] after the foundation of Echternach (698) by the Anglo-Saxon Willibrord, others followed in Hesse, the Main region, and in northern Bavaria through Boniface and his followers and pupils; here an initially closed German–Insular script province came into existence.[49] The Anglo-Saxon influence extended even as far as Regensburg with a certain strength.[50] Here, in Freising and in Benedictbeuern, and in other monastic foundations of Tassilo's time, it is clear that Bavaria was open to influence also from northern Italy.

Script regions with their own appearance were developed also on the upper Rhine, in the Lake Constance region, and in Rhaetia.[51] Of these, however, only St Gall has preserved original charters from the mid-eighth-century, and slightly later manuscripts, nine of which attest to the work of the monk Winithar as scribe and director of the scriptorium.

40 Lowe, ibid. 2, 389–98 and plates 75, 76, 77d, 79.
41 On the dissemination and influence of this style see above p. 104 f.
42 Luxeuil-script in Corbie codices: CLA v 633 and 671 (see above p. 105).
43 Cf. above p. 106.
44 The chronicle of Jerome in Valenciennes 495 (CLA vi 941; cf. f. 134ᵛ) should be added to the list in CLA vi, p. xxiii. For a differing view of these entries see F. Masai in H. Vanderhoven-F. Masai-P.B. Corbett, *Regula Magistri* (Brussels 1953) 37 ff.
45 Among these is the principal MS of the *Regula Magistri* (CLA v 633).
46 Cf. Lowe, CLA vi, p. xx f.
47 Cf. above p. 43 n. 39. For which see CLA x 1584. On the ex-libris saec. VIII cf. P. Gasnault, 'L'Ex-libris du VIIIe s. d'un manuscrit de S. Hilaire', *Scriptorium* 25 (1971) 49 ff. with plate 1.   48 Cf. the map in Riché, *Education*, 434.   49 See above p. 93 ff.
50 B. Bischoff, *Schreibschulen* 1, 172 f.   51 See above pp. 107 and 114.

The variety of writing practice in Francia at this time can be seen, just as in the manuscripts, in the small parchment slips that were presented as authentications of relic fragments and which are preserved in great numbers, for example in Chelles and St Maurice, and in the cathedral of Sens.[52] Their scripts are uncial, half-uncial, cursives and minuscules, amongst them some from well-known schools,[53] and sporadically also Insular scripts.

Of the hagiographical literature that is characteristic of the Merovingian period the Vita Wandregisili[54] is the only text that is transmitted separately in an uncial codex; in the case of a rich north-eastern French corpus of vitae of various origins the choice of the lives of St Medard (Venantius Fortunatus and Vita anonyma) perhaps offers a pointer to its circle of origin.[55] The substantial early transmission for the *Historia Francorum* by Gregory of Tours, with two manuscripts from the seventh century and three from the seventh/eighth, may be seen as a symptom of a strong interest in national history.[56]

The language of Merovingian texts is well-known for the fact that the grammatical system is to a greater or lesser extent in ruins. The uncertainty and confusion in orthography, above all in vocalism, penetrated even into liturgical and biblical manuscripts, as, for instance, in the Bobbio missal[57] and the gospel book of Gundohinus from 754.[58] Until well into the eighth century the outward appearance of some manuscripts is also very neglected, as in the parts of the miscellaneous manuscript Bern, Burgerbibl., MS 611[59] and the palimpsest Karlsruhe, Bad. Landesbibl., MS Aug. CCLIII.[60] Compared with the sobriety and practicality of a Roman law manuscript, the oldest (certainly not calligraphic) Wolfenbüttel manuscript of the Lex Salica, in which parodies of penalties are added, seems degenerated.[61]

But beside the decline in style in the century and a half from Gregory of Tours to the beginning of the carolingian reform, attempts were made either to recover the older forms in their calligraphic clarity or to arrive at entirely new ones. In various centres that have not yet been precisely located, uncial and half-uncial were written at least in the first half of the eighth century in set styles,[62] and in the psalterium duplex Vatican, MS Reg. Lat. 11[63] even in an artificial capitalis. It is to be assumed that familiarity with English scribal art made it possible to set the standard higher. Among the foremost achievements are the Missale

---

52 Saint-Maurice: ChLA I, Nr. 14–38; Sens: M. Prou, *Manuel de paléographie, Recueil de fac-similés* (Paris 1904), plate 5; Chelles: ChLA XVIII 669.
53 ChLA I 37 (Luxeuil); Prou, Nr. 4 (Laon). There are numerous examples of the b-type from Chelles.   54 CLA V 675.   55 Clm 3514, saec. VIII[1] or med. (CLA IX 1238).
56 CLA I 107 (very close to Gregory in date); V 670; VI 742a (b); VIII 1122.
57 CLA V 653; E.A. Lowe in *The Bobbio Missal, notes and studies*, Henry Bradshaw Society 61 (London 1924) 86 ff.   58 Steffens[2], *Lateinische Paläographie* 37; CLA VI 716.
59 CLA VII 604–604e.   60 CLA VIII 1099.
61 Cf. Bischoff, *Mittelalterliche Studien* 2, 67 n. 47.   62 See in CLA V 541 and 693b.
63 CLA I 101.

Gothicum vetus,[64] the 'Missale Francorum',[65] and two manuscripts of Gregory of Tours.[66]

In Italy, Spain, and the Frankish kingdom the first signs of ornamental and coloured book decoration which could be observed in the sixth century developed fully in precarolingian times in many local traditions.[67] By this time it concentrates on the opening of the book, its title, and its initials.[68] Fishes and birds are the preferred and widely disseminated motifs. In order to draw them a compass is often used for circles, bows, and star patterns, just as the ruler is used in the page-long Luxeuil initials. Elsewhere exuberant leaf-forms and luxuriant shoots are drawn in a free-swinging style. Geometrical patterns, the 8- or rope-motif, leaves and palmettes fill out the bodies of the initials. Interlace is very rare before the mid eighth century, so too a human head or hand. Imitation of insetting and of jewellery[69] is shown in the Old Latin Valerianus Gospel saec. VII*in*, probably deriving from the Latin Balkans.[70] Frontispieces with crosses[71] and ornamental titles are laid out in frames under arches. In the Gallican sacramentaries of the eighth century the UD-monogram appears of 'Vere Dignum'.[72] With its pictures of the Maiestas Domini and of the evangelists following earlier models, the Gundohinus gospel of 754 stands alone in the non-Insular book illumination of the time, like the Ashburnham Pentateuch of the seventh century, probably from Spain.

The Latin script and the Latin book that came with the Christian mission to Ireland in the fifth century encountered a cultural situation which already knew a script (Ogham) that was used for inscriptions, but not books, and which on the contrary had an established oral Celtic tradition.[73] In order for Christianity, its belief and its cult to take root, Ireland required an education in the Latin language and script. Patrick, in the tradition the great representative of the fifth-century conversion work, is supposed – according to a later legend – to have himself written '365 or more "abgetoria" ', abecedaria. An outspoken willingness among the Irish to adopt the new spiritual wealth and to come to grips with it made easier the initiation of a Latin education and even learning. It found its home in the great monasteries, of which many were founded in the sixth century.

When in Ireland Latin manuscripts were taken as models for their own home-produced books there must have been among them some that still displayed archaic features.[74] From the choice of scripts available the decision was to opt for

64 CLA I 93.   65 CLA I 103.   66 CLA V 670; VI 742b.

67 Zimmermann, *Vorkarol. Min.*, vols 1 and 2. J. Porcher in J. Hubert–J. Porcher–W. Fr. Volbach, *Frühzeit des Mittelalters*, Universum der Kunst (Munich 1968) 103–208, 360–4.

68 Nordenfalk, *Zierbuchstaben*.   69 Nordenfalk, ibid., 50.

70 CLA IX 1249; Nordenfalk, ibid., 158 and passim and plates III, 47–50; Zimmermann, *Vorkarol. Min.*, plates 4–10.   71 Bischoff, *Mittelalterliche Studien* 2, 289.

72 Nordenfalk, *Zierbuchstaben*, 162; A. Ebner, *Quellen und Forschungen zur Geschichte und Kunstgeschichte des Missale Romanum im Mittelalter* (Freiburg i. Br. 1896) 430 ff.; this also includes medieval allegorical and mystical interpretations.

73 For literature see p. 83 n. 1.   74 See above p. 20 f.

the most modern at that time, the later half-uncial; capitalis, uncial, older half-uncial, and cursive of the continental kind are not attested from Irish manuscripts. The alphabet was enlarged with alternative forms, and the script was wilfully stylised.

When the use of writing increased as a consequence of the invigoration of Irish learning, a narrower, more economical script, the Irish minuscule, and a system of extensive abbreviations developed; new possibilities of cursive writing were also tried. Thus Irish writing practice stands graded before us already in precarolingian times, from the bold round half-uncial of the gospels through library manuscripts in medial script size, up to the small, often tiny script of the Irish pocket gospel books toward which also the layout of the Palladium of the Patrician tradition, the Book of Armagh (c. 807), is oriented.[75] In Ireland writing stood in high regard as the pious handiwork of monks; many saints were famed as scribes.[76]

Ecclesiastical contacts existed at the outset with Rome and Gaul, and in the sixth century especially with Wales. Commercial contacts had existed for a long time with Spain; from the seventh century on the connection with Rome again became stronger, initially in southern Ireland. What was available in these ways in the realm of literature, beyond the most essential in a period of dissolution of the old Roman civilisation, must initially have depended very much on chance.[77] But there were amongst them works that were elsewhere forgotten or suppressed as either apocryphal or heretical, such as the Gospel of the Hebrews and the exposition of the Pauline epistles by the Briton Pelagius. When in the seventh and eighth centuries Irish learning, whose strongpoints were biblical exegesis, commentaries on Roman grammatical works, and computistical studies, began to stir itself, the book collections were rich, even if one-sided. Large collections of excerpts came into being: the learned ascetic Irish collection of canons[78] and the grammatical compilation *Donatus Ortigraphus* that was widely disseminated in various redactions.[79] In Ireland, from the seventh century onwards, glossing was carried out in the vernacular, while at the latest from the seventh century texts were being written in the Irish language.

The urge to undertake missionary activity and the drive for ascetic self-exile led the Irish to northern Scotland and Northumbria, Wessex and northern France, Burgundy and northern Italy, where Irish monastic foundations,

---

75 CLA II² 270
76 Christ–Kern in Milkau–Leyh, *Handbuch* 3/1², 314 f. (this includes the poem of the scribe in the forest, see Gerard Murphy (ed. and transl.), *Early Irish Lyrics* (Oxford 1956) 5).
77 The letter of Calmanus (Colmanus?) to Feradad (Feradach?) expresses the delight with which new, better and more complete texts were received; cf. Bischoff, *Mittelalterliche Studien* 1, 199. The letter is undated, but it mentions Isidore and should probably be assigned to the second half of the seventh century.
78 Cf. S. Hellmann, *Sedulius Scottus* (Munich 1906) 136 ff.
79 J. Chittenden (ed.), *Donatus Ortigraphus, ars grammatica*. CCSL Cont. Med. 40D (Turnhout 1982).   80 CLA II² 266–77.

centres of Irish influence and resting stages on the Irish pilgrim routes to Rome came into being. In such places on the continent as Bobbio, St Gall, Reichenau, and Würzburg, with a few exceptions, the still extant Irish manuscripts of the pre-Viking period were preserved. Their script was felt to be so distinctive that not only did the St Gall librarian form a separate section for 'libri Scottice scripti', but also other catalogues describe Irish – and occasionally Anglo-Saxon – manuscripts as 'scottica', 'Scotaica' and so forth.[81] The older Hiberno-Latin literature was in large part transmitted only through carolingian copies.

Irish script and book practice were taken over as a model not just in the other Celtic lands of Wales, Cornwall and Brittany.[82] From 635 on the northern part of England bordering on the already-Christianised land of the Picts was won over to Christianity by Irish monks from Lindisfarne. Thus was determined in large measure the history of literary culture in Anglo-Saxon England, since Irish script was transplanted to Northumbria.[83] A conflict of scripts too must have taken place as an accompaniment to the struggle between the Irish mission in the north and the Roman mission in the south initiated by Gregory the Great, which expanded from Canterbury, because uncial came from Rome as the script of the mission and of the many codices that were acquired by Anglo-Saxons such as Benedict Biscop. Hence it was extensively used in Kent and Mercia into the eighth century, even for charters, and eventually even for gospel books.[84] Half-uncial of continental type was also written in England,[85] but on the other hand the later Roman cursive is not attested there. From Canterbury the use of uncial was taken over also in Wearmouth and Jarrow in Northumbria and hence the Codex Amiatinus could be produced there, the uncial bible pandect that Ceolfrid in 716 had designated as a gift for St Peter's basilica in Rome. Here in Bede's monastery his work *De temporum ratione* was still copied in uncial, while the oldest manuscripts of his *Historia ecclesiastica* were written in Anglo-Saxon minuscule.[86]

For manuscripts of common texts the use of Anglo-Saxon minuscule established itself fully in the eighth century throughout England. Even the inmates of English nunneries were versed in writing and were active too as scribes. The

81 J.F. Kenney, *The Sources for the Early History of Ireland* 1 (New York 1929) 620 f., Nr. 449; Johanne Autenrieth, 'Insulare Spuren in Handschriften aus dem Bodenseegebiet bis zur Mitte des 9. Jahrhunderts', in *Paläographie* (1981) 145–57, plates 16–20.
82 See above p. 89 f.
83 Even after Irish monks had left Northumbria in 664 the monasteries and schools of Ireland remained a goal for many Anglo-Saxons. Irish and Anglo-Saxon features are mingled in Vat. Pal. Lat. 68 written by 'Edilberict filius Berictfridi' (CLA 1 78).
84 Lowe, *English Uncial*; cf. Bischoff, *Mittelalterliche Studien* 2, 328–39.
85 CLA II 237, and probably also VI 740.
86 *De temporum ratione*: Fragment in Darmstadt (MS 4262, CLA Addenda 1822) certainly copied before 735, and fragments in Bückeburg, Münster (CLA IX 1233 and S, p. 4; J. Petersohn in *Scriptorium* 20 (1966) 215–47 and plate 17 f.; and Braunschweig, Stadtbibl., Fragm. 70, this later MS in capitular uncial); *Hist. eccl.*: cf. Lowe, *Palaeographical Papers* 2, 441 ff.

oldest English ex–libris 'Cuthsuuithae boec thaere abbatissan' is probably her autograph from the period around 700.[87]

Of the size of English book collections that were deliberately built up for teaching some idea can be gleaned from the knowledge of literature in Aldhelm and Bede, and likewise from the catalogue of texts available in York cathedral library inserted by Alcuin into his poem on *The bishops, kings, and saints of York*.[88] Little has survived of these once great riches. But of the books that were written in England, and of the older books collected in Italy,[89] some have ended up in the Anglo-Saxon foundations on the continent like Echternach, Fulda, and Würzburg, and in the letters that Boniface and Lul directed home requests for books are a frequent theme.

The oldest remaining monuments of Insular book art[90] come from Ireland and from the Irish foundation at Bobbio (613). Already roughly at the beginning of the seventh century a typical characteristic form, the diminuendo initial group, occurs. In the Cathach of Columba, in which every psalm is distinguished by such a group, the enlarged letters are fashioned from Celtic motifs – though not without a knowledge of continental elements.[91] The dynamic handling of the contours which the Insular artists cultivate in the drawing of initials is already displayed there. In the Irish fragments from Durham[92] there first appears the interlace which, together with whirling spirals and subtly drawn interlaced animals, was to become the dominant decorative element in the book art of Ireland and Northumbria.

The style presents itself in full bloom in the great gospels of Durrow, Echternach, Durham A.II.17, and Lindisfarne written between 670 and 700, in which the Irish element has entered into combination with Northumbrian components.[93] These are arranged on the model of Irish gospel books which were also standard for Welsh and Breton gospels, hence probably established already in the first half of the seventh century. From these come the decorative pages filled with closely packed ornament ('carpet pages') in addition to pages on which the symbols of the four evangelists are brought together and others in which the decoration of Matthew I 18 ('Xpi autem generatio') is on a par with the opening of the gospels.[94]

87 Reprod.: Bischoff–Hoffmann, *Libri Sancti Kyliani* (Würzburg 1952) reprod. 13, cf. p. 88; CLA IX 1430a.

88 Cf. J.D.A. Ogilvy, *Books Known to the English, 597–1066* (Cambridge, Mass. 1967).

89 CLA II² 251; VIII 1139, 1196 (?); IX 1423a.b, 1430a.b.

90 C. Nordenfalk, *Celtic and Anglo-Saxon painting* (New York 1977).

91 C. Nordenfalk, 'Before the Book of Durrow', *Acta Archaeologica* 18 (1947) 155; D.H. Wright in A. Dold–L. Eizenhöfer, *Das irische Palimpsestsakramentar im Clm 14,429* (Beuron 1964) 37*ff.

92 Nordenfalk, 'Before the Book of Durrow', and idem, *Celtic and Anglo-Saxon painting*, plate 1.

93 See now George Henderson, *From Durrow to Kells. The Insular Gospel-Books 650–800* (London 1987) 32ff.

94 The first occurrence is probably in the Bobbio MS CLA III, 350. On other Irish symptoms, the initials outlined with red dots and the Irish ornamental capitals, see above p. 87.

Of the above-mentioned gospels, besides Lindisfarne, Echternach and Durham A.II.17 were possibly also written at Lindisfarne.[95] For Durrow, the oldest of them, Iona, the focal point of the Irish mission on the Scottish coast, has been suggested as the place of origin, but the text is classed as Northumbrian.[96] Two or three generations after Anglo-Saxon book-painting reached its peak with the Lindisfarne codex Irish art possessed the vigour that was required to create the ultimate masterpiece, the Book of Kells. Here the initials and other peripheral ornament are composed of human heads and interlaced bodies, realistic animals (cats and mice, moths and others), and even some fabulous ones. While Kells still retains the heavily stylised human representation, the switch to Roman art had taken place already in the evangelists' portraits of Lindisfarne, under the influence of Cassiodorus's Codex Grandior and other sources of Mediterranean provenance.

The Anglo-Saxon miniaturists in the eighth century advanced in these ways of approximating the early Christian and Italo-Byzantine book art and their portrait types. The Trier gospels (Domschatz MS 61), written at Echternach as a joint enterprise by an Anglo-Saxon named Thomas and a Frank, unites Northumbrian reminiscences and the decoration of an Italian exemplar. The miniatures of two codices from the school of Canterbury, the Vespasian Psalter and the Stockholm Codex Aureus, follow closely Italian manuscripts which probably rested there from the time of Gregory the Great and Augustine. Thus English book illumination leads up to that point where the carolingian renaissance begins.

95 T.J. Brown in *Codex Lindisfarnensis*, ed. T.D. Kendrick and others (Olten 1960) 89 f.
96 Reprod. in Zimmermann, *Vorkarol. Min.*, plate 198; Micheli, *L'Enluminure*, reprod. 7. The discovery of further fragments of this destroyed codex (CLA IV 466) by Mirella Ferrari supports an eighth-century date for the script; 'Spigolature Bobbiesi', *It. Med. e Um.* 16 (1973) 9–12 and plate 3. In evaluating the few extant monuments we should not overlook the fact that we have fragments of texts from a dozen more gospel books which, to judge from their scripts, might have had a similarly elaborate decoration.

The Carolingian period

By and large, it is only in the carolingian period[1] that what we now possess of the literary legacy of Roman antiquity and of the Latin patristic age was first preserved. This legacy nourished education and learning in the middle ages, which was in large measure dominated by the ancient authorities, until the influx of translations in the twelfth and thirteenth centuries resulted in a new orientation. Work with these texts is closely bound up with the literary production of the middle ages, is indeed a part of that production.

Because the history of manuscripts in the medieval period begins with this securing of the heritage, I would like to preface this section with a few remarks on how manuscripts were used in the middle ages.[2] Liturgical manuscripts, by virtue of their purpose, were truly functional books, and lectionaries were often supplied at a later date with introductory and closing formulae, while divisions into lections were often added in homiliaries and passionals. Chapter numbers and occasionally instructions for the lectio continua are often added to carolingian bibles in the twelfth and thirteenth centuries. Collations,[3] marginal notes by readers, 'nota' signs, and underlinings[4] with a stylus or red chalk are found nearly everywhere. Now and again such traces are clear symptoms of textual reworking,[5] as occurred in the innumerable canonistic, dogmatic, exegetical, and ethical compilations and florilegia. Industrious readers read pen in hand and used it diligently for explanatory or personal notes, as in the case of Ekkehard IV of St Gall[6] and several Constance clerics at the beginning of the Investiture Contest, amongst them the canonist Bernold.[7] Schoolbooks and books for study are generally those that most clearly bear the marks of use in their marginalia and glosses, often including vernacular glosses. But the Lenten readings in the

---

1 Cf. Christ–Kern in Milkau-Leyh, *Handbuch* 3/1², 335 ff.
2 Christ–Kern, 253 ff., 276 ff.
3 See below p. 205.   4 E.g. in Paris, BN, Lat. 12,242 ff.
5 Such as the autograph directions by Alcuin to his scribes (Bischoff, *Mittelalterliche Studien* 2, 12–19 with plate 1) and the signs of Florus of Lyons (Lowe, *Palaeographical Papers* 1, 323 ff. and plate 46). See also below p. 206.   6 Bruckner, *Scriptoria* 3, 46 n. 239.
7 Johanne Autenrieth, *Die Domschule von Konstanz zur Zeit des Investiturstreits* (Stuttgart 1956), with plate.

monasteries,[8] and the refectory readings[9] in monasteries and chapters were regular occasions for the use of books. From the ninth century on some lists of loans have been preserved.[10] For the purpose of working out from the accessible book holdings what use could be made of them and the intention in using them, those catalogues of medieval librarians and scholars are of special interest which indicate, besides the contents of their own libraries, those of others as well; this could be revealed by indication of those books that are missing from their own library but obtainable in the neighbourhood,[11] by the amalgamation of several catalogues,[12] or by lists of titles with references to where copies were available.[13]

Just as with the compilation of registers,[14] a simultaneous reflection of the active involvement with texts is also shown when, in the process of copying, they are deliberately placed in new textual environments which generate new lines of transmission. Typical occasions were the formation of corpora on a particular discipline or theme; examples can be cited for many disciplines and from all centuries of the middle ages.[15] If collections of poetry, historical works, travel literature, visions, prophecies, and many other subjects are often evidence of personal preference, some specialist collections too, like the twelfth-century corpora of texts relating to the study of Hebrew and biblical antiquities compiled in France and England, enjoyed a wide circulation.[16] Systematic arrangement

8　K. Christ, 'In caput quadragesimae', *Zentralbl. f. Bibliothekswesen* 60 (1944) 33–59; the list he cites on p. 44 as from Farfa is securely assigned to Cluny by A. Wilmart, 'Le couvent et la bibliothèque de Cluni vers le milieu du XIe siècle', *Rev. Mabillon* 11 (1921) 89–124. See also the ninth-century note in Clm 6300 (Bischoff, *Schreibschulen* 1, 143).

9　Notes on reading at table are collected in Lehmann, *Erforschung* 1, 22 f.; H. Hauke, 'Die Tischlesung im Kloster Tegernsee im 15. Jh. nach dem Zeugnis seiner Handschriften', *Stud. Mitteil. OSB* 83 (1972) 220–8. A full treatment is still needed.

10　The oldest catalogues come from Cologne, Dombibliothek (833; Becker, *Catalogi*, Nr. 16); Weißenburg (s. IX/X; Becker, Nr. 17); again from Cologne, Domb. (between 1010 and 1027; E. Dümmler in *Z. f. dt. Altertum* 19 (1876) 466 f.); from Freising (s. XI² and XII; Becker, Nr. 64 f.).

11　Metz, manuscripts of St Symphorien and St Vincent catalogued at St Arnould (saec. XI); *Catalogue général* 4° 5 (1879) 97.

12　The Sorbonne owned catalogues of Parisian monasteries (s. XIII); cf. R.H. Rouse, 'The early library of the Sorbonne', *Scriptorium* 21 (1967) 69 f. In Regensburg the catalogues of the monasteries were collected and copied (1347); cf. *Mittelalt. Bibliothekskat. Deutschl.* 4, 1, 152 f.

13　Cf. Lehmann, *Erforschung* 4, 172–83; on which see H. Silvestre in *Scriptorium* 15 (1961) 323–7 and 19 (1965) 90–6. The earliest come from England: the Franciscan 'Registrum librorum Angliae' (s. XIII ex.) and the 'Catalogus scriptorum ecclesiae' by Henry of Kirkstede of Bury St Edmunds (not John Boston of Bury) (s. XIV), which draws on 195 English libraries; see R.H. Rouse, 'Bostonus Buriensis and the author of the "Catalogus scriptorum ecclesiae"', *Speculum* 41 (1966) 471–99; there are illustrations of the Register in R.H. & M.A. Rouse, *Manuscripts at Oxford: R.W. Hunt Memorial Exhibition* (Oxford 1980) 42, 54 f.

14　See below p. 225.

15　See below on legendaries (p. 216), catalogues of writers (p. 206), and textbooks for the study of the liberal arts (p. 217). Other important examples are a collection of early commentaries on almost all the books of the Bible, in one volume, which goes back to Theodulf of Orleans (Paris, BN, Lat. 15,679), and 'Bedas Computus' (cf. Ch. W. Jones, *Bedae opera de temporibus* (Cambridge, Mass. 1943) 106 f.); D. Ó Cróinín, *Peritia* 2 (1983) 229–47.

16　A reference in Bischoff, *Mittelalterliche Studien* 2, 253.

may cast new light on individual texts.[17] Already in precarolingian times a critical and practical interest had led to the combination of two or three versions of the psalter in parallel columns.[18] In the same way, in the later period several recensions of translated works were copied side-by-side: two different versions of Aristotelian works[19] and three[20] or even four translations[21] of the writings of Pseudo-Dionysius the Areopagite.

That the great work of preservation and renewal of the transmission of ancient texts was possible at all was due to the political will of Charlemagne and to the understanding with which he took up the various proposals that were brought to him. In him an impetuous drive for education and an abhorrence of ignorance were deep-rooted. Both combined with the high concept he had of his duties as a ruler, and so he concerned himself with raising the educational level no less than with the moral elevation of his subjects and of the clergy. Like Pippin, who had carried out the unification of ecclesiastical chant in accordance with Roman usage, Charlemagne sought to see the liturgy, canon law, and the monastic mode of life standardised. To this end he determined to obtain authentic texts which would serve as the norm. He wanted a bible text purged of errors; the homiliary compiled by Paul the Deacon was recommended in an edict. Other works of this period that were destined for practical use probably also received his explicit approval: the commentary of Smaragdus on the liturgical gospels and epistles, and the *Liber glossarum* composed at Corbie.

That Charlemagne took a personal interest in books is attested not only by his biographer but also by the condition of the original manuscript of the *Libri Carolini*, the official manifesto of the iconoclastic controversy, with its marks of approbation, erasures and corrections, and the replacement of whole folios.[22] Nor was Charlemagne's care for books confined only to what was strictly necessary; he had the older transmission comprehensively gathered in the palace library, with which several extant volumes can still be associated.[23] The contri-

---

17 In Laon 273 and 279, both dating from the ninth century, the different parts of a commentary to the books of the Heptateuch are bound up with early Christian biblical poems (Ps. Hilary, Proba, Dracontius, Cyprianus Gallus, Alcimus Avitus). R. Peiper in MGH, AA 6/2 (Berlin 1883) liii ff.

18 The earliest Psalterium Quadruplex (Bamberg, Bibl. 44) was copied at St Gall in 909 with the Greek text included.

19 M. Grabmann, 'Forschungen über die lateinischen Aristoteles-Übersetzungen des XIII. Jahrhunderts', *Beitr. z. Gesch. d. Philos. d. Mittelalters* 17, 5/6 (Münster/W. 1916) 96 f.

20 Cf. eg. London, Lambeth Palace 382, s. XIII.

21 On Brussels, Bibl. Royale, MS 903, s. XV (from Hilduin to Traversari) cf. M. Grabmann, *Mittelalterliches Geistesleben* 1 (Munich 1926) 452.

22 Ann Freeman, 'Further studies in the Libri Carolini', *Speculum* 40 (1965) 203–22 with plate.

23 B. Bischoff in *Karl der Große, Lebenswerk und Nachleben* 2 (Düsseldorf 1965) 42–62 with 6 reprods; repr. *Mittelalterliche Studien* 3, 149–69, plates 5–10. I would like to add to this list Leningrad Q v I. 40, Tertullian, Apologeticum, one of the most beautifully written early carolingian manuscripts; see plate 12 infra.

bution of foreign scholars whom Charlemagne attracted to his court, and of others who knew the pleasure he took in the enlargement of its library, has often been summarised.[24] Amongst them Paul the Deacon, by his excerpts from Festus, did a service to a text that was later to be almost entirely lost.

The extent of the palace library is unkown; assembled from many sources, with books dating from five centuries, it was rich in rare texts and probably the largest library of its time. From this centre texts found in ancient manuscripts were once more put into circulation.[25] The uncial Puteanus of the third Decade of Livy probably belonged to it. Later in Corbie, it was copied c. 800 and was later at Tours. Somewhat later, under Louis the Pious, the codex of Augustine's Opuscula, Pal. Lat. 210, saec. VI–VII, was copied at the court into Paris, BN, N.A. Lat. 1448.[26] Old exemplars from other libraries were also brought to light. Thus a copy was made in Laon of the half-uncial Augustine *De civitate Dei*, an old Corbie possession.[27] From the Origen, saec. V–VI, Lyons MS 483 (from the cathedral library)[28] there descends – indirectly – the early carolingian manuscript, Paris, BN, Lat. 12,124. But most exemplars of carolingian copies are now lost, so that the transmission in general begins with the eighth/ninth or ninth century.

The first palace library was mostly dispersed after Charlemagne's death. However, under Louis the Pious a scriptorium at the palace supplied a new, select collection of books.[29] Likewise it appears that in a scriptorium writing in a style like that of Tours and affiliated to the palace a considerable number of manuscripts of *leges* and *formulae* was produced, as the public administration of justice required them;[30] their origin may date to the chancellorship of abbot Fridugis of St Martin (819–32). A monumental work of compilation that was undertaken in Louis's reign but which remained fragmentary must have had official character: a commentary on the bible in the form of catena on which work may have been carried out in more than one centre, because the manuscripts, which bear the unmistakable traces of excerpting, are widely distributed.[31]

It can be seen from carolingian exchanges of letters how manuscripts were exchanged between nearby and distant places for transcription or collation. Most informative are the letters of Lupus of Ferrières, whose correspondents ranged from abbot Altsig of York to pope Benedict III. Following Einhard's

24 Bischoff, ibid.   25 Bischoff, ibid.
26 B. Bischoff, *Lorsch im Spiegel seiner Handschriften* (Munich 1974) 56. Cf. also CLA Addenda 1825 (Philo, Quaestiones in Genesin, s. VII).
27 Cf. CLA vii 852 and v 635.   28 CLA vi 779.
29 Bischoff, 'Die Hofbibliothek unter Ludwig dem Frommen', in *Medieval Learning and Literature, Essays Presented to Richard William Hunt* (Oxford 1976) 3–22 with plate 1/2; repr. *Mittelalterliche Studien* 3, 171–86.
30 E.g. the Gemelli Berlin, Staatsbibl. Preuß. Kulturbes., Lat. qu. 150 and Warsaw 480; Vatic. Regin. Lat. 846, 852, 857, amongst others.
31 B. Bischoff, 'Die Bibliothek im Dienste der Schule', in *La scuola nell'occidente latino dell'alto medioevo* Settimane 19 (Spoleto 1972) 1, 413 f.; repr. *Mittelalterliche Studien* 3, 231–3.

example, he was concerned with collecting classical and patristic literature in accurate and complete copies, or with producing such texts. In a request addressed to Tours even a papyrus codex of Boethius' *In topica Ciceronis* is mentioned. He collated systematically; some of his collations have also passed over into copies made by his circle of pupils. For the emendation of a Solinus codex three different exemplars were drawn upon.[32] Book exchanges between St Denis and Reichenau are revealed by notices in the manuscripts themselves, which are confirmed by other items of information.[33] Exact textual comparisons will doubtless lead to still more disclosures concerning connections of this kind.

In the basic stock of the libraries, in which Latin patristic literature was predominant, the most necessary works came to be rapidly and widely distributed. Where one wished to extend the number of books beyond this nucleus, and to complete it, or fill the gaps in the œuvre of particular authors, one could resort to corpora and lists devoted to literary history in order to establish the desiderata.[34] Copies were also made of the newly-recovered Roman literature. For the needs of the school a narrower choice of textbooks and of such authors was achieved which could be read, together with a canon of early Christian poetry, in order to complement basic instruction in grammar. The uniformity of this staple diet in school libraries, the 'libri scholastici', which shows only minor variations up to the twelfth century, reflects the uniformity of education.[35]

The early carolingian period perfected a minuscule script which, for all its variations of stylistic expression from one scriptorium to another, possessed a clear legibility, elegant proportions, a natural flow in the formation of the individual letters and of the few ligatures that were retained in various groupings. The Anglo-Saxon script that was still written at Echternach, in the area of Boniface's mission, and at Werden, disappeared in stages in the first half of the ninth century, last of all at Fulda, where it had stood for some four decades in competition with caroline minuscule.[36]

As a means of giving greater clarity to the layout of the manuscripts three historic scripts were used almost everywhere along with the minuscule: uncial, capitalis, and monumental capitalis;[37] in Tours and in other schools half-uncial was also used as a fourth script.[38] The special purity of style of the capitalis written at the court of Louis the Pious[39] and in the circle of Lupus of Ferrières is inconceivable without the study of exemplars from antiquity. The layout too of

32 B. Bischoff, 'Paläographie und frühmittelalterliche Klassikerüberlieferung', in *La cultura antica nell'Occidente latino dal VII all'XI secolo*, Settimane 22 (Spoleto 1975) 79.

33 Karlsruhe, Aug CCXXVI, f. 1ᵛ and Milan, Ambros A. 220 inf.; cf. the letter about books in Escorial s.n. (reprod. in CLA XI 1628b).

34 R.A.B. Mynors (ed.), *Cassiodori Senatoris Institutiones* (Oxford 1937) xxxix ff.; W. Milde, *Der Bibliothekskatalog des Klosters Murbach aus dem IX. Jahrhundert*. Euphorion, Beih. 4 (Heidelberg 1968) 62 ff.; Bischoff, *Lorsch*, 64.

35 G. Glauche, *Schullektüre im Mittelalter*, Münchener Beiträge 5 (Munich 1970).

36 See above p. 117.   37 Above p. 59.   38 Above p. 77.

39 Bischoff, 'Die Hofbibliothek'.

such manuscripts (square proportions, two columns) was imitated in both these centres, occasionally even their linear decoration.[40] For several generations, at least in France, tironian notes were successfully revived as a useful instrument of school activity. From the ninth century on many liturgical books took on a new external aspect resulting from the invention of neumes.

The largest carolingian library catalogues, from Reichenau (822), Lorsch, St Gall, and Bobbio, indicate holdings of c. 400 to more than 600 volumes; Murbach achieved three hundred, St Riquier over two hundred. And these numbers can have been in no way unusual, especially since similar quantities of surviving items can still be demonstrated for several scriptoria. Book collections of individual magnates: Count Eberhard of Friaul and the west Frankish Count Heccard, are known from their wills; besides historical works, practical literature (on the art of warfare or agriculture) is also represented.[41]

The carolingian ideal blueprint for a monastery which is preserved in the monastic plan of St Gall envisaged a separate room for the 'sedes scribentium', and for two or three generations scriptoria were active in many places,[42] mostly copying for their own libraries and schools and their own liturgical requirements. Smaller churches were apparently provided for from episcopal sees,[43] in Charlemagne's time a number of nuns in the monastery of Chelles east of Paris, administered by Charlemagne's sister Gisela, took part in scribal activity; amongst other things they copied Augustine's commentary on the psalms for the cathedral church of arch-chancellor Hildebald of Cologne.[44] Behind the work of the scriptoria the initiative of well-known personalities can occasionally be recognised: the librarian Reginbert in Reichenau, the Salzburg archbishops Arn, Adalram, and Liuphram, the bishops Arbeo and Hitto in Freising, and Baturich at Regensburg.[45] The guiding hand in the great expansion of the

---

40 Cf. Cl. W. Barlow, 'Codex Vaticanus Latinus 4929', *Memoirs Amer. Acad. Rome* 15 (1938) esp. plates 14 and 17.

41 Eberhard: Schramm–Mütherich, *Denkmale*, 93 f.; Becker, *Catalogi*, Nr. 12; Heccard: E. Perard, *Recueil de plusieures pièces curieuses servant à l'histoire de Bourgogne* (Paris 1664) 25–7. Cf. P. Riché, 'Les bibliothèques de trois aristocrates carolingiens', *Le Moyen Age* 69 (1963) 87–104; repr. *Instruction et la vie religieuse dans le Haut Moyen Age* (London 1981) Nr. VIII.

42 On the 'oratio in scriptorio' cf. Battelli, *Lezioni³*, 116.

43 The large number of liturgical fragments copied at Freising and in a Mainz scriptorium support this conclusion. On the distribution of books on the Trinity (Alcuin) and on penance to priests at ninth–century regional synods cf. W. Hartmann, *Deutsches Archiv* 35 (1979) 375. Writing for profit is mentioned in a carolingian commentary on the Rule of St Benedict: W. Hafner, 'Der Basiliuskommentar zur Regula S. Benedicti', *Beitr. z. Gesch. d. alt Mönchtums u. d. Benediktinerordens* 23 (Münster/W. 1959), 139 f.

44 CLA VI, p. XXI f.; Bischoff, *Mittelalterliche Studien* I, 16–34. The production of the first copy of the Liber Glossarum in ab-script has been attributed to the nuns of a convent near the abbey of St Peter at Corbie; see T.A.M. Bishop, 'The prototype of Liber glossarum', in *Medieval scribes, Manuscripts & Libraries. Essays Presented to N.R. Ker* (London 1978) 69 ff. See also above p. 106 n. 93.

45 Above p. 118.

Corbie library in the third quarter of the ninth century was probably the librarian Hadoard.[46]

Thanks to the diversity in local styles of script among the c. seven thousand manuscripts and fragments from the late eighth and ninth century,[47] besides the roughly one hundred which can be localised, other still anonymous large, small, and very small groups can be distinguished but not identified. Some three hundred and fifty manuscripts still survive from Tours (i.e. basically from St Martin's), over three hundred from St Gall, roughly three hundred from Rheims (in which several scriptoria were involved), roughly two hundred from Corbie, over one hundred from Lorsch, Salzburg, Lyons, and Freising. Not only does Tours surpass the others in numbers but a full forty-five of the traceable codices are or were full in one volume bibles (pandects) of 420–450 leaves, with a format of c. 55 × 40 cm, written in two columns of fifty to fifty-two lines.[48] Between the last years of Alcuin (for whom Northumbrian bibles probably provided the model) and 850, St Martin's produced two such bibles every year for the Carolingians, for episcopal churches, and for monasteries.[49] These large-format bibles were imitated in other places, for example in Freising, and in two bibles dedicated to Charles the Bald, the Franco-Saxon Paris, BN, Lat. 2, and the Bible of San Paolo fuori le mura, in Rome.

The carolingian period is the first great epoch of book illumination on the continent since antiquity.[50] Its ornamental book art perpetuates types current in the Merovingian period and at the same time in many places reflects the influence of Insular decoration.[51] Furthermore, it harks back directly to motifs from antiquity (tendrils, palmettes, acanthus, meander) which then had the result that the repertoire of forms of the centuries immediately preceding were banished, or else mixed styles came about. In figural representation antique and early Christian models were followed closely and their study set free new and original facets of creativity.

A demonstration of what richness in initial forms and motifs a virtuoso and imaginatively inspired late-eighth-century miniaturist could employ is given by

---

46 Bischoff, *Mittelalterliche Studien* 1, 49–63.

47 For a survey up to the beginning of the ninth century see B. Bischoff in *Karl de Große, Lebenswerk und Nachleben* 2 (Düsseldorf 1965) 233–54, repr. *Mittelalterliche Studien* 3, 5–38.

48 In contrast the one-volume bibles from the circle of Theodulf, which document his critical work on the text, have a convenient format and are not bulky (c. 350 leaves of 34 × 24 cm, in two or three columns of normally 62 lines) because they use a disciplined, developed small and clear script.   49 B. Fischer in *Die Bibel von Moutier-Grandval* (Bern 1971) 64.

50 Florentine Mütherich, J. Porcher, K. Holter in *Karl der Große, Lebenswerk und Nachleben* 3 (Düsseldorf 1965) 9–114; J. Porcher in J. Hubert–J. Porcher–W. Fr. Volbach, *Die Kunst der Karolinger*, Universum der Kunst (Munich 1969), 69–208, 348–54; Fl. Mütherich–J.E. Gaehde, *Karolingische Buchmalerei* (Munich 1976); Fl. Mütherich, 'Malerei bis zum Ausgang des XI. Jahrhunderts', in *Propyläen-Kunstgeschichte*, Mittelalter 1 (Berlin 1969) 127–52 reprods 1–77; see also Porcher in *Frühzeit des Mittelalters*; Nordenfalk in *Das frühe Mittelalter*; in addition the literature cited in p. 87 n. 56.

51 Cf. G.L. Micheli, *L'Enluminure*.

the master craftsman who wrote the Gellone sacramentary.[52] The initial decoration in the great majority of manuscripts was, however, limited to a very narrow store of forms;[53] amongst them interlace[54] had become well-nigh indispensable. The older fish and bird motifs retreat and many manuscripts confine themselves to using enlarged capitalis letters. Important for the following period was a style of initials with broad and often intertwined foliate tendrils which makes its appearance in St Gall and Reichenau in the ninth century.[55] In Italy, the formation remains freer: for example, in the use of human heads. In the early carolingian period cruciform frontispieces are still frequent.[56]

The principal showcases of major book decoration are the gospel books with their canon tables and evangelists' portraits. In some illustrated manuscripts of the psalter and of the Apocalypse, and in the miniatures of three huge bibles, in part old cycles are renewed, in part individual pictorial innovation is at work.

The production of gospel books was the principal concern of the workshops that were established under Charlemagne at the court and which were still active in the time of Louis the Pious.[57] As to the style, two directions were followed: typical for the older 'palace school',[58] to which already the evangelistary of Godescalc belongs (781–3), is the extremely luxurious painting of the canon tables, portrait and initial pages, and the borders; early Christian pictorial sources from the Orient were reworked, and an Anglo-Saxon element too cannot be overlooked. In the gospel books of another, somewhat later, workshop tradition a classical simplicity was achieved both in the portraits and in the antique pedimental façades of the canon tables; the finest example is the Vienna coronation gospels on purple parchment.[59] Three illustrated classical manuscripts from Louis's time (Aratus, Terence) are indebted to the technical and artistic experience of these palace schools.[60]

52 CLA v 618; Bastard, *Peintures et ornements de manuscrits*, plates 49 to 61; smaller selections in Zimmermann, *Vorkarol. Min.*, plates 153–9, and E.A. Van Moë, *La lettre ornée dans les manuscrits du VIIIe au XIIe siècle* (Paris 1943). The lost manuscript made for Rachio, Bishop of Strasbourg, in 788 (CLA vi 835) should be compared; Bastard, *Peintures*, plates 46–8; cf. O. Homburger, 'Ein vernichtetes Denkmal merovingischer Buchkunst aus frühkarolingischer Zeit, der "Rachio-Codex" der Bongarsiana', in *Festschrift Hans R. Hahnloser* (Basel–Stuttgart 1961) 185–206.

53 Discussed in exemplary fashion by K. Holter in *Karl der Große* 3, 74–114 with 12 plates.

54 The construction of interlace using a network of dots can still be observed in some miniatures and initials where this has not been painted over. See E.J. Thiel, 'Studien und Thesen zur Initialornamentik des früheren Mittelalters', *Arch. f. Gesch. d. Buchwesens* 5 (1964) 1249–1330 with reprod.; idem, 'Neue Studien zur ornamentalen Buchmalerei des frühen Mittelalters', ibid. 11 (1970) 1057–1126 with reprod.

55 Cf. A. Merton, *Die Buchmalerei in St. Gallen vom neunten bis zum elften Jahrhundert*[2] (Leipzig 1923).   56 Bischoff, *Mittelalterliche Studien* 2, 289 ff.

57 Florentine Mütherich in *Karl der Große* 3, 9–59 with plate; on the dating of the latest MSS cf. Bischoff, 'Die Hofbibliothek', 12 ff.

58 Koehler, *Karol. Min.*2 (Berlin 1958), text and plates.

59 Koehler, *Karol. Min.*3 (Berlin 1960), text, 9–93, and plates 1–48.

60 Koehler–Mütherich, ibid. 4 (Berlin 1971) text, 73–115, and plates 28–95.

The artistic heritage of the later court school, whose quavering, excited style is masterfully expressed in the pen and ink drawings of the Utrecht Psalter and the evangelists' portraits of the Ebbo codex in Épernay, passed to the schools of Rheims and Hautvillers under Ebbo and Hincmar. At St Martin's at Tours[61] in Alcuin's time (†804) a local, initially monochrome style was still practised with canon arches and initials under Anglo-Saxon influence. However, here too the formation of a classical figure style and the adoption of antique motifs in the multicoloured or gold or silver initials soon followed. An intimate art that gives the direction to later development is shown in the boughs and leaf initials of the sacramentary written and painted for the Metz archbishop Drogo, in which the initials enclose pictures with tiny figures appropriate to each feastday.[62] A style from the second half of the century which is almost entirely devoid of figures and whose principal centres were St Amand and St Bertin at St Omer, is dependent on English decorative art, especially that of Northumbria. This style is distinguished by strongly geometrical frameworks and heavy initial forms which are filled out with narrow interlace patterns of the greatest precision. This 'Franco-Saxon' style is continued and developed in the tenth century not only in the neighbourhood of the old centres but also in Lower Germany and in England. Two bibles, one from St Martin's (the illustrated Vivian Bible, with a presentation portrait) and one from the Franco-Saxon workshop of St Amand were presented to Charles the Bald, who loved ostentation. When, in the sixties and seventies, he had ostentatious manuscripts made in one of his residences (probably Soissons), achievements made in the Rheims and Tours schools were also absorbed into the new court style. The Bible of San Paulo fuori le Mura written for Charles – which he probably bestowed on the church of Rome on the occasion of his coronation in 875 – is close to this eclectic, courtly style.[63] Of the works of German schools Hrabanus's *De laudibus s. crucis*, in which the pictures are integrated into fields of letters, became a much-admired and oft-copied artistic piece.[64]

Although Brittany had come under the supremacy of caroline script, a native tradition survived in book decoration until the beginning of the tenth century. In several gospels that are grouped around the centre of Landévennec the evangelists' symbols are represented by crudely drawn anthropomorphic figures to which the heads of the animal symbols are attached (horse-like in the case of Mark).[65]

61 Koehler, ibid. 1 (Berlin 1930–3) text 1/2 and plates.
62 Koehler, ibid. 3, text, 143–62 and plates 76–91.
63 The MSS of Charles the Bald in Schramm–Mütherich, *Denkmale*, Nr. (41) 42 ff., 51 f., 54 ff.
64 Hrabanus Maurus, *De laudibus sanctae crucis. Vollst. Faks.-Ausg. . . . des Codex Vindobonensis 652*; commentary K. Holter (Graz 1973). There is a collection of the manuscripts (roughly sixty) in H.-G. Müller, *De laudibus sancta* (!) *crucis*. Beih. z. Mittellat. Jahrb. 11 (Ratingen, etc. 1973) 36–9, and R. Kottje in *Rheinische Vierteljahrsblätter* 40 (1976) 279.
65 Reprod.: Micheli, *L'Enluminure*, fig. 145 f.; Porcher in *Die Kunst der Karolinger*, 203 ff.

3 The Carolingian period

Of the territories outside the carolingian empire England, which was raided by Vikings,[66] went through a period of profound stagnation; Lindisfarne was plundered in 793. The once flourishing monasteries of Ireland were the targets of annual Viking attacks from 795. All the more important, therefore, is the contribution to carolingian intellectual life of Irish scholars; of these Dungal, Sedulius Scottus, Iohannes Scottus, and Martin of Laon have left autograph specimens of their handwriting.[67] It is with them in particular and their Greek studies that bilingual manuscripts of the psalter, the gospels, and the Pauline epistles are associated. The considerable number of palimpsests in the Irish manuscripts of the ninth century suggests that Irishmen, when leaving home, brought with them older books that had belonged to their native libraries. Irishmen who had gone to the continent, and who there observed the difference between the old and the new kinds of writing current, are probably to be identified as the authors of the short catalogues of script-names from the late eighth and ninth century that contain partly confused but also partly authentic and important information.[68]

Much the greatest part of Spain lay under Arab rule, yet Christianity was in general not suppressed; bibles and large manuscripts of collected texts were produced by Mozarabs. A northern strip of territory which had maintained its independence became the heartland of the kingdom of Asturia, whence the Reconquista was to originate. Here, c. 780, the monk Beatus of Liébana composed his Apocalypse commentary with a cycle of illustrations derived from early Christian exemplars; this was for several centuries the most representative work of Spanish book illumination.[69] At the latest from the beginning of the tenth century, many manuscripts were adorned with the 'Cross of Oviedo' (with inscriptions such as 'PAX LVX REX LEX'), standing under an arch as a frontispiece, which was inspired by the golden standards of the Asturian kings in their wars against the Arabs.[70]

66 The Codex Aureus, now in Stockholm (CLA XI 1642), was bought back from Vikings. Another instance mentioned by Wattenbach, *Schriftwesen*, p. 545, results from an incorrect interpretation.

67 B. Bischoff, 'Irische Schreiber im Karolingerreich', in *Jean Scot Erigène et l'histoire de la philosophie*. Colloques Internationaux du CNRS, Nr. 561 (Paris 1977) 47–58; *Mittelalterliche Studien* 3, 39–54.

68 The older version in Sammelhandschrift Diez B Sant 66 (introduction B. Bischoff, Graz 1973) commentary, p. 32 f. The later catalogue (? by Sedulius Scottus) glossing 'Litterae unciales' (see above p. 184) mentions 'Virgilianae', 'Affricanae quae tunsae appellantur, quas in usu frequenti habemus' and 'longariae', Remigius replaces with 'quas . . . Scotti . . . habent'. Bischoff, *Mittelalterliche Studien* 1, 2.

69 W. Neuss, *Die Apokalypse des hl. Johannes in der altspanischen und altchristlichen Bibelillustration* 1, 2 (Münster/W. 1931); idem in J. Marqués Casanova–C.E. Dubler–W. Neuss, *Sancti Beati a Liebana in Apocalypsin codex Gerundensis* (Olten–Lausanne 1962) 44 ff.; A.M. Mundó–M.S. Mariana, *El commentário de Beato al Apocalipsis, Catálogo de los códices* (Madrid 1976).

70 Bischoff, *Mittelalterliche Studien* 2, 297 ff.; M.C. Díaz y Díaz, 'La circulation des manuscrits dans la Péninsule Ibérique du VIIIe au XIe siècle', *Cahiers de civilisation médiévale* 12 (1969) 385 f.

From the tenth to the twelfth century

In three generations the cultural renewal radiating from the court under Charlemagne had brought its fruits in the entire area of Carolingian rule. In the episcopal cities and in the monasteries libraries were created, many of them with hundreds of volumes. All important churches possessed splendid liturgical manuscripts in precious bindings which had been painted in carolingian workshops. But already, from the mid ninth century onwards, the security of the empire was under threat from Vikings and Saracens, and shortly after the turn of the century almost annually repeated attacks by the Hungarians began. Even cities like Trier (882) were set ablaze and many monasteries were destroyed; the monks in their flight were able to save the libraries of some of them, together with the relics of the monastic patron. In large parts of Germany, as a result of the Hungarian threat, cultural life could be eked out only with difficulty, or else it ceased entirely. Only after the victory against the Hungarians in 955 could a new resurgence get slowly under way, which was aided by the Gorze monastic reform. In Bavaria, which had been devastated, the reconstruction was undertaken by bishop Wolfgang of Regensburg with the help of monks trained at Trier. Among the centres that had remained untouched was St Gall, and because its monastic school was much visited and was also able to send teachers to various places such as Mainz, Speyer, and Salzburg, there was disseminated a minuscule with ligatures of an Irish kind, as well as the St Gall initial style and St Gall neumes. This wave also touched Freising, where Italian and Lotharingian influences came together.[1]

The library of Tegernsee, newly-founded by Hartwig of Trier, is an example of how losses of books could be made good.[2] Several generations of monks built up a substantial collection by the common labour of teachers (like Froumund) and pupils, and by obtaining exemplars from Freising, Regensburg, and per-

---

1 Natalia Daniel, *Handschriften des zehnten Jahrhunderts aus der Freisinger Dombibliothek.* Münchener Beiträge 11 (1973).
2 Christine Elisabeth Eder, *Die Schule des Klosters Tegernsee im frühen Mittelalter*, in *Stud. Mitteil. OSB* 83 (1972) = Beiheft der Münchener Beiträge; Chroust, *Monumenta* 2/1, plate 6 ff.

haps Augsburg, with a combined aim of providing for monastic study and for the school. When Benedictbeuern was reactivated as a monastery, Tegernsee manuscripts were copied there.[3] From the school of Tegernsee came the calligrapher Otloh, who later entered St Emmeram at Regensburg and whose manuscripts were much in demand beyond Bavaria.[4] His script, which he wrote in three levels of style, is a classic example of the slanted oval (Schrägoval) minuscule.

The cultural caesura in the Rhineland and in Lower Germany was less deep than in Bavaria; the Munich Hrotsvita manuscript is a witness to the fact that in a female foundation like Gandersheim the nuns too were capable of writing. Through the Ottonian colonisation and through the missionary work in Poland, Hungary, and the northern lands, in which the church organisation was reinforced by the erection of new bishoprics and the establishment of new monasteries, in the tenth and eleventh centuries the area of Latin script won extensive territories.

In France, which had also suffered heavily – Brittany in the early tenth century was for a generation almost depopulated – Cluny[5] (founded in 910), by virtue of the reform emanating from there, was a driving force behind a powerful regeneration of monasticism. Already in Odo's time a similarly organised centre of reform arose at Fleury, whence in the tenth century it could take root in England. The influence of Cluny itself extended over numerous monasteries of the Po valley, towards Rome and its environs, and to Monte Cassino and Catalonia. In Germany Hirsau attached itself to the Cluniac movement. In Belgium and Lotharingia Irish monks brought new impulses into the reform movement; their traces are found also in the script.[6]

The broad swell of monastic reform in the eleventh century gave new impetus to the provision of libraries.[7] The report of prior Burchard of Michelsberg near Bamberg for the years 1112–47,[8] in which the books written by the individual monks are listed name by name, gives an idea of how the leadership of an enthusiastic reforming abbot could be effective.

3 Christ–Kern in Milkau-Leyh, *Handbuch* 3/1², 408.   4 See above p. 120 n. 73.

5 The library which was created during the tenth century is characteristically carolingian. In the reforming centres of Cluny and Fleury, which were in lively contact with neighbouring and distant centres, various styles of writing came together. For Cluny, Monique-Cecile Garand, 'Le scriptorium', *J. des Savants* (1977) 257–83. For Fleury, J. Vezin, 'Leofnoth. Un scribe anglais à Saint-Bénoît-sur-Loire', *Codices Manuscripti* 3 (1977) 109–20 with plate; on a beneventan-trained scribe see above p. 111 n. 124.

6 See above p. 89. The 'Schottenmönche', who set up their first humble settlement in Germany in Regensburg in 1079, developed an Irish influenced minuscule, see Bischoff, *Mittelalterliche Studien* 1, 39.

7 Cf. R. Kottje, 'Klosterbibliotheken und monastische Kultur in der zweiten Hälfte des XI. Jahrhunderts', *Z. f. Kirchengesch.* 2 (1969) 145–62.

8 *Mittelalt. Bibliothekskat. Deutschl.* 3/3 (1939) 357–65. Karin Dengler-Schreiber, *Scriptorium und Bibliothek des Klosters Michelsberg in Bamberg von den Anfängen bis 1150*, Studien zur Bibliotheksgeschichte 2 (Graz 1978).

c. The manuscript in cultural history

In England the renewed care and expansion of libraries began under Alfred the Great (871–901). One of his achievements was the promotion of Anglo-Saxon literature through the translations and adaptations that he commissioned, and of which copies were made at his behest. His grandson Æthelstan (†941), a list of whose books survives, is well known as a donor of books to various churches.[9] As a result of the Benedictine reform which established itself in England in the mid tenth century the national script was largely superseded by caroline minuscule in the following generations for use in Latin texts; however, Anglo-Saxon retained a major place in English literary activity and through manuscripts of the tenth and eleventh centuries earlier poetry, including *Beowulf*, was saved.[10]

The Norman conquest also had decisive consequences for England's libraries. In all important places, in the cathedrals and in the large monasteries, they were modernised according to Norman standards.[11] The nucleus of the holdings was provided, with the aid of professional scribes,[12] by bibles in the largest format, together with works of the four great church Fathers, and those of Josephus and others, in large size. The example of Augustine's writings allows us to trace the penetration of texts transmitted on the continent, and the further passage of these texts thanks to the intercommunications of English centres.[13]

As was the case in Germany and France, under the pressure of external enemies, Hungarians and Saracens, in the late ninth and in the tenth century there came about a standstill, partly even a reverse in cultural matters in Italy too. In 949 the monks re-entered Monte Cassino and in the following centuries the monastery reached its apogee under abbot Desiderius (1058–87). One of his predecessors was the German Richer (1038–55), who came from Niederaltaich, one of the monasteries that had been ruled by Godehard of Hildesheim.[14] Through these monastic connections it is possible to explain the presence at Monte Cassino of a manuscript of Widukind of Corvey, the double preservation of Frontinus here and in Hersfeld (or Fulda), and the familiarity of the Monte Cassino historian Peter the Deacon with Tacitus's *Agricola*.[15] In Desiderius's time the beneventan script attained its most harmonised formation.[16] The

---

9 Th. Gottlieb, *Über mittelalterliche Bibliotheken* (Leipzig 1890) 278–80; J.A. Robinson, *The times of St. Dunstan* (Oxford 1923) 51 ff. The Heliand may have reached England because of links with the Saxon royal family; R. Priebsch, *The Heliand Ms. Cotton Caligula A.VII in the British Museum* (Oxford 1925).   10 Ker, *Catal. of MSS.*   11 Ker, *English MSS*, 10.
12 Ker, ibid., 4, 40.   13 Ker, ibid., 12 ff., 54–7.
14 K. Hallinger, *Gorze-Kluny* 1, Studia Anselmiana 22/23 (Rome 1950) 174 f.
15 Cf. L. Pralle, *Die Wiederentdeckung des Tacitus* (Fulda 1952) 57 n. 53.
16 Cf. above p. 110. A miniature shows Desiderius offering 'many wonderful books' to St Benedict, together with his buildings ('Cum domibus miros plures, pater, accipe libros'); M. Inguanez–Myrtilla Avery, *Miniature Casinesi del secolo XI illustranti la vita di S. Benedetto* (Monte Cassino 1934) plate 1; A. Pantoni, *Le vicende della basilica di Montecassino attraverso la documentazione archeologica*, Miscellanea Cassinese 36 (1973) frontisp. A.M. Stickler and others, *Codex Benedictus. Vat. Lat. 1202*, Codd e Vaticanis selecti quam simillime expressi

library that was compiled here possessed very rare works of classical literature: Varro, Seneca's Dialogues, Tacitus's Annals and Histories, as well as Apuleius.[17]

In Italy already in the early middle ages large format corpora are to be found: Florence, Bibl. Laur., Amiat. III (Hrabanus *In Genesim*, etc. 43 × 30 cm, saec. XI, with the monogram 'Benzo'); ibid., Conv. Soppr., MS 364 (49 × 32.5 cm) + Pl. 65.35 (c. 47.5 × 32 cm), a collection of secular and ecclesiastical learning. In the late-eleventh century a new type of large one-volume 'giant bible' appears, whose somewhat longish rectangular format was also applied to other large works (Augustine's psalm commentary, Gregory's *Moralia*) and collections (homiliaries, passionals). The bibles were illustrated, and in the initials the influence of Tours betrays itself.[18] These manuscripts were produced in an area stretching from northern Italy to Rome. In Rome the old Lateran library of the popes still existed; Deusdedit found there c. 1087 many sources for his canon collection; in the thirteenth century, however, it disappeared.

In southern Italy and Sicily the Normans had conquered Greek and Arab territories. When the king's rule was strengthened by Roger II a kind of aristocracy emerged which included Latins and members of the other two nations; we have in a Greek–Latin–Arabic three-column psalter (of 1153?)[19] a tangible documentary witness to this ethnic and linguistic community. In Sicilian manuscripts with miniatures a Byzantinising style predominated.[20]

Book practice in the Christian areas of Spain changed only slowly before the late eleventh century, when Roman and Cluniac influence began to penetrate and contribute to the decline of the Visigothic script.[21] To judge by the surviving manuscripts, the selection of works copied was rather narrowly delimited. However, they contain extensive subscriptions in which those concerned (scribes, painters, patrons) and the time of production are given in a detail unmatched anywhere else. The two particularly impressive groups that emerge from the transmission of the tenth and eleventh centuries are the full bibles

iussu Iohannis Pauli, pp. II, 1 (Stuttgart–Zürich 1981) f. 2ʳ. Cf. also F. Newton, 'The Desiderian scriptorium at Monte Cassino', *Dumbarton Oaks Papers* 30 (1976) 37–54 with plate.

17 F. Brunhölzl, 'Zum Problem der Casinenser Klassiküberlieferung', *Abh. Marburger Gelehrten Gesell.* (Jhg. 1971) 3, 111 f., suggests that the textual transmission of Varro, which depends on a Monte Cassino MS, and of other rare texts, took place in that region. Varro owned a villa near Casinum.

18 Cf. E.B. Garrison, *Studies in the History of Medieval Italian Painting* 1–4 (Florence 1953–62). An example from 1193 (?): *Catal. manoscr. datati* 1, plate 27/28.

19 London, BL, Harley MS 5786 (reprod.: *Pal. Soc.*, plate 132); *Catal. Dated and Datable MSS* 1, illustr. 84.

20 H. Buchthal, 'A school of miniature painting in Norman Sicily', in *Late Classical and Mediaeval Studies in Honor of Albert Mathias Friend Jr.* (Princeton 1955) 312–39 with 10 reproductions.   21 See above p. 99 ff.

written in two or three columns, and the illustrated Apocalypse commentaries of Beatus, with their extremely unnaturalistic, oriental-looking pictures.[22]

With the crusades Latin script was brought for a century and a half to Palestine and Syria.[23] A workshop of scribes and painters existed in the neighbourhood of the Church of the Holy Sepulchre; after 1187 this activity was transferred to St John of Acre. The scribes were predominantly in the French tradition. It is, however, the miniatures, initials, and scripts of titles in the books written here: 'anciennes estoires', and in the French translation of William of Tyre, that present the most noteworthy mixtures of western, Byzantine, and Armenian tastes.[24]

With the rise of the monastic orders of Cistercians, Premonstratensians, and Carthusians, a new upsurge of monastic scribal activity began. Because the first two founded an extremely large number of monasteries in the twelfth century in Germany, England, and Spain – and the Cistercians besides that in Italy – the penetration of the countries with written cultures, for example in Lower Saxony, Austria, and Bohemia, was fundamentally strengthened, while other territories acquired the first staging posts of such culture. The expansion of the Carthusian order followed more slowly before the end of the twelfth century, but this order, as no previous, envisaged writing as the duty of monks. In the *Consuetudines* redacted by Guigo, the fifth Carthusian prior, the writing equipment of the scribe is minutely detailed in the furnishing of the cell,[25] and the duty assigned to him is formulated thus: 'Quot enim libros scribimus, tot nobis veritatis precones facere videmur'.[26]

In the centralised orders the transmission and copying of texts took place in many ways within the orders. An example of the regional exchange of exemplars beyond such boundaries in the twelfth and early thirteenth centuries is provided by Bavarian and Austrian monasteries of the Regensburg and Passau dioceses that belonged to the Benedictine, Cistercian, and Premonstratensian orders. Here the giant codices of the *Glossarium Salomonis* with Greek–Latin colloquies originated,[27] and here the largest hagiographical compilation of the middle ages, the *Legendarium magnum Austriacum*, which filled six folio volumes, was collected and reproduced.[28] It is a keystone of a collecting and arranging activity in

---

22 See p. 211 n. 69.   23 See also below p. 227.

24 H. Buchthal, *Miniature Painting in the Latin Kingdom of Jerusalem* (Oxford 1957); J. Folda, *Crusader Manuscript Illumination at Saint-Jean d'Acre 1275–1291* (Princeton 1976).

25 See above p. 18 f.

26 Lehmann, *Erforschung* 3, 121 ff.; Gumbert, *Utrechter Kartäuser*, 308 ff.; reprod. of the Carthusian cell in Stiennon, *Paléographie*, 142.

27 G. Goetz, *Corpus glossariorum Latinorum* 1 (Leipzig 1923) 168.

28 A. Kern, 'Magnum Legendarium', in *Die Österreichische Nationalbibliothek, Festschrift Josef Bick* (Vienna 1948) 429–34. The relationship between the exemplars is outlined by W. Levison, MGH SRM 7 (1920) 534. The lending lists of Otto von Lonsdorf, Bishop of Passau c. 1260, reveal a vigorous exchange of books in his diocese; *Mittelalt. Bibliothekskat. Deutschl.* 4/1 (1977) 32 f.

this important field, which had begun in the eighth and ninth centuries, that saints' lives contained in booklets, often deriving from the cult centre itself, were brought together in great collections in the order of the calendar in accordance with local requirements, so as to serve for the office and for refectory reading.[29]

In the second half of the tenth century a change in education began to emerge. Gerbert of Aurillac, of southern French origin, who became familiar with Arabic mathematical science in Catalonia, was the first seriously to undertake the teaching programme of trivium and quadrivium. As his pupil Richer relates, he worked with demonstrations and models.[30] Knowledge of the nine Arabic number signs in the West begins with Gerbert's introduction of them into his lectures on the use of the abacus. The lessons of Gerbert, Fulbert of Chartres, and later famous scholastic scholars up to the brothers Anselm and Radulf of Laon, drew pupils from afar to Rheims, Chartres, Liège, Laon and other school centres long before Paris concentrated on higher study; from there they, in their turn, brought books back home, as did, for example, the monk Hartwic of St Emmeram, a pupil of Fulbert's at Chartres.[31] The school libraries had now to be supplemented with new aids.[32] Collections of textbooks of several *artes* were made,[33] and Thierry of Chartres finally combined in the 'Heptateuchos' the fundamental texts of all the seven liberal arts.

After Gerbert a shift in emphasis in the reading canon took place in the schools: the Christian poets no longer dominate so markedly as before; classical authors, amongst them the satirists, push to the fore.[34] In the area of theology the *Glossa ordinaria*, a work of commentary, came into existence from roughly 1100 and won an almost authoritative reputation. It was and remained written partly alongside the text, partly between the lines,[35] whence there resulted technical difficulties in the layout of the text when a better utilisation of the written space was sought.

29 On these booklets see Bischoff, *Mittelalterliche Studien* 1, 93–100; the St Gall listing of saints' lives according to the calendar, dating from the ninth to tenth century (*Mittelalt. Bibliothekskat. Deutschl.* 1, 91 ff.) refers to both kinds.

30 The tree-like or branch-like schemata in the margins of dialectical and rhetorical textbooks from this period probably reproduce the important distinctions which played so significant a role in the classroom (e.g. Clm 14,272, f. 153ʳ 'loci argumentorum') at the period of this revival of the *artes*. Gorze owned a 'Pagina (= Tabula) quomodo ex philosophia diversae diffinitiones quasi quidam fontes emanent' (*Rev. Bénéd.* 22 (1905) 10, lines 192 f.).

31 Bischoff, *Mittelalterliche Studien* 2, 80 ff.

32 In the last quarter of the tenth century Freising procured fundamental works of dialectic and rhetoric, in part from Metz; Daniel, *Handschriften der Freisinger Dombibliothek*, 84 ff., 140 ff. Cf. A. Van de Vyver, 'Les étapes du développement philosophique du haut moyen-âge', *Rev. Belge de philol. et d'histoire* 28 (1950) 425–52).

33 Cf. Bischoff, *Mittelalterliche Studien* 2, 80 f. A further example: London, BL, Burney 275, s. XIV (from the library of Charles V of France).

34 G. Glauche, *Schullektüre im Mittelalter*, Münchener Beiträge 5 (1970) 62 ff.

35 Cf. Beryl Smalley, *The Study of the Bible in the Middle Ages* (Oxford 1952) 46 ff. and plate 1. A connection is made between the later glossing of Peter the Lombard and the origins of the scholarly book-trade in Paris by C. de Hamel, *Glossed Books of the Bible and the Origin of the Paris Book-Trade* (Cambridge 1984).

c. The manuscript in cultural history

In the external appearance of the manuscript in post–carolingian centuries an increasing gradation of the script levels in relation to size, aesthetic appearance, and amount of abbreviation was recognised according to the purpose, which again was dependent on the contents. In library books and school books the space between the lines is frequently distinctly smaller than before. The forementioned innovations in teaching practice had their impact on writing practice: tiny commentary hands were used[36] and the tendency to abbreviate technical terms increased.[37] Neumes are now general in the appearance of liturgical manuscripts, and in the eleventh century the use of staves begins.

The twelfth century, which has been called a renaissance, marks a second highpoint after the carolingian era for the transmission of many classical authors and patristic literature, before the rise of scholasticism decisively changed the relationship to literature. That is due not only to the fact that in this century very many new monasteries were founded, and thereby new libraries. Rather, one can generalise and say that the educated men of the time had come to a consciousness of their own capacity with which they could face the entire transmission positively and openly, but also critically. Christian teaching based itself on the solid foundation of the Fathers of the church. But besides these the auctores, because of their formal qualities, were recognised as being indispensable for teaching and as examples for literature, and their sententious content was admired. The ethics of the moralists and philosophers were valued in humanistic openness. The classical authors were essential to education. So the increase in the transmission is an expression of this attitude, for which the great collection of Cicero's works which Wilbald of Stablo, abbot and statesman (†1158) compiled,[38] as well as the collection of Augustine's minor works in seven volumes, which was carried out in Clairvaux,[39] are impressive witnesses.

In the field of illumination[40] the carolingian experiences were not lost. The technical tradition became more secure and the iconographic continuity too was strengthened. The ancient recipes for making colour were newly edited in the eleventh century in the handbooks of 'Heraclius' and of Theophilus-Rugerus.[41]

---

36 A Liège commentary on Persius in St Gall 868 (s. XI ex.) is copied in a format of 12 × 12 cms with as many as 111 lines per page (p. 198B).   37 See above p. 154 f.

38 Lehmann, *Erforschung* 5 (1962) 131.

39 J. De Ghellinck, 'Une édition ou une collection médiévale des *Opera omnia* de Saint Augustin', in *Liber Floridus, Mittellateinische Studien Paul Lehmann . . . gewidmet* (St Ottilien 1950) 63–82.

40 Florentine Mütherich in L. Grodecki and others, *Die Zeit der Ottonen und Salier*, Universum der Kunst (Munich 1973) 86–255, 416–21 with plates; eadem, 'Malerei bis zum Ausgang des XI. Jahrhunderts', and 'Malerei des XII. Jahrhunderts', in *Propyläen-Kunstgeschichte, Mittelalter* 1/11 (Berlin 1969/72); Nordenfalk, *Das frühe Mittelalter*; idem, *Die romanische Malerei*; cf. also the literature cited in p. 187 n. 56.

41 H. Roosen-Runge studied the techniques of early medieval painters on the basis of his own experiments with these recipes. Cf. his *Farbgebung und Technik frühmittelalterlicher Buchmalerei* 1/2 (Berlin 1967).

218

Motifs, picture elements and compositions were diffused through model books of examples,[42] and Byzantine influence too was transmitted in this way, and probably also through the medium of illustrated manuscripts.[43] From southern France genuine or imitation friezes of Kufic script made their entry into western applied art;[44] in that way the miniaturists acquired a much-used filling element for borders. Already in the eleventh century there were laymen who practised the profession of miniaturists.[45]

The most widely-disseminated initial type in Germany, Switzerland, the Netherlands, and parts of France and northern Italy in post-carolingian times was the tendrilled initial,[46] which can be connected with the technique of interlace. The bodies of the letters, apparently cleft, constituted a strong narrow border and were frequently held together by realistic drawings of metal clasps which, in the case of gold initials, were offset with silver. In other areas thin interlace tendrils and stems with palmettes were preferred.[47] Towards the twelfth century coloured pen and ink initials, or initials in opaque colours with romanesque palmette motifs, become more frequent. Amongst the zoomorphic motifs dragons and lions become popular and from the eleventh century on the human figure is once more introduced as an ornament; fighting dragons and climbers among tendrils are quite typical. A precursor of the fleuronné style can be recognised towards the end of the twelfth century in the very expressive swinging contours that extend into the margin.[48] However, manuscripts in which the historiated initials fulfil an illustrative function also increase in number, as already in the carolingian period with the Gellone and Drogo sacramentaries and in the Corbie psalter. Thus the stories of biblical books or saints' lives[49] are made visible; in the bibles of large format these condensed pictures prepare the way towards the revival of independent illustration.

Many threads connect book illumination of the tenth and eleventh centuries –

---

42 R.W. Scheller, *A Survey of Medieval Model Books* (Haarlem 1963).

43 O. Demus, *Byzantine Art and the West* (New York 1970).

44 K. Erdmann, 'Arabische Schriftzeichen als Ornamente in der abendländischen Kunst des Mittelalters', *Akad. Wiss. u. Lit. Abh.*, geistes- und sozialwiss. Kl. (1953) 9. Kufic characters are already present in the model collection of Ademar of Chabannes (†c. 1030): Leiden, Voss Lat. 8° 15, f. 210ᵛ.

45 F. Masai, 'De la condition des enlumineurs et de l'enluminure a l'époque romane', *Bull. dell' Arch. Pal. Ital.* n.s. 2/3 (1956/7) 2, 135–44. Cf. also the picture of the Echternach scriptorium with a monk and a layman in C. Nordenfalk, *Codex Caesareus Upsaliensis* (Stockholm 1971) 114, and F. Mütherich in *Die Zeit der Ottonen und Salier*, 94. See in addition J.J.G. Alexander, 'Scribes as artists: the arabesque initial in twelfth-century English manuscripts', in *Medieval Scribes, Manuscripts & Libraries. Essays Presented to N.R. Ker* (London 1978) 87 ff. with reprod.

46 K. Löffler, *Romanische Zierbuchstaben und ihre Vorläufer* (Stuttgart 1927). For a carolingian precursor see above p. 210.

47 Examples in A.-E. Van Moë, *La lettre ornée dans les manuscrits du VIIIe au XIIe siècle* (Paris 1943).   48 Bruckner, *Scriptoria* 8, plate 31.

49 Cf., e.g. A. Boeckler, *Das Stuttgarter Passionale* (Augsburg 1923).

to carolingian art. Illuminated manuscripts from the palace schools of Charlemagne and Charles the Bald were studied in Fulda, in the upper Rhine region, and in Regensburg, while individual compositions were copied or modified. The Franco-Saxon style set the standard for the beginnings of painting in Lower-Saxony. To this Franco-Saxon style, and to that of other north-French schools, the art of England after 900 owes its new impulse.

In these two centuries German schools, among whose patrons were Ottonian and Salian rulers and the highest bishops of the empire, occupied leading positions. Otto III was a special friend of books;[50] through his teacher Gerbert of Rheims he had acquired manuscripts from France, and others he himself brought from Italy. A part of his book collection passed to Henry II, who donated them to his foundation, the cathedral church at Bamberg.[51]

The Reichenau school reached its apogee in the last third of the tenth century and was productive into the first half of the eleventh. Without being strongly rooted there, the 'Master of the Registrum Gregorii', one of the most important Ottonian book illuminators, whose activity had been in the upper Rhine region and in Trier, stood connected with it.[52] Reichenau manuscripts were in such demand that pope Gregory V 'pensionis nomine' requested that the abbot of the monastery should deliver a sacramentary, an epistolary, and a gospel book to Rome for the confirmation of his installation.[53] Otto III, Henry II, and archbishop Egbert of Trier were the highest ranked of those who commissioned books from the workshop. Three times there appears in the royal books the procession of the personified provinces paying homage, in which a motif from the late-antique Notitia dignitatum is transposed for contemporary use.[54] Egbert of Trier, by prefixing to his psalter the portrait sequence of the Trier bishops, strengthened the claims to the apostolic foundation of his see.[55] The Reichenau style spread into Switzerland and to northern Italy. The production of the Cologne school equalled it in breadth and attained the highest level with the sacramentary of St Gereon and the Hitda Codex.[56]

The school of St Emmeram at Regensburg, in which Henry II had a sacramentary made, began its activity at the end of the tenth century with restoration work on the Codex Aureus of Charles the Bald, and motifs from that manuscript reappear in the principal work of the school, the evangelistary of the abbess Uta of Niedermünster. Under Henry III, Echternach played the rôle of a

---

50 Schramm–Mütherich, *Denkmale*, Nr. 80 ff. (to 109).   51 Ibid., Nr. 110 ff. (to 141).

52 C. Nordenfalk, 'The chronology of the Registrum Master', in *Kunsthistorische Forschungen, Otto Pächt zu seinem 70. Geburtstag* (Salzburg 1972) 62–76 with reprod.

53 I.B. De Rossi in H. Stevenson, *Codices Palatini* I (1886) lxxxvii; Th. Klauser in *Jb. f. Liturgiewiss.* 11 (1931) 329.

54 See Schramm–Mütherich, *Denkmale*, Nr. 82 and 108.

55 H.V. Sauerland–A. Haseloff, *Der Psalter Erzbischof Egberts von Trier* (Trier 1901).

56 P. Bloch–H. Schnitzler, *Die ottonische Kölner Malerschule* 1/2 (Düsseldorf 1967/70); see esp. Nr. IV and V.

palace workshop that prepared gospels for Speyer and Goslar for the emperor.[57] The style of the painting school at Vyšehrad in Prague was dependent on Bavarian illumination of the eleventh century.[58] In the late eleventh century Salzburg entered the front rank and it remained the most prominent school of the German south-east until 1200; here Byzantine influence was especially marked.[59]

In the twelfth century, illustration with pen-and-ink drawings was very widespread; in Bavaria and Austria, Swabia and Alsace. Here the monumental work of the *Hortus deliciarum*, with 344 religious and didactic pictures, was illustrated by the nun Herrad of Landsberg in the monastery of Odilienberg.[60] In the Rhineland originated the now lost Wiesbaden codex of the *Scivias* of Hildegard of Bingen, with boldly coloured pictures of the visions seen by her, the miniatures of the Speyer evangelistary[61] executed in lighter colours, and those of the *Speculum virginum*.[62] Amongst the schools of Lower Saxony, Helmarshausen is distinguished by its connection with Henry the Lion who had, amongst other things, a precious gospel book written and painted there.[62a]

In France[63] there are no centres in the tenth and eleventh centuries that were comparable to Reichenau or Cologne; however, miniaturists were active in many places and important works are not lacking. In an impressive stylistic modification of the Beatus Apocalypse the Apocalypse of St Sever (saec. XI) was painted in bright colours, a work of the greatest expressiveness. Noteworthy workshops could be found in Limoges,[64] Angers, in the Paris abbey, and in north-east France, the old home of the Franco-Saxon style whose severe, complicated interlace decor was still practised into the eleventh century. Here in the late tenth and eleventh centuries, in St Amand, Marchiennes, Arras, and St Bertin at St Omer (where the abbot Odbert, 986–1008, was himself active as a miniaturist) many manuscripts were illustrated in which a strong impulse from English style is obvious. Around 1100 (to 1120) canon Lambert of St Omer collected and illustrated his encyclopaedia, *Liber floridus*.[65] The production of this region

57 Schramm–Mütherich, *Denkmale*, Nr. 154 and 155; C. Nordenfalk, *Codex Caesareus Upsaliensis*, commentary.   58 See above p. 61.

59 G. Swarzenski, *Die Salzburger Malerei von den ersten Anfängen bis zur Blütezeit des romanischen Stils* (Leipzig 1913).

60 A. Straub–G. Keller, *Herrade de Landsberg, Hortus deliciarum* 1/2 (Strasbourg 1901); J. Walter, *Herrade de Landsberg, Hortus deliciarum* (Strasbourg–Paris 1953); Rosalie Green and others, *Herrad of Hohenburg, Hortus Deliciarum* 1, 2 (London–Leiden 1979).

61 K. Preisendanz–O. Homburger, *Das Evangelistar des Speyerer Domes* (Leipzig 1930).

62 Colour reprods in A. Boeckler, *Deutsche Buchmalerei vorgotischer Zeit* (Königstein 1952) 51.

62a *The Gospels of Henry the Lion*, introd. by Christopher de Hamel. Sotheby's Sales Catal., 6 Dec. 1982.

63 J. Porcher, *Französische Buchmalerei* (Recklinghausen 1959).

64 Danielle Gaborit-Chopin, *La décoration des manuscrits à Saint-Martial de Limoges et en Limousin du IXe au XIIe siècle* (Paris–Geneva 1969).

65 Edition of the Ghent original: Ae. I. Strubbe–A. Derolez, *Lamberti S. Audomari canonici Liber Floridus* (Ghent 1968).

continues also in the twelfth century. It influenced the revival of book art in the neighbouring style-region on the Maas; in the mature 'Maas school' of the twelfth century, book illumination and the art of enamelling influenced one another.

English book art[66] was revitalised, after the caesura in the ninth century, through the study of French models, and it rapidly acquired a noteworthy indepndence. The virtuoso pen and ink style of the Utrecht Psalter was taken over and the codex itself was twice copied in England. English artists learned from this the capacity for expression in the human figure, which is pushed almost to eccentricity, and the angular drapery folds of their own drawings,[67] on which they worked with various colours and with delicate gradation of the strokes. The agitated drawing of the contours also dominates in the pictures in opaque colours in the Benedictional of St Æthelwold and its relatives, whose framework was a riot of acanthus, taken over from Franco-Saxon models. Numerous monasteries participated in this 'Winchester style'.

In the art of initials a preference is shown for interlace and bird-and-dragon motifs which echo the smooth, fluid type of the older Canterbury style, paired with wildly agitated and knotted tendrils and acanthus forms. Even before 1066 human figures appear in England in the initials.[68] In the twelfth century, English artists illustrated the books of the bible with a preference for historiated initials.[69]

In early medieval Italy the principal centre of book painting lay at first in the south, in Campania and Apulia. From the tenth to the thirteenth century this was the homeland of illustrated liturgical Easter rolls.[70] In most of these rolls Byzantine influence is manifest. In Monte Cassino, where in 1023 the oldest illustrated manuscript of Hrabanus's encyclopaedia was made,[71] the miniaturists, particularly under Desiderius, endeavoured to cling closely to Byzantine style.

The most important object of book painting in the eleventh and twelfth centuries, in a European trend, is the Bible in large format. The Catalan bibles of

66 W. Oakeshott, *The Sequence of English Medieval Art, Illustrated Chiefly from Illuminated Manuscripts 650–1450* (London 1950); F. Wormald in L. Grodecki and others, *Die Zeit der Ottonen und Salier*, Universum der Kunst (Munich 1973) 226–255 with reprods; E.G. Millar, *La miniature anglaise du Xme au XIIIme siècle* (Paris 1926); O. Elfridi Saunders, *Englische Buchmalerei* 1 (Florence–Munich 1927); Elzbieta Temple, *Anglo-Saxon Manuscripts 900–1066*, Survey of the manuscripts illuminated in the British Isles 2 (London 1976).

67 Francis Wormald, *English drawings of the tenth and eleventh century* (London 1952).

68 Idem, 'Decorated initials in English manuscripts from A.D. 900 to 1100', *Archaeologia* 91 (1945) 107 ff.; repr. *Collected Writings* 1 (Oxford 1984) 47–75.

69 C.M. Kauffmann, *Romanesque Manuscripts 1066–1190*, Survey 3 (London 1975).

70 See above p. 111.

71 A. Amelli, *Miniature sacre e profane dell'anno 1023 illustranti l'enciclopedia medievale di Rabano Mauro* (Monte Cassino 1896); Marianne Reuter, *Text und Bild im Codex 132 der Bibliothek von Montecassino 'Liber Rabani de originibus rerum'*, Müncher Beiträge 34 (Munich 1984).

Roda and Ripoll ('Farfa Bible') from the beginning of the eleventh century,[72] and a bible from Arras only slightly younger, are still isolated. In the second half of the eleventh century in northern and central Italy and in Rome began the production of 'giant bibles';[73] stimulated by the Italian example, the Salzburg school produced several illuminated bibles in the twelfth century.[74] Shortly before 1100 the creation of illuminated bibles also begins in France, and this continues without interruption into the thirteenth century; this was facilitated by contacts with English book-painting. Thus in the decoration of the four-volume bible of abbot Stephen Harding of Citeaux (†1133), who was himself an Englishman, English hands participated. A love of pictures and a striving after motifs in the decoration of initials which had dominated in early Citeaux art were, however, sharply objected to by Bernard of Clairvaux, and for his order the 1134 statutes laid down: 'litterae unius coloris fiant et non depictae'.[75]

A new genre of religious illuminated manuscripts, psalters introduced by full-page pictures from the life of Christ, was probably initiated in England.[76] From there at any rate comes the earliest example, the St Albans psalter in Hildesheim from c. 1115.[77] Precious books of this kind, which served the purpose of prayer and contemplation, were painted principally for princely and higher noble-women until the advent of the books of hours.

In the most varied places, England, France, Germany, and Monte Cassino from the tenth century on, the lives of the respective patron saints were illustrated in codices which could bear witness to the pride of the abbeys as well as to the fame of the saints.[78] Most impressive of these is the sequence of three illustrated Vitae S Amandi from the eleventh and twelfth centuries in Ottonian, early romanesque, and high romanesque styles.[79] Most of the surviving manuscripts are unique copies, so we must presume that very many others have been lost.

---

72 W. Neuss, *Die katalanische Bibelillustration um die Wende des ersten Jahrtausends und die altspanische Buchmalerei* (Bonn–Leipzig 1922).   73 Cf. Garrison, *Studies*.

74 G. Swarzenski, *Die Salzburger Malerei*.

75 Ch. Oursel, *Miniatures cisterciennes (1109–1134)* (Mâcon 1960) 13; Nordenfalk, *Die romanische Malerei*, 182. A different intellectual criticism of 'superbia librorum' (saec. XIII) in L. Delisle, *Le cabinet des manuscrits de la Bibliothèque Nationale* 3 (Paris 1884) 378 f.

76 An earlier English example is in the psalter, London, BL, Cotton Tib. C IV (c. 1050) with a set of full-page illustrations which is not yet standardized; F. Wormald, *Collected Writings* 1 (Oxford 1984) 123–37 and illustr. 124–54.

77 O. Pächt–C.R. Dodwell–F. Wormald, *The St. Albans Psalter (Albani Psalter)* (London 1960). The illustration of the journey to Emmaus in this psalter is one of the clearest pieces of evidence that illuminators depicted scenes from liturgical drama; O. Pächt, *The Rise of Pictorial Narrative in Twelfth Century England* (Oxford 1962) 33 ff. and plate 7.

78 Cf. F. Wormald, 'Some illustrated manuscripts of the Lives of the saints', *Bull. John Rylands Library* 35 (1952) 248–266, esp. 261 f.

79 Reprod. in Nordenfalk, *Die romanische Malerei*, 185, 187, 194.

V

The late middle ages

With the entry into the gothic period the medieval book system experiences the most profound changes of its entire history.[1] If, up to that time, it was bound up with clerical institutions (the monasteries and chapters), now new forces were at work which resulted in an enormous increase in book production: the scholarly activities that were organised in the universities, the increased practice of preaching,[2] the deepening of religious life through mysticism, above all in the female religious orders, the spread of written education among the laity,[3] and their interest in literature, especially in the vernaculars. Writing, of course, still continued in the religious communities, but a large part of the professional production of books passed over to the civilian professional scribes in the cities.[4] Outside the world of books and of formal charters writing became a tool in daily life, for administration, trade and crafts, for which book-keeping became indispensable. In city schools writing and arithmetic were taught, and formulae for letters also belonged to the instruction.[5] However, there were apparently still in the thirteenth and fourteenth centuries not a few canons and monks who excused themselves from the duty of witnessing legal transactions because of their inability to write.[6]

1 Cf. Mazal. *Gotik*; Christ–Kern in Milkau-Leyh, *Handbuch* 3/1², 426 ff.
2 Cf. J.B. Schneyer, *Geschichte der katholischen Predigt* (Freiburg i. Br. 1969) 109 ff., 189 ff.
3 The Cathar sects had their own rituals and doctrinal texts. From the thirteenth century their persecution, and the church's struggle against heresy, was supported by the Inquisition, through whose hands the sole surviving example of such a text, Florence, Bibl. Naz. I. II. 44, probably passed. Cf. A. Dondaine, *Un traité neomanichéen du XIIIe siècle. Le liber de duobus principiis suivi d'un fragment de rituel cathare* (Rome 1939).
4 139 professional scribes, including two women, are known from Bologna in the period 1265–8; Cencetti, *Lineamenti*, 219.
5 F. Rörig, 'Mittelalter und Schriftlichkeit', *Die Welt als Geschichte* 13 (1953) 38 ff.; Helga Hajdu, *Lesen und Schreiben im Spätmittelalter* (Pécs–Fünfkirchen 1931); W. Schmidt, 'Vom Lesen und Schreiben im späten Mittelalter', in *Festschrift für Ingeborg Schröbler zum 65. Geburtstag* (Tübingen 1973) 309–27.
6 F.W. Oediger, *Über die Bildung der Geistlichen im späten Mittelalter* (Leiden–Cologne 1953), 135 n. 8; A. Wendehorst, 'Monachus scribere nesciens', *Mitteil. Inst. Österr. Geschichtsforschung* 71 (1963) 67–75.

The book was now more rationally designed. Clearer division made reading and usage easier.[7] Foliation, which after sporadic earlier appearance was frequent from the twelfth century on, and the somewhat later practice of paginating – both of which could be expanded by numbering the columns – made citation easier; in Oxford manuscripts of the thirteenth century even the lines are numbered.[8] From the thirteenth century onwards indices were supplied.[9] One principal type derives from the division of the work into books and chapters divided into sections that are indicated by letters of the alphabet, and is thus independent of the individual exemplar. Another type indicates the folio or even page numbers of the book.[10] The popularisation of the book, which now became the personal property of innumerable people, was facilitated by the introduction of paper. In scholastic garb Richard of Bury, chancellor of England and bishop of Durham, and himself a great book-collector, expresses his intimacy with learned books in his *Philobiblon*, when he complains in expressive terms about their enemies and scorners.[11]

The 'third great power of the middle ages', the *studium*, made its first appearance when, after modest beginnings, the medieval science of Roman law originated,[12] and canon law was raised to the status of a science in the twelfth century through the systematic and didactic direction given by Gratian. In the Italian universities, above all in Bologna, the textbooks of both subjects, laid out with apparatus, received their characteristic form. Many of these manuscripts were decorated with miniatures in the titles that related to the act of promulgation; numerous manuscripts of the *Decretum* were also decorated with miniatures of the *causae* of the second book.[13] In no category of manuscripts are Hebrew entries more frequently found than in these law codices; they were

7 Cf. M.B. Parkes, 'The influence of the concept of Ordinatio and Compilatio on the development of the book', in *Medieval Learning and Literature, Essays Presented to Richard William Hunt* (Oxford 1976) 115–41 with plates 9–16.
8 Extensive details in Lehmann, *Erforschung* 2, 1–59.
9 Cf. Anna-Dorothee von den Bricken, 'Tabula alphabetica', in *Festschrift für Hermann Heimpel* 2 (Göttingen 1972) 900–23. For other aids see R.H. Rouse , 'La diffusion en occident au XIIIe siècle des outils de travail facilitant l'accès aux textes autoritatifs', in *L'enseignement en Islam et en Occident au Moyen Age*, Islam et Occident au Moyen Age 1 (Paris 1978) 113–147. There is a draft of an alphabetical encyclopaedia, s. XIII, in Clm 29,670/19.
10 The index to John of Abbéville in Brussels, Bibl. Roy., II 1051, which has 'chaldaean' foliation, is especially noteworthy. There is a plate in Bischoff, *Mittelalterliche Studien* 1, plate VII.
11 M. MacLagan (ed.), *Richard de Bury, Philobiblon. The Text and Translation of E.G. Thomas* (Oxford 1960). W. Schmidt sees the Philobiblon as a piece of social criticism, in 'Richard de Bury – ein antihöfischer Höfling', *Philobiblon* 19 (1975) 156–88.
12 P. Classen discusses the official consultation of the early Codex 'Pisanus' (which became the 'Florentinus' after 1204) by delegations of Bologna lawyers when there was uncertainty about the text, in 'Burgundio von Pisa', *Sitzungsber. Heidelberger Akad. Wiss.*, phil.-hist. Kl. (1974) 4, 39 ff.
13 A. Melnikas, *The Corpus of the Miniatures in the Manuscripts of Decretum Gratiani* 1–3, Studia Gratiana 16–18 (Rome 1975).

written by Jewish moneylenders while the books were in their temporary possession.

The new trend in the disciplines practised in the faculties of arts and medicine demanded translations of the complete works of Aristotle and the writings of the Greek, Arabic, and Jewish doctors. Among the theologians the rise up the academic stepladder was itself connected with the multiplication of books through commentaries on the *sententiae* and *Quaestiones disputatae* and *quodlibetales*.

When, in the thirteenth century, an expansion took place in the studies that were very closely bound up with the textbooks of the faculties and the masters' commentaries and glossing apparatus, the universities recognised the necessity for controlling the reliability of the texts whose multiplication was indispensable for these studies. For this purpose the institution of the *stationarius* was created, with whom standard copies were deposited, and these were then given out for copying in *peciae* to professional scribes.[14] Paris, Oxford, Bologna, and Naples experienced very similar developments in this regard during the thirteenth and fourteenth centuries. The reception of new academic literature in the lists of the *stationarii* was in itself a form of publication. The younger universities, however, did not take over this practice; in the German universities textbooks were written by the students from the dictation of the master (the 'pronuntiatio').

The very rapid, elastic script, using very economical abbreviations, enabled the hearers to transcribe even from lectures, the 'reportatio'.[15] Such texts even passed into circulation, whether authorised or not.

In most medieval universities – though not in Bologna, where the professors owned their own specialist libraries – there grew up from legacies of the masters, or from the bequests of princely patrons, academic libraries which were either the property of the whole university or of individual faculties. The largest and most important, and the most rapid in growth, was that of the Sorbonne (founded 1257), which in 1290 comprised 1,017 volumes, and in 1328 already 1,722 volumes.[16] Of the multitude of donors of every nationality, numbering roughly 170, Gerhard of Abbéville (c. 1271) was distinguished by the size as well as by the value of his gifts, because they contained a large part of the books that Richard of Fournival, chancellor of the church in Amiens, had prudently gathered and described in his *Biblionomia* using the image of a garden.[17] The Sorbonne library was divided up into the 'great' reference library with its *libri catenati*, and the 'small' library, which was made up of duplicates, and whose books – to judge from the loan indices – were much used.

14 On the pecia see above p. 43 f.
15 For a reportatio of lectures by Hugh of St Victor see Bischoff, *Mittelalterliche Studien* 2, 182–7.
16 R.H. Rouse, 'The early library of the Sorbonne', *Scriptorium* 21 (1967) 42–71, 227–51.
17 R.H. Rouse, 'Manuscripts belonging to Richard de Fournival', *Rev. d'hist. des textes* 3 (1973) 253–69 with plate.

A learned library which was a close second to that of the Sorbonne in extent was that of the Avignon popes. It was the third papal book collection, for after the disappearance of the Lateran library[18] another was assembled anew in Rome in the course of the thirteenth century, that which was called the 'Bonifatiana' after Boniface VIII, and which remained in Rome after the transfer of the curia to Avignon; but this was neglected and eventually dispersed. The library at Avignon, which was drawn into involvement in the schism, also had an unfortunate fate. None the less around seven hundred manuscripts (of its over two thousand) are preserved in almost equal numbers in Paris and in the Borghesiani collection in the Vatican.[19] Avignon was at the same time a large book market,[20] like Constance and Basel during the conciliar years.[21]

No collection better illustrates the extent to which book-ownership fluctuated in the late middle ages than that of the Rhenish Magister Amplonius Ratinck (†1435), still today for the most part preserved in Erfurt, which likewise comprised all subjects and into which had flowed manuscripts from the most varied regions of the German and Roman world. Amongst them were found even carolingian books from the Cologne cathedral library (Fol. 42 and 64) and a volume from the church of Nazareth with its catalogue of around one hundred volumes in the library there (Qu. 102, saec. XII*ex*).

Of the new orders the Dominicans from the beginning were committed to studies; however, they preferred to have their books written by others rather than to copy them themselves.[22] As excerptors they carried out the most extensive collective scholarly work of the middle ages: the *Specula* directed by Vincent of Beauvais and the first comprehensive verbal concordances of the bible.[23] Later Dominicans worked also as miniaturists. The fact that already in the mid thirteenth century Dominicans and Franciscans were uniformly prescribing the notation with square notes[24] for use in their liturgical books contributed considerably to their adoption.

Iohannes Gerson (†1429) directed his treatise *De laude scriptorum* to a Carthusian, summing up his twelve *considerationes* in these verses:

18 See above p. 215.

19 Christ–Kern in Milkau–Leyh, *Handbuch* 3/1², 467 f.

20 Cf. *Mittelalt. Bibliothekskat. Deutschl.* 4, 1, 112; Hlaváček, 'Studie k dějinám knihoven v českém statě v dobĕ předhusitskĕ', in *Acta Universitatis Carolinae* (1965) 6, 60 f.; Th. Gottlieb, *Über mittelalterliche Bibliotheken* (Leipzig 1890) 35 f., Nr. 72; M. Dvořák, 'Die Illuminatoren des Johannes von Neumarkt', *Jahrb. der Kunstsammlungen des Allerhöchsten Kaiserhauses* 22/1 (1901) 74 ff.; repr. in *Gesammelte Aufsätze zur Kunstgeschichte* (Munich 1929) 128 ff.).   21 Lehmann, *Erforschung* 1 (1941) 253–80.

22 A. Walz, 'Vom Buchwesen im Predigerorden bis zum Jahre 1280', in *Aus der Geisteswelt des Mittelalters*, Beitr. z. Gesch. d. Philos u. Theol. d. Mittelalters, Suppl. 3 (Münster/W. 1935) 1, 111–127.   23 Lehmann, *Erforschung* 4, 361 f., 366 f.

24 See above p. 175. Cf. P. Wagner, *Neumenkunde*² (Leipzig 1912) 313, 328. The Franciscan *Statutum pro libris choralibus scribendis* in S.J.P. van Dijk, *Sources of the Modern Roman Liturgy. The Ordinals by Haymo of Faversham and Related Documents* 2 (Leiden 1963) 362–4.

Praedicat atque studet scriptor, largitur et orat,
Affligitur, sal dat, fontem lucemque futuris,
Ecclesiam ditat, armat, custodit, honorat.[25]

The order still remained true to the task of writing in the late middle ages,[26] and the remains of the libraries of various houses, Erfurt, Mainz, Cologne, and Basel,[27] and their catalogues, are among the largest of the middle ages.

This monastic activity of the Carthusians was adopted as a model by two late-medieval movements in Holland and Lower Germany. Of these the reformed Augustinian canons at Windesheim, who devoted themselves principally to the copying of learned literature, were the more similar to the Carthusians. If, on the other hand, the 'Brethren of the Common Life', who were also termed 'broeder van de penne', write, they do so with the aim of earning their keep with meaningful work.[28] Their writing practice is precisely graded according to content; from their hands came innumerable liturgical books and vernacular texts of *devotio moderna*.

In Upper Germany the civilian book industry was more strongly represented, and the profession of 'stool scribe' ('cathedralis') was frequently connected with the activity of notary. Bavarian Benedictine monasteries like St Emmeram,[29] Tegernsee, and Scheyern,[30] ordered extensive collections of sermons, theological and ascetical works, encyclopaedias, and even liturgical manuscripts from lay scribes.

A south-Italian speciality are the bilingual codices of the Greek psalter and the Greek liturgies with Latin translation dating from the thirteenth and fourteenth centuries, which go back to the activity of the Basilian abbot Nektarios of Casole near Otranto (†1235).[31]

Much was written and painted too in nunneries belonging to various orders.[32] They saved in particular the writings of the German mystics. The Cologne convent of the Poor Clares and the Cistercian nunnery of Lichtenthal near

25 Iohannes Gerson, *Œuvres complètes*, ed. P. Glorieux, 9 (Paris 1973) 423–34.
26 Lehmann, *Erforschung* 3, 121–42; Gumbert, *Utrechter Kartäuser*, 311 ff.
27 Bruckner, *Scriptoria* 10 (1964) 81–94 with plate 38 ff.
28 B. Kruitwagen, *Laatmiddeleeuwsche Palaeographica, Palaeotypica, Liturgica, Kalendalia, Grammaticalia* (The Hague 1942) 25–78; W. Oeser, 'Die Brüder vom gemeinsamen Leben in Münster als Bücherschreiber', *Arch. f. Gesch. d. Buchwesens* 5 (1964) 197–398.
29 *Mittelalt. Bibliothekskat. Deutschl.* 4, 1, 117.
30 C. Wehmer, 'Augsburger Schreiber aus der Frühzeit des Buchdrucks', *Beitr. z. Inkunabelkunde*, n.F. 2 (1938) 108–27, esp. 123 ff.
31 J.M. Hoeck–R.J. Loenertz, *Nikolaos-Nektarios von Otranto, Abt von Casole* (Ettal 1965) 74 ff., plates 1–3.
32 A. Bruckner, 'Zum Problem der Frauenhandschriften im Mittelalter', in *Aus Mittelalter und Neuzeit. Festschrift zum 70. Geburtstag von Gerhard Kallen* (Berlin 1957), 171–83; idem, 'Weibliche Schreibtätigkeit im Spätmittelalter', in *Festschrift Bernhard Bischoff* (Stuttgart 1971) 441–8. An uncalligraphic entry by 'arme Engilbirne', probably a recluse (s. XIII¹), in Petzet-Glauning *Deutsche Schrifttafeln*, plate 21.

Freiburg are well known as workshops of book painting. Clara Hätzlerin in Augsburg (†after 1476) was a civilian professional female scribe seven of whose manuscripts are still known.[33]

For book decoration new international fashions appeared.[34] The more modest opening letters have the heavy bulging forms of gothic majuscule (Lombards). The colours used almost exclusively are blue and red in alternation, and these colours are also contrasted when the bodies of larger initials are ornamentally cleft; they are used above all in fleuronée or filigree work. This was developed in the first half of the thirteenth century in France. In this way the interior of the compact body of the initial and its surrounding area are filled with florid spirals or other patterns and ornamental strokes, while fine bundles of swinging lines run out into the margin in free play; here too bodies and ornaments are drawn in the respective contrasting colours.[35] A simpler emphasis on the large letters suitable for the pen occurs through doubling of the principal lines that can crisscross; masks are often drawn in. These are the 'cadella' (derived from 'capitalis'), a genuine invention of the writing masters.

From the thirteenth century on the borders extending out from the initials belong to the general decoration. They first appear in France and England, where they are heavily notched and set with thorny leaves. The margins are the stage for drolleries in which wit and often grotesque fantasy are deployed.[36] When, in the late middle ages, the margins are covered with broad rows of tendrils or closed broad frames, there are mixed into them naturalistically painted insects, flowers, fruit, and other things.

Book illumination had acquired a great freedom in the eleventh and twelfth centuries, especially in the formation of historiated initials illustrating the text. On the other hand, in actual illustration it reached out only into occasional individual works: encyclopaedias, historical works, and chivalric poetry, beyond the wide-ranging ecclesiastical, biblical, and hagiographical themes with inher-

---

33 Cf. E. Gebele in *Neue Deutsche Biographie* 7 (Berlin 1966) 455 f.

34 Cf. Mazal, *Gotik*; H. Köllner–Sigrid v. Borries–H. Knaus, in *Zur Katalogisierung mittelalterlicher und neuerer Handschriften*, Zentralbl. f. Bibliothekswesen u. Bibliogr. Sonderheft (1963) 142–54; see in addition the literature cited p. ooo n. 56. For heraldry as a means of studying manuscripts of the Gothic and Renaissance periods see M. Pastoureau, 'L'héraldique au service de la codicologie', in *Codicologica* 4 [Litterae textuales] (Leiden 1978) 75 ff. Late romanesque initials, fleuronné and what is more fantasias reached Iceland in simple forms; cf. H. Hermannsson, *Icelandic Illuminated Manuscripts of the Middle Ages*, Corpus Codicum Islandicorum (Copenhagen 1935) Medii Aevi 7.

35 Ellen J. Beer, *Beiträge zur oberrheinischen Buchmalerei in der ersten Hälfte des 14. Jahrhunderts unter besonderer Berücksichtigung der Initialornamentik* (Basel–Stuttgart 1959) 17 ff., 50 ff.; G. Schmidt, *Die Malerschule von S. Florian*, Forschungen zur Geschichte Oberösterreichs 7 (Linz 1962) 173 ff.; Mazal, *Gotik*, 50 f.

35a Most extensively by Jean Miélot, a secretary to Philip the Good, in Brussels, Bibl. Roy., MS 9249–50 (1449): *Mss. datés*, Belgique 3, plates 517–28.

36 Mazal, *Gotik*, 51 ff.; Lilian M.C. Randall, *Images in the Margins of Gothic Manuscripts* (Berkeley–Los Angeles 1966); Rosy Schilling in *Reallex. z. Deutsch. Kunstgesch.* 4, 577 ff.

ited pictorial sequences. From the thirteenth century on, however, the delight in illustration knows no further bounds. Amongst illuminated manuscripts the liturgical ones and those intended for private devotion: pontificals, breviaries, psalters, and books of hours (livres d'heures), which take over the rôle of psalters,[37] occupy a prominent place. Just as the biblical, liturgical, and legendary scenes depicted in them, so too the pictures of the months in their calendars finally develop into small pictures in their own right. In the biblical literature the iconographic types were regularised, as in other areas: the typological mirroring of the redemption in the Old Testament is canonised partly in the enormous collection of illustrations to the 'Bible moralisée', partly in the poor memorial pictures of the 'biblia pauperum' and the *Speculum humanae salvationis*. In the literature of the new disciplines of legal science, astrology, alchemy, and warfare, illustrations also begin to appear. Of literature in the narrower sense, the religious and profane poetry and prose of the vernaculars seem to have been more often provided with pictures than the Latin ones; illumination matched the desires of the readers.

The artistic richness of French gothic book painting[38] and its radiation to the other countries of Europe demand that it be given pride of place. Its great period begins around 1220 under Philip II Augustus. It had its centre in Paris, its masters worked for kings and aristocratic ladies. In the principal thirteenth-century works the kind of presentation, formal construction, and the motifs in the repertoire[39] of miniatures are extremely similar to contemporary glass painting, for example in the manuscripts of the 'Bible moralisée', a huge typological illustrated commentary on scripture,[40] in the psalter of Louis IX, and in other manuscripts painted for the king.

From the late thirteenth century on, many Paris book painters are known by name. Those that can be connected with surviving works are Maître Honoré, who illuminated a breviary for Philip the Fair, and Jean Pucelle, active around 1325–30. He was one of the first to use grisaille technique and took up trends from Italian art, which was the dominant one on French soil, at Avignon.[41] With the sons of Johann the Good (†1364), who was himself a lover of fine books, Charles V (1364–80), Louis of Anjou (†1384), Philip the Bold of Burgundy (†1404), and Jean Duc de Berry (†1416), there appeared a generation of bibliophiles such as had not existed in the middle ages. The library of the learned

37 See e.g., the lavishly illustrated catalogues of all these types from French libraries by V. Leroquais (Paris 1927–41).

38 Porcher, *Französische Buchmalerei* (Recklinghausen 1959); Mazal, *Gotik*, 55–66; F. Avril, *Buchmalerei am Hofe Frankreichs 1310–1380* (Munich 1978).

39 Compare the biblical typology given in the English handbook 'Pictor in carmine' which dates from around 1200; M.R. James in *Archaeologia* 94 (1951) 141–66.

40 *Bible moralisée. Faksimile-Ausgabe . . . des Codex Vindobonensis 2554.* 1/2; commentary; R. Haussherr (Graz–Paris 1973).

41 Where Simone Martini, from Siena, painted the title page of Petrarch's manuscript at Vergil. (See M. Dvořák, 'Die Illuminatoren des Johannes von Neumarkt.')

Charles V[42] numbered over one thousand manuscripts. It contained, besides French epics and romances, and ostentatious manuscripts of the bible and liturgy, the many French translations from classical authors, church Fathers, and medieval works that the king had had made. Even painters from distant towns and foreign parts were drawn to Paris by his orders, amongst them Flemings and Italians. The name of the Duc de Berry is inseparably linked to his books of hours (Belles heures, Très belles heures, Petites heures, Grandes heures, Très riches heures), for which he employed artists of the first rank like the brothers Limburg and perhaps even the brothers Van Eyck.[43] In the succeeding decades there worked in Paris the anonymous 'Bedford Master', who participated in the 'Terence des ducs', the 'Marshal Boucicaut Master', and the Master of the 'Rohan Hours', who painted moving pictures of death. The last outstanding French miniaturist of the gothic period was Jean Fouquet (†c. 1480); he completed the Josephus that was begun for the Duc de Berry and he illustrated the 'Grandes chroniques de France', with their valuable topographical views, the book of hours of Etienne Chevalier, and the Munich Boccaccio *Des cas des nobles hommes et femmes'*.

Of the Burgundian dukes it was Philip the Good (1419–67) whose lavish patronage encouraged Flemish book painting, which already stood under the influence of the brothers Van Eyck, to its full development.[44] The apogee lasted into the early sixteenth century; its greatest artist is the 'Master of Mary of Burgundy'.[45] The north-Dutch book painting of the fifteenth century was closely related to the Flemish, but it lacked the courtly component.[46]

English book art[47] of the thirteenth century still produced illuminated bibles, psalters, and bestiaries. A wholly new genre that was practised there and in northern France until the fourteenth century were the illustrated Apocalypses.[48] The transition to gothic which took place in close contact with France was completed around 1220. The school of St Alban's represented relatively independent English style in which the important chronicler Matthew Paris deter-

42 L. Delisle, *Recherches sur la librairie de Charles V* (Paris 1907); *La librairie de Charles V* (Exhibition catalogue, Paris 1968).

43 Cf. M. Meiss, *French Painting in the Time of Jean de Berry. The Late Fourteenth Century and the Patronage of the Duke*. Text, plates (London 1969); idem, *The Limbourgs and their Contemporaries* 1/2 (London–New York 1974).

44 Fr. Winkler, *Die flämische Buchmalerei des XV. und XVI. Jahrhunderts* (Leipzig 1925); L.M.J. Delaissé, *La miniature flamande, le mécénat de Philippe le Bon* (Brussels 1959).

45 G.I. Lieftinck, *Boekverluchters uit de omgeving van Maria van Bourgondie c. 1475–c. 1485*, text, plates (Brussels 1969); J.J.G. Alexander, *The Master of Mary of Burgundy* (New York 1970).

46 A.W. Byvanck, *La miniature dans les Pays-Bas septentrionaux* (Paris 1937); L.M.J. Delaissé, *A century of Dutch manuscript illumination* (Berkeley–Los Angeles 1968).

47 O. Elfrida Saunders, *Englische Buchmalerei* 2 (Florence–Munich 1927); E.G. Millar, *La miniature anglaise du Xme au XIIIme siècle* (Paris 1927); idem, *La miniature anglaise du XIVe et XVe siècle* (Paris–Brussels 1928).

48 L. Delisle–P. Meyer, *L'Apocalypse en français au XIIIe siècle* (Paris 1901).

mined the style of the workshop as director of the scriptorium, and he himself probably worked as painter and illustrator of his own works; several picture sequences for English saints' lives belong to this school.[49]

The influence of Parisian art is more noticeable in the 'palace school' in which were gathered artists working on behalf of Henry III of England and in which laymen too worked as illuminators, and also in monastic centres like Canterbury. A particular jewel of this tendency is the 'Queen Mary Psalter' of around 1300, which, besides a large picture cycle from the Old Testament and psalter illustrations, contains hundreds of smaller pictures beneath the text.[50] With on the one hand an extreme refinement, and on the other a forcefulness of expression which does not fall short of excess, the 'East Anglian school' that flowered from roughly 1300 to 1325 in Norfolk and Suffolk, and especially in the village of Gorleston near Yarmouth, with its gothic decorative elements of marginal borders and drolleries, attains the most astonishing results. The greatest works are again psalters: the Ormsby psalter, the Gorleston psalter, the St Omer psalter, and, as a latecomer, the Luttrell psalter. In the fifteenth century, during which Paris was for a lengthy period occupied by the English, French book art surpasses the English.

In Italy[51] native traditions, Byzantinising tendencies, and French gothic cross and influence each other. Scientific illustration especially was here given rewarding tasks in the rich didactic, astronomical–astrological, medical, and medico-botanical literature; in Bologna the continuity of miniaturist art was bound up with book production for the university.[52] Monuments of the religious painting that flourished in many places are the initials of the large choir books which often border on paintings in themselves. Many artists strove to depict the fantastic scenes and stirringly described encounters in Dante's *Divina commedia*.[53]

In Spain for the first time an outstanding centre of book art activity arose at the court of Alfons X the Wise (1252–84), who had his 'Cantigas de Santa Maria', his collections of laws, his 'chess-book', and his 'lapidary book', and the compilations from Arabic and western sources created at his request, all richly illustrated.[54] His artists, laymen, learnt from the French gothic. Later, in the widespread productions for kings, ecclesiastical and secular lords, churches and

49 R. Vaughan, *Matthew Paris* (Cambridge 1958).

50 G. Warner, *Queen Mary's Psalter, Miniatures and Drawings by an English Artist of the Fourteenth Century* (London 1917).

51 P. d'Ancona, *La miniature italienne du Xe au XVIe siècle* (Paris–Brussels 1925); M. Salmi, *La miniatura italiana* (Milan 1956); Bernhard Degenhart–Annegret Schmitt, *Corpus der italienischen Zeichnungen 1300–1450*, pt. 1, 4 vols (Berlin 1968); pt. 2, 3 vols (Berlin 1980).

52 See above p. 225.

53 P. Brieger–M. Meiss–Ch. S. Singleton, *Illuminated manuscripts of the Divine Comedy* 1/2 (Princeton 1969).

54 J. Domínguez-Bordona, *Die spanische Buchmalerei vom 7. bis 17. Jahrhundert* (Munich–Florence 1930) 2, plates 81–92.

monasteries, besides French influence, Italian and finally Flemish influence had come into play.

In Germany the shift to gothic was once again accompanied by an impulse from Byzantine exemplars through which it is possible to explain the elegant, lively modelled figures of the Goslar Gospels.[55] German gothic book painting[56] begins very late by comparison with France; a Thuringian-Saxon school, whence came the psalters made for the landgrave Hermann of Thuringia (†1217),[57] and the school of the Benedictine monastery of Scheyern, which likewise was at work in the first half of the thirteenth century (using amongst others Regensburg exemplars),[58] still belong stylistically to late romanesque. In monastic workshops the simple typological cycles of the 'biblia pauperum'[59] and the *Speculum humanae salvationis*[60] were copied. The former was more widely disseminated in the south east, the latter more in the west.

Those artistic terrains of the German-speaking regions that were especially productive for book painting in the late thirteenth century and the fourteenth are the Rhineland, with Cologne as focal point, where French influence worked most strongly, the upper Rhine region, Franconia, and Austria. In south-west Germany and the German part of Switzerland the interest of aristocratic circles favoured the development of book art; here the Manesse and Weingarten song books and numerous German world chronicles were written and decorated. In Franconia and Austria monastic art dominates initially. Worthy of mention among higher ecclesiastical patrons are the archbishops Balduin of Luxembourg (†1354) and Kuno of Falkenstein (†1388).

When Prague under Charles IV became a centre of European art it was above all his chancellor Johann of Neumarkt (†1380)[61] and other prelates who commissioned precious liturgical manuscripts. Amongst the artists active for this circle was Johann of Troppau, who in 1368 wrote a gospel book for Albrecht III in Austria entirely in gold and illuminated in the most sumptuous manner.[62] The

55 A Goldschmidt, *Das Evangeliar im Rathause zu Goslar* (Berlin 1910); Demus, *Byzantine Art and the West* (New York 1970) 163 ff., esp. 197 ff.
56 H. Swarzenski, *Die lateinischen illuminierten Handschriften des XIII. Jahrhunderts in den Ländern an Rhein, Main und Donau.* Text, plates (Berlin 1935); A. Boeckler, *Deutsche Buchmalerei der Gotik* (Königstein i. T. 1959).
57 A. Haseloff, *Eine thüringische-sächsische Malerschule des 13. Jahrhunderts* (Strasbourg 1897).
58 J. Damrich, *Ein Künstlerdreiblatt des 13. Jahrhunderts aus Kloster Scheyern* (Strasbourg 1904).   59 G. Schmidt, *Die Armenbibeln des XIV. Jahrhunderts* (Graz–Köln 1959).
60 E. Breitenbach, *Speculum humanae salvationis* (Strasbourg 1930).
61 M. Dvořák, *Die Iluminatoren des Johannes von Neumarkt* 22/1 (1901) 35–126 (repr. in *Gesammelte Aufsätze zur Kunstgeschichte* (Munich 1929) 74–207).
62 E. Trenkler, *Das Evangeliar des Johann von Troppau* (Vienna 1948); G. Schmidt, 'Johann von Troppau und die vorromanische Buchmalerei', in *Studien zur Buchmalerei und Goldschmiedekunst des Mittelalters. Festschrift für Karl Hermann Usener* (Marburg 1967), 275–93 with reprods; *Katal. dat. Hss.*, Österreich 1, plates 150 f. In the initial E of f. 9r, which shows Christ teaching the Lord's Prayer, Johannes produced a virtuoso example of microscopic writing, which was later especially popular: on the sheet which Christ is holding, which measures 14 × 6–7mm, the text of the Lord's Prayer is copied in 19 lines of clearly legible script.

tradition founded here continued under king Wenceslas, who had several bibles (amongst them one in German in six volumes), law manuscripts, the 'Willehalm', astronomical works, and others written and luxuriously illustrated.[63] The area of influence of the Prague style extended as far as Austria and southern Germany. Amongst the German book painters of the fifteenth century one can also number Stephen Lochner.

In the last century of the middle ages the desire and inclination towards illustration of many works of MHG literature, which until then had received no illumination, such as the Niebelungenlied, increased.[64] It was principally paper manuscripts ('popular manuscripts') that were enriched with simple or lightly coloured pen and ink drawings. The workshop of Diebold Lauber in Hagenau, who is traceable from 1425 to 1467, occupies a prominent place in this production, in which there appeared many freely invented cycles and from which fifty manuscripts and several sales lists are still preserved.[65] The palatine court ordered several books from Lauber. In the second half of the century the Württemberg duchess Margarete of Savoy and the humanistically inclined Duke Eberhard im Bart[66] had manuscripts written and painted.

After the chronicle of the Constance council by Ulrich of Richental contemporary history comes more strongly into vogue in illustrated local chronicles. New branches of practical book illustration came into being with the fencing and wrestling manuals, and the books on warfare and firearms. Closely related to these, the culturally valuable 'medieval housebook' contains one of the richest cycles of the children of the planets.[67] The printed prayerbook of Maximilian (1513) to whose marginal drawings the best artists of the time contributed – Dürer, Cranach, Baldung Grien, Altdorfer, and others – is among the last testimonies of the great medieval art of book painting.

63 J. Krasa, *Rukopisy Václava* IV. (Prague 1971). Facs.: *Die Goldene Bulle* (*Codex Vindobonensis*, 338); commentary A. Wolf (Graz 1977).

64 Cf. Hella Frühmorgen-Voss, *Text und Illustration im Mittelalter*, ed. with introd. by N.H. Ott (Munich 1975) 1–56.

65 R. Kautzsch, 'Diebold Lauber und seine Werkstatt in Hagenau', *Zentralbl. f. Bibliothekswesen* 12 (1895) 1 ff., 57 ff. (esp. 108–11).

66 W. Hoffmann in *Graf Eberhard im Bart von Württemberg im geistigen und kulturellen Geschehen seiner Zeit* (Stuttgart 1938) 45–65.

67 H. Th. Bossert–W.F. Storck, *Das mittelalterliche Hausbuch, nach dem Original im Besitz der Fürsten von Waldburg-Wolfegg-Waldsee* (Leipzig 1912).

The age of humanism

In northern Italy laymen interested in literature, and active members of the notarial or judicial profession, already in the thirteenth century discovered copies of rare or forgotten authors from old ecclesiastical libraries and used them in their works. Thus Albertanus of Brescia (†c. 1248) copied from a carolingian codex of the letters of Seneca which he provided with marginal comments and sketches.[1] The Paduan scholars Lovato dei Lovati (1241–1309), Geremia di Montagnone (†1321) and Iohannes de Matociis, mansionarius of the cathedral at Verona,[2] were lucky to make genuine discoveries. Amongst these were Catullus, Tibullus, Propertius, Varro *De re rustica*, the *Scriptores historiae Augustae*, and letters of Cicero; treasures of the Verona cathedral library which Rather had seen in the tenth century were rediscovered. For Lovato a second source was the library of Pomposa; the best manuscript of Seneca's tragedies that he used was written there in the eleventh century.

The effect of these discoveries could have remained limited for a long time to local literature and their use in florilegia, if Petrarch[3] had not incorporated them in the comprehensive picture of Roman antiquity which from his youth he had sought to recover. In the course of his efforts to acquire newer and better texts external circumstances came to his assistance; through his sojourn at the curia in Avignon he was able to establish valuable contacts. In the course of extensive journeys he himself made discoveries but he also utilised the old Veronese codices. Petrarch copied and collated a great deal; his first great achievement was the unification of the three Decades of Livy in one single volume.[4]

In his time the library of Monte Cassino became known as a hoard of ancient

---

1 Claudia Villa, 'La tradizione delle "Ad Lucilium" e la cultura di Brescia dall'età carolingia ad Albertano', *It. Med. e Um.* 12 (1969) 9–51 with reprod.
2 L.D. Reynolds–N.G. Wilson, *Scribes and Scholars* (Oxford 1974) 109 ff.; idem, *D'Homère à Erasme* (Paris 1984) 85 ff. For the whole section see A. Petrucci (ed.), *Libri, scrittura e pubblico nel Rinascimento. Guida storica e critica* (Rome-Bari 1979).
3 Idem, *Scribes and Scholars*, 112 ff.; idem, *D'Homère*, 87 ff. Ibid., 114 ff.
4 G. Billanovich, 'Petrarch and the textual tradition of Livy', *J. Warburg and Courtauld Inst.* 14 (1951) 137–208. Idem, *La tradizione del testo di Livio e le origini dell'umanesimo 2. Il Livio del Petrarca e del Valla, British Library, Harleian 1492 riprodotto integralmente* (Padua 1981).

texts thanks to Zanobi da Strada and Boccaccio (Apuleius, Tacitus, Varro *De lingua Latina*) and its codices, written in Beneventan, later made their way to Florence. In Florence it was Coluccio Salutati, a collector and humanist in Petrarch's sense, who passed on the master's ideal to a younger generation, of whom the papal secretary Poggio Bracciolini was most prominent as the most successful discoverer of unknown classical texts. A participant in the council of Constance, he brought a rich booty home from the monasteries of the surrounding region, as well as from his extensive journeys in Germany and France.

References to rarities and even manuscripts were also sent to the humanists by Germans; Nicholaus of Cusa brought the twelve comedies of Plautus (unknown in the middle ages) to Italy, while the Hersfeld monk Henry of Grebenstein brought the minor works of Tacitus.[5] The search was no longer left to chance;[6] when in 1431 a papal mission went to Germany, Niccolo Niccoli, Poggio's friend, was able to give to the mission a detailed inventory of classical codices to be obtained from Reichenau, Fulda, Hersfeld, and Cologne.[7] In this way old libraries which, since the early middle ages, had been expanded only in the area of indispensable legal literature, now become interesting once more. However, false hopes were raised too by rumours of the recovery of lost Decades of Livy and Cicero's *De re publica*.[8]

From Poggio comes the successful practical realisation of a reform in writing which Petrarch strove for before him; for the second type of humanistic script, the cursive, Niccoli's personal hand became the basis.[9] Thus a new path was indicated for the scribes, and personalities like Giovanni Aretino, Antonio Sinibaldi and Bartolomeo Sanvito aimed to realise the new script as an art in the age which also sought to establish the harmony of epigraphic script. The scribes prepared the ground for the greatest achievements of the early printers, Nicolaus Jenson's antiqua (Venice 1470) and the cursive of Aldus Manutius (Venice 1501).

In Italy a resurgence of book art accompanied the triumph of humanism. Ecclesiastical and secular princes and patrons vied to have libraries assembled in

---

5 L. Pralle, *Die Wiederentdeckung des Tacitus* (Fulda 1952). A portion of this carolingian manuscript, a quire of the Agricola, is preserved in the humanist Codex Aesinas (from Jesi); R. Till, *Handschriftliche Untersuchungen zu Tacitus' "Agricola" und "Germania" mit einer Photokopie des Codex Aesinas* (1943). Florence, Laur. XLVII 29, Priscian, s. IX is a ninth-century Priscian manuscript completed in humanistic script.

6 Many ancient classical manuscripts, once they had been copied and were no longer of interest, were neglected and destroyed. Others disappeared because it was the custom well into the sixteenth century to print from somewhat corrected original manuscripts; see Reynolds-Wilson, *Scribes and Scholars*, 123; idem, *D'Homère*, 95. All too clear traces of this practice are also found in the manuscripts of Hrotswitha (Clm 14,485) and in manuscripts of Bede; cf. Bischoff, *Mittelalterliche Studien* 1, 112 ff.

7 R.P. Robinson, 'The inventory of Niccolo Niccoli', *Classical Philology* 16 (1921) 251 ff.; N. Rubinstein, 'An unknown letter by Jacopo di Poggio Bracciolini on discoveries of classical texts', *It. Med. e Um.* 1 (1958) 385–400.

8 Lehmann, *Erforschung* 1, 280–95; 4, 95–106.   9 See above p. 147 f.

which were brought together the classical texts whose numbers were now increased, the new translations from the Greek, works of church Fathers, and of the humanists, and already some Greek manuscripts. Humanistic book decoration began with small initials with white shoots ('bianchi girari') in coloured panels which reveal their derivation from Italian manuscripts of the romanesque age.[10] Soon, however, all the decoration was concentrated on the title pages often with architectural borders, and this brought the antiquarian tendencies into play once more; putti, half-length figures and other antique motifs, along with coats of arms, emblems and medallions of the patrons. Great collections were founded in Florence by the Medici, by the Este in Ferrara,[11] by Federigo da Montefeltro (1474–82) in Urbino,[12] by Malatesta Novello (†1465) in Cesena, by the Arragonese kings of Naples,[13] by the Sforza who had inherited the Lombard-Gothic library of the Viscontis in Pavia and continued it in humanistic taste,[14] and by others. Through Nicholas V (1447–55), who had belonged to the circle of Florentine humanists, the Vaticana, the fourth papal library, was founded.[15] Several of the aforementioned were among the customers of the Florentine book dealer Vespasiono da Bisticci (†1498), author of the humanist *Vitae*. He had thoroughly organised book production, which required the cooperation of scribes and miniaturists; he employed forty-five copyists at times. In Florence, in the workshops of Attavante dei Attavanti and others, King Matthias Corvinus of Hungary (1458–90) also had many of his most magnificent manuscripts written and painted.[16]

Of Federigo da Montefeltro, Bisticci wrote that he would have been ashamed to receive a printed book into his select library.[17] The printed book, which had come into the world with Gutenberg's 42-line Bible (Mainz, between 1450 and 1456) in an unsurpassed masterpiece, was the mechanised continuation of the late gothic and humanistic book. The printed work and the manuscript continued for a while side by side and many manuscripts were still being copied from printed books in the fifteenth century.[18] The miniaturists too saw a remunerative field of activity in the painting of opening pages and initials in

---

10 O. Pächt, 'Notes and observations on the origin of Humanistic book-decoration', in *Fritz Saxl. A Volume of Memorial Essays* (London 1957) 189.   11 Now in Modena.
12 Now in the Vatican.
13 Cf. Elisabeth Pellegrin, *La bibliothèque des Visconti et de Sforza, ducs de Milan* (Paris 1955), supplement (plates; Florence–Paris 1969).
14 T. de Marinis, *La Biblioteca Napoletana dei re d'Aragona* 1–4 (Milan 1947/52), esp. vols 3 and 4 (Tavole) and also Supplement 1/2 (Verona 1969).   15 See above pp. 215 and 227.
16 Cs. Csapodi–Klara Csapodi–Gárdonyi, *Bibliotheca Corviniana* (Budapest 1969).
17 Bömer–Widmann in Milkau-Leyh, *Handbuch* 3/1², 521 n. 1.
18 C.F. Bühler, *The Fifteenth-Century Book: the Scribes, the Printers, the Decorators* (Philadelphia 1960) 34 ff.; O. Mazal, *Paläographie und Paläotypie. Zur Geschichte der Schrift im Zeitalter der Inkunabeln* (Stuttgart 1984); T. Brandis, 'Handschriften- und Buchproduktion im 15. und frühen 16. Jahrhundert'; L. Grenzmann–K. Stackmann (edd), *Literatur und Laienbildung im Spätmittelalter und in der Reformationszeit*, Symposion Wolfenbüttel 1981 (Stuttgart 1981) 176–193.

printed books, exactly along the lines of the manuscripts,[19] and into manuscripts (prayerbooks) engravings (printed) pictures were pasted.

But by 1470 at the latest, when the printing industry experienced a huge expansion, the twilight of the age of manuscripts was already at hand. Since the victory of the printed book was not to be halted, it could only be a well meaning but in the long run futile labour for abbot Johannes Trithemius (†1516), in his little book *De laude scriptorum manualium*[20] that he had printed in Mainz in 1494, to extoll once again the copying of books as a monastic occupation and to describe how the non-writing brothers could also participate in the creation of the book.

19 H.J. Hermann, *Die Handschriften und Inkunabeln der italienischen Renaissance*, 3. Beschreibendes Verzeichnis der illuminierten Handschriften in Österreich, 8 6 (Leipzig 1930–2).

20 I. Busaeus (ed.), *Iohannis Trithemii Spanhemensis opera pia et spiritualia* (Mainz 1604) 742–64; *Johannes Trithemius, De laude scriptorum. Zum Lobe der Schreiber*. Edited, with transl. and introd., by K. Arnold, Mainfränkische Hefte 60 (Würzburg 1973); *Johannes Trithemius, In Praise of Scribes*, ed. with introd. by K. Arnold, transl. by R. Behrendt (Lawrence, Kansas 1974).

Plates

1a.   ex]emplis ut hac casti maneant in (rel)igione nepotes et
maneat nostros ea cura nepo
tes et carosque nepotes et pugnent ipsique nepotesque et
centum conplexa nepotes et anne
aliquis magna de stirpe nepotum et animamque nepotis et
famamque et facta nepotum

1b.   IMMINET ET LENTAE TEXVNT VMBRACVLA
VITES
HVC ADES INSANI FERIANT SINE LITORA
FLVCTVS
QVID QVAE TE PVRA SOLVM SVB NOCTE
CANENTEM
AVDIERAM NVMEROS MEMINI SI VERBA
TENEREM
DAPHNI QVID ANTIQVOS SIGNORVM SVSPICIS
ORTVS

Bibliography: Florence, Biblioteca Laurentiana, pl. 39.1, f.6ᵛ. CLA III 296. Fols
222, 215 × 155 mm; 29 lines. Vergilius 'Mediceus' (*Ecl.* 9.42–10.2) + scholia. Complete
facsimile in E. Rostagno, *Il codice Mediceo di Virgilio*, 2 vols (Rome 1931).

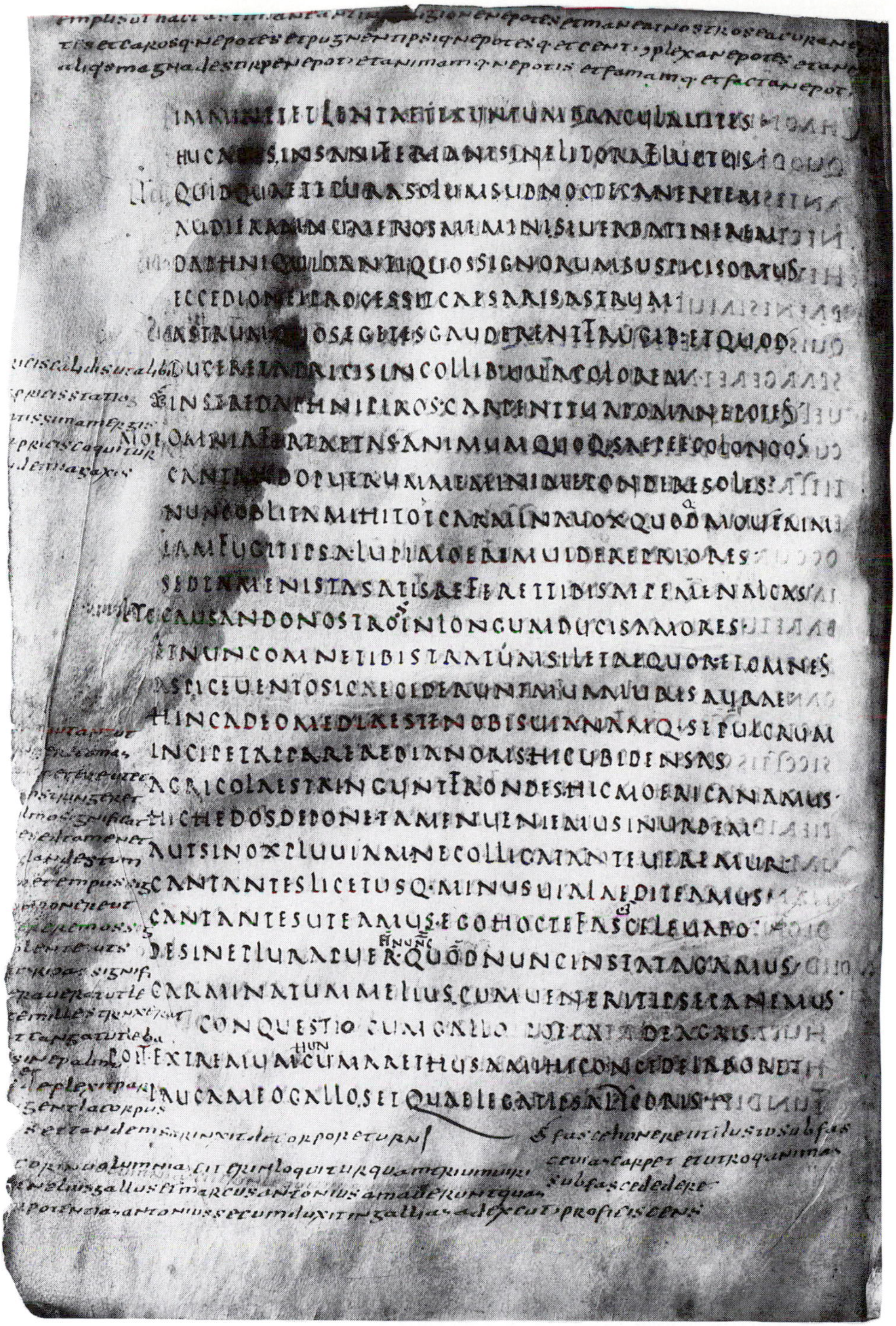

1. Capitalis, *ante* 494; sloping half-uncial (cf. pp 78, 184)

2a. SICVLORV]M VRBES SIGNIS MONVMENTISQVE
POP]VLI R · MAXIME · LAETARI · ARBITRABATVR
COL]LOCARET K · DENIQVE · ILLE · IPSE
MISERICORDIAM VICTI · FIDEM ·
SOCIIS IN EO BELLO CONSVLVIT VERVM
ETIAM ·

2b.] · TVM · IMPERI
QVE · PRAEFECTÍ
] · SATIS · POLLÉRENT
]VS · ATQVE · ANTIOCH[VS
GE]NERIS · DESPECTI ·

Bibliography: (2a) Giessen, Universitätsbibliothek, Pap. Jand. 90. CLA VIII 1201.
Fragm. c.160 × c.155 mm, 1 col.; 8 lines visible. Cicero, *In Verrem*, Actio II, II 3–4. R.
Seider, *Paläographie der lateinischen Papyri* 2/1, Nr. 1 (Stuttgart 1978) 31–33.
 (2b) London, British Library, Pap. 745. CLA II 207. One leaf, 87 × 52 mm, 10 lines.
Fragmentum *De bellis Macedonicis*. R. Grenfell-A.S. Hunt, *Oxyrhynchus Papyri* 1 (London
1898) 59–60.

2a.   Older roman cursive, s. I (cf. pp 57, 62)

2b.   Calligraphic roman majuscule, s. I–II (?) (cf. pp 9, 68, 69, 73, 182).

3.

]entia nostra dulcissi
]abilis gloria fruges uiuē
]e manducantes qui g(e)ne
]es prudentiae uictus
]fius hilara imago he

Bibliography: Manchester, John Rylands Library, Pap. 472. CLA S 1720. Fragm. 187 × 156 mm, 22 lines. Liturgical fragment. C.H. Roberts, *Catalogue of the Greek and Latin papyri in the John Rylands Library Manchester* 3 (Manchester 1938) 49–56.

3.   Older (eastern) half-uncial, s. IV (cf. p 74).

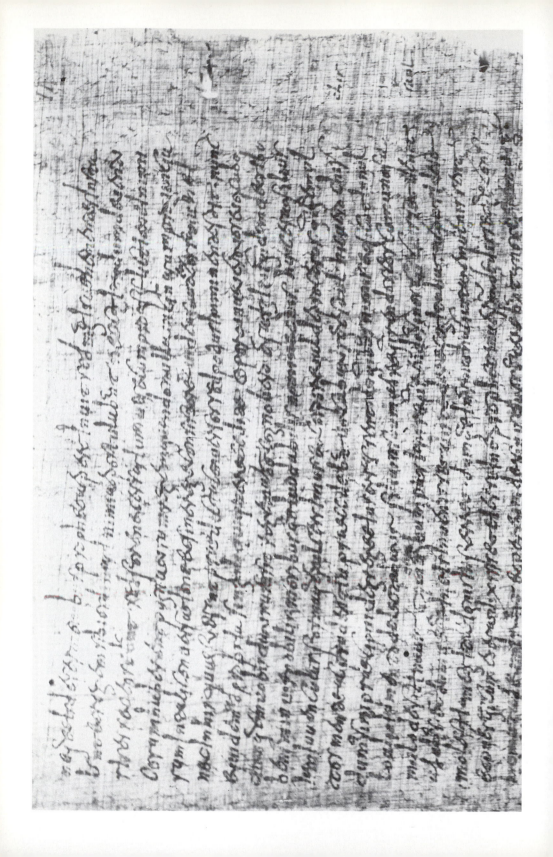

4. New roman cursive, s. VI (cf. pp 102, 182).

4. neque eis de sermonibus prophetae pertinuit sed magis uehementer insta
bant et regem sibi ordinari nimiae postulabant nec cogitandum de uentu
ris esse censebant sed fore necessarium uere cum pro afflictione inimi
corum haberent pugnaturum regem quando nulla uicinarum prouincia
rum in tali conversatione et sine rege consisteret uidens aut^{em} eos
samuhel

Bibliography: Milan, Biblioteca Ambrosiana, Cim. MS. 1, p. 11. CLA III 304. Fols
92, 340 × 240 mm, 30–39 lines. Josephus, *De antiquitatibus Iudaicis* VI 3–4. R. Seider,
Paläographie der lateinischen Papyri 2/1, Nr. 67, 163–5.

5 col. 2 DUM AUTEM HAEC AGERENTUR
AUDINI FILIUS QUI LIBRUM IPSUM
PROTULERAT IPSA DIE A FEBRE
CORREPTUS DIE TERTIA EXPIRA
UIT. POST HAEC NOS TRANSMI[SIMUS

Bibliography: Vatican, Biblioteca Apostolica, MS. Reg.Lat. 689 bis, f. 324^V. CLA I
107. Fols 7, 310 × 265 mm, 2 cols, 31 lines. Gregory of Tours, *Historia Francorum* IX 30.

...us obnixis igy
...rex hanc urbem
...ecolli ins tribu
...sin...uit sic
...uit animo chil
...us post patris
...regnans nihil
...ecullo tribuit
...ecurbs ad gra
...eouit nunc
...otestatis uestrae
...incenseatis tri
...in non seduidi
...quid noceatis
...eius sacramen
...ulare dispontius
...dicente respon
...ecellibrum prae
...habimus in quo
...quic populo est in
...eteco aio liber
...ist thesauro de la
...est nec umquam
...onuallis tan nos
...mirum enim si pro
...shorum ciuium
...eus est iudicauit
...super eos qui pro
...uium nostrorum
...etantitemporis
...eospatioprotuleru...

DUMAUTEMHAECAGERENTUR
AUDINITIUS QUILIBRUMIPSI
PROTULERAT IPSADIE ...FEBRE
CORREPTUS DIETERTIA EXPIRA
UIT POSTHAECNOSTRANS MI
SIMUS NUNTIOS ADREGEM
UTQUIDDEHACCAUSANUBERET
MANDATAREMITTERET SED
PROTINUS EPISTULAM CUMM
AUCTORITATE MISERUNTNEPO
PULUSTORONICUSPROREUE
RENTIASCIMARTINIDISCRIBI
RITUR QUIBUSRELICTIS STATI
UIRIQUIADHAECMISSIFUERAN
ADPATRIAMSUNTREGRESSI
XXI GUNTHCHRAMNUS...
EXERCITUMCOMMOUITINSEP
TIMANIAM AUSTROUALDUS
AUTEMDUXPRIUS CARCASSO
NAMACCEDENS SACRAMEN
TASUSCIPIRAT IPSOSQPOPU
LOSDITIONISUBEGERAT REGIAE
REXAUTEMADRELIQUAS CIUI
TATES CAPIENDAS BOSONEM
CUMANTESTIODISTINAT QUI
ACCEDENS CUMSUPERBIA
DISPECTOAUSTROUALDODUCE
ATQ CONDEMNATO CURABSQ
EO CARCASSONAMINGREDI
PRAESUMPSISSET IPSECUM
SANCTONICIS PETROCORICIS

5.   Uncial, s. VII (cf. pp 153, 196).

Ideo habentes hanc ministrationem iux
ta quod misericordiam consecuti sumus
non deficimur sed abdicamus occulta
dedecoris non ambulantes in astutia ne
que adulterantes uerbum...

6. Palimpsest. Lower script: late half-uncial, s. VII. Upper script: Visigothic minuscule, s. IX (cf. pp 25, 96, 193)

6a.   Ideo habentes hanc ministrationem iux
col. i   ta quod misericordiam consecuti sumus
non deficimus sed abdicamus occulta
dedecoris non ambulantes in astutia ne
que adulterantes uerbum dei sed manifes[tatione

6b.   Tamquam in heresim declinantes et litteras mittit quibus omnes si
mul absque discretione ab ecclesiastico federe segregaret. Sed
hoc non omnibus placebat episcopis quin potius et e contra
rio scribentes iubebant ut magis que pacis sunt agerent et
concordie adque unianimitati studerent. Denique ex

Bibliography: León, Archivio Cathedralicio, MS. 15, f.84^v. CLA xi 1636. Fols 185, c. 444 × 320 mm, 2 cols, 72–76 lines. Lower script: Biblia: 2 Cor 4:2–13; 5:10–6:5. Upper script: Eusebius-Rufinus, *Historia Ecclesiastica* V 24, 9–14. B. Fischer, 'Ein neuer Zeuge zum westlichen Text der Apostelgeschichte', in J.N. Birdsall & R.W. Thomson (edd), *Biblical and patristic studies in memory of Robert Pierce Casey* (Freiburg 1963) 33–62.

7, 6–7   XXII De his* qui non uoluntate sed cassu homicidium
perpetrauerunt
----
* his *corr. ex* hiis

12–15   canones anciritanes
ISti canones priores quidem sunt nicenis kanonibus
expositis sed tamen niceni primo accepti sunt
propter auctoritatem sancti et magni concilii quod factum est in
niceam

Bibliography: Cologne, Diözesan- u. Dombibliothek, MS. 213, f. 19^v. CLA VIII
1163. Fols 143, 328 × 230, 22–25, 27 long lines. Collectio canonum Sanblasiana. R.
McKitterick, 'Knowledge of canon law in the Frankish kingdoms before 789: the manuscript
evidence', *Journal of Theological Studies*, n.s., 36 (1985) 110–14.

xxiii De his qui uirginitatem pollicita prnceuam(?)
caeasunt prpessione contempta

xxiiii Si quis adulterium commiserit

xx De mulieribus q̄ fornicantur et partus suos necant

xxi De his qui uoluntarie homicidium fecerint

xxii De his qui nōuoluntate sed casu homicidium
perpetrauerint

xxiii De his qui auguria auspicia uel diuinationesqu
ci aba secundum more gentium obseruant

xxiiii Si quis sponsam habens sorori eius fornicari
uoluerit uiolentiam expli tituli incipiunt
canones anicitia ies

Zi canonis priores quidesm sunt nichil sp kanonib:
expositur sed tamen nichil primo accepta sunt
propter auctoritatem ysn et magni concilii quod factum est inniceam

7. Anglo-Saxon half-uncial, minuscule, cursive minuscule, s. VIII (cf. p 91).

8 col.1,   iob Ingredieris in habundan

1–5   dantia sepulcrum sicut infertur acer
uus tritici in tempore suo. Gregorius.
Quid enim sepulcri nomine nisi contemplati
ua signatur quae nos quasi ab hoc mundo mortuos

col.2,   discipulus qui testimonium perhibuit ueritati de his et scripsit haec

20–21 et scimus quia uerum est testimonium eius sunt au[tem

Bibliography: Dublin, Trinity College, MS. 52 'Book of Armagh', f. 103^r. CLA II 270. Fols 215, 195 × 145 mm, 2 cols, 34–40 lines. Novum Testamentum, Patriciana, Martiniana. Left: *Moralia* VI 37, 56 (MPL 75, 760); right: *Moralia* V 6, 9 (MPL 75, 684); centre: *Evang. Ioh.* 21: 20–5. J. Gwynn, *Liber Ardmachanus, the Book of Armagh* (Dublin 1913); E. Gwynn, *Book of Armagh, the Patrician documents* (Dublin 1937); R. Sharpe, 'Palaeographical considerations in the study of the Patrician documents in the Book of Armagh', *Scriptorium* 36 (1982) 3–28.

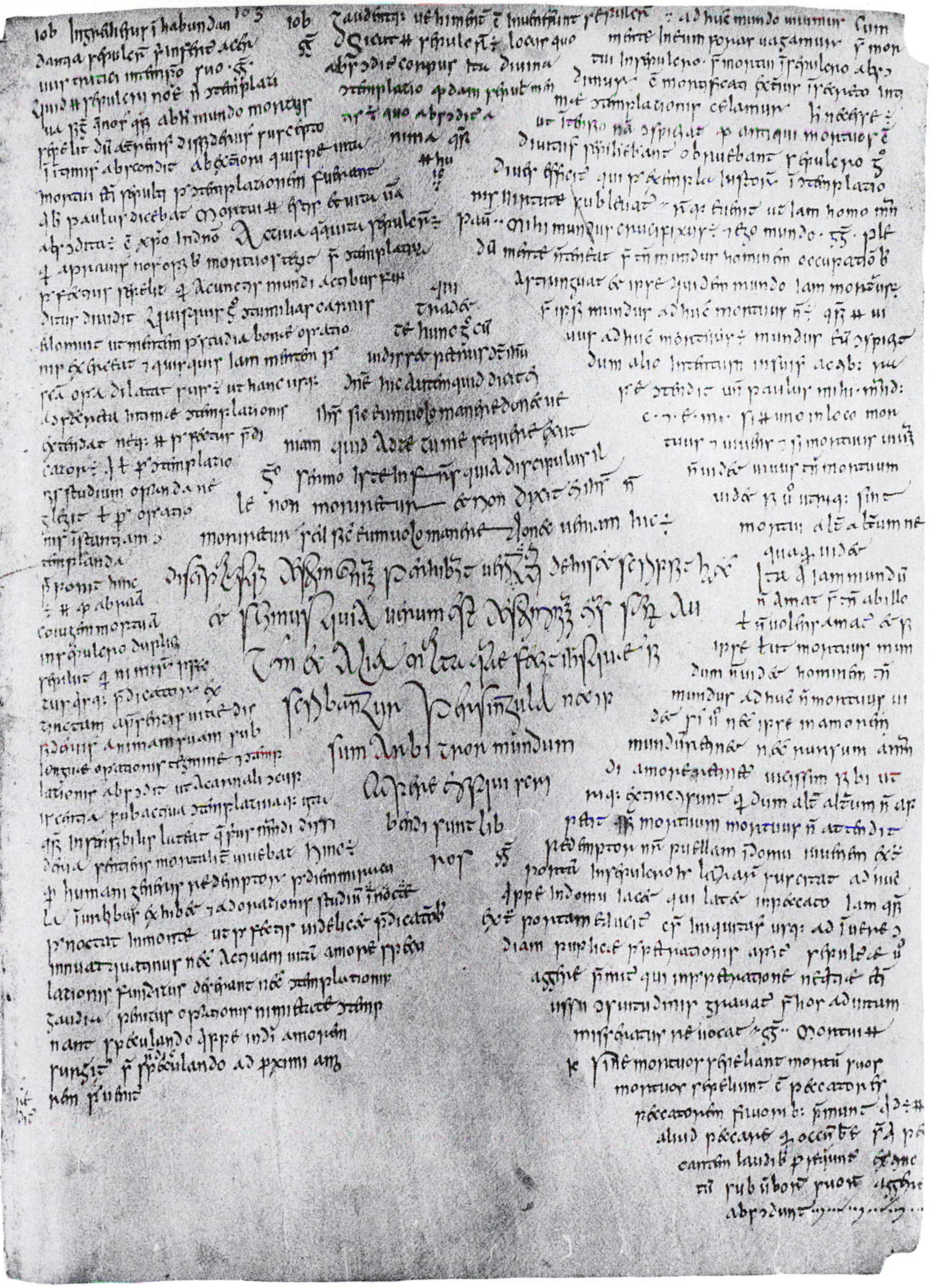

8. Irish cursive minuscule, ca. 807 (cf. pp 86, 198).

9. quod iusta remissio poterat expiare. Redeant* ergo in suum
statu uolontaria. redintegratione coniugia neque ullo modo
ad opproprium male uolontatis trahatur. quod conditio neces
sitatis extorsit. quoniam sicut hae mulieres quae reuerti ad uiros
suos noluerunt impiae sunt habendae. ita ille quae in affec[tum

---

*R *corr. ex* S

Bibliography: Verona, Biblioteca Capitolare, MS. LXII (60) f.84ʳ. CLA IV 512.
Fols 99, 290 × 177 mm, 25–29 lines. Cresconius, *Concordia canonum* c. 226 (MPL 88, 918).
E. Camsi – W.M. Lindsay, *Monumenta paleografici Veronesi* 2 (Vatican 1934) p. 7, pl. 33.

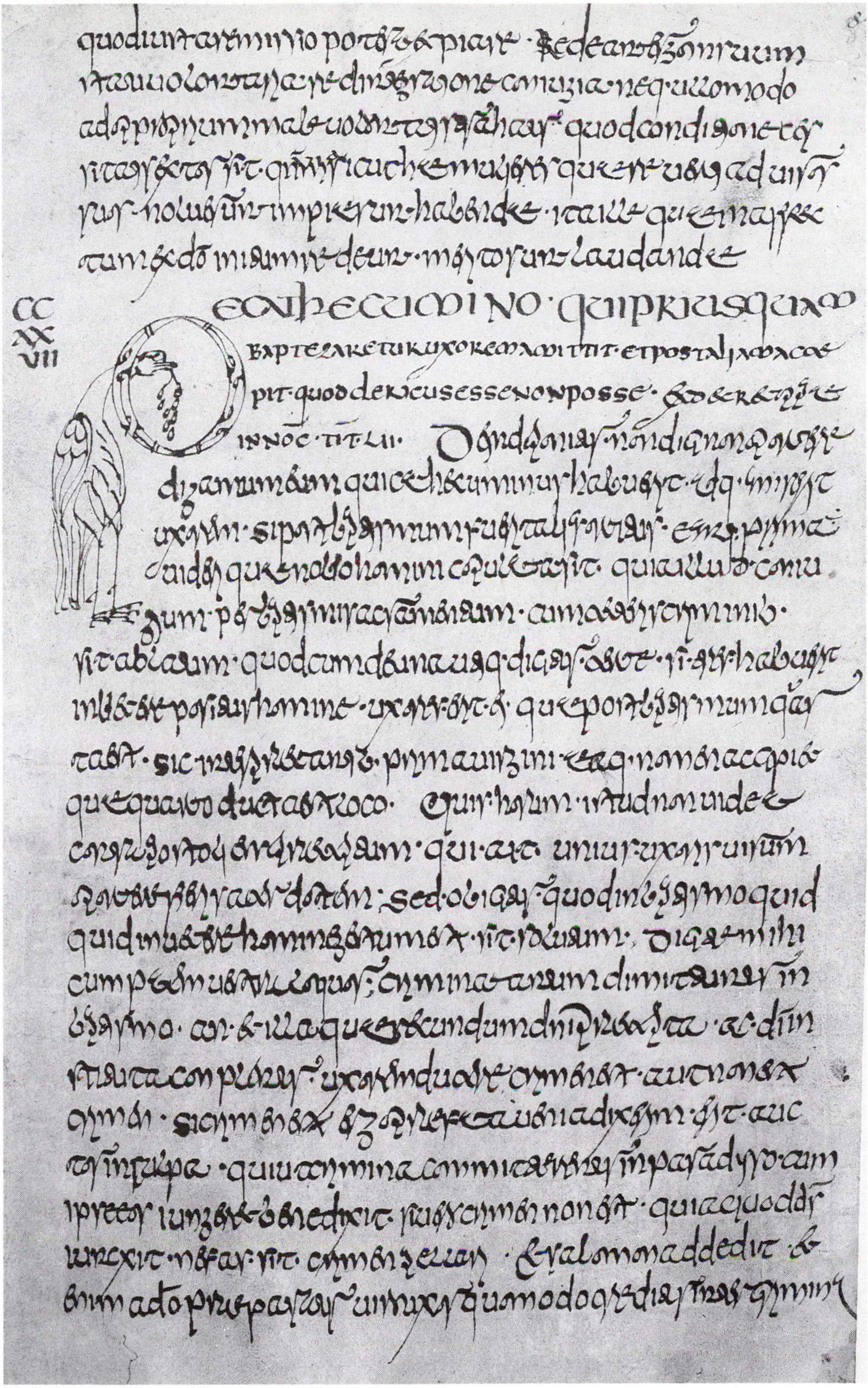

9. Cursive minuscule (Italian), s. VIII (cf. p 102).

10 col.1,Austroaldus sigalis I. splenis I. auenae I.
3–7   Leodo tridici I. splenis I. ordei I. semis
        Arnegisilus ordei I.
        Aunobertus tridici II. ordei I. unigrania I.
        Chadolenus tridici I. auenae I. *De uilla**

----

        *Nota Tironiana

Bibliography: Paris, Bibliothèque Nationale, Nouv.Acq.Lat. 2654, Nr. 11. ChLA XVIII 659. P. Gasnault & J. Vezin (edd), *Documents comptables de Saint-Martin de Tours à l'époque mérovingienne*. Collection de documents inédits sur l'histoire de France (Paris 1975) 53.

10.   Cursive minuscule (French), s. VII.

11,   t]estimonium   sed quando glorificatus est dominus iesus tunc recor
marg.,   er]go perhibebat   dati sunt. quia haec erant scribta de eo. et haec
text   tur]ba que erat   fecerunt ei.
       cu]m eo quando   XXXIII LEGENDUM IN AUTENTICA
                             EBDOMADA
       la]zaro uo[cabit] SECUNDA FERIA AD MATUTINOS

Bibliography: Paris, Bibliothèque Nationale, MS. Lat. 9427, f.96^v. CLA v 579. Fols 246, 285 × 180, 22 lines. Lectionarium Luxoviense. P. Salmon, *Le lectionnaire de Luxeuil.* Collectanea Biblica Latina 7, 9 (Rome 1944, 1953) 82–83. E.K. Rand–L.W. Jones, *The earliest book of Tours, with supplementary descriptions of other manuscripts of Tours.* Studies in the script of Tours 2 (Cambridge, Mass. 1934) 55, pl. XXXIV.

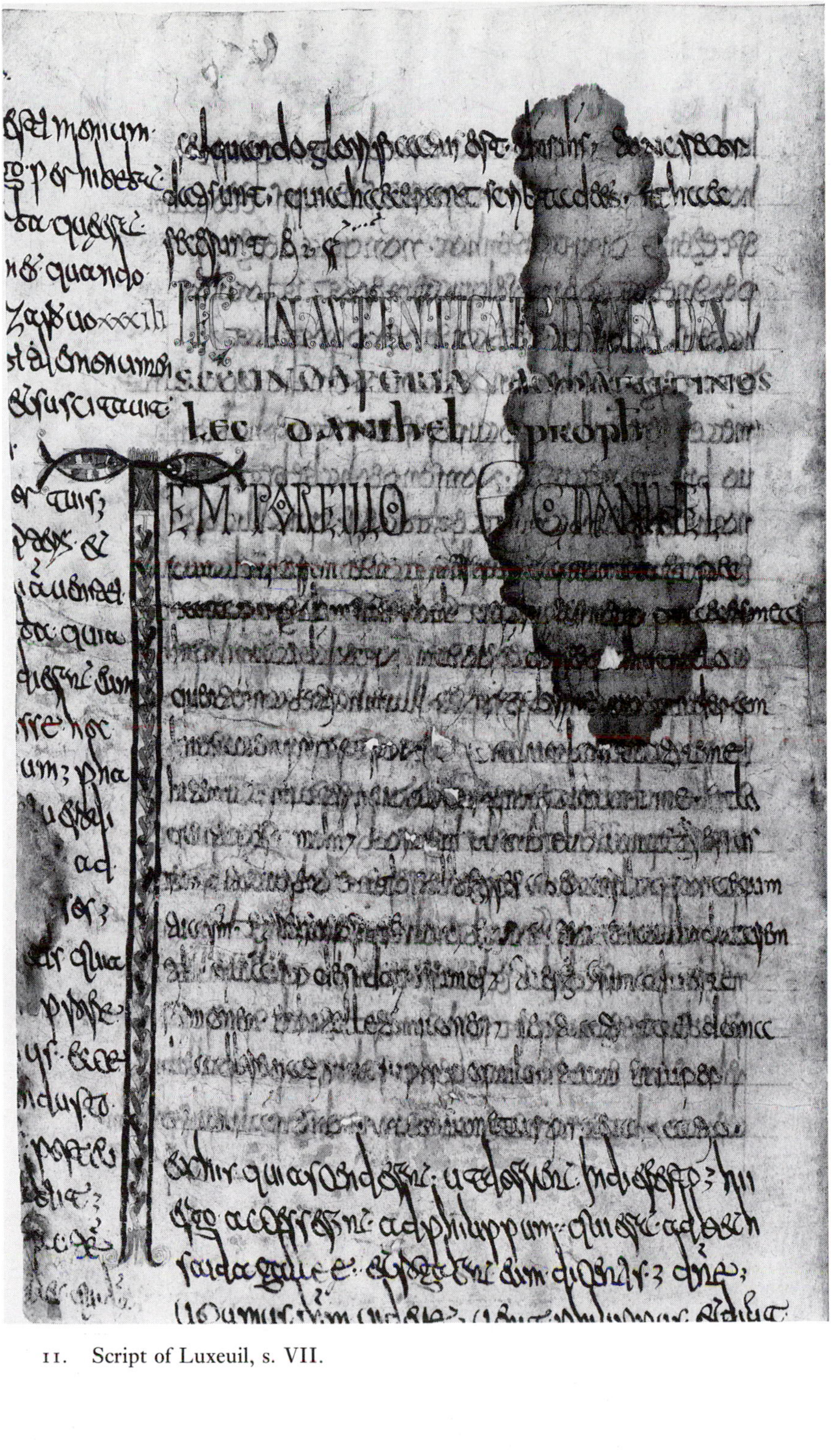

11. Script of Luxeuil, s. VII.

12.   APOLOGYTICUM TERTULLIANI
col.1/2 I DE IGNORANTIA IN CHRISTO IESU
        S I N O N
        licet uobis romani imperii
        antistites in aperto et edito

Bibliography: Leningrad, Publichnaya Biblioteka im. M.E. Saltikova-Shchedrina, MS. Q.v.I.40, f.1ʳ. Fols 61, 205 × 170 mm, 2cols, 21 lines. Tertullian, *Apologeticum* c. 1, 1–3. A. Staerk, *Les manuscrits latins de la Bibliothèque Impériale de St. Petersbourg* (St Petersburg 1911) 130–31; B. Bischoff, *Mittelalterliche Studien* 3 (Stuttgart 1981) 160.

DE IGNORANTIA INXPO IHV

SINON

licet uobis romani imperii
antistites inaperto & edito
ipso fere uertice ciuitatis prae
sidentibus ad iudicandum palam
dispicere &coram examina
re quid sit liquido incausa
xpianorum · siad hanc solam
speciem auctoritas uestra

Nihil decausa sua deprecatur.
quia nec deconditione mira
tur; scit se peregrinam in
terris agere. inter extrane
os facile inimicos inuenire
Ceterum genus. sedem. spem
gratiam. dignitatem incaelis
habere. unum gestit inter
dum. neignorata damnetur·
Quid hic deperit legibusin suo
regno dominantibus. siaudia
tur. An hoc magis gloriabi

12.   Caroline minuscule, s. VIII–IX (cf. p 204).

13. te mirabiliter dextera tua. Sagitte tue
acute potentissime. populi sub te cadent. In
corda inimicorum regis. Sedes tua deus in seculum
seculi. uirga recta est uirga regni tui. Di
lexisti iustitiam et odisti iniquitatem. propterea

Bibliography: Naples, Biblioteca Nazionale, MS. VI.E.43, f.103ᵛ. Fols 283, 245 × 155 mm, 30 lines. Breviarium. E.A. Lowe, *Scriptura Beneventana* (Oxford 1929) pl. 81; idem, *The Beneventan script* (Rome 1980) 1, 67; 2, 101.

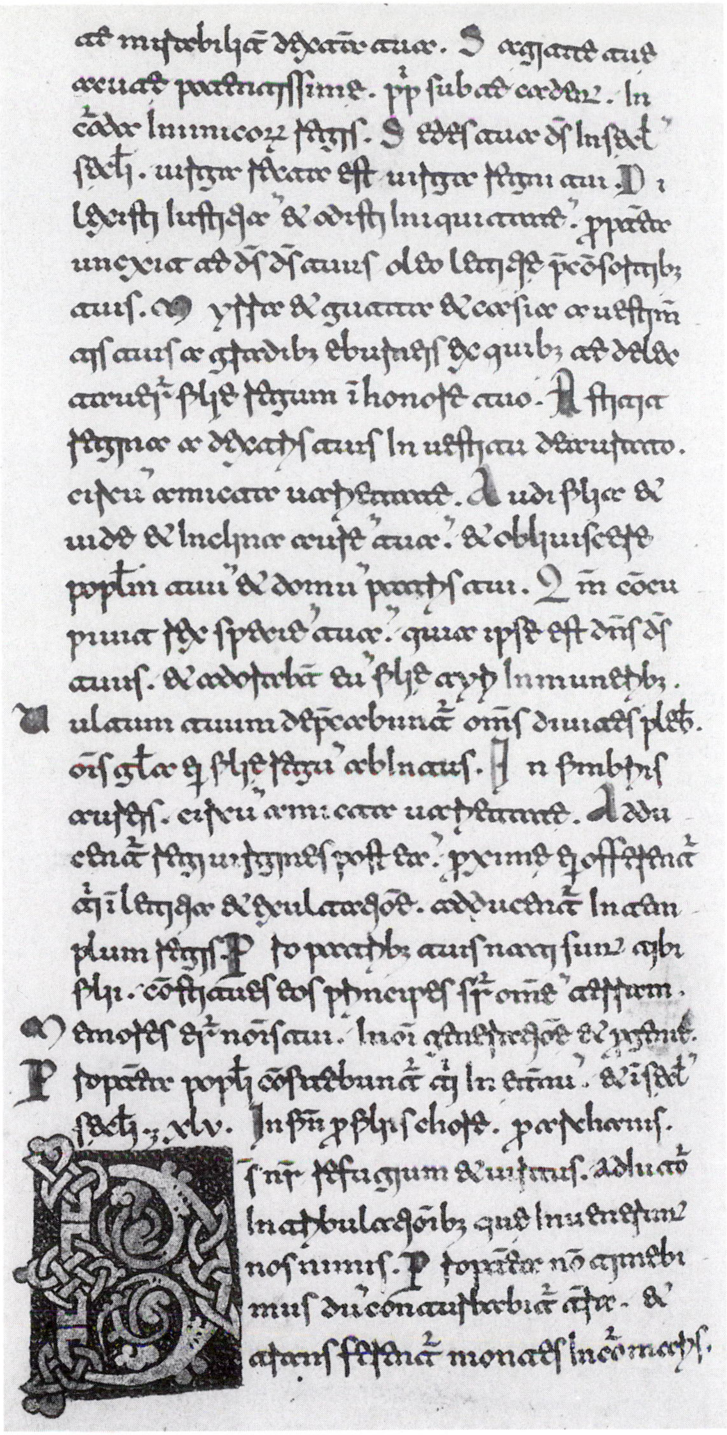

13. Beneventan script, 1099–1118.

14. la]pidem. qui portare debuerat iugum domini. Asi
nus ergo ad molam. caecus ad lapidem. genti
lis ad saxum. qui adorat eum quem non ui
det nec agnoscit. Deus enim non in manu
factis habitat. nec in metallo aut saxo cog[noscitur

Bibliography: Berlin, Staatsbibliothek Preussischer Kulturbesitz, MS. Theol.lat.fol. 270, f.224ᵛ. Fols 249, 380 × 250 mm, 2 cols. Homiliary of Lach, copied by Lambert of Affligem. Maximus of Turin, *Sermo* 48 (CCSL 23, 190); *Sermo in sollemnitate omnium sanctorum* (MPL 94, 452). V. Rose, *Verzeichnis der lateinischen Handschriften der königlichen Bibliothek zu Berlin* 2/1 (Berlin 1901) 136–150.

pidem : qui portare debuerat iugum dñi. Asi
nus ergo ad molam. cecus ad lapidem. genti
lis ad saxum : qui adorat eum quem non ui
det nec agnoscit. Ds enim non in manufa
ctis habitat : nec in metallo aut saxo cog
noscit. hic ergo gentilis populus cum psecu
tionem xpiano intulerit. hac plectit : ut
cum sua sacrilega mola iudicandi seculi
fluctibus dimergatur. DE ROGA IN

Rabani Archiepiscopi.

SOLLEOPNITATE

OONNIVOS SCORVOS.

egimus in ecclesiasticis
hystoriis. quod scs bonefacius qui quartus
a beato gregorio romane urbis episcopatum
tenebat. suis precibus a foca cesare impetrarit
donari eccłe xpi templũ rome. quod ab anti
quis pantheon ante uocabatur. quia hoc quasi
simulachrũ omniũ uideretur esse deorum :
in quo eliminata omni spurcitia. fecit eccłam
sce̊ di genitricis marie. atq̃ omniũ martyrũ
xpi : ut exclusa multitudine demonũ. multi
tudo ibi scõrum in memoria haberetur : et
plebs uniuersa in capite kalendarum nouem
brium. sicut in die natalis dñi ad eccłam in
honore omniũ scõx consecratam conueniret :
ibiq̃ missarum sollempnitate a presule sedis
aplice celebrata. omnib; q̃ rite pactis. unuscq̃
in sua cum gaudio remearet. Ex hac ergo con
suetudine sce̊ romane eccłe. crescente religione
xpiana decretum est : ut in ecclesiis di que per

14.   Transitional script, s. XII.

15.   nostre salutis auxilium   P V Er
col. 1/2 peruenire concede. per   NA
         Prephacio. Quia per incarna   TVS
         ti uerbi. Et. Communicantes. ut   Est
         supra. Communicacionem.   nobis et
                                    filius datus

Bibliography: Munich, Bayerische Staatsbibliothek, Clm 10072, f.13ᵛ. Fols 272. Missale Romanum copied at Bologna in 1374.

15. Gothic Textualis (Rotunda), 1374.

16a.   (Assit principio sancta maria meo)
Text   MAxima cognicio na
         ture et sciencia demon
         strans ipsam est in corporibus
         et in aliis magnitu
         dinibus et in passionibus et in mo[tibus

16b.   Comm.
         inquid quod aristotiles intendebat per motus motus locales
         quibus non mutatur sunstancia rei mote. et intendebat per
         passiones mutaciones. quibus mutatur substancia rei. et com
         plementum istarum transmutacionum sunt qualitates sensibiles
         et quomodocumque sint. isti sermones propinqui sunt. Deinde

Bibliography: Oxford, Balliol College, MS. 244, f.2^r. Fols 134, 360 × 233 mm, 31 lines of text, 62 lines of gloss. Averroes, *In Aristotelis Libro de caelo*. Copied by Richard of Manchester for William de Mundham in 1308. R.A.B. Mynors, *Catalogue of the manuscripts of Balliol College Oxford* (Oxford 1963) 265–66.

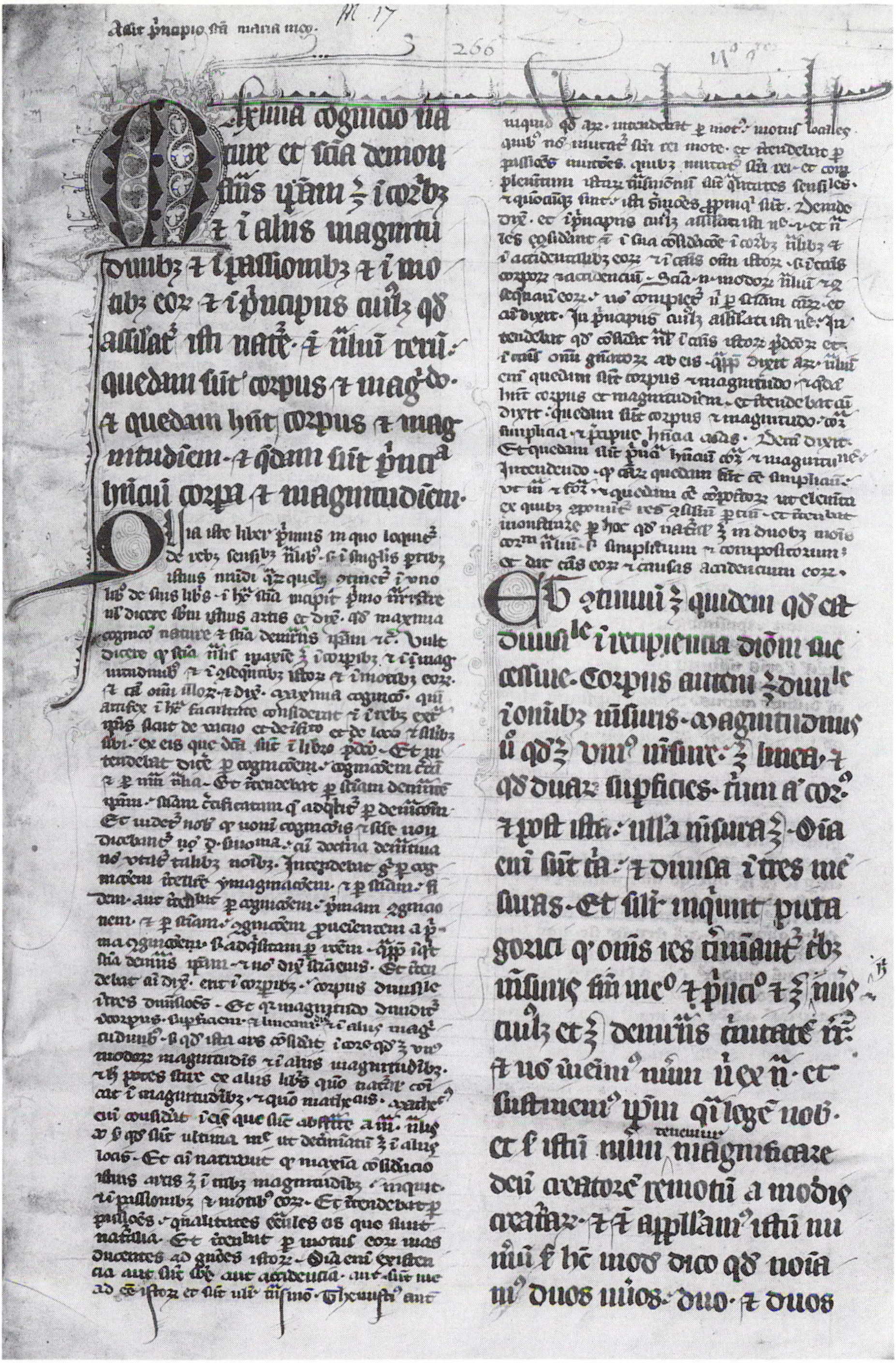

16. Gothic Textualis, 1308.

17 col.1,73 (line 21 from below)
    confitendo 6⁰ Utrum possit confessio differri 7⁰ Utrum
    veniale teneamur confiteri . . . 1 isa(ie)

17 col.2, 51–59 (lines 47–39 from below)
    in generali de venialibus . . . emendare § Circa 5(?) medicus
    corporalis necesse habet inquirere omnes circumstancias
    corporis ergo plus spiritualis item
    bonus rethor in foro non solum que . . . . . sunt sed nichil
    ommittit
    de contingentibus. ergo . . . . cuilibet . . . . . in foro penitencie
    quia contingencia(?) . . . sciri non prost (= prodest ?)
    contra infinite sunt et . . . . . . nec possunt omnes ad
    memoriam sed . . . .
    requiret circumstans esset confitendum . . . .
    Respond . . quod circumstancie . . . d . . .
    trahunt in genus peccati et he confitende . . . . vel sol . .
    omnes
    que agrauant rem(?) sunt confitende quia qualitas emende debet
    esse secundum
    qualitatem et quantitatem culpe.

Bibliography: Paris, Bibliothèque Nationale, MS. Lat. 15652. f.77ʳ. Fols. 221
295 × 200 mm, 2 cols, at least 90 lines. The volume contains various booklets of different
dimensions. Augustinus, *De LXXXVI Quaestionibus, Reportationes variae, De Libro
Appolloni regis Tyri*, Tullius, *De divinatione* (Tusculans). Plate shows *Distinctiones 18–20 in
Sententiis A. Putheorumvilla* (A. de Pouzolles). M. Chenu, *Maîtres et bacheliers de l'Université
de Paris v. 1240. Description du manuscrit Paris, Bibl.Nat.lat. 15652.* Études d'histoire
littéraire et doctrinale du XIIIᵉ siècle (Paris-Ottawa 1932) 11–39

17.   Gothic cursive, s. XIII (cf. p 138).

18a.   Dom]inus illuminacio mea
col.1   sal]us mea quem timebo
         do]minus protector vite
            a quo trepidabo. Dum
         adpro]piant super me nocen[tes

18b.   Miserere mei deus secundum magnam
col.2   misericordiam tuam Et secundum
         multitudinem miseracionem tuarum. dele
         iniquitatem meam Amplius laua
         me ab iniquitate mea et a peccato

Bibliography: s'Gravenhage (The Hague), Königliche Bibliothek, MS. 76 D 45, IV A. Advertisement sheet of Hermann Strepel, 1447. Ps. 26: 1–2; Ps. 50: 2–4; *Salve regina*. G. Lieftinck, *Manuscrits datés conservés dans les Pays-Bas: Catalogue paléographique des manuscrits en ecriture latine portant des indications de date* (Amsterdam 1964) No. 90, p. 38. The attribution to Münster is questioned by W. Oeser, 'Die Brüder des Gemeinsamen Lebens in Münster als Bücherschreiber', *Archiv für Geschichte des Buchwesens* 5 (1962) 197–398: cols 251–2.

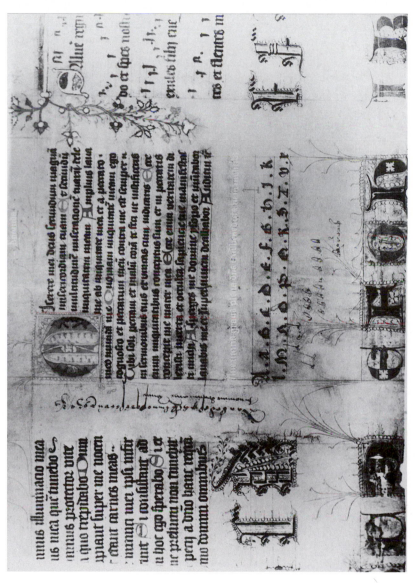

18. Gothic scripts: Textualis, 'lettres cadeaux', initials, Lombards, notation, 1447.

ꝛ ans anꝰ sm ansaugnidinonen
abccdeefghiklm . ansmgmdino
ansmgmdni aamsingndnomen
ansmgn aabbccdid☙ defi
ansmgn dinonanennpnenam
. emonans . an maria mater gra tmate

. aabbcdoid☙ ā . ansi an
ana m maria t mata t hec dies no p
ansmgmdminanenampnenenmane
abccr aꝝ aabbct ddefghikl
a . abccabcddoeffgghiklm
aaaabbcddd defgg
. aaabccddefgghikkmnopp
ū a..arbcddefgghik

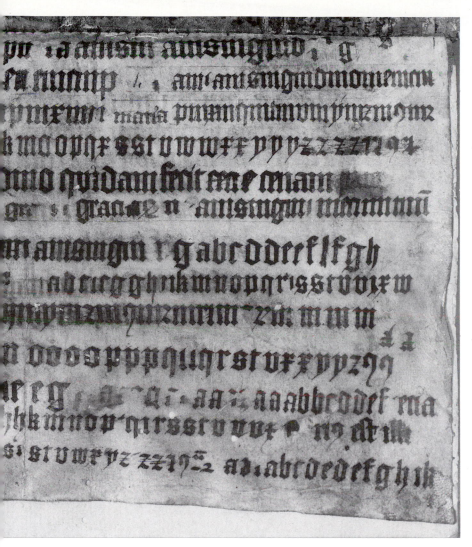

19. Gothic Textura, s. XV (cf. p 39). Lucerne, Zentralbibl., MS. Pap. 25, flyleaf. Writing exercises.

20.   Pater tuus et ego; De eodem.
        dolentes querebamus te et cetera
        ¶Illud quod est maxime causa recuperationis
        rei perdite est solicitudo inquisitionis luce   Querite
        et inuenietis et cetera Ratio enim sumitur per opositum quia res

Bibliography: Padua, Biblioteca Antoniana, Cod. XXI.508, f.13^r. G. Abate & G. Luisetto, *Codici e manoscritti della Biblioteca Antoniana col catalogo delle miniature*, 2 vols (Vicenza 1975) 511. *Introductiones dominicales* (Luc. 2:48, etc.).

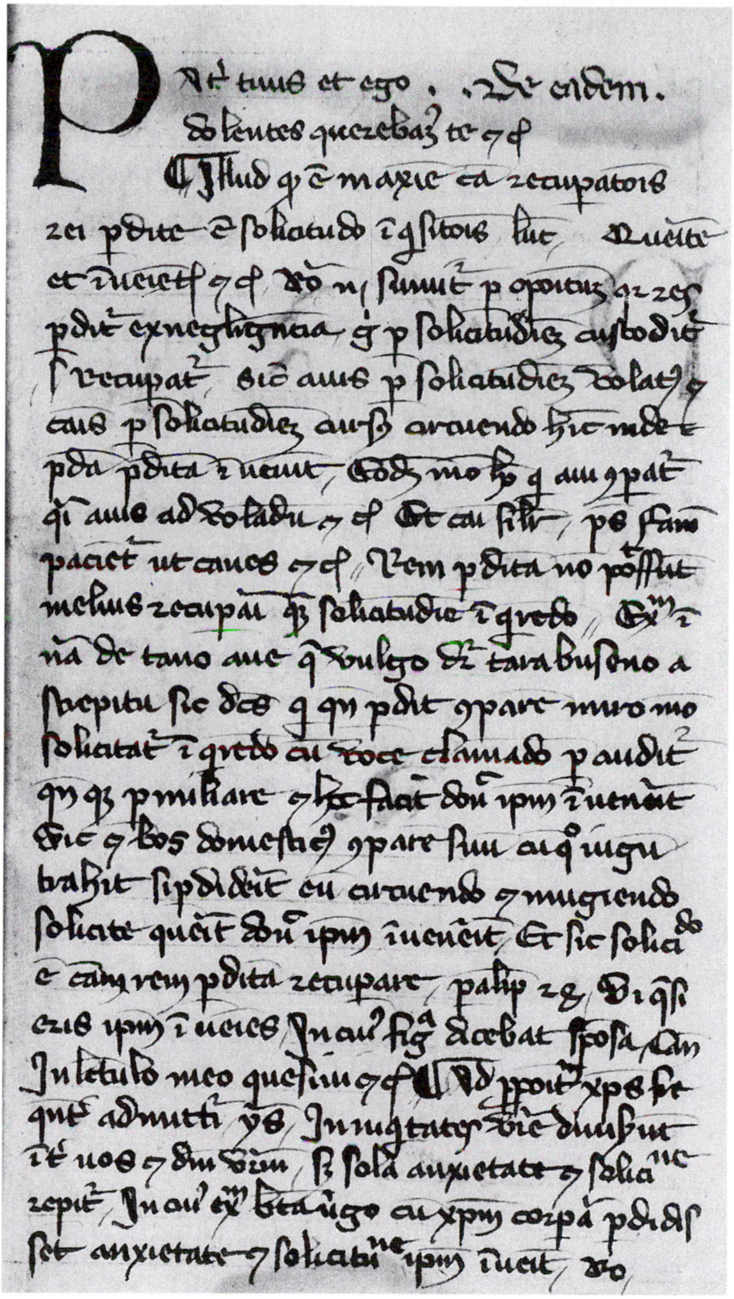

20. Gothic cursive, 1391.

21.   positus sum et liberare.   Et tu
         domine qui genus humanum
         cum in custodia recepisti et
         omni credulitate deposita in
         paradisum cum proprio san]guine

Bibliography: Vienna, Österreichische Nationalbibliothek, Cod. Lat. 1929, f.137ᵛ. Fols 154, 177 × 123 mm, 17 lines. Book of Hours in Latin and French copied between 1458 and 1473 for the daughters of Charles VII of France. O. Pächt-D. Thoss, *Die illuminierten Handschriften und Inkunabeln der Österreichischen Nationalbibliothek* 1, Französische Schule 1 (Vienna 1974) 29–32.

politus sum et liberare. Et tu
domine qui genus humanu
cum in custodia recepisti et
omni arduitate depositum in
paradisum cum proprio san
guine mercatus es. Et inter
homines et angelos fecisti pa
cem. Tu domine dignare
cum tua misericordia inter
me et inter inimicos meos sta
bilire et firmare concordiam
et veram pacem et gratiam tu
am semper michi ostende li
berare etiam me digneris de
omni tribulatione et angustia
in qua politus sum et de insi
diis inimicorum meorum. Et

21. Bastard ('Bourguigonne'), s. XV.

POMERIVM DICITVR HOC OPVS COMPILATVM

8–11   Instantiae tuae uenerande pater
ac domine Michael Rauennatis
ecclesiae archidiacone abruere ne
queo qui non ut appetitui tuo satis[faciat

Bibliography: Berlin, Deutsche Staatsbibliothek, MS. Hamilton 570, f. 1ʳ. Fols 224, 335 × 230 mm, 31 lines. Venice c. 1470. Riccobaldus Ferrariensis, *Pomerium Ravennatis Ecclesiae*. H. Boese, *Die lateinischen Handschriften der Sammlung Hamilton zu Berlin* (Wiesbaden 1966) 279.

POMERIVM . DICITVR . HOC . OPVS . CŌPILATVM
STVDIO . ET . LABORE . RICOBALDI . FERARIENSIS
ANNO . CRISTI . MCCLXXXXVII . QVIA . SICVT
POMERIA . FIVNT . AD . OBLECTAMENTA . VISVS .
ET . GVSTVS . ITA . HOC . OPVS . EST ÆDITVM . AD .
IOCNDITATEM . ANIMI . ET . CORPORIS . PER FRVC
TS . EXEMPLER . RER . GESTAR . INCIPIT . FOELICTER ..

Nstante tue uenerande pater
ac domine michael Rauennatis
ecclesie archidiacone abnuere ne
queo qui non ut appetitu tuo satis
faciat me ad hoc impellis, sed quibus
dam mediocriter litteratis elubrare
studiam cronicum beati hyeronimi
opus quod marachiuo Rauennantis
ecclesie sorduerat obsoletu tamen quia
artificiose contextum, tum quia eius scp
ur peruetuste unaqueq, lincola una i
dictio uidentur Vtq, ipsi operi auctentica
memorie digna inferam . Que & iocis ac se
rys legentium animos alliciant dum legunt .
porro mihi persuadendo persuades opere pretia
ore nos modernos qui a priscis uiris tanta multi
plicium rerum emolumenta percepimus pręteri
ti aliquid utilitatis afferre opi quidem maiorum
sumptibus & laboribus nostre utilitati sunt urbiu
menia basilice edes publice deriuationes fluminu
arborum sactiones liberalium artium monumenta ut
inquam tue obtempero uisioni . Ceterum codicis seriem
intellectu difficilem & ad transferendum membranis dispe
diosam uiderent seriei ordinem mutare decreui pluta que

22. Humanistic minuscule, ca. 1470.

23,   Ad Illustrissimum Principem et Excellen
lines   tissimum dominum. dominum Borsium Clarissimum
1/2,   - - - - -
9–11   sapientia fu reputato. Le cui famosiss^ime lege
           suono anchora a li presenti huomini chiara
           testimonianza de la anticha Iusticia Era

Bibliography: Berlin, Deutsche Staatsbibliothek, MS. Hamilton 112. Fols 61, 215 × 140 mm, 21 lines. Bornius de Sale, *Liber de virtutibus*. Boese, *Die lateinischen Hss.*, 64.

Ad Illustrissimum Principem z Excellen-
tissimum dominu. dnm Borsiuz Clarissiuz
Ducem Mutine ac Regij Rodiggij ez Co-
mitem ac Marchionem Esten. zc.:—

SOLONE IL CVI E-
BVRNEO PECTO
VNO HVMANO
TEMPLO DE DIVINA

sapientia, fu reputato Le cui famosissme lege
suono anchora a li presenti huomini chiara
testimonianza, de la anticha Iusticia Era
segondo che dicono alcuni spesse volte vsa-
to de dire. Ogni Principato Republica,
ouer regimento si come noi andare et
stare sopra, doi pedi Diquali cum matura
grauita affirmaua, il destro non Lasciare
alcun diffecto comesso impunito et il sini-
stro ogni ben facto remunerare agiungen-
do che qualuncha de le doe cose gia decte
per vitio o per negligentia sottraeua
et men che ben si seruaua, senza num
dubio quella Re pu. chel-facto

23. Humanistic cursive, s. XV.

Bibliography

This summary list of bibliographical references follows in the main the order in which the subjects concerned are discussed in the text, with this difference, that the references on the history of script are placed at the beginning.

Periodicals, bibliographies, collected papers

LEONARD E. BOYLE, *Medieval Latin palaeography, a bibliographical introduction*. Toronto 1984. Very important.

Palaeographia Latina. Ed. by W.M. LINDSAY. 1–6, Oxford 1922–9.

Scriptorium. Revue Internationale des études rélatives aux manuscrits, Brussels 1946/7 ff.

Bullettino dell' Archivio Paleografico Italiano. 1–5, Perugia 1908–18. n. s. 1–4/5, Rome 1955–8/9. ser 3, 1 ff., 1962 ff.

Studie o rukopisech, Prague 1962 ff.

Revue d'histoire des textes, Paris 1971 ff.

Codices manuscripti, Vienna 1976 ff.

Scrittura e Civiltà, Turin 1977 ff.

Italia Medioevale e Umanistica, Padua 1958 ff.

Litterae textuales, Amsterdam 1972 ff.

Gazette du livre médiéval, Paris 1982 ff.

BERNHARD BISCHOFF, Paläographie, in HERMANN HEIMPEL–HERBERT GEUSS (edd), Dahlmann-Waitz, *Quellenkunde der deutschen Geschichte*[10], Stuttgart 1967, (Abt. 14).

T. JULIAN BROWN, Palaeography, in *New Cambridge Bibliography of English Literature* 1, Cambridge 1974, 209 ff.

JAN-OLOF TJÄDER, Latin palaeography, in *Eranos* 75 (1977) 131–61; 78 (1980) 65–97; 80 (1982) 63–92; 82 (1984) 66–95.

IRMGARD FISCHER, *Die Handbibliothek in Handschriftenlesesälen. Überlegungen zu ihrer Entstehung, Aufgabe und Benutzung*, Arbeiten aus dem Bibliothekar-Lehrinstitut des Landes Nordrhein-Westfalen, H. 44, Cologne 1974.

BERNHARD BISCHOFF, *Mittelalterliche Studien*. 1–3, Stuttgart 1966–67, 1981.

PAUL LEHMANN, *Erforschung des Mittelalters* see p. ix.

JEAN MALLON, *De l'écriture. Receuil d'études*, Paris 1982.

E.A. LOWE, *Palaeographical Papers*, see p. ix.

JOSEFINA MATEU IBARS – MA. DOLORES MATEU IBARS, *Bibliografía paleográfica*, Barcelona 1974.

JOAN GIBBS (ed.), *University of London Library, The Palaeography Collection* 1/2, Boston Mass. 1968.

Bayerische Staatsbibliothek. *Handbibliothek der Handschriftenabteilung. System und Katalog*. Wiesbaden 1978 ff.

Bibliography

Nature and methods of palaeography

LUDWIG TRAUBE, *Vorlesungen und Abhandlungen*, 1–3, Munich 1909–20.

ALFIO ROSARIO NATALE, *Ludwig Traube e la nuova metodologia paleografica*, Milan 1957.

GIORGIO PASQUALI, Paleografia quale scienza dello spirito, in *Nuova Antologia* 355 (1931) 342 ff. (reprinted in PASQUALI, *Pagine stravaganti*, Lanciano 1933, 196 ff.).

T. JULIAN BROWN, Latin Palaeography since Traube, *Transact. of the Cambridge Bibliographical Society* 3 (1959/60) 361 ff. (reprinted in *Codicologica* 1. *Théories et principes* (Litterae textuales; Amsterdam 1976) 27 ff.).

FICHTENAU, *Mensch und Schrift* see p. viii.

PAVEL SPUNAR, Définition de la paléographie, in *Scriptorium* 12 (1958) 108 ff.

JEAN MALLON, Qu'est ce que la paléographie? in *Paläographie*, 1981, 47–52.

ANDRÉ BOUTEMY, Évolution de la paléographie latine, in *Phoibos, Bulletin du Cercle de philologie classique et orientale de l'Université libre de Bruxelles* 10–12 (1955–58, published 1962) 25 ff. (cf. *Scriptorium* 18, 1964, 548).

AUGUSTO CAMPANA, Paleografia oggi. Rapporti, problemi e prospettive di una 'coraggiosa disciplina', in *Studi in onore di Arturo Massolo* 2 (Studi Urbinati di storia, filosofia e letteratura 41, n. s. 1/2, 1967) 1013 ff.

HEINRICH FICHTENAU, Paläographie, in *Enzyklopädie der geisteswissenschaftlichen Arbeitsmethoden*, Munich–Vienna 1976, 125 ff.

WILHELM KÖHLER, Paläographie und Kunstgeschichte in *Göttingische Gelehrte Anzeigen* 193, 1931, 332 ff.

FRANÇOIS MASAI, La paléographie gréco-latine, ses tâches, ses méthodes, in *Scriptorium* 10 (1956) 281 ff. (reprinted with a postscript by Albert DEROLEZ in *Codicologica* 1. *Théories et principes* (Litterae textuales; Amsterdam 1976) 34 ff.).

ALESSANDRO PRATESI, Paleografia greca e paleografia latina o paleografia greco-latina?, in *Studi storici in onore di Gabriele Pepe*, Bari 1969, 161–72.

LÉON GILISSEN, *L'Expertise des écritures médiévales*, Gent 1973.

WALDEMAR SCHLÖGL, *Die Unterfertigung deutscher Könige von der Karolingerzeit bis zum Interregnum durch Kreuz und Unterschrift*. Münchener Historische Studien, Abt. Geschichtl. Hilfswissenschaften 16, Kallmünz 1978.

EKKEHARD KRÜGER, *Die Schreib- und Malwerkstatt der Abtei Helmarshausen bis in die Zeit Heinrichs des Löwen*, 1–3. Quellen und Forschungen zur hessischen Geschichte 21, Darmstadt–Marburg 1972.

PAVEL SPUNAR, Palaeographical Difficulties in Defining an Individual Script, in *Miniatures, Scripts, Collections. Essays Presented to G.I. Lieftinck* 4 (Litterae textuales), Amsterdam 1976, 62 ff.

GUY FINK-ERRERA, Contribution de la macrophotographie à la conception d'une paléographie générale, in *Bulletin de la Société Internationale pour l'Étude de la Philosophie Médiévale* 4 (1962) 100 ff.

Les techniques de laboratoire dans l'étude manuscrits. Colloques internationaux du CNRS., Nr. 548, Paris 1972, Paris 1974.

ALPHONSE DAIN, *Les manuscrits*², Paris 1964.

FRANÇOIS MASAI, Paléographie et codicologie, in *Scriptorium* 4 (1950) 273 ff.

L.M.J. DELAISSÉ, Towards a History of the Medieval Book, in *Codicologica* 1. *Théories et principes* (Litterae textuales; Amsterdam 1976) 75 f.

GERARD ISAAK LIEFTINCK, *Paleografie en handschriftenkunde*, Amsterdam 1963.

ALBERT GRUIJS, *Codicologie of boek-archeologie? Een vals dilemma*, Nijmegen 1971.

—De la 'Bücherhandschriftenkunde' d'Ebert à la 'Codicologie' de Masai, in *Codicologica* 1. *Théories et principes* (Litterae textuales; Amsterdam 1976) 27 ff.

Bibliography

ALBERT DEROLEZ, Codicologie ou archéologie du livre? Quelques observations sur la leçon inaugurale de M. Albert Gruijs à l'Université Catholique de Nimègue, in *Scriptorium* 27 (1973) 47 ff.

EMMANUELE CASAMASSIMA, Per una storia delle dottrine paleografiche dall' Umanesimo a Jean Mabillon 1, in *Studi Medievali*, ser 3, 5 (1964) 525 ff.

General history of script

HUBERT NÉLIS, *L'écriture et les scribes*, Brussels 1918.

PAUL SATTLER–GÖTZ VON SELLE, *Bibliographie zur Geschichte der Schrift bis in das Jahr 1930*. Archiv für Bibliographie, Beiheft 17, Linz 1935.

ALOIS BÖMER–WALTER MENN, Die Schrift und ihre Entwicklung, in MILKAU–LEYH, *Handbuch*, 1², Wiesbaden 1952, 1 ff.

HANS JENSEN, *Die Schrift in Vergangenheit und Gegenwart³*, Berlin 1969.

CHARLES HIGOUNET, *L'Écriture* (Que sais-je? 653), Paris 1955.

MARCEL COHEN, *La grande invention de l'écriture et son évolution*, 1–3, Paris 1958.

JAMES G. FÉVRIER, *Histoire de l'écriture*, Paris 1959.

DAVID DIRINGER, *The Hand-Produced book*, London 1953, New York 1954.

DAVID DIRINGER–REINHOLD REGENSBURGER, *The Alphabet³*, 1/2, London 1968.

JAN TSCHICHOLD, *Geschichte der Schrift in Bildern*. Hamburger Beiträge zur Buchkunde⁴, Hamburg 1961.

MATTHIAS MIESES, *Die Gesetze der Schriftgeschichte. Konfession und Schrift im Leben der Völker*, Vienna–Leipzig 1919.

ADOLF PETRAU, *Schrift und Schriften im Leben der Völker. Ein kulturgeschichtlicher Beitrag zur vergleichenden Rassen- und Volkstumskunde*. Veröfftl. d. Hochschule für Politik, Forschungsabt. Volkstumskunde 2, Berlin 1939.

Alfabetismo e cultura scritta nella storia della società italiana, Perugia 1979.

STANLEY MORISON, *Politics and Script. Aspects of Authority and Freedom in the Development of Graeco-Latin Script from the Sixth Century B.C. to the Twentieth Century A.D.*, Oxford 1972.

Selected essays on the History of Letter-Forms in Manuscript and Print, ed. D. McKitterick 1/2, Cambridge 1981.

Survey of Latin script

EDWARD MAUNDE THOMPSON, *An Introduction to Greek and Latin Palaeography*, Oxford 1912 (repr. New York 1965).

BERTHOLD LOUIS ULLMAN, *Ancient Writing and Its Influence*. Introd. by JULIAN BROWN, Cambridge, Mass. 1969.

HERBERT HUNGER, Antikes und mittelalterliches Buch- und Schriftwesen, in *Geschichte der Textüberlieferung der antiken und mittelalterlichen Literatur*, 1, Zürich 1961, 25 ff.

STEFFENS², see p. xi.

BATELLI, *Lezioni³*, see p. vii.

CENCETTI, *Lineamenti*, see p. viii.

Compendio, see p. viii.

FOERSTER, *Abriß²*, see p. ix.

STIENNON, *Paléographie*, see p. xi.

BERTHOLD BRETHOLZ, *Lateinische Paläographie*. Grundriß der Geschichtswissenschaft, ed. by A. MEISTER, 1, 1², Leipzig 1926.

EDMOND H.J. REUSENS, *Éléments de paléographie*, Louvain 1899.

Bibliography

MAURICE PROU–ALAIN DE BOÜARD, *Manuel de paléographie latine et française*[4], Paris 1924.

OLGA ANTONOVNA DOBIASH-ROZHDESTVENSKAYA, *Istoriya pisma v srednie veka. Rukovodstvo k izucheniyu paleografii.* History of script in the Middle Ages. An introduction to the study of palaeography, Moscow 1936.

WLADIMIR SEMKOWICZ, *Paleografia łacińska*, Krakow 1951.

VIKTOR NOVAK, *Latinska paleografija*, Belgrade 1952.
Paleografija i slovensko-latinska symbioza od 7–15 stoletja (with English summary), in *Istoriski časopis* 7 (1957) 1 ff.

ALEKSANDRA DMITRIEVNA LJUBLINSKAJA, *Latinskaya paleografiya*, Moscow 1969.

ALEKSANDER GIEYSZTOR, *Zaryzs dziejów pisma łacińskiego*, Warsaw 1973.

IVAN HLAVÁČEK, *Uvod do latinské kodikologie* (Introduction to Latin codicology), Prague 1978.

E.A. LOWE, *Handwriting, our medieval Legacy*[2], Rome 1969.

JOHN, *Latin Paleography*, see p. ix.

ROBERT MARICHAL, De la capitale romaine à la minuscule, in MARIUS AUDIN (ed.), *Somme typographique*, 1, *Les origines*, Paris 1948.
L'Écriture latine et la civilisation occidentale du Ier au XVIe siècle, in MARCEL COHEN (ed.), *L'Écriture et la psychologie des peuples*, Paris 1963, 199 ff.

PAUL LEHMANN, *Lateinische Paläographie bis zum Siege der karolingischen Minuskel. Einleitung in die Altertumswissenschaft*, ed. by ALFRED GERCKE–EDUARD NORDEN, 1, 10, Leipzig 1925.

CHARLES PERRAT, Paléographie médiévale, in CHARLES SAMARAN (ed.), *L'Histoire et ses méthodes*. Encyclopédie de la Pléiade 11, Paris 1961, 585 ff.

JOHS. BRØNDUM-NIELSEN (ed.), *Palaeografi A. Danmark og Sverige*. Nordisk Kultur 28, Stockholm–Oslo–Copenhagen 1943.

DIEDRIK ARUP SEIP, *Palaeografi B. Norge og Island*, ibid., 1954.
Nomenclature, see p. x.

RUDOLF KAUTZSCH, *Wandlungen in der Schrift und in der Kunst*. Kleine Drucke der Gutenberg-Gesellschaft 10, Mainz 1929.

STANLEY MORISON, *Notes on the Development of Latin Script from Early to Modern Times*, Cambridge 1949.

HERMANN DELITSCH, *Geschichte der abendländischen Schreibschriftformen*, Leipzig 1928.

OTTO HURM, *Schriftform und Schreibwerkzeug. Die Handhabung der Schreibwerkzeuge und ihr formbildender Einfluß auf die Antiqua bis zum Einsetzen der Gotik*, Vienna 1928.

EDWARD JOHNSTON, *Writing & Illuminating & Lettering*, rev. ed., London 1939.

FRANTISEK MUZIKA, *Die schöne Schrift in der Entwicklung des lateinischen Alphabets*, 1/2, Hanau 1965.

BÉNÉDICTINS DU BOUVERET (edd) *Colophons de manuscrits occidentaux des origines au XVIe siècle*, 6 vols, Fribourg 1965–82.

PAUL LEHMANN, Autographe und Originale namhafter lateinischer Schriftsteller des Mittelalters, in *Erforschung* 1, 359 ff.

Latin script in antiquity

LUIGI SCHIAPARELLI, *La scrittura latina nell'età romana*, Como 1921.

JEAN MALLON, *Paléographie romaine* (Scripturae 3), Madrid 1952.
Paléographie romaine, in CHARLES SAMARAN (ed.), *L'Histoire et ses méthodes*. Encyclopédie de la Pléiade 11, Paris 1961, 553 ff.

JAN–OLOF TJÄDER, Die Forschungen Jean Mallons zur römischen Paläographie, in MIÖG 61 (1953) 385 ff.

ROBERT MARICHAL, Paléographie et épigraphie latines, in *Actes du 2ᵉ Congrès International d'épigraphie grecque et latine* (Paris 1952), Paris 1953, 180 ff.

L'Écriture latine et l'écriture grecque du 1ᵉʳ au 6ᵉ siècle, in *L'Antiquité classique* 19 (1950) 113 ff.

Paléographie précaroline et papyrologie, in *Scriptorium* 1 (1946/7) 1 ff.; (1950) 127 ff.

CHARLES PERRAT, Paléographie romaine, in *X Congresso Internazionale di Scienze Storiche* (Rome 1955), Relazioni 1, Florence 1955, 345 ff.

RICHARD SEIDER, *Paläographie der latienischen Papyri* 1, 2/1, 2/2 Stuttgart 1972 ff.

GIORGIO CENCETTI, Note paleografiche sulla scrittura dei papiri latini dal I al III secolo D.C., in *Accad. delle Scienze dell' Istituto di Bologna, Cl. di scienze morali, Memorie*, ser 5, 1 (1950) 3 ff.

ROBERT MARICHAL, L'Écriture latine de la chancellerie impériale, in *Aegyptus* 32 (1952) 336 ff.

CHRISTIAN COURTOIS, LOUIS LESCHI, CHARLES PERRAT, CHARLES SAUMAGNE, *Tablettes Albertini, Actes privés de l'époque vandale (fin du Vᵉ siècle)*, Paris 1952.

JAN–OLOF TJÄDER, *Nichliter. lateinische Papyri*, see p. xi.

Considerazioni e proposte sulla scrittura latina nell' età romana, in *Palaeographica, Diplomatica e Archivistica, Studi in onore di Giulio Batelli* 1, Rome 1979, 31–62.

'Some ancient letter-forms in the later Roman cursive and early medieval script of the notarii, in *Scrittura e Civiltà* 6 (1982) 5–21.

La misteriosa 'scrittura grande' di alcuni papiri revennati e il suo posto nella storia della corsiva latina e nella diplomatica romana e bizantina, dall' Egitto a Ravenna, in *Studi Romagnoli* 3 (1952) 173 ff.

GIOVANNA PETRONIO NICOLAI, Osservazioni sul canone della capitale libraria romana fra I e III secolo, in *Miscellanea in memoria di Giorgio Cencetti*, Turin 1973, 3 ff.

ALESSANDRO PRATESI, Considerazioni su alcuni codici in capitale della Biblioteca Apostolica Vaticana, in *Mélanges Eugène Tisserant* 7 (*Studi e Testi* 237), Vatican City 1964, 243 ff.

JAN–OLOF TJÄDER, Der Ursprung der Unzialschrift, in *Basler Z. für Geschichte und Altertumskunde* 1974, 9 ff.

DAVID FORBES BRIGHT, *The Origins of the Latin Uncial Script*, Diss. Univ. of Cincinnati 1967.

E.A. LOWE–E.K. RAND, *A sixth-century fragment of the letters of Pliny the Younger*, Washington 1922 (from LOWE, 'The Palaeography of the Morgan Fragment' reprinted in LOWE, *Pal. Papers* 1, 103 ff.).

ARMANDO PETTRUCCI, L'onciale romana, in *Studi Mediev.*, ser 3, 12 (1971) 75 ff.

E.A. LOWE, *English Uncial*, Oxford 1960.

BERNHARD BISCHOFF, (review of LOWE, *English Uncial*) in *Ma. Studien* 2, 328 ff.

DAVID H. WRIGHT, Some notes on English uncial, in *Traditio* 17 (1961) 441 ff.

ROBERT MARICHAL, L'Écriture du Paul de Leyde, in G.G. ARCHI et al., *Pauli Sententiarum Fragmentum Leidense (Cod. Leid. B. P. L. 2589)*, (Studia Gaiana 4), Leiden 1956, 25 ff.

BRUNO BREVEGLIERI, Materiali per lo studio della scrittura minuscola latina: i papiri letterari, in *Scrittura e Civiltà* 7 (1983) 5–49.

E.A. LOWE, A hand-list of half-uncial manuscripts, in *Miscellanea Francesco Ehrle* 4 (*Studi e Testi* 40), Rome 1924, 34 ff.; introd. repr. *Palaeographical Papers* 1, 139–41.

ALFIO ROSARIO NATALE, Marginalia, La scrittura della glossa dal V al IX secolo, in *Studi in onore di Carlo Castiglioni (Fontes Ambrosiani* 32), Milan 1957, 615 ff.

Bibliography

ARMANDO PETRUCCI, Scrittura e libro nell'Italia altomedievale, in *A. Giuseppe Ermini,* Spoleto 1970 (*Studi Mediev.*, ser 3, 10,2) 157 ff.

BERNHARD BISCHOFF, Die alten Namen der lateinischen Schriftarten, in *Ma. Studien* 1, 1 ff.

See also plates: Bassi, *Écriture latine*, CLA, ChLA, Zangemeister-Wattenbach, Chatelain (*Uncialis scr.*).

Tachygraphy (shorthand) and tironian notes

ARTHUR MENTZ–FRITZ HAEGER, *Geschichte der Kurzschrift²*, Wolfenbüttel 1974.

CHRISTIAN JOHNEN, *Allgemeine Geschichte der Kurzschrift⁴*, Berlin 1940.

Geschichte der Stenographie im Zusammenhang mit der allgemeinen Entwicklung der Schrift und der Schriftkürzung 1. *Die Schriftkürzung und Kurzschrift im Altertum, Mittelalter und Reformationszeitalter*, Berlin 1911.

HERBERT BOGE, *Griechische Tachygraphie und Tironische Noten. Ein Handbuch der antiken und mittelalterlichen Schnellschrift*, Berlin 1973.

ARTHUR MENTZ, Die Tironischen Noten. Eine Geschichte der römischen Kurzschrift, in *Arch. f. Urk.* 16 (1939) 287 ff. and 17 (1942) 155 ff.; also Berlin 1944.

EMILE CHATELAIN, *Introduction à la lecture des notes tironiennes*, Paris 1900 (repr. New York n.d.).

ULRICUS FRIDERICUS KOPP, *Palaeographia critica*, 1–4, Mannheim 1817–29 (Vol. 1.2 *Tachygraphia veterum exposita et illustrata*. Vol. 2 published as *Lexicon Tironianum* ed. by BERNHARD BISCHOFF, Osnabrück 1965).

GIORGIO COSTAMAGNA-M.F. BARONI-L. ZAGNI, *Notae Tironianae quae in lexicis et in chartis reperiuntur novo discrimine ordinatae*. Fonti e studi del corpus Membranarum Italicarum, ser 2, Fonti Medievali 10, Rome 1983.

GUILELMUS SCHMITZ (ed.), *Commentarii notarum Tironianarum*, Leipzig 1893.

PAUL LEGENDRE, *Etudes tironiennes. Commentaire sur la VIᵉ églogue de Virgile, tiré d'un manuscrit de Chartres*, Bibliothèque de l'École des Hautes Études 165, Paris 1907 (pp. 50–67 Les manuscrits tironiens).

LUIGI SCHIAPARELLI, Tachigrafia sillabica latina in Italia. Appunti, in *Bollettino della Accademia Italiana di Stenografia* 4 (1928) 11 ff., 80 ff., 157 ff.

GIORGIO COSTAMAGNA, *Il sistema tachigrafico sillabico usato dai notai medioevali italiani* (sec. VIII-XI), Genoa 1953.

ARTHUR MENTZ, Gabelsberger und die Tironischen Noten, in *Franz Xaver Gabelsberger, gest. 4. Januar 1849*, ed. by A. MENTZ, Wolfenbüttel 1948.

Insular scripts

LUDWIG BIELER, Insular palaeography, present state and problems, in *Scriptorium* 3 (1949) 267 ff.

W.M. LINDSAY, *Early Irish minuscule script*. St. Andrews University Publications 6, Oxford 1910.

Early Welsh Script (idem, 10), Oxford 1912.

D.H. WRIGHT in Alban DOLD–Leo EIZENHÖFER, *Das irische Palimpsestsakramentar im Clm 14,429 der Staatsbibliothek München*. Texte und Arbeiten 53/54, Beuron 1964, 35*f.

PATRICK MCGURK, The Irish pocket Gospel Book, in *Sacris Erudiri* 8 (1956) 249 ff.

T. JULIAN BROWN, The Lindisfarne Scriptorium, in T.D. KENDRICK, T.J. BROWN et al., *Evangeliorum quattuor codex Lindisfarnensis*, Olten-Lausanne, 1960, 89 ff.

E.A. LOWE, A key to Bede's scriptorium. Some observations on the Leningrad manuscript of the 'Historia ecclesiastica gentis Anglorum', in *Scriptorium* 12 (1958) 182 ff. (reprinted *Pal. Papers* 2, 441 ff.).

WOLFGANG KELLER, *Angelsächsische Paläographie. Die Schrift der Angelsachsen mit besonderer Rücksicht auf die Denkmäler in der Volkssprache*, 1.2 (*Palaestra* 43), Berlin–Leipzig 1906.

N.R. KER, *Catalogue of Manuscripts Containing Anglo-Saxon*, Oxford 1957.

FRANCIS WORMALD, The Insular Script in Late Tenth Century English Latin Manuscripts, in *Atti del X Congresso Internazionale di Scienze Storiche*, Rome 1955, 160 ff.

GEORG BAESECKE, *Der Vocabularius Sancti Galli in der angelsächsischen Mission*, Halle 1933.

HERRAD SPILLING, Angelsächsische Schrift in Fulda, in A. Brall (ed.), *Von der Klosterbibliothek zur Landesbibliothek*, Stuttgart 1978, 47–98.

See also plates: Zimmermann, CLA, ChLA, Sanders.

Visigothic script; Sinai script

AGUSTÍN MILLARES CARLO, *Tratado de paleografía española*, 1–3, 3rd ed., Madrid 1983.

ZACARÍAS GARCÍA VILLADA, *Paleografía española*, 1/2, Madrid 1923.

ANTONIO CHRISTIANO FLORIANO CUMBREÑO, *Paleografía y diplomática españolas.* Oviedo 1945.

CHARLES UPSON CLARK, *Collectanea Hispanica.* Transactions of the Connecticut Acad. of Arts and Sciences 24, Paris 1920.

AGUSTÍN MILLARES CARLO, *Contribución al 'Corpus' de códices visigóticos*, Madrid 1931. *Nuevos estudios de paleografía española*, Mexico 1941.

LUIGI SCHIAPARELLI, Note paleografiche intorno all'origine della scrittura visigotica, in *Arch. stor. ital.*, ser 7, 12 (1929) 165–207.

ANSCARI M. MUNDÓ, Para una historia de la escritura visigótica, in *Bivium: Homenaje a Manuel Cecilio Díaz y Díaz*, Madrid 1983, 175–96.

RODNEY POTTER ROBINSON, *Manuscripts 27 (S. 29) and 107 (S. 129) of the Municipal Library of Autun. A Study of Spanish Halfuncial and Early Visigothic Minuscule and Cursive Scripts.* Mem. of the Amer. Acad. in Rome 16, New York 1939.

AUGUSTÍN MILLARES CARLO, *Consideraciónes sobre la escritura visigótica cursiva*, León 1973.

MANUEL GÓMEZ-MORENO, *Documentación goda en pizarra.* R. Acad. de la Historia, Madrid 1966.

MANUEL C. DÍAZ y DÍAZ, Los documentos hispano-visigóticos sobre pizarra, in *Studi Medievali.*, ser 3, 7 (1966) 75 ff.
Libros y librerias en la Rioja altomedieval, Logroño 1979.
Códices visigóticos en la monarquía leonesa, León 1983.

ANSCARI M. MUNDÓ, El commicus palimpsest Paris lat. 2269 amb notes sobre litúrgia i manuscrits visigótics a Septimánia i Catalunya, in *Liturgica* 1, *Cardinal I.A. Schuster in memoriam*, Montserrat 1956, 173 ff.

E.A. LOEW, Studia Palaeographica. *A contribution to the history of early Latin minuscule and to the dating of Visigothic manuscripts.* MSB 1910, Abh. 12 (reprinted in LOWE, *Pal. Papers* 1, 2 ff.).

ANSCARI M. MUNDÓ, La datación de los códices liturgicos visigóticos toledanos, in *Hispania Sacra* 18 (1965) 1 ff.

MANUEL C. DÍAZ y DÍAZ, La circulation des manuscrits dans la Péninsule Ibérique du VIIIe au XIe siècle, in *Cahiers de civilisation médiévale* 12 (1969) 219 ff., 383 ff.

See also plates: Burnam, Ewald-Loewe, Canellas.

Bibliography

E.A. LOWE, An unknown Latin Psalter on Mount Sinai, in *Scriptorium* 9 (1955) 177 ff., (reprinted *Pal. Papers* 2, 417 ff.).
Two New Latin Liturgical Fragments on Mount Sinai, in *Rev. Bénéd.* 74 (1964) 252 ff. (reprinted *Pal. Papers* 2, 520 ff.).
Two Other Unknown Latin Liturgical Fragments on Mount Sinai, in *Scriptorium* 19 (1965) 3 ff. (reprinted *Pal. Papers* 2, 546 ff.).

Beneventan

E.A. LOEW, *The Beneventan Script*, Oxford 1914; 2nd enlarged ed. 1/2 Rome 1980.
VIKTOR NOVAK, *Scriptura Beneventana*, Zagreb 1920.
GUGLIELMO CAVALLO, Struttura e articolazione della minuscola beneventana libraria tra i secoli X-XII, in *Studi Medievali*, ser 3, 11 (1970) 343 ff.
MYRTILLA AVERY, *The Exultet Rolls of South Italy*, Princeton–London–The Hague 1936.
GUGLIELMO CAVALLO, *Rotoli di Exultet dell'Italia Meridionale*, Bari 1973.
See also plates: Loew.

Precaroline script in Italy and in the kingdom of the Franks

KARL BRANDI, Ein lateinischer Papyrus aus dem Anfang des 6. Jahrhunderts und die Entwicklung der Schrift in den älteren Urkunden, in *Arch. f. Urk.* 5 (1914) 269 ff.
Der byzantinische Kaiserbrief aus St. Denis und die Schrift der frühmittelalterlichen Kanzleien, *Arch. f. Urk.* 1 (1908) 65 ff.
PAUL RABIKAUSKAS, *Die römische Kuriale in der päpstlichen Kanzlei*. Miscellanea Historiae Pontificiae 20, Rome 1958.
LUIGI SCHIAPARELLI, Note paleografiche. Intorno all'origine della scrittura curiale romana, in *Arch. stor. ital.*, ser 7, 6 (1926) 165 ff.
JAN-OLOF TJÄDER, Le origini della scrittura curiale romana, in *Bull. dell'Arch. Pal. Ital.*, ser 3, 2/3 (1963/4) 8 ff.
ALFONSO GALLO, La scrittura curiale napoletana nel Medio Evo, in *Bull. dell'Istituto Storico Italiano* 45 (1929) 17 ff.
Contributo allo studio delle scritture meridionali nell'alto Medioevo, *Bull. dell'Istituto Storico Italiano* 47 (1932) 333 ff.
FRANCO BARTOLONI, La nomenclatura delle scritture documentarie, in *X Congresso Internazionale di Scienze Storiche, Roma 1955*, Relazioni 1 (Florence 1955) 434 ff.
Semicorsiva o precarolina?, in *Bull. dell'Arch. Pal. Ital.* 12 (1943) 2.
Note paleografiche. Ancora sulle scritture precaroline. in *Bull. dell'Istituto Storico Italiano per il Medio Evo* 62 (1950) 139 ff.
LUIGI SCHIAPARELLI, *Influenze straniere nella scrittura italiana dei secoli VIII e IX. Note paleografiche (Studi e Testi 47)*, Rome 1927.
PAOLO COLLURA, Studi paleografici. *La precarolina e la carolina a Bobbio*, Milan 1943 (repr. Florence 1965).
PIUS ENGELBERT, Zur Frühgeschichte des Bobbieser Skriptoriums, in *Rev. Bénéd.* 78 (1968) 220 ff.
ALFIO ROSARIO NATALE, Influenze merovingiche e studi calligrafici nello scriptorium di Bobbio (secoli VII-IX), in *Miscellanea G. Galbiati 2. Fontes Ambrosiani* 26, Milan 1951, 1 ff.
Studi paleografici. Arte e imitazione della scrittura insulare in codici bobbiesi, Milan 1950.
ARMANDO PETRUCCI, Scrittura e libro nella Tuscia altomedievale (secoli VIII-IX), in *Atti del 5º Congresso Internazionale di studi sull'alto medioevo*, Spoleto 1973, 627 ff.

Libro, scrittura e scuola, in *La scuola nell'occidente latino dell'alto medioevo (Settimane 19)*, Spoleto 1972, 1, 313 ff.

LUIGI SCHIAPARELLI, Note palcografiche. Intorno all'origine e ai caratteri della scrittura merovingica, in *Arch. stor. ital.*, ser 7, 16 (1932) 169 ff.

PIERRE GASNAULT–JEAN VEZIN, *Documents comptables de Saint-Martin de Tours à l'époque mérovingienne*. Collection de documents inédits sur l'histoire de France, Paris 1975.

E.A. LOWE, The script of Luxeuil. A title vindicated, in *Rev. Bénéd.* 63 (1953) 132 ff. (reprinted in *Pal. Papers* 2, 389 ff.).

OLGA ANTONOVNA DOBIASH–ROZHDESTVENSKAYA, *Histoire de l'atelier graphique de Corbie de 651 à 830 reflétée dans les Corbeienses Leninopolitani*. Acad. des sciences de l'URSS. Travaux de l'Inst. de l'hist. de la science et de la technique, ser 2, 3, Leningrad 1934.

LESLIE WEBBER JONES, The Scriptorium at Corbie 1.2, in *Speculum* 22 (1947) 191 ff., 375 ff.

EDWARD KENNARD RAND, *The Earliest Book of Tours*. Studies in the Script of Tours 2, Cambridge, Mass. 1934.

BERNHARD BISCHOFF, Ein wiedergefundener Papyrus und die ältesten Handschriften der Schule von Tours, in *Ma. Studien* 1, 6 ff.

MICHAEL HOCIJ, Die westlichen Grundlagen des glagolitischen Alphabets, in *Südostdeutsche Forschungen* 4 (1940) 509 ff.

See also plates: CLA, ChLA, Zimmermann, Bonelli, Natale.

Caroline minuscule up to the twelfth century

BERNHARD BISCHOFF, La nomenclature des écritures livresques du IXe XIIIe siècle, in *Nomenclature*, 7 ff.

Die karolingische Minuskel, in *Karl der Große, Werk und Wirkung* (exhibition catalogue) 207 ff. (French.: La minuscule caroline et le renouveau culturel sous Charlemagne, in *Institut de Recherche et d'Histoire des Textes, Bulletin* 15, 1967/8, 333 ff.); repr. in *Ma. Studien* 3, 1–4.

ALFRED HESSEL, Zur Entstehung der karolingischen Minuskel, in *Arch. f. Urk.* 8 (1923) 201 ff.

HARALD STEINACKER, Zum liber Diurnus und zur Frage nach dem Ursprung der Frühminuskel, in *Miscellanea Francesco Ehrle* 4 (*Studi e Testi* 40), Rome 1924, 105 ff.

GIORGIO CENCETTI, Postilla nuova a un problema vecchio: L'origine della minuscola 'carolina', in *Nova Historia* 7 (1955) 1 ff.

BERNHARD BISCHOFF, Paläographie und frühmittelalterliche Klassiküberlieferung, in *La cultura antica nell'occidente latino dal VII all'XI secolo (Settimane 22)* Spoleto 1975, 1, 59 ff.; repr. in *Ma. Studien* 3, 55 ff.

Panorama der Handschriftenüberlieferung aus der Zeit Karls des Großen, in *Karl der Große, Lebenswerk und Nachleben* (ed. WOLFGANG BRAUNFELS) 2, Düsseldorf 1965, 233 ff. (see also Index: Frühkarolingische Handschriften und ihre Heimat, in *Scriptorium* 22, 1968, 306 ff.); repr. *Ma. Studien* 3, 39 ff.

Die Hofbibliothek unter Ludwig dem Frommen, in *Medieval Learning and Literature, Essays Presented to Richard William Hunt*, Oxford 1976, 3 ff.; repr. *Ma. Studien* 3 170 ff.

Lorsch im Spiegel seiner Handschriften (Münchener Beiträge, Beiheft), Munich 1974.

W.M. LINDSAY–PAUL LEHMANN, The early Mayence scriptorium, in *Palaeographia Latina* 4 (1925) 15 ff.

LESLIE WEBBER JONES, *The Script of Cologne from Hildebald to Hermann*, Cambridge, Mass. 1932.

BERNHARD BISCHOFF–JOSEF HOFMANN, *Libri Sancti Kyliani. Die Würzburger Schreibschule und die Dombibliothek im VIII. und IX. Jahrhundert*. Quellen und Forschungen zur Geschichte des Bistums und Hochstifts Würzburg 6, Würzburg 1952.

BERNHARD BISCHOFF, *Die südostdeutschen Schreibschulen und Bibliotheken in der Karolingerzeit* 1, *Die bayrischen Diözesen*, Leipzig 1940³ (Wiesbaden 1974); 2. *Die vorwiegend österreichischen Diözesen*, Wiesbaden 1980.

Kalligraphie in Bayern. Achtes bis zwölftes zahrhundert, Wiesbaden 1981.

Eine Sammelhandschrift Walahfrid Strabos (Cod. Sangall 878), in *Ma. Studien* 2, 34 ff.

HERRAD SPILLING, Das Fuldaer Skriptorium zur Zeit des Hrabanus, in R. Kottje – H. Zimmermann (edd), *Hrabanus Maurus*. Akad. d. Wiss. u.d. Lit. Mainz, Abh. d. geistes- u. sozialwiss. Kl., einzelveröffentlichung 4, Wiesbaden 1982, 165–91.

KARL FORSTNER, *Die karolingischen Handschriften und Fragmente in den Salzburger Bibliotheken. Ende des 8. Jahrhunderts bis Ende des 9. Jahrhunderts*. Mitteilungen der Gesellschaft für Salzburger Landeskunde, Erg.-Bd. 3, Salzburg 1962.

Das Verbrüderungsbuch von St. Peter in Salzburg. Vollst. Faksimile-Ausgabe. Codices selecti 51, Graz 1974.

BONIFAZ FISCHER, Die Alkuin–Bibeln; ALBERT BRUCKNER, Der Codex und die Schrift, in *Die Bibel von Moutier-Grandval, British Museum Add. MS. 10,546*, Bern 1971, 49 ff., 99 ff.

EDWARD KENNARD RAND, *A Survey of the Manuscripts of Tours*, 1.2. Studies in the Script of Tours 1, Cambridge, Mass. 1929.

BERNHARD BISCHOFF, Die Kölner Nonnenhandschriften und das Skriptorium von Chelles, in *Ma. Studien* 1, 16 ff.

T.A.M. BISHOP, The Script of Corbie, A Criterion, in *Essays Presented to G.I. Lieftinck* 1 (Litterae textuales), Amsterdam 1972, 9 ff.

JEAN VEZIN, Les manuscrits copiés à Saint-Denis en France pendant l'époque carolingienne, in *Paris et Ile-de-France*, Mémoires publiés par la féderation des sociétés historiques de Paris et de l'Ile-de-France . . . 32, 1981, 273 ff.

BERNHARD BISCHOFF, Hadoardus and the manuscripts of classical authors from Corbie, in *Didascaliae, Studies in Honor of Anselm M. Albareda*, New York 1961, 41 ff. (German tr. Hadoard und die Klassikerhandschriften aus Corbie, in *Ma. Studien* 1, 49 ff.).

FREDERICK M. CAREY, The scriptorium of Reims during the archbishopric of Hincmar (845–882 A.D.), in *Classical and mediaeval studies in honor of Edward Kennard Rand*, Menasha, Wis., 1938, 41 ff.

CHARLES HENRY BEESON, *Lupus of Ferrières as Scribe and Text Critic. A Study of his Autograph Copy of Cicero's De Oratore*, Cambridge, Mass. 1930.

ELISABETH PELLEGRIN, Les manuscrits de Loup de Ferrières, in *Bibl. Éc. Chartes* 115 (1957) 5 ff.

D. GABORIT-CHOPIN, *La décoration des manuscrits à Saint-Martial de Limoges et en Limousin du IXᵉ au XIIᵉ siècle*. Paris–Geneva 1969.

BENIAMINO PAGNIN, Formazione della scrittura carolina italiana, in *Atti del Congresso Internazionale di diritto e di storia del diritto* 1, Milan 1951, 245 ff.

LUIGI SCHIAPARELLI, *Il codice 490 della Biblioteca Capitolare di Lucca e la scuola scrittoria lucchese (secolo VIII-IX). Contributi allo studio della minuscola precarolina in Italia (Studi e Testi 36)*, Rome 1924.

TERESA VENTURINI, *Ricerche paleografiche intorno all'arcidiacono Pacifico di Verona*, Verona 1929.

GIORGIO CENCETTI, Scriptoria e scritture nel monachesimo benedettino, in *Il monachesimo nell'alto medioevo e la formazione della civiltà occidentale* (*Settimane* 4) Spoleto 1957, 206 ff.

PAOLA SUPINO MARTINI, Carolina romana e minuscola romanesca: in *Studi Medievali*, ser 3, 15 (1974) 769 ff.

ETTORE CAU, Scrittura e cultura a Novara (secoli VIII-IX), in *Ricerche Medievali* 6-9 (1971-4) 1 ff.

PHILIP LEVINE, Lo '*scriptorium*' *Vercellese da S. Eusebio ad Attone*. Quaderni dell'Istituto di Belle Arti di Vercelli 1, Vercelli 1958.

ALFRED HESSEL, Studien zur Ausbreitung der karolingischen Minuskel, I. Spanien, in *Arch. f. Urk.* 7 (1921) 197 ff.; II. Großbritannien und Italien, idem. 8 (1923) 16 ff.

NATALIA DANIEL, *Handschriften des zehnten Jahrhunderts aus der Freisinger Dombibliothek* (Münchener Beiträge 11), Munich 1973.

CHRISTINE ELISABETH EDER, Die Schule des Klosters Tegernsee im frühen Mittelalter im Spiegel der Tegernseer Handschriften, in *Stud. Mitt. OSB* 83 (1972) 1 ff. (also Münchener Beiträge, Beiheft).

LESLIE WEBBER JONES, The Script of Tours in the tenth century, in *Speculum* 14 (1939) 179 ff.

The Art of Writing at Tours from 1000 to 1200 A.D., in *Speculum* 15 (1940) 286 ff.

MONIQUE-CECILE GARAND, Manuscrits monastiques et scriptoria au XIe et XIIe siècles, travail au scriptorium, in *Codicologica* 3 (Litterae Textuales), 1980, 9 ff.

Le scriptorium de Cluny, carrefour d'influences au XIe siècle, Le ms. Paris, BN, Nouv. Acq. Lat. 1548, in *Journal des Savants* 1977, 257 ff.

JEAN DUFOUR, *La bibliothèque et le scriptorium de Moissac*, Geneva-Paris 1972.

JEAN VEZIN, *Les scriptoria d' Angers au XIe siècle*, Paris 1974.

MEYER SCHAPIRO, The Parma Ildefonsus, a romanesque illuminated manuscript from Cluny and related works, n.p. 1964.

JEAN VEZIN, Une importante contribution à l'étude du 'scriptorium' de Cluny à la limite des XIe et XIIe siècles, in *Scriptorium* 21 (1967) 312 ff.

J.J.G. ALEXANDER, *Norman Illumination at Mont St. Michel 966–1100*, Oxford 1970.

CHRISTIAN DE MERINDOL, *La production des livres peints à l'abbaye de Corbie au XIIème siècle. Étude historique et archéologique*, 1–3, Lille 1976.

JACQUES STIENNON, Le scriptorium et le domaine de l'abbaye de Malmédy du Xe au début du XIIIe siècle, d'après les manuscrits de la Bibliothèque Vaticane. Bulletin de l'Institut Historique Belge à Rome 26, 1950/1, 5 ff.

ADRIAAN VERHULST, L'Activité et la calligraphie du scriptorium de l'abbaye Saint-Pierre-au-Mont-Blandin de Gand à l'époque de l'abbé Wichard (†1058), in *Scriptorium* 11 (1957) 37 ff.

ARMANDO PETRUCCI, Censimento dei codici dei secoli XI-XII. Istruzioni per la datazione, in *Studi Medievali*, ser 3, 9 (1968) 1115 ff.

MARIA ANTONIETTA MAZZOLI CASAGRANDE, I codici Warmondiani e la cultura a Ivrea fra IX e XI secolo, in *Ricerche Medievali* 6-9 (1971-4) 89 ff.

MARIA VENTURINI, *Vita ed attività dello 'scriptorium' veronese nel secolo XI*, Verona 1930.

MARIA LUISA GIULIANO, *Cultura e attività calligrafica nel secolo XII a Verona*, Padua 1933.

T.A.M. BISHOP, *English Caroline Minuscule*, Oxford 1971.

Bibliography

KARIN DENGLER-SCHREIBER, *Scriptorium und Bibliothek des Klosters Michelsberg in Bamberg von den Anfängen bis 1150.* Studien zur Bibliotheksgeschichte 2, Graz 1978.

CARL PFAFF, *Scriptorium und Bibliothek des Klosters Mondsee im hohen Mittelalter.* Österr. Akad. d. Wiss., Veröffentlichungen der Kommission für Geschichte Österreichs 2, Vienna 1967.

MIROSLAW FLODR, *Skiptorium olomoucké. K počátkům písařské tvorby v českých zemích (The scriptorium at Olmutz. The beginnings of written culture in the Czech lands).* Spisy univ. v Brně filos. fakulta 65, Prague 1960.

HREINN BENEDIKTSSON, *Early Icelandic Script as Illustrated in Vernacular Texts from the Twelfth and Thirteenth Centuries,* Reykjavik 1965.

HARALD SPEHR, *Der Ursprung der isländischen Schrift und ihre Weiterbildung bis zur Mitte des XIII. Jahrhunderts,* Halle a. S. 1929.

OTTO MAZAL, *Buchkunst der Romanik,* Graz 1978.

WALTER BERSCHIN, *Griechisch-lateinisches Nittelalter. Von Hieronymus zu Nikolaus von Kues,* Bern-Munich 1980.

Early gothic and Gothic script

ERNST CROUS–JOACHIM KIRCHNER, *Die gotischen Schriftarten,* Berlin 1928.

OTTO MAZAL, *Buchkunst der Gotik,* Graz 1975.

WILHELM MEYER, *Die Buchstaben–Verbindungen der sogenannten gotischen Schrift.* Abh. der Ges. der Wiss. zu Göttingen, n.F. 1, 6, Berlin 1897.

CARL WEHMER, Die Namen der 'gotischen' Buchschriften. Ein Beitrag zur Geschichte der lateinischen Paläographie, in *Zbl. f. Bw.* 49 (1932) 11 ff., 169 ff., 222 ff.

G.I. LIEFTINCK, Pour une nomenclature de l'écriture de la période dite gothique. Essai s'appliquant spécialement aux manuscrits originaires des Pays-Bas médiévaux, in *Nomenclature* (see above, p. 12) 15 ff.

J.P. GUMBERT, *Utrechter Kartäuser,* see above p. viii.

Nomenklatur als Gradnetz. Ein Versuch an spätmittelalterlichen Schriftformen, in *Codices manuscripti* 1 (1975) 122 ff.

A Proposal for a Cartesian Nomenclature, in *Miniatures, Scripts, Collections. Essays presented to G.I. Lieftinck* 4 (Litterae textuales) Amsterdam 1975, 45 ff.

KARIN SCHNEIDER, Gotische Schriften in deutscher Sprache 1. Vom späten 12. Jahrhundert bis um 1300. Text, plates, Wiesbaden 1987.

THOMAS FRENZ, Gotische Gebrauchsschriften des 15. Jahrhunderts: Untersuchungen zur Schrift lateinisch-deutscher Glossare am Beispiel des 'Vocabularius Ex quo', in *Codices Manuscripti* 7 (1981) 14 ff.

W. OESER, Das 'a' als Grundlage für Schriftvarianten in der gotischen Buchschrift, in *Scriptorium* 25 (1971) 25 ff., 303.

GAINES POST, A general report: Suggestions for future studies in late medieval and Renaissance Latin paleography, in *Relazioni del X⁰ Congresso Internazionale di Scienze Storiche, Roma 1955,* 1, Florence 1955, 407 ff.

BRYGIDA KÜRBISÓWNA, *Rozwój pisma gotyckiego (The development of Gothic script).* Sprawozdania Poznánskiego Towarzystwa Przyjaciól Nauk 44/45, 1955.

T.V. LUIZOVA, Ob istoricheskich usloviyach voznikoveniya tak nazyvaemogo goticheskogo pisma (On the historical prerequisites for the origin of the 'Gothic' script), in *Srednie veka* 5 (1954) 269 ff.

JACQUES BOUSSARD, Influences insulaires dans la formation de l'écriture gothique, in *Scriptorium* 5 (1951) 238 ff.

N.R. KER, *English Manuscripts*, see above, p. ix.

R.A.B. MYNORS, *Durham Cathedral Manuscripts to the end of the twelfth century*, Oxford 1939.

LÉOPOLD DELISLE (ed.), *Rouleau mortuaire du B. Vital, abbé de Savigni, contenant 207 titres écrits en 1122–1123 dans différentes églises de France et d'Angleterre, éd. phototypique*, Paris 1909.

GERARD ISAAC LIEFTINCK, *De librijen en scriptoria der westvlaamse cistercienserabdijen Ter Duinen en Ter Doest in de 12e en 13e eeuw en de betrekkingen tot het atelier van de kapittelschool van Sint Donatiaan te Brugge*. Mededelingen van de koninkl. Vlaamse Acad. voor wetenschappen, letteren en schone kunsten van België, Kl. d. letteren, 15, 1953, 2.

VERA LOROVNA ROMANOVA, Rukopisnaya kniga i goticheskoe pismo vo Francii v XIII-XIV vv. (The manuscript book and the Gothic script in France, saec. XIII-XIV), Moscow 1975.

BENIAMINO PAGNIN, *Le origini della scrittura gotica padovana*. R. Univ. di Padova, Pubbl. della fac. di lettere e filos. 6, Padua 1933.

    La 'Littera bononiensis'. Studio paleografico. Atti del R. Istituto Veneto di scienze, lettere ed arti 93, 1933/34, pp. 1593 ff.; reprinted in *Ricerche Medievali* 10–12 (Pavia 1975–7) 93–168.

JEAN DESTREZ, *La 'pecia' dans les manuscrits universitaires du XIIIe et du XIVe siècle*, Paris 1935.

ANTOINE DONDAINE, *Secrétaires de Saint Thomas*, 1/2, Rome 1956.

ARMANDO PETRUCCI, *La scrittura di Francesco Petrarca* (*Studie e Testi* 248), Vatican City 1967.

T.A.M. BISHOP, *Scriptores regis. Facsimiles to identify and illustrate the hands of royal scribes in original charters of Henry I, Stephen, and Henry II*, Oxford 1961.

LYUDMILA ILINICHNA KISELEVA *Goticheskii kursiv XIII-XV vv.*, Leningrad 1974.

GIANFRANCO ORLANDELLI, Ricerche sulla origine della 'littera bononiensis'. Scritture documentarie bolognesi del secolo XII, in *Bullet. dell'Arch. Pal. Ital.*, n.s. 2/3 (1956/7).

STEPHAN HAJNAL, *Vergleichende Schriftproben zur Entwicklung und Verbreitung der Schrift im 12.–13. Jahrhundert*, Budapest etc. 1943.

    L'Enseignement de l'écriture aux universités médiévales[2] (ed. L. MEZEY), Budapest 1959.

WALTER HEINEMEYER, Studien zur Geschichte der gotischen Urkundenschrift 1/2/3 in *Arch. f. Dipl.* 1 (1955) 330 ff.; 2 (1956) 250 ff.; 5/6 (1959/60) 308 ff.

FRIEDRICH UHLHORN, *Die Großbuchstaben der sogenannten gotischen Schrift mit besonderer Berücksichtigung der Hildesheimer Stadtschreiber* (separatum from *Z. für Buchkunde*), Leipzig 1924.

N. DENHOLM-YOUNG, *Handwriting in England and Wales*, Cardiff 1954.

M.B. PARKES, English *Cursive Book Hands 1250–1500*, Oxford 1969.

C.E. WRIGHT, *English Vernacular Hands from the Twelfth to the Fifteenth Centuries*, Oxford 1960.

PAVEL SPUNAR, L'Évolution et la fonction de la bâtarde en Bohême et en Pologne in *Studia zródłoznawcze* 6 (1961) 1 ff.

    Genese české bastardy a její vztah k českým prvotiskům (The origin of Czech Bastarda and its connection with early Czech printing), in *Listy filolologické* 3 (78. 1955) 34 ff.

BONAVENTURA KRUITWAGEN, *Laat-middeleeuwsche paleografica, paleotypica, liturgica, kalendalia, grammaticalia*, The Hague 1942.

W. OESER, Die Brüder des Gemeinsamen Lebens in Münster als Bücherschreiber, in *Arch. für Geschichte des Buchwesens* 5 (1964) esp. pp. 197 ff.

Bibliography

S.H. STEINBERG, Medieval Writing-masters, in *The Library*, ser 4, 22 (1942) 1 ff.
CARL WEHMER, Die Schreibmeisterblätter des späten Mittelalters, in *Miscellanea Giovanni Mercati* 6 (*Studi e Testi* 126) Vatican City 1946, 147 ff.
Augsburger Schreiber aus der Frühzeit des Buchdrucks, 1/2, in *Beiträge zur Inkunabelkunde*, n.F. 1 (1935) 78 ff.; 2 (1938) 108 ff.
ALFRED HESSEL, *Die Schrift der Reichskanzlei seit dem Interregnum und die Entstehung der Fraktur*. Nachr. d. Ges. d. Wiss. in Göttingen, n.F., Fachgruppe 2,2, 1936/9.
H.A. GENZSCH, Kalligraphische Stilmerkmale in der Schrift der luxemburgisch-habsburgischen Reichskanzlei. Ein Beitrag zur Vorgeschichte der Fraktur, in *MIÖG* 45 (1931) 205 ff.
Untersuchungen zur Geschichte der Reichskanzlei und ihrer Schriftformen in der Zeit Albrechts II. und Friedrichs III. Diss. Marburg 1930 (abstract).
HEINRICH FICHTENAU, *Die Lehrbücher Maximilians I. und die Anfänge der Frakturschrift*, Hamburg 1961.
FRITZ RÖRIG, Mittelalter und Schriftlichkeit, in *Welt als Geschichte* 13 (1953) 29 ff.
HELGA HAJDU, *Lesen und Schreiben im Spätmittelalter*. Elisabeth-Univ., Pécs, Schriften aus dem Dt. Inst. 1, Pécs 1931.
FRIEDRICH WILHELM OEDIGER, *Über die Bildung der Geistlichen im späten Mittelalter*, Leiden–Cologne 1953.
WIELAND SCHMIDT, Vom Lesen und Schreiben im späten Mittelalter, in *Festschrift für Ingeborg Schröbler zum 65. Geburtstag*, Tübingen 1973, 309 ff.
GERHART BURGER, *Die südwestdeutschen Stadtschreiber im Mittelalter*. Beiträge zur schwäbischen Geschichte 1/5, Böblingen 1960.
CURT F. BÜHLER, *The Fifteenth-Century Book, the Scribes, the Printers, the Decorators*, Philadelphia 1960.
LZUDMILA IKINIČNA KISELEVA, *Zapadnoevropejskaja Kniga XIV-XV vv.* (The west-European book of the 14th and 15th c.), Leningrad 1985.
STANLEY MORISON, *The Art of Printing*. Proceedings of the British Academy 23, 1937. (German edition.: ST. MORISON, *Schrift, Inschrift, Druck*, Hamburg 1948.)
OTTO MAZAL, *Paläographie und Paläotypie. Zur Geschichte der Schrift im Zeitalter der Inkunabeln*, Stuttgart 1984.
See also plates: Kirchner (*Script. Goth. libr.*), Thomson.

Humanistic script

BERTHOLD LOUIS ULLMAN, *The Origin and Development of Humanistic Script*, Rome 1960.
ALFRED HESSEL, Die Entstehung der Renaissanceschriften, in *Arch. f. Urk.* 13 (1933) 1 ff.
GIULIO BATTELI, Nomenclature des écritures humanistiques, in *Nomenclature* (see above, p.x) 35 ff.
ALBINIA C. DE LA MARE, Humanistic Script, in J.J.G. ALEXANDER–A.C. DE LA MARE, *The Italian Manuscripts in the Library of Major J.R. Abbey*, London 1969, pp. xxii-xxiii.
The Handwriting of Italian Humanists 1, Facsimiles 1, Oxford 1973.
JAMES WARDROP, *The Script of Humanism. Some Aspects of Humanistic Script, 1460–1560*, Oxford 1963.
AUGUSTO CAMPANA, Scritture di umanisti, in *Rinascimento* 1 (1950) 227 ff.
JOHN P. ELDER, Clues for Dating Florentine Humanistic Manuscripts, in *Studies in Philology* 44 (1947) 127 ff.

Bibliography

MILLARD MEISS, Toward a more comprehensive Renaissance palaeography, in *The Art Bulletin* 42 (1960) 97 ff.

GIOVANNI MARDERSTEIG, (ed.), *Felice Feliciano Veronese, Alphabetum Romanum*, Verona 1960.

EMMANUELE CASAMASSIMA, *Trattati di scrittura del Cinquecento italiano*, Milan 1966.

KARL SCHOTTENLOHER, Handschriftenforschung und Buchdruck im 15. and 16. Jahrhundert, in *Gutenberg-Jahrbuch* 6 (1931) 73 ff.

Modern script, German script

KARL PIVEC, Paläographie des Mittelalters – Handschriftenkunde der Neuzeit?, in LEO SANTIFALLER (ed.), *Festschrift zur Feier des zweihundertjährigen Bestandes des Haus-, Hof- und Staatsarchivs* 1, Vienna 1949, 225 ff.

STANISLAV POLÁK, Studium novověkého písma. Problémy paleografie, Příbram 1973.

C. BONACINI, *Bibliografia delle arti scrittorie e della calligrafia*. Biblioteca bibliografica italica 5, Florence 1953.

WERNER DOEDE, *Bibliographie deutscher Schreibmeisterbücher von Neudörfer bis 1800*, Hamburg 1958.

Schön schreiben, eine Kunst. Johann Neudörffer und seine Schule im XVI. und XVII. Jahrhundert. Bibliothek des Germ. National-Mus., Nürnberg, zur deutschen Kunst- und Kulturgeschichte 6, Nürnberg 1957.

ALBERT KAPR, *Johann Neudörffer der Ältere, der große Schreibmeister der deutschen Renaissance*, Leipzig 1956.

KARL BRANDI, *Unsere Schrift. Drei Abhandlungen zur Einführung in die Geschichte der Schrift und des Buchdrucks*, Göttingen 1911.

HANS HIRSCH, *Gotik und Renaissance in der Entwicklung unserer Schrift*, Vienna 1932 (reprinted in *Aufsätze zur mittelalterlichen Urkundenforschung*, Darmstadt 1965, 276 ff.).

HERIBERT STURM, *Einführung in die Schriftkunde²*, Neustadt a. d. Aisch 1961.

See also plates: Dülfer-Korn, Santifaller.

Abbreviations

LUIGI SCHIAPARELLI, *Avviamento allo studio delle abbreviature latine nel medioevo*, Florence 1926.

IOANNES LUDOLFUS WALTHERUS, *Lexicon diplomaticum, abbreviationes syllabarum et vocum in diplomatibus et codicibus e saeculo VIII ad XVI usque occurentes exponens*, Göttingen 1747 (new edition, Ulm 1756; reprint 1966).

ADRIANO CAPPELLI, *Lexicon abbreviaturarum, quae in lapidibus, codicibus et chartis praesertim medii aevi occurrunt. Dizionario di abbreviature latine ed italiane⁵*, Milan 1954. (German edition: *Lexicon abbreviaturarum. Wörterbuch lateinischer und italienischer Abkürzungen²*, Leipzig 1928).

AUGUSTE PELZER, *Abréviations latines médiévals. Supplément au ,Dizionario di abbreviature latine ed italiane' di Adriano Cappelli*, Louvain 1964.

PAUL LEHMANN, *Sammlungen und Erörterungen lateinischer Abkürzungen in Altertum und Mittelalter*. Abh. d. Bayer. Akad. d. Wiss., phil.-hist. Abt., n.F. 3, 1929.

LUDWIG TRAUBE, *Nomina Sacra*, see above, p. xi.

C.H. TURNER, The 'Nomina Sacra' in early Latin manuscripts, in *Miscellanea Francesco Ehrle 4 (Studi e Testi 40)*, Rome 1924, 62 ff.

Bibliography

A.H.R.E. PAAP, *Nomina Sacra in the Greek Papyri of the first five centuries A.D.* Papyrologica Lugduno-Batava 8, Leiden 1959.

W.M. LINDSAY, *Notae Latinae*, see above, p. ix.

DORIS BAINS, *A Supplement to Notae Latinae (Abbreviations in Latin Mss. of 850 to 1050 A.D.)*, Cambridge 1936. (reprinted Hildesheim 1965).

JOSÉ LÓPEZ DE TORO (ed.), *Abreviaturas hispánicas*, Madrid 1957.

M.-H. LAURENT, *De abbreviationibus et signis scripturae Gothicae*, Rome 1939.

EMIL SECKEL, Paläographie der juristischen Handschriften des 12. bis 15. und der juristischen Drucke des 15. und 16. Jahrhunderts, in *Z. der Savigny-Stiftung für Rechtsgeschichte* 45 (1925), Roman. sect. 1 ff. (see also separate publication, Weimar 1925).

Punctuation

MARTIN HUBERT, Corpus stigmatologicum minus, in *Archivum Latinitatis medii aevi* 37 (1970) 14 ff.; 39 (1974) 55 ff.

Le vocabulaire de la 'ponctuation' aux temps médiévaux, *Archivum Latinitatis medii aevi* 38 (1972) 57 ff.

RUDOLF WOLFGANG MÜLLER, *Rhetorische und syntaktische Interpunktion. Untersuchungen zur Pausenbezeichnung im antiken Latein*, Diss. Tübingen 1964.

E. OTHA WINGO, *Latin Punctuation in the Classical Age*, The Hague 1972.

JEANNETTE MOREAU–MARÉCHAL, Recherches sur la ponctuation, in *Scriptorium* 22 (1968) 56 ff.

JEAN VEZIN, Le point d'interrogation, un élément de datation et de localisation des manuscrits. L'exemple de Saint-Denis au IXe Siècle, in *Scriptorium* 34, 1980, 181 ff.

ALFONSO MAIERÙ (ed.), Grafia e interpunzione del Latino nel Medioevo. Seminario Internazionale Roma, 22–27 settembre 1984. Lessico Intellettuale Europeo 41, Rome 1987.

Musical notation

WALTER LIPPHARDT – LUTHER DITTMER – MARTIN RUHNKE, 'Notation', in *Musik in Geschichte und Gegenwart* 9 (Kassel 1961), esp. 1611 ff.

JOHANNES WOLF, *Handbuch der Notationskunde*, 1, Leipzig 1913.

Musikalische Schrifttafeln. *Für den Unterricht in Notationskunde*, pts. 1–10. Veröffentlichungen des Fürstl. Inst. für Musikwissenschaftliche Forschung zu Bückeburg, Reihe 2,2, Leipzig 1922/3.

JACQUES HOURLIER, (ed.), *La notation musicale des chants liturgiques latins. Présentée par les moines des Solesmes*, Solesmes 1963.

GREGORI M. SUNYOL, *Introducció a la paleografía musical gregoriana*, Montserrat 1925 (French tr.: *Introduction à la paléographie musicale grégorienne*, Tournai 1935).

PETER WAGNER, *Neumenkunde²*. *Einführung in die gregorianischen Melodien 2*, Leipzig 1912.

EWALD JAMMERS, *Tafeln zur Neumenkunde*, Tutzing 1965.

Die paläofränkische Neumenschrift, in *Scriptorium* 7 (1953) 235 ff.

SOLANGE CORBIN, *Répertoire de manuscrits médiévaux contenant des notations musicales*, 1–3, Paris 1965 ff.

(CORBIN) Die Neumen. Vol. 1, 3 in W. Arlt (ed.), *Paläographie der Musik*, Cologne 1977.

BRUNO STÄBLEIN, Schriftbild der einstimmigen Musik, in *Musikgeschichte in Bildern* 3, Leipzig 1975.

Bibliography

Numbers

KARL MENNINGER, *Zahlwort und Zahl²*, Göttingen 1958.
GEORGE FRANCIS HILL, *The Development of Arabic Numerals in Europe*, Oxford 1915.
GUY BEAUJOUAN, Étude paléographique sur la 'rotation' des chiffres et l'emploi des apices du 10ᵉ au 12ᵉ siècle, in *Revue de l'histoire des sciences* 1 (1948) 301 ff.
MARCEL DESTOMBES, Un astrolabe carolingien et l'origine de nos chiffres arabes, in *Archives Internationales d'Histoire des Sciences*, no. 58/9 (1962) 3 ff.
BERNHARD BISCHOFF, Die sogenannten 'griechischen' und 'chaldäischen' Zahlzeichen des abendländischen Mittelalters, in *Ma. Studien* 1,67 ff.

Ciphers

FRANZ STIX, Geheimschriftkunde als historische Hilfswissenschaft, in *MIÖG*, supplementary vol. 14 (1939) 453 ff.
ALOYS MEISTER, *Die Anfänge der modernen diplomatischen Geheimschrift*, Paderborn 1902.
Die Geheimschrift im Dienste der päpstlichen Kurie von ihren Anfängen bis zum Ende des 16. Jahrhunderts, Paderborn 1906.
BERNHARD BISCHOFF, Übersicht über die nichtdiplomatischen Geheimschriften des Mittelalters, in *MIÖG* 62 (1954) 1 ff. (see also separate publication, Graz–Cologne 1954).
RENÉ DEROLEZ, *Runica manuscripta, the English tradition*. Rijksuniversiteit te Gent, Werken uitgegeven door de faculteit van de wijsbegeerte en letteren, 118. afl., Brügge 1954.

Codicology

ARMANDO PETRUCCI, La descrizione del manoscritto – storia, problemi, modelli, Rome 1984.
FRIEDRICH ADOLF EBERT, *Zur Handschriftenkunde* 1, Leipzig 1825.
WILHELM WATTENBACH, *Das Schriftwesen im Mittelalter³*, Leipzig 1896.
I.H.M. HENDRIKS, Pliny, Historia Naturalis XIII, 74–82, and the Manufacture of Papyrus, in *Z. f. Papyrologie u. Epigraphik* 37 (1980) 121 ff.
WILHELM SCHUBART, *Einführung in die Papyruskunde*, Berlin 1918.
Das Buch bei den Griechen und Römern². Handbücher der Staatlichen Museen zu Berlin, Berlin–Leipzig 1921.
FREDERICK G. KENYON, *Books and Readers in Ancient Greece and Rome²*, Oxford 1951.
GUGLIELMO CAVALLO (ed.), *Libri, editori e pubblico net mondo antico, Guida storica e critica*, Rome-Bari 1975.
(ed.), *Libri e lettori nel medioevo. Guida storica e critica*, Rome-Bari 1977.
ARMANDO PETRUCCI (ed.), *Libri, scrittura, e pubblico nel Rinascimento*, Guida storica e critica, Rome-Bari 1979.
SANTIFALLER, *Beiträge*, see above, p. xi.
C.H. ROBERTS-T.C. SKEAT, *The birth of the Codex*, Oxford 1983.
ERIC G. TURNER, *The Typology of the Early Codex*, Philadelphia 1977.
KARL LÖFFLER, *Einführung in die Handschriftenkunde*, Leipzig 1929.
KARL LÖFFLER – PAUL RUF, Allgemeine Handschriftenkunde, in MILKAU-LEYH, *Handbuch* 1² (1952) 106 ff.
L. D. REYNOLDS (ed.), *Texts and Transmission. A Survey of the Latin Classics*, Oxford 1973.

—N.G. WILSON, *D'Homère à Erasme. La transmission des classiques grecs et latins.* 2nd enlarged ed. Paris 1984.

JOACHIM KIRCHNER, *Germanistische Handschriftenpraxis. Ein Lehrbuch für die Studierenden der deutschen Philologie²*, Munich 1967.

LESNE, *Livres*, see above, p. ix.

G.S. IVY, The Bibliography of the Manuscript Book, in Francis WORMALD – C.E. WRIGHT, *The English Library before 1700*, London 1958.

LÉON GILISSEN, *Prolégomènes à la codicologie*, Ghent 1977.

CARLA BOZZOLO-EZIO ORNATO, *Pour une histoire du livre manuscrit au moyen âge*, Paris 1980.

RONALD REED, *Ancient Skins, Parchment and Leathers*, London 1973.
The Nature and Making of Parchment, Leeds 1975.

ALBAN DOLD, Palimpsesthandschriften, ihre Erschließung einst und jetzt, ihre Bedeutung, in *Gutenberg-Jahrbuch* 1950, 16 ff.

GILBERT OUY, Histoire 'visible' et histoire 'cachée' d'un manuscrit, in *Le Moyen Age* 64 (1958) 115 ff.

JOHN BENTON, Digital image-processing applied to the photography of manuscripts, in *Scriptorium* 33 (1979) 40 ff.

E.A. LOWE, Codices Rescripti. A list of the oldest Latin palimpsests with stray observations on their origin, in *Mélanges Eugène Tisserant* 5 (*Studi e Testi* 235) Vatican City 1964, 67 ff. (reprinted *Pal. Papers* 2, 480 ff.).

BERNHARD BISCHOFF, *Der Fronto-Palimpsest der Mauriner* (*MSB* 1958, 2).

FRITZ HOYER – HANS H. BOCKWITZ, *Einführung in die Papierkunde*, Leipzig 1941.

ARMIN RENKER, *Das Buch vom Papier*, Leipzig 1934.

HEINZ ROOSEN-RUNGE, Die Tinte des Theophilus, in *Festschrift Luitpold Dussler*, Berlin 1972, 87 ff.

HANS LOUBIER, *Der Bucheinband von seinen Anfängen bis zum Ende des 18. Jahrhunderts²*, Leipzig 1926.

HELLMUTH HELWIG, *Handbuch der Einbandkunde*, 1–3, Hamburg 1953–5.

ERNST KYRISS, *Verzierte gotische Einbände im alten deutschen Sprachgebiet*, Text, 3 vols, plates, Stuttgart 1951–8.

LÉON GILISSEN, *La reliure occidentale antérieure à 1400*, Turnhout 1983.

Book decoration

D.M. ROBB, *The Art of the Illuminated Manuscript*, Cranbury, N.Y. 1973.

FRANZ UNTERKIRCHNER, *Die Buchmalerei, Entwicklung, Technik, Eigenart*, Vienna 1974.

MAURICE SMEYERS, *La miniature.* Typologie des sources du moyen âge occidental, Fasc. 8, Turnhout 1974.

KURT WEITZMANN, *Ancient Book Illumination*, Cambridge Mass. 1959.
Spätantike und frühchristliche Buchmalerei, Munich 1977.

CARL NORDENFALK, *Celtic and Anglo-Saxon painting*, New York 1977.

JOHN WILLIAMS, *Frühe spanische Buchmalerei*, Munich 1977.

FLORENTINE MÜTHERICH – JOACHIM GAEHDE, *Karolingische Buchmalerei*, Munich 1976.

J.J.G. ALEXANDER, *Initialen in großen Handschriften*, Munich 1978.

RICHARD MARKS-NIGEL MORGAN, *Englische Buchmalerei der Gotik 1200–1500*, Munich 1980.

FRANÇOIS AVRIL, *Buchmalerei am Hofe Frankreichs 1310–1380*, Munich 1978.

Bibliography

J.J.G. ALEXANDER, *Buchmalerei der italienischen Renaissance im 15. Jahrhundert*, Munich 1977.
WILHELM KOEHLER, *Buchmalerei des frühen Mittelalters. Fragmente und Entwürfe aus dem Nachlaß*, Munich 1972.
HEINZ ROOSEN-RUNGE, *Farbgebung und Technik frühmittelalterlicher Buchmalerei 1/2*, Berlin 1967.
ROBERT WALTER SCHELLER, *A Survey of Medieval Model Books*, Haarlem 1963.
LILLIAN M.C. RANDALL, *Images in the Margins of Gothic Manuscripts*, Berkeley 1966.
In the following items I refer to the works listed in vols 5 to 7 of the Propylaen Kunstgeschichte:
HERMANN FILLITZ (ed.), *Das Mittelalter*, I, Berlin 1969, 313 ff.
OTTO VON SIMSON (ed.), *Das Mittelalter* II, Berlin 1972, 440, 442 f., 444, 446 ff., 452 ff.
JAN BIAŁOSTOCKI (ed.), *Spätmittelalter und beginnende Neuzeit*, Berlin 1972, 434 ff.

Facsimiles, series

HANS ZOTTER, *Bibliographie faksimilierter Handschriften*, Graz 1976.
Codices Graeci et Latini photographice depicti duce Scatone DE VRIES *(et post eum* G.I LIEFTINCK)*, Leiden 1897 ff.
Codices e Vaticanis selecti, Rome 1899 ff.
Codices e Vaticanis selecti . . . iussu Iohannis Pauli II, Zürich 1981 ff.
Armarium codicum insignium, Turnhout 1980 ff.
Umbrae codicum occidentalium, Amsterdam 1960 ff.
Codices selecti, Graz 1960 ff.
Deutsche Texte in Handschriften, Cologne-Graz 1962 ff.
Litterae. Göppinger Beiträge zur Textgeschichte, Göppingen 1971 ff.
Early English Manuscripts in Facsimile, Copenhagen 1951 ff.
Corpus codicum Danorum medii aevi, Copenhagen 1960 ff.
Corpus codicum Suecicorum, Copenhagen 194 ff.
Corpus codicum Islandicorum, Copenhagen 1930 ff.
Manuscripta Islandica, Copenhagen 1954 ff.
Early Icelandic Manuscripts in Facsimile, Copenhagen 1958 ff.

Albums of plates principally concerned with book hands

Palaeographical Society, see above, p. x.
New Palaeographical Society, see above, p. x.
Catalogue des manuscrits datés, see above, p. vii.
Manuscrits datés, Belgique, see above, p. x.
Manuscrits datés, Pays-Bas, see above, p. x.
Catalogo dei manoscritti datati, see above, p. vii.
Katalog der datierten Handschriften, Österreich, see above, p. ix.
Katalog der datierten Handschriften, Sweden, see above, p. ix.
Catalogue of the dated manuscripts, Switzerland, see above, p. viii.
DEGERING, *Schrift*, see above, p. viii.
STEFFENS[2], see above, p. x.
ARNDT-TANGL[4], see above, p. vii.
KIRCHNER, *Scriptura Latina libraria*[2], see above, p. ix.

HANS FOERSTER, *Mittelalterliche Buch- und Urkundenschriften*, Bern 1946.

ERNESTO MONACI, *Esempi di scrittura latina dal secolo I dell' era moderna al XVIII*, Rome 1898 (new edition 1906).

FRANCO BARTOLONI, *Esempi di scrittura latina dal secolo I a. C. al secolo XV*, Rome 1934.

EHRLE-LIEBAERT, see above, p. viii.

Exempla scripturarum, see above, p. viii.

CHROUST, see above, p. viii.

BRUCKNER, *Scriptoria*, see above, p. vii.

Recueil des fac-similés à l'usage de l'École des Chartres, Fasc. 1–4, Paris 1880–7.

Album paléographique ou Recueil de documents importants relatifs à l'histoire et à la littérature nationales, reproduits en héliogravure d'après les orginaux des bibliothèques et des archives de la France par la Société de l'École des Chartres, Paris 1887.

Archivio Paleografico Italiano, see above, p. vii.

J. VAN DEN GHEYN, *Album Belge de paléographie. Recueil de spécimens d'écritures d'auteurs et de manuscrits belges (VIIe–XVIe siècles)*, Brussels 1908.

FRANCESCO CARTA-CARLO CIPOLLA-CARLO FRATI, *Atlante paleografico-artistico, Monumenta palaeografica sacra*. Text and plates, Turin 1899.

GIROLAMO VITELLI-CESARE PAOLI, *Collezione Fiorentina di facsimili paleografici greci e latini*, 1/2, Florence 1897.

EDWARD MAUNDE THOMPSON–GEORGE FREDERIK WARNER (edd), *Catalogue of Ancient Manuscripts in the British Museum*, 1/2, London 1881–4.

LÉOPOLD DELISLE, *Le cabinet des manuscrits de la Bibliothèque (Impériale) Nationale*, 1–3, Plates, *Histoire générale de Paris* 5, Paris 1868–81.

RUDOLF BEER (ed.), *Monumenta palaeographica Vindobonensia. Denkmäler der Schreibkunst aus der Handschriftensammlung des habsburg-lothringischen Erzhauses*, 1/2, Leipzig 1910–13.

ÉMILE CHATELAIN, *Paléographie des classiques latins* 1/2, Paris 1884–1900.

MAXIMILIANUS IHM, *Palaeographia Latina*. Text and plates, Leipzig 1909.

SCATO DE VRIES (ed.), *Album palaeographicum. Tabulae 54 selectae ex cunctis iam editis tomis codicum Graecorum et Latinorum photographice depictorum*, Leiden 1909.

RUDOLF MERKELBACH–HELMUT VAN THIEL, *Lateinisches Leseheft zur Einführung in Paläographie und Textkritik*, Göttingen 1969.

HELMUT VAN THIEL, *Mittellateinische Texte, ein Handschriften-Lesebuch*, Göttingen 1972.

Codices Latini Antiquiores (CLA), see above, p. viii.

Chartae Latinae Antiquiores (ChLA), see above, p. viii.

ZIMMERMANN, *Vorkarolingische Miniaturen*, see above, p. xi.

KOEHLER (KÖHLER), *Karolingische Miniaturen*, see above, p. ix.

KOEHLER-MÜTHERICH, *Karolingische Miniaturen*, see above, p. ix.

STELIO BASSI, *Monumenta Italiae graphica*, 1/2, Cremona 1956–7.

CAROLUS ZANGEMEISTER–GUILELMUS WATTENBACH, *Exempla codicum Latinorum litteris maiusculis scriptorum*, and *Supplementum*, Heidelberg 1876–9.

AEMILIUS CHATELAIN, *Uncialis scriptura codicum Latinorum novis exemplis illustrata*, Paris 1901.

E.A. LOWE, *Codices Lugdunenses antiquissimi. Le scriptorium de Lyon*. Documents paléographiques, typographiques, iconographiques 3/4, Lyon 1924.

CARLO CIPOLLA, *Codici Bobbiesi della Biblioteca Nazionale Universitaria di Torino*. Text and plates, Milan 1907.

ENRICO CARUSI–W.M. LINDSAY, *Monumenti paleografica veronesi*, 1/2, Rome 1929–34.

GIUSEPPE TURRINI, *Millennium scriptorii Veronensis, dal IV° al XV° secolo*, Verona 1967.

Bibliography

E.A. LOWE, *Scriptura Beneventana, Facsimiles of South Italian and Dalmatian manuscripts from the sixth to the fourteenth century*, 1/2, Oxford 1929.

ENRICO CARUSI–VINCENZO DE BARTHOLOMAEIS, *Monumenti paleografici degli Abbruzzi*, 1,1, Rome 1924.

GIUSEPPE BONELLI, *Codice paleografico lombardo. Riproduzione in eliotipia e trascrizione diplomatica di tutti i documenti anteriori al 1000 esistenti in Lombardia, Secolo VIII*, Milan 1908.

ALFIO ROSARIO NATALE, *Il museo diplomatico dell' Archivio di Stato di Milano* 1, 1.2, Milan 1971.

VINCENZO FEDERICI, La scrittura delle cancellerie italiane dal secolo XII al XVII. Text and plates, Rome 1934.

PAULUS EWALD–GUSTAVUS LOEWE, *Exempla scripturae Visigoticae XL tabulis expressa*, Heidelberg 1883.

JOHN M. BURNAM, *Palaeographia Iberica, Fac-similés de manuscrits espagnols et portuguais (IXe–XVe siècles)*, Paris 1912–25.

ANGEL CANELLAS, *Exempla scripturarum Latinarum in usum scholarum*, 1/2, Saragossa 1963–6.

EDUARDO NUNES, *Album de paleografia portuguesa*, Lisbon 1969 ff.

W.B. SANDERS, *Facsimiles of Anglo-Saxon Manuscripts*, 1–3, Southampton 1878–84.

CHARLES JOHNSON–HILARY JENKINSON, *English Court Hand, A. D. 1066–1500. Illustrated Chiefly from the Public Record*, 1/2, Oxford 1915.

HILARY JENKINSON, *The later court hands in England from the XVth to the XVIIth century. Illustrated Chiefly from the Commonpaper of the Scrivener's Company of London, the English Writing Masters and the Public Records*. Text and plates, Cambridge 1927.

KIRCHNER, *Scriptura Gothica libraria*, see above, p. ix.

THOMSON, *Bookhands*, see above, p. x.

WILHELM SCHUM, *Exempla codicum Amplonianorum Erfurtensium saeculi IX–XV*, Berlin 1882.

PETZET-GLAUNING, see above, p. x.

GERHARD EIS, *Altdeutsche Handschriften*, Munich 1949.

MAGDA ENNECCERUS, *Die ältesten deutschen Sprachdenkmäler*, Frankfurt/M. 1897.

BAESECKE, *Lichtdrucke*, see above, p. vii.

KOENNECKE, Bilderatlas, see above, p. ix.

FISCHER, *Schrifttafeln*, see above, p. viii.

RUDOLF THOMMEN, *Schriftproben aus Basler Handschriften des XIV.–XVI. Jahrhunderts*, Berlin 1908.

CARL ROTH–PHILIPP SCHMIDT, *Handschriftenproben zur Basler Geistesgeschichte des XV. und XVI. Jahrhunderts*, Basel 1926.

GEORG MENTZ, *Handschriften aus der Reformationszeit*, Bonn 1912.

OTTO CLEMEN, *Handschriftenproben nach Originalen der Zwickauer Ratsschulbibliothek*, 1, Zwickau 1911.

JULIUS FICKER–OTTO WINCKELMANN, *Handschriftenproben des sechzehnten Jahrhunderts nach Straßburger Originalen*, 1.2, Strasbourg 1902–5.

KURT DÜLFER–HANS–ENNO KORN, *Schrifttafeln zur deutschen Paläographie des 16.–20. Jahrhunderts²*, 1/2, Marburg 1967.

KARL GLADT, *Deutsche Schriftfibel. Anleitung zur Lektüre der Kurrentschrift des 17.–20. Jahrhunderts*, Graz 1976.

LEO SANTIFALLER, *Bozner Schreibschriften der Neuzeit 1500–1851. Beiträge zur Paläographie*. Schriften des Inst. für Grenz- und Auslanddeutschtum an der Univ. Marburg 7, Marburg 1930.

Index of Manuscripts Cited

Throughout this book manuscripts are often cited by their number of *Codices Latini Antiquiores* or *Chartae Latinae Antiquiores*, but without their shelf-number in the relevant library. To help the reader, the translators of the French edition supplied the missing shelf-numbers, and that practice has been followed here. Where manuscripts figure in CLA, the reference is given in brackets (Roman numerals for volume number, Arabic for the serial number); items discussed in the *Chartae* follow the same pattern, but with the abbreviation *ChLA* preceding.

Superscript numbers refer to footnotes.

ABERDEEN
Pap. 2a (II 118) 58[33]
Pap. 2c (II 120) 66

AMIENS
6, 7, 9, 11, 12 195
12, fol. 1 (VI 708) 194[33]
18 219
87 et 88 (VI 709) 42[32]
220 (VI 716) 107[98]

ANGERS
675 42[31]

ANN ARBOR, Univ. of Michigan
P. Inv. 1320 (P. Mich. III 159) (ChLA V 280) 55[13]
P. Inv. 1804 (P. Mich. III 164) (ChLA V 281) 73[138]
P. Inv. 5271e (P. Mich. 592) (ChLA V 298) 65[80]
Pap. 459 (CLA S 1781) 57

ARRAS
435 223

AUTUN
3 (CLA S 2) (VI 716) 107[98], 196[58]
4 (CLA S 3), fol. 6–24 (VI 717b) 114[8]
24 (CLA S 28) (VI 724) 194[33]
27 (CLA S 29) (VI 727a, 728) 96, 96[2], 99[20]
107 (CLA S 129) (VI 729) 96[8]

BALTIMORE, Walters Art Gallery
Ms. 71 120[72]

BAMBERG
Bibl. 44 204[18]
Bibl. 140 120
Lit. 1 117[47]
Lit. 7 et 8 26
Patr. 4 (VIII 1028) 27[64]
Patr. 5 9[11]
Patr. 87 (VIII 1031) 77[171], 79[191], 185[42], 191[7]

BARCELONA, Fundació san Luc evangeliste
Pap. Barc. (CLAS 1782) 152[13]

BASEL
F. III. 15b, ff. 1–19 (VII 844) 93[76]
F. III. 15d (VII 847) 87[26]
F. III. 15e 95[97]
F. III. 15f (VII 848) 93[76]
N. I. 4A (VII 852) 205[27]
O. IV. 17 (VII 853) 26[56]

BERKELEY, Univ. of California
P. Inv. 1422–3010 (P. Tebt. 686ª et ᵇ) (ChLA V 304) 7[2], 39[9], 63[71]

BERLIN, Aeg. Museum
P. 6757 (VIII 1033) 72[136], 79[191]
P. 6760 (VIII 1036) 11[28]
P. 8507 (VIII 1038) 55[14]
P. 11 323 (VIII 1039) 73[145]
P. 11 325 (VIII 1041) 73[145]
P. 11 753 (VIII 1042) 73[145], 150[4]
P. 11 229 A + B (VIII 1043) 26[49]
Deutsche Staatsbibl.
Phillipps 1676 (VIII 1057) 115[15]

Index of names and subjects

Index of authors whose works are cited in the notes

Index of authors cited